Allegro non troppo

ANIMATION: KEY FILMS/FILMMAKERS

Series Editor: Chris Pallant

Titles in the Series:
Toy Story: How Pixar Reinvented the Animated Feature
edited by Susan Smith, Noel Brown, and Sam Summers
Princess Mononoke: Understanding Studio Ghibli's Monster Princess
edited by Rayna Denison
Norman McLaren: Between the Frames
by Nichola Dobson
Hayao Miyazaki: Exploring the Early Work of Japan's Greatest Animator
by Raz Greenberg
Snow White and the Seven Dwarfs: New Perspectives on Production, Reception, Legacy
edited by Chris Pallant and Christopher Holliday

Allegro non troppo

Bruno Bozzetto's Animated Music

Marco Bellano

BLOOMSBURY ACADEMIC
NEW YORK • LONDON • OXFORD • NEW DELHI • SYDNEY

BLOOMSBURY ACADEMIC
Bloomsbury Publishing Inc
1385 Broadway, New York, NY 10018, USA
50 Bedford Square, London, WC1B 3DP, UK
29 Earlsfort Terrace, Dublin 2, Ireland

BLOOMSBURY, BLOOMSBURY ACADEMIC and the Diana logo are trademarks of
Bloomsbury Publishing Plc

First published in the United States of America 2021
This paperback edition published 2022

Copyright © Marco Bellano, 2021

For legal purposes the Acknowledgments on p. ix constitute an extension
of this copyright page.

Cover design: Louise Dugdale
Cover photograph courtesy of Fondazione Teatro Donizetti / Comune di Bergamo;
Archivio Fondazione Teatro Donizetti

This work is published subject to a Creative Commons Attribution Non-commercial No Derivatives License. You may share this work for non-commercial purposes only, provided you give attribution to the copyright holder and the publisher.

Bloomsbury Publishing Inc does not have any control over, or responsibility for, any third-party websites referred to or in this book. All internet addresses given in this book were correct at the time of going to press. The author and publisher regret any inconvenience caused if addresses have changed or sites have ceased to exist, but can accept no responsibility for any such changes.

Library of Congress Cataloging-in-Publication Data
Names: Bellano, Marco, author.
Title: Allegro non troppo : Bruno Bozzetto's animated music / Marco Bellano.
Description: New York : Bloomsbury Academic, 2021. | Series: Animation: key films/filmmakers; book 9 | Includes bibliographical references and index.
Identifiers: LCCN 2021006736 (print) | LCCN 2021006737 (ebook) | ISBN 9781501350863 (hardback) | ISBN 9781501350870 (ebook) | ISBN 9781501350887 (pdf)
Subjects: LCSH: Allegro non troppo (Motion picture : 1976)
Classification: LCC PN1997.2.A44455 B45 2021 (print) | LCC PN1997.2.A44455 (ebook) | DDC 791.43/72–dc23
LC record available at https://lccn.loc.gov/2021006736
LC ebook record available at https://lccn.loc.gov/2021006737

ISBN: HB: 978-1-5013-5086-3
PB: 978-1-5013-7628-3
ePDF: 978-1-5013-5088-7
eBook: 978-1-5013-5087-0

Series: Animation: Key Films/Filmmakers

Typeset by Newgen KnowledgeWorks Pvt. Ltd., Chennai, India

To find out more about our authors and books visit www.bloomsbury.com
and sign up for our newsletters.

This one is for my grandfather, Ferdinando (1919–1997). Thanks for the many unforgettable Saturday afternoons we spent chatting about the mysteries of the universe, classical music, dinosaurs, comics, and animation. You showed me the wondrous and kind side of the world.

CONTENTS

Acknowledgments ix
Preamble xi
Foreword xiii

Introduction: Sketching around Bozzetto 1

Part One: The Whole Picture 21

1. Bruno Bozzetto's Life and Works: From the Short Format to the Feature Film 23

2. *Allegro non troppo* at a Glance 63

3. The Path to *Allegro non troppo* 101

Part Two: The Episodes and Their Frame 131

Premise 133

4. The Live-Action Frame 139

5. *Prélude à l'après-midi d'un faune* 149

6. *Slavonic Dance Op. 46 No. 7* 159

7. *Boléro* 165

8. *Valse triste Op. 44 No. 1* 177

9 *Concerto in C Major RV 559* 185

10 *The Firebird Suite* (1919 Version) 193

Finale(s) 203

A Guide to Further Research 213
Appendix 1 215
Appendix 2 225
Bibliography 231
Index 249

ACKNOWLEDGMENTS

I am deeply thankful to Bruno Bozzetto for the time and patience he generously dedicated to my questions and observations on *Allegro non troppo* and his other works. The talks I had with him have been among the best experiences I encountered during the making of this book.

I also owe a lot to Giannalberto Bendazzi. He provided invaluable advice and support to my research; he selflessly shared his immense knowledge in the history of animation with equal amounts of authoritativeness and amiability.

I am grateful to the Department of Cultural Heritage of the University of Padova, the only Italian academic institution where the history of animation gets a chance to be researched and taught; specifically, I wish to thank Prof. Alberto Zotti Minici; Prof. Rosamaria Salvatore, who never spares herself in her dedication to help; and Prof. Jacopo Bonetto, the head of the department, whose trust in my work has always honored and motivated me.

Prof. Bonetto was also decisive in backing my application to chair and bring to Padova the 29th Annual Conference of the SAS—Society for Animation Studies. This book was born on the wake of that 2017 event, which to me was a unique occasion of professional growth. For this reason, I address a sincere thank you to the SAS board and to its then president, Dr. Nichola Dobson.

During my researches, I have received data, materials, and feedbacks from several institutions and individuals, which I would like to mention here with gratitude: Anita and Irene Bozzetto; Maurizio Nichetti; Carlo Re; the Registry Office at the Municipality of Milan; Giancarlo Ripa and Vittorio Miccichè at San Paolo Multimedia; the Teatro Donizetti; and in particular the archivist, Clelia Epis.

A special thanks goes to the Bloomsbury Academic team, and in particular to Chris Pallant, Erin Duffy, and Katie Gallof. They literally made this book possible, also by helping me get through unforeseen obstacles with great patience and swift effectiveness.

I would like to remember here also some of the most important mentors I had during my studies at the Conservatory of Vicenza. Their teachings have fundamentally influenced the way I understand and practice music: the pianist Antonio Rigobello, the composer Enrico Pisa, and the conductor Giancarlo Andretta.

I wish to thank my family, and especially my mother Elina, my father Mauro, and my maternal grandmother Lucia. Their relentless support and trust were some of the most important ingredients in the mix of events that made my interest in animation into a career.

Finally, I have infinite gratitude for Faranak, my wife. The time I spent on this book was graced by her love, intelligence, and creativity; and so was everything else in my life.

PREAMBLE

About a century ago, humankind created a language that could be understood by everybody everywhere and called it animation. Making use of animation, Bruno Bozzetto created short and feature films that brought about admiration and fame to him, all over the world. His best achievement was *Allegro non troppo* (1976).

The specialists of animation recognized his genius and wrote extensively about him: books, essays, articles.

But in Italian only.

Pressed by the needs of international affairs, mankind had understood that a *verbal* means of communication was needed, too, and had decided to use English as the second common language of all.

Easier said than done.

Italians gave up when they clashed with "Worcestershire" and "choir." Hence, everybody trying to write on Bruno Bozzetto for the rest of the world gave up.

The gallant knight who saved the day, as you already know since you have this book in your hands, was Marco Bellano.

Therefore, this story has a merry ending.

Even merrier than its title of *Allegro non troppo*, which literally translated means "Cheerful … not too Much."

Happy reading!

Giannalberto Bendazzi

FOREWORD

Alberto Zotti Minici*

The US theatrical poster proclaimed it "a gorgeous send-up of *Fantasia*!" But was it just a send-up? More than forty years have passed since the release of *Allegro non troppo*, and yet the question is still a valid one. Apparently, the black-and-white live-action interstitial sequences that introduce the music-based animated shorts in color make the point clear: all the comedy in the film is about stealing from Disney's "concert feature." The running joke works like this: the hosts in the live-action sequences feign ignorance about the existence of *Fantasia*, while surreptitiously borrowing as much as possible from the previous feature. However, then, why is the animation so creative and different from that of its alleged model? The first American spectators of the film might have noticed that, while iterating Disney's concept of "seeing the music and hearing the picture," Bozzetto's animated shorts ventured into unexpected territories. They did not shy away from the grotesque, the sensual, the pathetic, and the ridicule; their visual approaches were wildly eclectic, very far from the polished "illusion of life" of *Fantasia*, and yet so right for the tales they told. More importantly, while foregrounding some memorable imagery with a high potential to become timeless (like the close-up of the Coca-Cola bottle littered by space travelers or the deep sad eyes of the cat who meets ghosts from his past), *Allegro non troppo* did not conceal that it was an Italian film of the 1970s. It is not necessary to know about the social turmoil, the terroristic attacks, and the economic crisis that plagued the director's country in that decade to enjoy the feature. Still, all those elements are part of the show, tightly intertwined with the art and the gags and with a decisive role in defining the tone and meaning of *Allegro non troppo*. It is not far-fetched to say that the

---

* Alberto Zotti Minici is Associate Professor in History and Technique of Photography at the Department of Cultural Heritage of the University of Padova, Italy. He is the director of the Padova Museo del PRECINEMA, a permanent exhibition of optical and audiovisual devices that predate cinema. It was established in 1998 by the lanternist Laura Minici Zotti (http://www.minicizotti.it).

US audience might have found the film much quirkier than it appeared to Italians, most likely because of this subtext.

Such rich cultural duplicity is at the core of the historical and critical study of *Allegro non troppo* featured in this book. The work is part of Marco Bellano's continuing study on music in animation, a topic he can tackle from the vantage point of someone who is competent both in film studies and music composition and performance, being also a pianist and conductor. To see his interdisciplinary approach unfold its potential has been, and still is, both thought-provoking and exciting.

The book acknowledges and details the Italian quality of the film while situating it in an international panorama. In fact, Bozzetto's animation has been crossing national borders since its 1958 debut in Cannes, up to and beyond the 2013–14 exhibition that the Walt Disney Family Museum dedicated to the director.

Curiously, a minor intercultural issue showed up also in the case of that exhibition, unbeknownst to many. The title of the event was "Animation, Maestro!": the musical reference was clearly intended to appeal to the familiarity the American audience has with *Allegro non troppo*. However, the curators maybe did not know that no one should ever call Bozzetto a "maestro": he cordially dislikes that honorific. It is not a matter of false modesty at all; first of all, he considers himself more of an artisan. Then, he just prefers other forms of courtesy, as he favors a positive candidness in human relationships. So, could the whole "send-up of Fantasia" joke in *Allegro non troppo* be a natural expression of this side of Bozzetto's personality? He has always looked up to Disney and his heritage, but he would have never tried to compete with him. This was not because he considered himself inferior; he was just aware of being different. He did not want to be yet another maestro, but just to be recognized as Bruno. *Allegro non troppo* is one of Bruno's best portraits; this book tries to tell why.

Introduction: Sketching around Bozzetto

Ideas, Lines, Images, and Their Circumstances

"A drawing is an idea with a line around it."[1] Bruno Bozzetto (Milan, Italy, March 3, 1938) has repeated this favorite quote of him so many times that it became indissolubly bounded to him and his art. Bozzetto acknowledges an unnamed child[2] with the paternity of this phrase, even though it sounds quite similar to a motto[3] ascribed to the French painter Henri Matisse (1869–1954); anyhow, it remains the most elegant short commentary on Bozzetto's approach to animation. Ideas are the main fuel of his films, while the visual style is instrumental to them: after all, because of a poetic coincidence, Bozzetto's surname means "sketch" in Italian, and another of

---

[1] "Un disegno è un'idea con una linea intorno." Bozzetto can be heard saying this in the documentary film *Bozzetto non troppo* (2017), dir. Marco Bonfanti, Italy: Istituto Luce Città, at 1:14:7.

[2] According to Bozzetto, the child who said that was a participant in a discussion about Bozzetto's animation during a class taught by Massimo Maisetti, a scholar and writer specialized in animation. Maisetti later informed the director about the remark of the child. Bozzetto in the documentary *L'arte è un delfino. Intervista a Bruno Bozzetto* (Stefania Gaudiosi, September 30, 2019). https://www.artribune.com/television/2019/09/video-l-arte-e-un-delfino-intervista-a-bruno-bozzetto/ (accessed December 14, 2019).

[3] "Dessiner met une ligne autour d'une idée." For example, the quote inspired the title of an exhibition at the Gagosian Gallery in Genève, Switzerland: "A line (a)round an idea," May 2–July 27, 2019, https://gagosian.com/exhibitions/2019/a-line-around-an-idea-selected-works-on-paper/ (accessed July 1, 2019).

his catchphrases is that he cannot actually draw well.[4] This is why, for his films, he mostly relied on the graphic competences of a selected group of colleagues and friends. Bozzetto's self-taught drawing skills might be limited to two-dimensional characters, made of simple shapes and angular lines, but his design is always cleverly functional to comedy and satire and, more importantly, it consistently stays easily readable and highly expressive. In terms of communicative effectiveness, in spite of his own judgment, Bozzetto can be considered a major visual artist. In fact, he did not shy away from illustrating books or providing newspapers with cartoons featuring his most famous character, Mr. Rossi. He also mentions Saul Steinberg, R. O. Blechman,[5] and Ronald Searle[6] among the main references of his drawing style.

It is in filmmaking, though, that Bozzetto's art showed its outstanding qualities at best. *Mistertao* (1988) won a Golden Bear for the Best Short Film at the 1990 Berlin International Film Festival; *Cavallette* (*Grasshoppers*, 1990) received an Academy Award Nomination for Best Animated Short Film in 1991; from November 21, 2013, to March 17, 2014, the Walt Disney Family Museum in San Francisco hosted the exhibition "Bruno Bozzetto: Animation, Maestro!" More than by honors and awards, though, the worth of Bozzetto's body of work is proved by the unwaveringly positive audience response that continues to the present day in respect to the new, self-produced shorts he keeps releasing online through his YouTube account, BrunoBozzettoChannel.

Many reasons justify Bozzetto's domestic success and international recognition. Among the most important ones there might be a widely relatable thematic choice, which is to say the parodistic exposition of the foolish inclination of humans to pursue self-destructive life choices, while appeasing a greedy pursue of power. Since his first animated short film, *Tapum! La storia delle armi* (*Tapum! The History of Weapons*, 1958), Bozzetto has adopted a consistent satirical strategy, based on the estrangement of the viewer from the subject. Many of his films show, in caricature, the absurdity of the human behavior. The events, often graphically violent and dramatic, are however presented in the fashion of a documentary; a mockingly authoritative voiceover sometimes reinforces this impression. A faraway point of view completes the disengagement of the spectator. As Bozzetto often remarked, even the most tumultuous crowd, from a distance, looks like a bunch of insects. That is why he has sometimes been called

---

[4]Anna Antonini, "Bruno Bozzetto: Wit and Wisdom," *Animation Journal* 25 (2017): 38.
[5]Bozzetto in Roberto Tirapelle (wrongly attributed to Alessandro Camon), ed., *Il cinema di Bruno Bozzetto. Sequenze 9* (Verona: Nuova Grafica Cierre, 1990), 9.
[6]Bozzetto in Ivan Manuppelli, "Intervista a Bruno Bozzetto," *Piero Tonin Blog*, December 12, 2014, http://pierotonin.blogspot.com/2014/12/intervista-bruno-bozzetto_12.html (accessed October 17, 2019).

the entomologist of mankind.⁷ The viewers are thus invited to laugh at the miseries of the human race from a safe position, while, ironically, the film is actually targeting them. This lingering irony, which is in some ways close to the disenchantment of Voltaire's *Candide*, is a distinctive trait of Bozzetto's narrative style and one of the foundations of its universal appeal.

Another distinguishing feature of Bozzetto's works, and one that firmly secured them a place in the panorama of contemporary animation, is their affinity with the stylized visual approach championed by many authors and schools around the world between the 1950s and 1970s. Bozzetto's first inspiration was Ward Kimball, and in particular the daringly stylized (for the Disney canon) animated documentary *Toot, Whistle, Plunk and Boom* (1953);⁸ this choice brought Bozzetto in the same artistic area of other films he knew and esteemed, those by the United Productions of America (UPA), like *Gerald McBoing Boing* (Robert Cannon, 1951) and *Rooty Toot Toot* (John Hubley, 1951), as well as of the abstract designs of the Zagreb School of Animated Film, nurtured by the talents of Dušan Vukotić, Borivoj Dovniković, Ante Zaninović, Zlatko Bourek, Zlatko Grgić, Vladimir Jutriša, Aleksandar Marks, Vatroslav Mimica, and Nedeljko Dragić; they were identified as a school by Georges Sadoul in 1958, the same year of Bozzetto's debut at the second edition of the Rencontres Internationals du Film d'Animation, a subsection of the Cannes Film Festival (its next edition, in 1960, would have become the Festival international du film d'animation d'Annecy). The director also lists Norman McLaren and the works of the National Film Board of Canada (NFB) among the main drives of his early inspiration: they revealed to him that it was possible to make animation without anthropomorphic animals.⁹ However, as Bozzetto himself remarked,¹⁰ the NFB and Zagreb films were mostly intended for a niche audience at festivals; he wanted instead to reach average filmgoers and people. This is why his choice of Kimball as a first source of inspiration proved to be strategic: Kimball had a somewhat radical approach to animation design (which was also in tune with Bozzetto's own drawing skills), but it was framed within the Disney model that had among its main tenets the ability to achieve a widespread appeal, "anything that a person likes to see, a quality of charm, pleasing design, simplicity, communication and magnetism," in the words of the

---

⁷Antonini, "Bruno Bozzetto: Wit and Wisdom," 39. Bozzetto himself acknowledged this definition of his in the documentary *Bozzetto non troppo*, at 1:05:00.
⁸Bozzetto during a meeting with the author in Bergamo, Italy, on January 4, 2019; also mentioned in the English biography published on Bozzetto's official website, https://www.bozzetto.com/pdf/longbio_bb.pdf (accessed September 24, 2020).
⁹Bruno Bozzetto, "Adagio, accelerando," in *Fantasmagoria. Un secolo (e oltre) di cinema d'animazione*, ed. Davide Giurlando (Venezia: Marsilio, 2017), 79.
¹⁰Bozzetto during a meeting with the author in Bergamo, Italy, on July 5, 2019.

Disney veterans Frank Thomas and Ollie Johnston.[11] In addition to that, shortly after Bozzetto's debut, the bidimensional and stylized approach to narrative animated drawings cemented itself as a popular standard in the Western world, thanks to the international successes of the TV series and sitcoms in limited animation of the Hanna-Barbera Productions, like "The Flintstones" (1960–5). Such stylistic trend encountered the Italian audience in a crucial moment: the airing of the evening TV advertising program "Carosello" ("Carousel"), which between 1957 and 1977 remained the only time slot available to commercials in the programming of the single-channel (two-channel from 1961) Italian state television, RAI.[12] Limited animation with a strong design proved functional to the increasing need for relatively cheap but highly appealing short ads. In fact, some of the Hanna-Barbera characters were even licensed to the Italian Studio Pagot, which animated commercials with the Flintstones, the Jetsons, Yogi Bear, and Huckleberry Hound.[13] Bozzetto's natural alignment with those market requirements granted him a preeminent position in the panorama of the "Carosello" animated ads; some of the most successful and well-remembered characters of the program came from Bozzetto's studio, including the American Indian Unca Dunca and the beavers Pildo, Poldo, and Baffoblù. Bozzetto, though, also directed live-action commercials for "Carosello." As a filmmaker, he has always affirmed that he was interested in cinema as a whole, even though animation had his unquestioned preference;[14] this is why his filmography comprises several live-action works, including his fourth and last full-length feature, *Sotto il ristorante cinese* (*Under the Chinese Restaurant*, 1987). However, commercials had never been a preferred outlet to Bozzetto's creativity. He considered the average "Carosello" animations quite crude in terms of technical standard, and he felt that they appealed only to children, while he has always wanted to speak to adults.[15] This is also why he had a mixed opinion on the Hanna-Barbera series, notwithstanding the apparent visual similarities between them and his own films. Anyway, Bozzetto had always aimed at making his commercials with uncompromised quality, but his decision to embark in such productions was mostly dictated by necessity. In fact, he was able to fund his short and features mostly because of the revenue from the commercials. Bozzetto's commitment with "Carosello" started just by chance, because of a suggestion from a friend of his who

---

[11] Frank Thomas and Ollie Johnston, *The Illusion of Life: Disney Animation* (New York: Disney Editions, 1981), 68.
[12] See Piero Dorfles, *Carosello* (Bologna: Il Mulino, 1998).
[13] Fulvio Fiori and Marco Pagot, eds., *The Art of Pagot* (Milano: Edizioni BD, 2008), 91–3.
[14] Bozzetto in the documentary film *Gente di Milano—I mondi di Bruno Bozzetto* (Daniela Trastulli), in the DVD "I corti di Bruno Bozzetto," part of the DVD collection "Tutto Bozzetto (o quasi)" (Roma: Multimedia San Paolo, 2005), at 00:16:20.
[15] Bozzetto during a meeting with the author in Bergamo, Italy, on July 5, 2019.

worked for the automotive firm Innocenti; at the beginning of the 1960s, the director was about to sell out all his cinematographic equipment, with the intention to leave animation for good (because of how unprofitable it was) and to study for a university degree.[16] The decision to work for "Carosello" gave a new chance to his career, but he remained sourly skeptical about the life models and consumerism ideals that those ads promoted; such are the roots of the pungent parodies of ads and average buyers abundantly present in his works, and prominently so in the feature film *Vip, Mio fratello superuomo* (*Vip, My Superman Brother*, 1968).

Italian Animation: An Overview, from Its Origins to the 1970s

The involvement of the director with "Carosello" points out another decisive reason behind the consolidation of Bozzetto's reputation: he started his career and produced his most renowned works during the years when Italian animation peaked, in terms of quality, originality, and sociocultural relevance; Bozzetto himself was one of the driving forces of this "golden age," but he also benefited from the favorable circumstances. In 1957, when "Carosello" debuted, the impact of Italian animation on the audiovisual culture of the country was almost nonexistent. While the Disney films enjoyed a rapidly growing fame and appreciation, also thanks to a series of rapid-fire releases during the 1940s that made up for the films that had never reached Italian cinemas due to the Second World War,[17] the domestic animated production was scarce, mostly derivative and limited to hand-drawn short films, which were still being made with makeshift means and an amateurish approach. Only a few film studios used part of their resources to make animations, like the Istituto Nazionale Luce or the INCOM (Industria CortiMetraggi; "Short Film Industry"), a production company founded in 1938 by Sandro Pallavicini to make propaganda shorts and newsreels for the fascist regime (1922–43); it kept producing newsreels until 1967, the

---

[16]Bozzetto in Gianni Rondolino, *Bruno Bozzetto Pubblicitario* (Torino: STIP, 1969), quoted in Massimo Scaglioni, "La pubblicità: da Carosello allo spot," in *La fabbrica dell'animazione. Bruno Bozzetto nell'industria culturale italiana*, ed. Giannalberto Bendazzi, Raffaele De Berti (Milano: Editrice Il Castoro, 2003), 43.
[17]*Snow White and the Seven Dwarfs* was released in Italy during the 1938/1939 season; then, after the War hiatus, *Saludos Amigos* was released on April 15, 1946; *Fantasia* on September 19, 1946; *Pinocchio* on November 4, 1947; *Bambi* on February 11, 1948; *Dumbo* on October 3, 1948; *The Three Caballeros* on July 14, 1949; *Snow White* was rereleased between December 1949 and January 1950; *Make Mine Music* opened in cinemas on December 16, 1949 and *Song of the South* in April 1950. See Nunziante Valoroso, "Stagioni cinematografiche Walt Disney Italia 1938–2000," *Cabiria* 171 (2012): 45–6.

year when it was bought by the Istituto Nazionale Luce.[18] During the 1930s and 1940s, small animation studios were starting business and then closing down after a short while: such were the cases of the Milion Film, founded by the brothers Carlo (1907–1964) and Vittorio Cossio (1911–1984), or of the Macco Film, established in Rome by Luigi Giobbe in 1942 and then destroyed by a fire in 1943.[19] In 1935, the composer, director, actor, and cinematographer Romolo Bacchini (1872–1938)[20] embarked his studio Cartoni Animati Italiani Roma (CAIR) on the production of *Le avventure di Pinocchio* (*Pinocchio's Adventures*), a full-length animated feature that would have been Italy's first. However, it remained unachieved, just like a previous feature film attempt by another director, Guido Presepi's *Vita di Mussolini* (*Mussolini's Life*, 1925-7).[21] Another example of a short-lived animation production company was the CARAN in Turin, opened in January 1942 by the painter and illustrator Alessio De Barberis with the live-action director Jacopo Comin; however, the only source that tells about this studio is a single magazine article; no one of its films seems to have survived or even been released.[22]

This dire situation persisted during the whole first half of the twentieth century, its causes having been the competition with the unmatchable animated films from the United States and many technical inadequacies: the artists and animators did not have access to professional animation stands or cameras, which were not produced in Italy or were out of reach because of their high cost, and did not know the detail of the cel animation technique, the key to the efficient and seemingly faultless animated drawings imported from America. So, the devices and processes had to be reinvented from scratch each time a new production facility was set up. For example, in 1921 Giovanni Bottini (aka Jean Buttin) devised an analogue to the transparent cel technique for his short *La cura contro il raffreddore* (*The Treatment for the Common Cold*);[23] during the 1940s, two of the most relevant authors

---

[18]Marco Scollo Lavizzari, "INCOM," in *Enciclopedia del Cinema* (Roma: Treccani, 2003), http://www.treccani.it/enciclopedia/incom_%28Enciclopedia-del-Cinema%29/ (accessed July 7, 2019).
[19]Francesco Maurizio Guido, aka Gibba, *Diario. Un uomo di grande insuccesso* (Alassio: Città di Alassio, 2008), 33–4.
[20]Bacchini is thought to have been the very first composer of original music for silent films; in 1906 he wrote the scores to two films credited to Gaston Velle, *Nozze tragiche* (*Tragic Wedding*) and *La malia dell'oro* (*The Enchantment of Gold*). See Sergio Miceli, *Musica per film. Storia, estetica, analisi, tipologie* (Milano: Ricordi LIM, 2009), 69.
[21]Marco Bellano, "Origini dell'animazione italiana: epopee di pionieri solitari," in *Fantasmagoria. Un secolo (e oltre) di cinema d'animazione*, ed. Davide Giurlando (Venezia: Marsilio, 2017), 46.
[22]Raffella Scrimitore, *Le origini dell'animazione italiana. La storia, gli autori e i film animati in Italia 1911–1949* (Latina: Tunué, 2013), 55.
[23]Raffaella Scrimitore, Mario Verger, and Emiliano Fasano, "Chronology of Italian Animation, 1911–2017," *Animation Journal* 25 (2017): 9.

in the history of Italian animation, the brothers Nino (1908–1972) and Toni Pagot (1921–2001), did their animated drawings by using transparent sheets produced by the Rhodia firm in Rho, near Milan;[24] hence the name that, for many years, Italian animation attached to the cel: *rodovetro* ("glass of Rhodia"; it has now been substituted by the English loan word "cel"). The Pagot brothers also engineered an animation camera with the help of their father Umberto, by modifying a regular camera with gears and sprockets made with cutaway pieces from a broomstick.[25] They even recreated independently the Technicolor process, unavailable in Italy because of postwar commercial sanctions.[26] Bozzetto himself, later, made his first animated film, *Tapum!*, with a 16mm camera mounted on a tilted ironing board.[27] Even with those ingenious and moneysaving strategies, though, the production costs remained a major hindrance to the development of Italian animation, as they did not have any chance to be compensated by the sales or even by the share on box-office revenue that the Italian government conceded to production companies during the 1930s.[28] Here is how a film critic, Joseph-Marie Lo Duca, described the situation in early 1949:

> What is most surprising is that there is no regular production of animated drawings and puppets in Italy. When I speak of unemployed specialists, I do so because I do not ignore the efforts that had been done in this field. For ten times cohesive groups of artists, animators, inkers, and so on, teamed up. By wasting paper, celluloid, India ink and tempera, each one of them learned a craft. As they achieved a certain skillfulness, after the production of their first film—which was by no means infamous— the group collapsed. In Milan, in Rome or in smaller cities, many tried themselves regularly with animated drawings. In animated cartoons, the efforts usually resulted in a success. But the absence of a market and of some effective help made projects and endeavors sink. That Italy is the ideal place for animated drawings and puppets is just common saying. The crafty intelligence—that sometimes imitates art—is still strongly alive among us and it could be worthy of that new technical-artistic form that is the animated drawing. But the market is poor, and the future has been jeopardized by the routine. What could an Italian producer of

---

[24]Roberto Della Torre, "Le straordinarie avventure dei fratelli Pagot," in *The Dynamite Brothers. Una storia molto animata*, ed. Roberto Della Torre and Marco Pagot (Milano: Il Castoro, 2004), 41.
[25]Della Torre, "Le straordinarie avventure dei fratelli Pagot," 41.
[26]Fulvio Lombardi, "Ferma, ferma lì! ... Ci siamo anche noi," in *The Dynamite Brothers. Una storia molto animata*, ed. Roberto Della Torre and Marco Pagot (Milano: Il Castoro, 2004), 4.
[27]Bozzetto in Tirapelle, *Il cinema di Bruno Bozzetto*, 12.
[28]Scrimitore, *Le origini dell'animazione italiana*, 56.

animated drawings hope, in the present state of things? To lose two or three million per film.²⁹

As Lo Duca said, notwithstanding the unfavorable context, several early Italian animations proved to be far from infamous, and actually rose to historical fame in hindsight. Not much can be said of the 1911 paint-on-film experiments of the futurist brothers Ginanni Corradini, Arnaldo Ginna (1890–1976), and Bruno Corra (1892–1982), as they are today lost; they might have been the very first examples of Italian animation, even though some scholars differ on this point, like Carlo Montanaro, who pointed out how their work was probably intended just as a substitute for light projections in live performances. He instead sees a starting point for Italian animation in the short stop-motion tricks featuring animated shoes of Arrigo Frusta's live-action short *La storia di Lulù* (*Lulù's story*, 1909).³⁰ Other stop-motion sequences, this time with animated toy soldiers, appeared later in the Second World War propaganda films *Il sogno del bimbo d'Italia* (*The Dream of the Italian Child*, Riccardo Cassano, 1915) and *La Guerra e il sogno di Momi* (*The War and Momi's Dream*, 1917); the latter was directed by the Spanish specialist of "trick films" Segundo de Chomón (1871–1929). Stop-motion "tricks" were thus the first kind of animation practiced in Italy; however, during the 1920s, when the purpose of animation shifted from being a circumscribed attraction in a live-action context to embracing the whole visual and narrative horizon of a film, Italian artist consistently chose to employ drawn animation; that is to say, they based animation on the popular visual culture of comics and book illustrations (and of painting, secondarily), by following the lead of the United States. Stop-motion animated films were rare exceptions, even though Italy has

---

[29]

Quel che è più sorprendente è che in Italia non esista una produzione regolare di disegni e di pupi animati. Quando parlo di specialisti disoccupati è perché non ignoro gli sforzi fatti in questo campo. Dieci volte si formarono gruppi omogenei di disegnatori, animatori, inchiostrartici ecc. Sciupando carta, celluloide, inchiostro di China e tempera, ognuno imparava un mestiere. Raggiunta una certa abilità, finito il primo film—assolutamente non infame—il gruppo crollava. Regolarmente, a Milano, a Roma, in città minori, molti si cimentarono col disegno animato. Generalmente gli sforzi furono coronati dal successo per quanto riguarda i disegni animati. Ma l'assenza d'un mercato e d'un aiuto efficace faceva naufragare progetti e realizzazioni. Affermare che l'Italia sia il paese ideale per i disegni animati e per i pupi è un vero luogo comune. L'intelligenza artigianale—che a volte simula l'arte—è ancora vivissima tra noi e sarebbe degna di questa nuova forma tecnico-artistica che è il disegno animato. Ma il mercato è povero e l'avvenire compromesso dalle abitudini. Allo stato di cose attuale, che può sperare un produttore di disegni animati in Italia? Perdere due o tre milioni per film. (Joseph-Marie Lo Duca, "Alice al paese delle meraviglie," *Cinema Nuova Serie*, I, 6 (January 15, 1949): 176–7. English translation by the author)

³⁰Carlo Montanaro, "C'era una volta l'animazione italiana," *Cabiria* 177 (2014): 9–10.

a secular puppet theater tradition, part of which is a UNESCO World Heritage (i.e., the Sicilian Opera dei Pupi). That theater was mostly used as material for live-action films featuring puppets (*I quattro moschettieri*, *The Four Musketeers*, Carlo Campogalliani, 1936);[31] animated puppet films remained a minority. The only animated restitution of the Opera dei Pupi was Ugo Saitta's *Teste di legno*, or *Pisicchio e Melisenda* (*Wooden Heads* or *Pisicchio and Melisenda*, 1938); Carlo Cossio, instead, directed a now-lost Western film parody with puppets, *Tompitt e i banditi del Far Prest* (*Tompitt and the Fare Fast Outlaws*, 1931). This niche repertoire of early Italian animation features also works by animators who worked in Italy but had East European origins, which granted them a special connection with strong national traditions of puppet theater and animation. Paul Bianchi (1902–1958), who was born in Ukraine, directed films like *Il topo di campagna e il topo di città* (*The Country Mouse and the City Mouse*, 1935), which is now lost, and *Un'avventura nella foresta* (*An Adventure in the Forest*, 1942); Giuseppe Šebesta (1919–2005), whose father was from Czechoslovakia, directed *Novelletta* (*Short Story*, 1949).

Among the scattered and visually inconsistent repertoire of early Italian animation, a few works stood out and earned historical reputation. Among them there are the refined and highly personal shorts (e.g., *Nel paese dei ranocchi*, *In the Land of Frogs*, 1942) by Antonio Rubino (1880–1964), an illustrator, poet, composer, and one of the founders of the renowned magazine for children *Il Corriere dei Piccoli* since its establishment in 1908; he was an artist who brought to Italian comics a unique style, in open contrast with the local and American traditions. During the fascist years, another distinct voice was that of Luigi Liberio Pensuti (1903–1946), an anarchic intellectual who first directed animated shorts based on texts by the Roman and anti-fascist poet Trilussa (such films were later called back and destroyed by the regime)[32] and then worked for INCOM. His educational and scientific shorts brought Italian animation in the territories of the animated documentary and, notwithstanding the evident technical limitations, testified a conscious care in reaching communicative effectiveness through clear layouts, appealing drawings, and well-timed animated acting.[33] Another memorable contribution was that of Francesco Maurizio Guido, aka Gibba[34] (1924–2018); his first short film *L'ultimo sciuscià* (*The Last Shoeshine*, 1947) was the only attempt to translate into

---

[31] Scrimitore, *Le origini dell'animazione italiana*, 45.
[32] Scrimitore, *Le origini dell'animazione italiana*, 118.
[33] See Raffaella Scrimitore, "Luigi Liberio Pensuti, film d'animazione oltre la propaganda," *Cabiria* 178 (2014): 47–56; Cristina Formenti, "Note sul documentario animato italiano e il suo periodo delle origini," *Immagine. Note di storia del cinema* 15 (2017): 65–77.
[34] Cristina Formenti, "Dal neorealismo al documentario animato scientifico: le animazioni 'realiste' di Gibba," *Cabiria* 178 (2014): 4–19.

animation the neorealist poetics of directors such as Roberto Rossellini and, in particular, Vittorio De Sica; the child in the short is in fact voiced by Luciano De Ambrosis, the protagonist of De Sica's *I bambini ci guardano* (*The Children Are Looking at Us*, 1943). The film is a retelling of Hans Christian Andersen's *The Little Matchgirl* in the context of the Allied invasion of Italy; while the drawing style roughly mimics the Disney shorts of the 1940s, the story is historically circumstantiated, has a bittersweet tone, and a tragic ending.

Italian animation started to produce full-length features in 1949, quite late in respect to other European countries. Germany had already had Lotte Reiniger's *Die Abenteuer des Prinzen Achmed* (*The Adventures of Prince Achmed*) in 1926, while Spain produced Arturo Moreno's *Garbancito de la Mancha* (*Little Garbanzo Bean from the Mancha*) in 1945 and Denmark released Svend Methling's *Fyrtøjet* (*The Tinderbox*) in 1946. Italy's case was unique, though, because two "first animated features" were released at the same time: Nino Pagot's *I fratelli Dinamite* (*The Dynamite Brothers*) and Anton Gino Domeneghini's *La rosa di Bagdad* (*The Rose of Bagdad*, or *The Singing Princess*).[35] They did not prove to be game changers for the Italian industry of animation, as no other full-length animated feature was produced in the country until 1965. Both films were first screened during the 1949 Venice Film Festival; *The Rose of Bagdad* even won the first prize in the category "Film per ragazzi" ("Films for young people"); *The Dynamite Brothers* was screened in the section "Film a soggetto" ("Narrative films").[36] However, after an unsuccessful cinema release around Christmas 1949,[37] *The Dynamite Brothers* sunk into oblivion. It seldom reappeared before its 2004 DVD release, as in the case of its black-and-white broadcast during the TV show "Mille e una sera," on RAI's Secondo Canale, at 9:15 p.m. on May 1, 1971. The ticket sales of *The Rose of Bagdad* were comparatively more successful, and the film reached the foreign markets of the UK, the Netherlands, France, and Belgium; however, the real profit was marginal, because of the massive production costs, the inadequate theatrical distribution, and Domeneghini's poor financial decisions. He was probably the only real producer-entrepreneur that Italian animation has ever had,

---

[35]Even though Domeneghini's *The Rose of Bagdad* debuted at the Venice International Film Festival on August 22, 1949, just like *The Dynamite Brothers*, the latter was registered at SIAE (the Italian copyright office) in 1947; its registry number was 672. *The Rose of Bagdad* was registered in 1949 (no. 799). However, it is controversial whether a SIAE registration could establish the legal existence of a film in a certain date, or not. Giannalberto Bendazzi, "The First Italian Animated Feature Film and Its Producer: Anton Gino Domeneghini," *Animation Journal* 3, no. 2 (Spring 1995): 14–15.

[36]Giannalberto Bendazzi, "Un produttore e il suo film. Anton Gino Domeneghini e The Rose of Bagdad," in *Il movimento creato. Studi e documenti di ventisei saggisti sul cinema d'animazione*, ed. Giannalberto Bendazzi, Guido Michelone (Torino: Edizioni Pluriverso, 1993), 131.

[37]Della Torre, "Le straordinarie avventure dei fratelli Pagot," 42.

but his penchant for grandiosity, often connected with his firm believe in the fascist ideals, had him promise to repay his creditors with the double of the loaned sums. When he evened out the production costs, he raised his offer to three times the due amount.[38] The two films did not thus kickstart the Italian animation market; however, they had several artistic merits and they favored encounters and connections between creatives that would have later contributed to the "golden age" of Carosello. *The Rose of Bagdad* and *The Dynamite Brothers* were profoundly different: the former was helmed by Domeneghini (1897–1966), a fascist advertising businessman who sought to emulate and even surpass Disney. His advertising agency, IMA (Idea-Metodo-Arte; "Idea-Method-Art"), which was established in 1929, was converted into an animation studio to face the crisis of the advertising market due to the War; the resulting film was a fairy tale inspired by *One Thousand and One Nights*, based on a close moviola study of a *Snow White and the Seven Dwarfs* print and enriched by the contributions of fine illustrators like Angelo Bioletto (1906–1987) and Libico Maraja (1912–1983), and of the renowned composer Riccardo Pick-Mangiagalli. The director of *The Dynamite Brothers*, Nino Pagot (1908–1972), was too a fine illustrator; with his brother Toni (1921–2001), the animator and musician Ferdinando Palermo (1913–1988), and the obscure but brilliant composer Giuseppe Piazzi (1903–1969), he created a film in four episodes that was ideally connected with the tradition of Collodi's *Pinocchio*; it dealt with the mischievous deeds of the triplets Dynamite and their redemption. The film was less technically polished but more daring, imaginative, and dynamic than *The Rose of Bagdad* (Piazzi's music even imitated Igor Stravinsky, and not the melodic style of US animation).[39] The production of both films was anyway slowed down and hampered by the War, even though the Pagot brothers were on the opposite front of Domeneghini, as they gave shelter to antifascists and people persecuted by the regime in their studios in Milan. Toni was also deported to Germany. In the end, *The Dynamite Brothers* was the more influential of the two, also because the Pagot brothers would have continued their careers by animating many memorable characters for "Carosello," including the black chick Calimero, while Domeneghini, after two experimental shorts, returned to a managerial role in the advertisement business. The work of the Pagot brothers was also an epitome to the panorama of early Italian animation: it showed how to make the best of the energetic diversity of styles and approaches that marked the early history

---

[38] Bendazzi, "Un produttore e il suo film," 131.
[39] See Marco Bellano, "'Oh ... Musica moderna!'. Hollywood, satira e 'modernismo' nella musica di Giuseppe Piazzi per *I fratelli Dinamite*," *Cabiria* 178 (2014): 57–70; and also Bellano, "*I fratelli Dinamite* di Nino Pagot (1949) e l'idea di 'bello' in musica," in *Estudios sobre la influencia de la canción popular en el proceso de creación de música incidental*, ed. Sergio De Andrés Bailón (Salamanca: Ediciones Universidad de Salamanca, 2016), 335–57.

of this medium in Italy, while celebrating the ability to bypass the technical impairments with confident ingenuity.

The real game changer for Italian animation was advertising. Since the 1920s, when commercials started to be screened in Italian cinemas, the demand for short and visually compelling commercials had been steadily growing. Attilio Giovannini wrote in 1957 that the first blows to the Italian perception that Disney was the "embodiment" of animated drawings came precisely from the authors of animated commercials.[40] Gec (Enrico Gianeri, 1900–1984), a journalist and cartoonist who was also among the first animation historians of Italy, reported that the first advertising cartoon, for a garment bag,[41] was authored by the Cossio Brothers in 1929 at the IPC (Impresa Pubblicità Cinematografica—"Cinema Advertising Enterprise")[42] of Bruno Ditz and Marcello Maestro; Bruno Munari, who would have later become a renowned designer, worked for the same company and collaborated to the Cossios' animations.[43] Cinema advertisement offered frequent job opportunities also to other Italian animators during the 1930s and 1940s, as in the case of Gustavo Petronio, who created a well-received pair of characters for the Arrigoni food company in Trieste, *Arrigo e il suo tigrotto* ("Arrigo and his tiger cub"). Two other authors of animations destined to be remembered, Paul Bianchi and Nino Pagot, started their career in advertisement; they worked for the Publi-Enic company of the Leoni Brothers, one of the two major agencies for cinema advertising in Italy until 1950, together with the Publicitas company. Meanwhile, as already pointed out, Domeneghini's IMA had already started business in 1929. In the postwar years, advertising became a main player in the economic recovery of Italy. The push to produce and sell claimed for more advertising agencies that mostly opened in the city of Milan. In 1951 Osvaldo Cavandoli, who previously worked with the Pagots and was destined to fame with his later "Carosello" character La Linea ("The Line"), established the short film studio Pupilandia ("The Land of Puppets") with the photographer Ugo Gelsi; in the same period, the Studio 3P was born from an initiative of Elena Pellegrini and Osvaldo Piccardo, another former collaborator of the Pagots who later, with his brother Marcello and Bruno Munari, promoted and coordinated a major experimental center in film and advertising, the Studio di Monte Olimpino, near Como (1962–72).[44] The Gamma Film of the brothers Gino and Roberto Gavioli was legally registered in 1949;[45] its

---

[40]Attilio Giovannini, *Guida alla pubblicità cinematografica* (Milano: L'ufficio moderno, 1957), 166.
[41]Scrimitore, *Le origini dell'animazione italiana*, 41.
[42]Enrico Gianeri, aka Gec, *Storia del cartone animato* (Milano: Omnia Editrice, 1960), 192.
[43]Piero Zanotto and Fiorello Zangrando, *L'Italia di cartone* (Padova, Liviana, 1973), 25–6.
[44]http://nuke.monteolimpino.it/Default.aspx (accessed on July 9, 2019).
[45]Marcello Zane, *Scatola a sorpresa. La Gamma Film di Roberto Gavioli e la comunicazione audiovisiva in Italia da Carosello a oggi* (Milano: Jaca Book, 1998), 22–3.

first animated advertisements were for the Lever agency, but the Gaviolis built their reputation at Guido and Oscar Maestro's Opus (that bought the Publi-Enic in 1950), starting with the short *Night and Day* (1951); the Gamma Film later worked for Ferry (Ferdinando) Mayer, a cousin of the Leoni brothers of Israeli origins, who founded his own agency in 1950, after a period as an employee at Opus. Most of the interest that Italian industries had in promoting their business through animated commercials goes to Mayer's merit.[46] Another major player in the pre-"Carosello" years of animated advertising was the Pagot Film studio, which had already been releasing animated commercials since 1936 (for the Leoni brothers);[47] in the early 1950s it changed its name into Opec—Organizzazione Pagot & C. ("Pagot Organization and Company") that remained active until 1972, when Nino Pagot died; it was later reopened as Rever by the sons of Nino, Marco and Gi (Gina), and is still active in 2021. The production was further stimulated by the establishment of competitions for commercials only; in 1951, the Mostra Internazionale del Cinema al Servizio della Pubblicità ("International Exhibition of Cinema at the Service of Advertising") opened at the Milan Fair; in 1954, the Festival Internazionale del Film Pubblicitario ("Advertising Film International Festival") had its first edition in Venice, but, after a second edition in Monte Carlo, it later moved to Cannes; it alternated between the latter and Venice until (1984) it settled in the French city, where it still takes place under the name Festival International de la Publicité Cannes Lions.

Such a productive context, now richer in resources and competences and fueled by an unprecedented demand for animation, paved the way to the debut of "Carosello" in 1957 and naturally attracted many young talents into its welcoming force field. Bozzetto was among them; and so was his studio, the Bruno Bozzetto Film (Studio Bozzetto & Co. since 2000), established in 1960 in Milan, via Melchiorre Gioia.

At the end of the two "Carosello" decades, Italian animation had changed its face. There still was not an industrial production, and an equal competition with the animated films imported from the United States was out of question; however, many studios had managed to stay active well beyond their opening and first works, fostering thus the consolidation of stylistic traditions and the continuous training of the skills of many practitioners. Such studios were more artisanal workshops than industrial facilities; there was not a single production model but a flexible disposition to modify or reinvent the animation pipeline according to the specific necessities of each

---

[46]Roberto Della Torre, "È nata un'idea! La produzione pubblicitaria cinematografica dei fratelli Pagot," in *Un mondo perfetto. Le pubblicità cinematografiche dei fratelli Pagot*, ed. Roberto della Torre and Marco Pagot (Milano: Il Castoro, 2005), 13.
[47]Della Torre, "Le straordinarie avventure dei fratelli Pagot," 38.

film, even by means of "trial and error" processes. In this respect, Bozzetto has always liked to call himself an "eternal amateur,"[48] always ready to learn a new craft from scratch; this is maybe one of the reasons of the visceral discontent he feels when someone addresses him with the word "maestro." Productivity and creativity were anyway fiercely stimulated by the "Carosello" requirements: the deadlines and format imposed by the RAI were in fact quite restrictive so that directors and scriptwriters had to keep devising clever narrative and visual solutions in order to make the best out of those limitations. Each commercial could not last more than two minutes and fifteen seconds, which is sixty-four meters and twenty-six centimeters of film length.[49] The actual promotional message had to stay in the last thirty seconds only.[50] Each short could not be repeated (but there were some exceptions); every evening the "Carosello" time slot had to last ten minutes (from 8:50 to 9:00 p.m.), which allowed for a total of four shorts. This meant 1,460 new commercials per year, both animated and live-action.[51] This is why the RAI, which initially wanted to self-produce the commercials, outsourced the films to private studios that kept multiplying through the whole country; even though Rome and Milan were the main productive centers, other film companies appeared also in smaller cities. Among those specialized in animation, for example, there were Paul Campani's Paul Film in Modena or the Studio K of Francesco Misseri, Pier Francesco Tamburini, and Renzo Tarchi in Florence. The already-mentioned Gamma Film, in Milan, was one of the most active: in its first three years of work for Carosello (1958–1960) it produced 110 commercials; they became 290 in 1961–3.[52] Many famous stop-motion "carosellos" were produced by Armando Testa in Turin; the Corona Cinematografica of the brothers Ezio, Fulvio, and Elio Gagliardo, active in Rome from the late 1940s through 1997, besides its contribution to the advertising market by means of its association with the Ondatelerama company in 1960, which was for a short time known as Publicorona,[53] deserves also to be mentioned because of a peculiar production of animated documentaries and experimental shorts.

---

[48]"Eterno dilettante." Mario Serenellini, "La medietà made in Italy nella saga nata 45 anni fa. Dialogo tra il Signor Rossi e il Signor B," in *Bruno Bozzetto. Cinquant'anni di cartoni animati*, ed. Dino Aloi (Torino: Edizioni Il Pennino, 2005), 56.
[49]Vito Molinari, *Carosello... e poi tutti a nanna. 1957–1977: i vent'anni che hanno cambiato l'Italia* (Sestri Levante: Gammarò edizioni, 2019), 23-4. Through the years, the allowed length changed to 2:30 in 1959, it went back to 2:15 in 1960, then it became 2:05 in 1973, and 1:40 in 1974. See Viviana Giovannetti, ed. *Ai margini del cartoon. Supplemento a Cineclub 25* (Roma: FEDIC, 1995), 33.
[50]Dorfles, *Carosello*, 17.
[51]Marco Giusti, *Il grande libro di Carosello* (Segrate: Frassinelli, 2004), 13.
[52]Zane, *Scatola a sorpresa*, 60.
[53]Giusti, *Il grande libro di Carosello*, 16.

Other than by the proliferation of studios with a continued activity, the new florid condition of Italian animation was signaled by the quality and quantity of films made with no advertising purposes. Those works, mostly short films, were often produced out of the desire of artists and directors to put to test the abilities they honed with "Carosello," but there was also room for films by traditional artists who, in the words of Giacomo Ravesi, saw animation as "a fertile land to extend their artistic search beyond the canvas and develop original connections between art, painting, and animation."[54] Such were the cases of Cioni Carpi (1923–2011), Manfredo Manfredi (1934), Alberto Mastroianni (1903–74), and Magdalo Mussio (1925–2006).

With no real audience, apart from the people at the animation festivals that had started to appear in Europe in those years (like in Cannes, 1960, and Zagreb, since 1972), those short films embodied the liberation of the artistic desires of a generation. There was actually a marginal interest in theatrical success; a 1965 law[55] instituted a state award called "Premio di qualità" ("quality award") that sustained the most deserving short films productions, destined to be screened in cinemas with full-length features; but the winners were usually not animations but "artsy" documentaries made with the prospective funding in mind only.[56] Sometimes cinema operators did not even program them,[57] as they feared they would have irritated the audience.[58]

This situation freed the directors and animators from the competition with Disney; a plurality of visual styles could thus be researched and expressed without almost no concern, except the budgetary ones. For example, the theater and opera scenographer Emanuele Luzzati (1921–2007) and the cinematographer Giulio Gianini (1927–2009) initiated in 1960 (*I paladini di Francia*, The Paladins of France) a series of shorts wherein using stop-motion are animated cut-out collages of poor materials, including "fabric, paper, splinters of wood, plastic or glass, doilies for cakes, basically everything in reach."[59] The final result bridged together the historical Italian

---

[54] Giacomo Ravesi, "Painted Screens: Italian Experimental Artists-Animators," *Animation Journal* 25 (2017): 62.
[55] Law 1213/1965; http://www.prassicoop.it/Norme/L%201213_65%20A.pdf (accessed July 19, 2019). See also Marco Bertozzi, *Storia del documentario italiano. Immagini e culture dell'altro cinema* (Venezia: Marsilio, 2008), 125.
[56] See Bruno Di Marino, "Vite in scatola: opere e autori del cinema d'animazione," in *Storia del cinema italiano 1965/1969*, ed. Gianni Canova (Venezia: Marsilio, 2003), 227.
[57] Bertozzi, *Storia del documentario italiano*, 125.
[58] Bozzetto, "Adagio, accelerando," 82–3.
[59] "Stoffe, carte, pezzetti di legno, plastica o vetro, centrini delle torte, praticamente qualunque cosa gli capitasse a tiro." Carla Rezza Gianini, "Animazione per passione," in *Gianini e Luzzati. Cartoni animati*, ed. Alfio Bastiancich and Carla Rezza Gianini (Milano: Silvana Editoriale, 2013), 23.

puppetry with the most refined styles of illustration for children; many of Gianini and Luzzati's stories did not use dialogue, but their character acted in close synchronization with music from the opera repertoire. Two of their works based on opera symphonies by Gioachino Rossini went on to receive Academy Award nominations: *La gazza ladra* (*The Thieving Magpie*, 1964) and *Pulcinella* (1973, based on Rossini's *Il turco in Italia*, *The Turk in Italy*). Other artists who contributed to the ebullient variety of approaches to animation of the 1960s and 1970s were Giorgio "Max" Massimino-Garniér (1924–1985), Guido Gomas (Luigi Guido Gonzo; 1936–2005), Lorenzo Taiuti (1943), and Pino Zac (Giuseppe Zaccaria; 1930–1985).

This expressive renovation was encouraged also by new Italian initiatives that recognized the artistic value of animation, like the international meetings that took place in 1969 and 1970 in Busto Arsizio, Mantova, and Abano Terme, resulting in the creation of the Istituto per lo Studio e la Diffusione del Cinema di Animazione (ISCA—"Institute for the Study and Diffusion of Animated Cinema"), in the spring of 1970. In the same year, until 1971, the second RAI channel inaugurated "Mille e una sera" ("One Thousand and One Evenings"), a program that every Saturday broadcasted renowned animated features from the past, including *Vynález skázy* (*The Fabulous World of Jules Verne*, Karel Zeman, 1958), *Le Théâtre de monsieur et madame Kabal* (*Mr. and Mrs. Kabal's Theatre*, Walerian Borowczyk, 1967), and the two Italian pioneering full-length features of 1949. From 1970 and 1973, another program "Gli eroi di cartone" ("Cartoon Heroes") aired biweekly thematic anthologies of animated shorts, during the afternoon time slot of the first RAI channel dedicated to children's shows; it featured also films by Winsor McCay, Władysław Starewicz, and Norman McLaren.

Another major consequence of this situation was the reappearance of full-length animated features: in 1965, Bozzetto directed *West and Soda* (1965), an animated spaghetti-western whose ideation actually anticipated Sergio Leone's genre-defining *Per un pugno di dollari* (*A Fistful of Dollars*, 1964), but that was released later only because of the longer time required by animation production. Two more feature were completed in the 1960s, Bozzetto's *Vip, Mio fratello superuomo* (*Vip, My Brother Superman*, 1968) and Gino and Roberto Gavioli's *Putiferio va alla Guerra* (*The Magic Bird*, 1968), plus a film that alternated live-action with an extended animated sequence by Pino Zac, *Gatto Filippo licenza d'incidere* (*Philip the Cat—Licence to Hack*, 1966). But it was during the 1970s that animated feature films started to populate the Italian cinema repertoire more conspicuously, even though the numbers remained far from overwhelming. With the exclusion of the live-action works with animated sequences, the final count is of eight, among which there were some record-setters, like the first Italian hand-drawn version of Collodi's *Pinocchio* (*Un burattino di nome Pinocchio*; *The Adventures of Pinocchio*, 1971) and the debut of an animated pornographic comedy feature film in Italy, *Il nano e la strega* (*King Dick*, Gibba 1975). Four out of those eight features were by Bozzetto: three films featuring Mr. Rossi that however were broadcasted in small installments on TV[60] (*Il signor Rossi cerca la felicità, Mr. Rossi in Search of Happiness*, 1976; *I sogni del signor Rossi, Mr. Rossi's Dreams*, 1977; *Le vacanze del signor Rossi, Mr. Rossi's Vacations*, 1978) and, above all, *Allegro non troppo* (1976).

Approaching *Allegro non troppo*

Allegro non troppo is, as of 2021, the third and last animated full-length feature that Bozzetto directed on the basis of an original concept and with an audience of young adults in mind (the Mr. Rossi films are usually not counted, because they are just collections of short films for children, based on a preexisting character). *Allegro non troppo* came at the very end of the "Carosello" era, and it retrospectively feels like a farewell to it, as well as a celebration of the history of Italian animation up to that point. In fact, in content and style, the film resumes major characteristics such as the accent on the short format (it is made of separate shorts alternated with a live-action continuing story), the use of cel animation (but there is also a brief sequence in stop-motion clay animation), a plurality of visual approaches (each short has a different design and animation style), a deep accordance between visual and musical rhythms (like in the films by Gianini and Luzzati), a mocking stance on advertising and consumers, and a blatant reference to Disney animation: the film is a parodistic remake of *Fantasia* (James Algar and others, 1940).

However, at the same time, *Allegro non troppo* also superseded all those traits and showed how far Italian animation could go. The short format is encased into a long continuity, and some of the animated stories overflow into the framing sequences, by mixing drawings with live-action footage; cel animation is used in unconventional ways, as in the bravura piece that is the episode on Maurice Ravel's *Boléro*, where the animators had to draw intricate *sfumato* shadows in pencil on the bodies of the numerous creatures that populate the scenes; the stylistic diversity is used in close accordance with the expressive content of the music and storylines; the choreographic connection between music and movement is explored in depth; the parody on consumerism expands to a wider array of ecological and social issues, but it also deeply connects with the Italian context of the 1970s, which leaves a deep cultural mark on a film that anyway retains an international appeal; and, finally, the reference to the Disney model is by no means due

---

[60]Maurizio Nichetti in Mario Querin, ed., *Bruno Bozzetto* (Trento: Centro di Documentazione Visiva, 1992), 27–8.

to marketing reasons or to a scarcity of original ideas, but it is a heartfelt homage to it and a deep rethinking of the very idea of "concert feature," as Disney initially wanted to call *Fantasia*.

Allegro non troppo was also a landmark in Bozzetto's career. In 1976, after eighteen years of activity, he had already directed two animated features and eighteen animated theatrical shorts, which earned respect and interest among critics and spectators at international festivals. A great number of short TV animations, like "carosellos," program intros, and small specials, added to the count of his works. In the 1970s, he was also in the middle of a renewed interest for live-action films, favored by his encounter with the actor and screenwriter Maurizio Nichetti (Bozzetto practiced live-action during his stints as a filmmaker before his 1958 official debut); when Nichetti played the role of an animator in the interstitials of *Allegro non troppo*, he had already starred in three shorts by his friend. A premise to *Allegro non troppo*'s format, which reunites multistylistic fragments into a larger unitary structure, is found in *Sottaceti* (*Pickles*, 1971), which packs in mere twelve minutes thirteen episodes plus an epilogue, all making fun of the absurd human ways to deal with major sociohistorical issues like war, pollution, and so on; the animation is continuously varied and very stylized (everything in it is exceptionally drawn and colored by Bozzetto himself,[61] just like it happens in one of the shorts of *Allegro non troppo*). Moreover, Bozzetto had already played with humorous uses of music from "high" repertoires in *Opera*, a 1973 short he codirected with one of his key collaborators, Guido Manuli, and that is based on surreal gags synchronized with excerpts from Italian operas.

Where This Book Stands

The aim of the present book is to introduce *Allegro non troppo* to English-speaking readers; it is both a historical record and an analytical commentary, but also a gateway to details on the history of Italian animation and Bozzetto's career, which have been largely absent from the discourses of international animation studies because of a language barrier.

The book is divided into two main parts. Part 1 ("The Whole Picture") is of three chapters; it is about *Allegro non troppo* from a general point of view. It has an informative scope and follows a historical criterion. Chapter 1 ("Bruno Bozzetto's Life and Works: From the Short Format to the Feature Film") outlines the director's biography, with special attention

---

[61]Giannalberto Bendazzi, *Bruno Bozzetto. Animazione primo amore* (Milano: ISCA, 1972), reprinted in Alfio Bastiancich, ed., *Bruno Bozzetto: 1958–1988* (Savona: Centro Promozionale Coop, 1988), 27–8.

to his professional efforts and the building of his view on animation and audiovisual aesthetics. The reader will be provided with extra elements of history of Italian animation when necessary. The critical transition to the full-length feature in Italian animation is discussed there, in order to stress the groundbreaking impact of Bozzetto's exploration of this field. Chapter 2 ("*Allegro non troppo* at a Glance") is an overall description of the film: its narrative content, its relationship with the Italian society and history of the 1970s, and its communicative strategies. The conclusive section of this chapter will be dedicated to the comparison between *Allegro non troppo* and Walt Disney's *Fantasia*. Chapter 3 ("The Path to *Allegro non troppo*") informs about the history of the preproduction and production of the film. It will also provide a few biographical sketches of the main artistic contributors to the work (e.g., Giuseppe Laganà, Guido Manuli, and Maurizio Nichetti). The chapter will report on all-new information about discarded episodes of *Allegro non troppo*, based on conversations with Bruno Bozzetto and archival material.

Part 2 ("The Episodes and Their Frame") approaches the several episodes of *Allegro non troppo* individually. There is a chapter for each one of them, plus one chapter on the live-action sequences that connect the animated parts and one chapter on the animated multiple conclusions of the film. Each chapter is structured as follows: (1) a description and summary of the episode; (2) "program notes," which is to say a commentary accessible to a wide audience but based on scholarship from musicology, music history, animation history, and animation theory. The structure of Part 2 will thus be modeled after *Allegro non troppo* itself. After an explanation of the methodology that will be used during the audiovisual analysis, Chapter 1 will deal with "The Live-Action Frame"; the live-action sequences in *Allegro non troppo* will be explained in light of their satirical and structural relevance. The rest of the chapters will be titled after the pieces of music used in the episodes: *Prélude à l'après-midi d'un faune* (Claude Debussy), *Slavonic Dance Op. 46 No. 7* (Antonín Dvořák), *Boléro* (Maurice Ravel), *Valse triste Op. 44 No. 1* (Jean Sibelius), *Concerto in C Major RV 559* (Antonio Vivaldi), and *The Firebird Suite* (1919 Version) (Igor Stravinsky). The last chapter is about the "Finale(s)," and the finale of the book itself, providing also its conclusion.

Some of the preproduction notes by Bozzetto have been translated and organized in two appendixes. Appendix 1 lists the titles of all the musical works that the director considered to use during his creative process, alphabetically ordered by composer. The plot ideas that the director wrote down near to some of the composition titles have also been reported. However, when such ideas were more extensively developed, they have been translated and collected in Appendix 2, ordered again by composer name.

A peculiar feature of this book is that the director himself is one the sources of its research. Over a whole year (2018–19), Bozzetto has kindly agreed to meet the author to share his own recollections, archives, and expertise. This firsthand material on *Allegro non troppo* (and his other works) was cross-checked, integrated, and sometimes amended, when compared with other literature and testimonies on the topic, as it usually happens when interviews are involved in a scholarly work; however, it constituted an unvaluable sources of insights and research leads, which the author received with deep gratitude and which will be presented to the reader in the next pages.

PART ONE

The Whole Picture

1

Bruno Bozzetto's Life and Works: From the Short Format to the Feature Film

The Italian Disney?

"The Italian Disney" or "the anti-Disney": there is no middle ground, in the formulas the Italian press employs when talking about Bruno Bozzetto.[1] The recurring comparison with Disney tells a lot about the average Italian idea of animation and how it has been forged by the works of the American entrepreneur. However, both comparisons are misleading. It is true that Bozzetto has repeatedly voiced his unconditioned admiration for Disney: *Allegro non troppo* is directly inspired by *Fantasia*, a film the director saw in theater more than a dozen times,[2] and that he calls "a revelation, something essential to me, a part of my life."[3] Bozzetto has also a personal attachment to *Bambi* (David Hand and others, 1942): "[it] educated me. ... There I learned what is man to nature";[4] "from that moment, I think that my poetics got influenced by it for good."[5] Moreover, the Disney short *Toot,*

---

[1] Massimo Maisetti, "Bruno Bozzetto: l'anti Disney," in *Bruno Bozzetto: 1958–1988*, ed. Alfio Bastiancich (Savona: Centro Promozionale Coop, 1988), 70.
[2] Bozzetto in Bastiancich, *Bruno Bozzetto*, 12.
[3] "Una rivelazione, qualcosa di imprescindibile, una parte della mia vita." Personal communication to the author via Skype, January 20, 2019.
[4] "*Bambi* mi ha formato. ... Da lì ho capito che cosa era l'uomo per la natura." Andrijana Ružić, "Un romanzo corale," in *Allegro non troppo. Un tesoro dell'arte italiana*, ed. Chiara Cereda, Shirin Chehayed, Priscilla Mancini, and Andrijana Ružić (Milano: Agema, 2016), 24.
[5] "Da quel momento credo che la mia poetica ne fu influenzata per sempre." Fabrizio Dividi, "Bruno Bozzetto: 'L'ecologia? L'ho scoperta grazie a *Bambi* della Disney'," *Corriere Torino* (July 10, 2019), https://torino.corriere.it/cultura/19_luglio_10/

Plunk, Whistle and Boom was not only among his early main sources of graphic inspiration (see the Introduction) but also a strong motivation to overcome his hesitations and see a professional future in the same field of Disney:

> It was inconceivable to make films like he did, with such a rich animation, so technically advanced ... You get scared even before you start! ... [With *Toot, Plunk, Whistle and Boom*] I discovered that it was possible to make an "intelligent" film, a parody of everyday life, with a bare drawing style ... just like mine! So, after all, it was Disney again that directed me towards this job.[6]

The director never sought an artistic confrontation with his colleague in Hollywood, though. He conceded once that his own style might be "a mixture between Walt Disney and McLaren, and those two are diametrically opposed characters!"[7] adding soon after that "I always advice to not imitate Walt Disney."[8] In fact, Bozzetto never did so; as Bendazzi argued, the only thing he might have in common with Disney is that "he remained in the path of the same tradition (a tradition Disney is only part of, because it was born 'before' Disney); that is to say, he made humorous films, with caricatural characters, whose vicissitudes are worthy of the purest slapstick comedy."[9]

So, the recurring labeling of Bozzetto as a new Disney is just part of the easy parlance of the Italian press, which holds Disney as the only reference in animation. However, it is also true that Bozzetto has been the only popularly known director of Italian animation for many years, at least until the late-1990s commercial successes of the full-length animated features

---

bruno-bozzetto-l-ecologia-l-ho-scoperta-grazie-bambi-disney-910bb784-a2f8-11e9-a4d9-199f0357bdd6.shtml (accessed July 18, 2019).

[6]
> Non era pensabile fare dei film come li faceva lui, con quel tipo di animazione così ricca e con una tecnica così avanzata ... Ti spaventi ancora prima di incominciare! [Con *Toot, Plunk, Whistle and Boom*] ho scoperto che si poteva fare un film "intelligente," una parodia della vita normale, realizzandolo con un disegno scarno ... come quello che sapevo fare anch'io! Quindi in definitiva è stato ancora Disney a spingermi verso questo lavoro.

Bruno Bozzetto, Intervista, in Maria Francesca Botticini, "Allegro non troppo. Bruno Bozzetto, Cartoonist italiano" (thesis, Università degli Studi di Bologna, 1993), II, quoted in Antonio Vincenzo Boscarino, *L'estetica di Bruno Bozzetto. Teoria e prassi tra movimento e spettacolo* (Roma: Bulzoni Editore, 2002), 16–17.

[7]Bozzetto (1968), in Bastianich, *Bruno Bozzetto*, 12.
[8]Ibid.
[9]"È pur rimasto nel solco della tradizione stessa (una tradizione di cui Disney è solo parte, perché nata "prima" di Disney); ha cioè fatto film umoristici, con personaggi caricaturali, con vicende degne della più pura *slapstick comedy*." Giannalberto Bendazzi, *Bruno Bozzetto. Animazione primo amore* (Milano: ISCA, 1972), reprinted in Alfio Bastianich, ed., *Bruno Bozzetto: 1958–1988* (Savona: Centro Promozionale Coop, 1988), 30.

by Enzo D'Alò (*La gabbianella e il gatto*, *Lucky and Zorba*, 1998); the association with Disney's name was thus also based on his fame. Moreover, when Bozzetto started making full-length animated films in the 1960s, the only popular model of animated feature was the Disney one. Bozzetto himself, when initially prompted by Attilio Giovannini to try his skills with the long format, instinctively played the proposal down by saying, "I am no Disney company."[10] As explained by Bendazzi in 1972, "whoever prepares to the one hour and half trial in animation is at a crossroad: a competition on par with Disney, to give the audience what is already in their desires, or a competition to negate Disney and try to attract the audience with innovation."[11] Nonetheless, Bozzetto seems to have found a third way: being innovative without negating Disney altogether, but sublimating his legacy into an alternative aesthetics. The present chapter will deal with Bozzetto's own way to animation and to the animated feature through a biographical sketch, mostly focused on the events that provide insight into the reasons of his stylistic and production choices.

The Early Years

Bruno Bozzetto's birthdate, March 3, 1938, tells that the director was born in the middle of one of the darkest periods in Italian and European history. In Germany, on February 4, Adolf Hitler abolished the War Ministry and created the Oberkommando der Wehrmacht (High Command of the Armed Forces), so to have the military power under his direct control; similarly, on March 30, the Italian dictator Benito Mussolini was granted equal power over the Italian military to that of the king. On March 12, the *Anschluss* happened: Nazi Germany invaded and annexed Austria. Later that year, the vicious racist side of the totalitarian regimes manifested itself in the proclamation of the Italian racial laws and the November 9–10 *Kristallnacht* (Night of Broken Glass), a Nazi pogrom against Jews. Meanwhile, the Spanish Civil War, which started in 1936, was still raging. A tragic stage was being prepared for the Second World War.

However, Bozzetto does not retain dramatic memories from the war years. On the contrary, his recollections of his first eleven years of life are mostly fond. His family moved away from Milan to settle in Bergamo, a small city where the future director was to find an ideal rural and bucolic environment. That wise choice spared Bozzetto from the bombings that devastated Milan

---

[10] "Mica sono la Disney." Dividi, "Bruno Bozzetto."
[11] "Chi si accinge al cimento dell'ora e mezzo in animazione, si trova dunque di fronte a un bivio: concorrere con Disney mettendosi sullo stesso piano, per dare al pubblico ciò che esso già desidera, o concorrere con Disney negandolo e tentando di attrarre il pubblico con la novità." Bendazzi, *Animazione primo amore*, 22.

in 1940, and also offered fuel to an ecological and nostalgic humanism that would have later surfaced in his films. In Bozzetto's words, Bergamo was a "city-cradle, the cotton wool of childhood, the warmth of the first friendships. ... In Bergamo, I grew up surrounded by greenery, in an idyll of natural friendships and harmonies."[12] It is the place where he still lives in 2021. A big shock was anyway bound to happen during his early years, and it was precisely about his living place: his parents moved back to Milan in 1949, to settle in an apartment in Corso Matteotti, near Piazza San Babila. Bozzetto commented,

> I still remember the arrival ... at the Central Station, in the fog, with the impending city all around it. ... I immediately felt caged. In a cage of fog. For sure, my idealizations of uncontaminated nature were born from that childhood trauma. Or also because I suddenly found myself alone, an only child, without my friends of Bergamo. Maybe I started to do cinema because of that: to recreate a world I felt I had lost.[13]

Bozzetto remained an only child, and his parents gave unconditioned support to his career, both morally and financially. His family had an artist in it: Bozzetto's maternal grandfather, Girolamo Poloni (1877–1954), an academic fresco painter from Martinengo (near Bergamo), whose sumptuous and realistic use of light had him called by his teacher Lodovico Pogliaghi "a man born three centuries too late. His age would have been 1600, given how much of the air and impression of those times he manages to infuse in color."[14] Bozzetto used to visit his grandfather's atelier and to be spellbound by the artist's ability to breathe life into flat figures with lines and paint. The director reckons that his own drawing style and skills are nothing like his

---

[12] "Città-culla, l'ovatta dell'infanzia, il calore delle prime amicizie. ... A Bergamo ero cresciuto nel verde, in un idillio d'amicizie e armonie naturali." Mario Serenellini, "Dialogo tra il Signor Rossi e il Signor B," in *Bruno Bozzetto. Cinquant'anni di cartoni animati*, ed. Dino Aloi (Torino: Edizioni Il Pennino, 2005), 50.

[13] Mi ricordo ancora l'arrivo ... alla Stazione Centrale, nella nebbia, con la città incombente tutt'attorno. ... Io mi sono sentito subito in gabbia. Una gabbia di nebbia. Sicuramente, le mie idealizzazioni della natura incontaminata nascono da quel trauma infantile. Anche perché mi sono ritrovato di colpo solo, figlio unico, senza gli amici conosciuti a Bergamo. È forse per questo che ho cominciato a fare cinema: per ricrearmi un mondo che sentivo d'aver perduto. (Serenellini, "Dialogo tra il Signor Rossi e il Signor B," 50)

[14] "È un uomo nato in ritardo di tre secoli. La sua epoca sarebbe stata il Seicento tanto egli sa trasfondere nel colore l'aria e l'impressione di quel tempo." Lodovico Pogliaghi in Chiara Moretti, "Girolamo Poloni," in *I pittori bergamaschi dell'Ottocento*, ed. Rossana Bossaglia (Azzano San Paolo: Bolis, 1992), now at https://girolamo-poloni.weebly.com (accessed July 19, 2019).

grandfather's; nonetheless, he holds dear one of Poloni's frescos, on a wall of his private studio.

Bozzetto's parents were not artists, but they were well-to-do and provided for a welcoming and encouraging domestic environment. The director remembers his mother, Maria Giovanna Poloni (affectionately nicknamed Tiny), for her "sweetness, good personality and discretion (a trait I inherited from her),"[15] but he is especially grateful to his father Umberto, "a creative and brilliant fellow like few others, ... I feel that, in respect to my human and professional education, I basically owe everything to him";[16] "the creativity is mine, by I owe to him all about the practical side and how to face life."[17] In fact, Bozzetto considered him an inventor, "a technical genius";[18] he recalls that "the several houses where we lived were full of his little clever technical inventions, made just for the simple pleasure of creating something new, and not for necessity."[19] Umberto studied electrical engineering. He created and directed the sales branch of an industry he cofounded with his two brothers; it produced chemicals for the production of textiles. A member of the Alpini Corps of the Italian army, he was also a lover of contemplative mountain walks, which reinforced Bozzetto's budding interest in the natural landscape and also provided him with ideas for some later works (like *Mistertao*, 1990). Umberto transmitted to his son several interests: "for classical music, for good literature and, when I was a child, for the humor of some comics, and ... for novelties and technologies."[20] He was initially not interested in cinema at all, just like Bozzetto's mother,[21] but he slowly changed his mind as he saw how much his son cared for it. The story about Umberto building Bozzetto's first animation stand in the middle of the living room of their house with an ironing board (see the Introduction) is one of the episodes the director is most fond of; Bozzetto's second, more professional animation stand was designed by Umberto as well and built by Luciano Marzetti,

---

[15] "La dolcezza, la bontà di carattere e la riservatezza (che ho ereditato da lei)." Bruno Bozzetto, "Era mio padre," in *Bruno Bozzetto. Cinquant'anni di cartoni animati*, ed. Dino Aloi (Torino: Edizioni Il Pennino, 2005), 15.
[16] "Una figura creativa e geniale come poche, ... sento che a lui, nella mia formazione umana e professionale, devo praticamente tutto." Bozzetto, "Era mio padre," 15.
[17] "La creatività è mia, ma tutto ciò che riguarda la parte pratica e il modo di affrontare la vita lo devo a lui." Alberta Voltolini, "Bruno Bozzetto. 'Campiglio quanto m'ispiri'," *CampiglIO* 4 no. 6 (Summer 2018): 18.
[18] "Un genio della tecnica." Voltolini, "Bruno Bozzetto. 'Campiglio quanto m'ispiri'," 18.
[19] "Le diverse case in cui abitammo erano piene di sue piccole geniali invenzioni tecnologiche, fatte non per necessità, quanto per il semplice piacere di crear cose nuove." Bozzetto, "Era mio padre," 15–16.
[20] "La musica classica, la buona letteratura e, da piccolo, anche l'umorismo di certi fumetti, ... le novità e le tecnologie." Bozzetto, "Era mio padre," 15.
[21] Tina Porcelli and Fabrizio Liberti, "Bruno Bozzetto," *Cineforum*, http://www.cineforum.it/rubrica/Il_film_che/Bruno_Bozzetto (accessed July 20, 2019).

who was to become an expert animation cinematographer.[22] Another key moment in this father–son relationship eased Bozzetto's crucial decision about making a full-length feature. *West and Soda* was going to cost about a hundred million liras. "'If we make the film and then it is a total fiasco, will we be able to go on living, afterwards?', asks Umberto. 'Yes', is Bruno's answer. 'Then let's do it!', says his father."[23]

First Attempts

Bozzetto's earliest attempts at cartooning were the illustrations that he drew in the spur of the moment, out of the inspiration he took from the books he read during his youth.[24] Even though Max Massimino-Garniér called him "a cultured man without books,"[25] because of the charming naiveté that his films use while conveying a sharp and well-informed vision of the world, Bozzetto has always relished reading a wide variety of literary texts, from narrative to popular science essays. Ernest Hemingway was among his early favorites, because of his attitude to "stylization";[26] then came J. D. Salinger, Saul Bellow's *Herzog* (1964), and Bernard Malamud, among others. He said to have read twelve times Dino Buzzati's *Il deserto dei tartari* (*The Tartar Steppe*, 1940). He used to be a comic book fan, too; among his favorites there were Hal Foster's *Prince Valiant*, Lee Falk's *The Phantom* and *Mandrake*, Lyman Young's *Tim Tyler's Luck*, and the Mickey Mouse daily strips by Floyd Gottfredson. He claims that the Donald Duck and Uncle Scrooge comics by Carl Barks liberated his imagination much more than classics of children literature like *Pinocchio* or Ferenc Molnár's *A Pál utcai fiúk* (*The Paul Street Boys*, 1906).[27]

Bozzetto's distinctive curiosity and need for gathering firsthand knowledge nurtured in him a keen ability to observe and interpret his surroundings; this is why several of the amateur films he shot before and

---

[22]Bozzetto, "Era mio padre," 16.
[23]"'Se noi facciamo il film ed è un fiasco totale, possiamo continuare a vivere dopo?', chiede Umberto. 'Sì' è la risposta di Bruno. 'Allora facciamolo!' dice il padre." Roberto Davide Papini, "Tutto iniziò da un'asse da stiro," in *Bruno Bozzetto. Cinquant'anni di cartoni animati*, ed. Dino Aloi (Torino: Edizioni Il Pennino, 2005), 38.
[24]Bozzetto, "Adagio, accelerando," in *Fantasmagoria. Un secolo (e oltre) di cinema d'animazione*, ed. Davide Giurlando (Venezia: Marsilio, 2017), 79.
[25]Bendazzi, *Animazione primo amore*, 32.
[26]Paolo Di Stefano, "Bruno Bozzetto: 'Ora il mio signor Rossi diventerà un blogger'," *Corriere della Sera* (september 29, 2018). https://www.corriere.it/cronache/18_settembre_29/bruno-bozzetto-ora-mio-signor-rossi-diventera-blogger-fb6c27ec-c420-11e8-af74-9a32bd2d1376.shtml?refresh_ce-cp (accessed July 21, 2019).
[27]Giannalberto Bendazzi, "Intervista a Bruno Bozzetto," in Roberto Tirapelle, *Il cinema di Bruno Bozzetto. Sequenze 9* (Verona: Nuova Grafica Cierre, 1990), 53.

soon after his 1958 professional debut are short live-action documentaries about nature (*Piccolo mondo amico, Small Friendly World*, 1955; *I gatti che furbacchioni, The Cats Are So Slick*, 1956; *A filo d'erba, On a Blade of Grass*, 1957; *Il solito documentario, The Usual Documentary*, 1959). Before making those films, however, Bozzetto was to refine his self-taught graphic and storytelling abilities by providing with satirical cartoons a column ("Dietro la coda del cavallo si mormora"; "Behind the Tail of the Horse, Rumor Has It") of the high school paper *Il rudere* (*The Wreck*),[28] while he attended the high school "Cesare Beccaria" in Milan. Bozzetto considered himself a rather lazy student, but several experiences he did in his high school years decisively stimulated his interest in film and animation. During a school trip to London, Bozzetto deserted usual destinations like the British Museum and instead sneaked into cinemas to watch animated films.[29] It was at the Cameo-Poly Cinema[30] (now Regent Street Cinema), a theater then specialized in up-market foreign films, that he enthusiastically discovered Tex Avery and the MGM "Tom & Jerry" series:[31] for the first time, the horizon of his cartoon knowledge went beyond Disney.[32] From history classes, instead, he received a rather drastic impression: he felt that mankind was not into anything else but building weapons. This conclusion would have later blossomed into *Tapum! The History of Weapons*. Outside of the classroom, he nurtured his passion for cinema by joining the Cineclub Milano, a social circle whose members shared in turn their homemade films. Its programs included also animation, giving thus to Bozzetto the impression that the Italian interest in this medium was growing.[33] In particular, the director remembers some cartoons by a Cineclub member, Turolla,[34] who suggested him to contribute to the club with animations of his own.[35]

Those were in fact also the times of Bozzetto's first probing into the territory of self-made amateur films. When he was about 15, he started to make flipbooks out of bloc-notes. Around 1953, his father came home with an 8mm camera; Umberto never had a chance to use it for himself, as Bozzetto confiscated it for his cinema experiments. The first of Bozzetto's homemade animated film was born soon after: it was not based on new

---

[28]Papini, "Tutto iniziò da un'asse da stiro," 39.
[29]Di Stefano, "Bruno Bozzetto."
[30]Ivan Manuppelli, "Intervista a Bruno Bozzetto," *Piero Tonin Blog* (December 12, 2014), http://pierotonin.blogspot.com/2014/12/intervista-bruno-bozzetto_12.html (accessed October 17, 2019).
[31]Bozzetto, "Adagio, accelerando," 79.
[32]Di Stefano, "Bruno Bozzetto."
[33]Bozzetto, "Adagio, accelerando," 79.
[34]Bozzetto during a class for the History of Animation course at the Department of Cultural Heritage, University of Padova, Italy, November 25, 2014.
[35]Boscarino, *L'estetica di Bruno Bozzetto*, 129.

characters, but it was an attempt at a Donald Duck cartoon (1953).[36] The black and white film features Donald walking in a street, who suddenly stops when he reads a title on a newspaper abandoned on the ground: "The Martians are coming."[37] He then raises a sign that says, "Let's flee, then." The ending titles promise a next episode. Bozzetto did not have any knowledge about cel animation, so he had to redraw the background in each image. That is why all the lines are continuously wobbling, and Donald has an oversimplified and rough design; notwithstanding those shortcomings, there is a dramatic close-up on the newspaper headline (that could not be done with a real zoom, but only by recreating the camera movement image by image) that reveals how Bozzetto had already a grasp on some basics of film cartoon storytelling. In 1954, he animated *Fantasia indiana* (*An Indian Fantasy*) that foreshadows the theme of one of his "Carosello" series with the American Indian Unca Dunca and shows a more convincing use of narrative rhythm; cel animation is also attempted. Then, in 1955, the director-to-be worked on an unfinished science-fiction stop-motion animated short with robot puppets.[38] The series of amateur animations ended shortly after Bozzetto's professional debut with *Tapum!*; in 1958 he scratched directly on film *Tico-Tico*, a work evidently inspired by Norman McLaren and based on a musical piece, a Brazilian samba. Bozzetto saw McLaren's films for the first time at a film festival in Rapallo, where he submitted one of his documentaries about insects, *Small Friendly World* (that also won an award there). *Tico-Tico* is probably Bozzetto's first conscious attempt at using music as the sole rhythmic guide to an animation. While it verges on the purely abstract, the action on screen always seeks to remain understandable and communicative. A similar preoccupation emerges in *Partita a dama* (*A Game of Checkers*, 1958), a paper cut-out animation that brings to life nonanthropomorphic objects and, according to Bendazzi,[39] references again McLaren, and in particular his short *Rhythmetic* (1956).

The 8mm camera was later substituted by a 16mm Bolex Paillard, the camera that was used to shoot *Tapum!*. Umberto set up a studio dedicated to his son's filmmaking in a room of their apartment, where there was also a small moviola. Bozzetto improved his animation skills with it, by studying frame by frame some rented prints of American cartoons.[40]

---

[36]Bendazzi, *Animazione primo amore*, 29.
[37]The theme of the story is vaguely similar to that of the first Donald Duck comic ever authored in Italy, *Paolino Paperino e il mistero di Marte* (*Donald Duck and the Mystery of Mars*, Federico Pedrocchi, 1937). However, it was reprinted only in 1938, the year of Bozzetto's birth, and then no more until 1994; so, Bozzetto might have never read it.
[38]Bendazzi, *Animazione primo amore*, 29.
[39]Ibid., 30.
[40]Bozzetto during a class for the History of Animation course at the Department of Cultural Heritage, University of Padova, Italy, November 25, 2014.

Before that, the 8mm camera was also put to use in a series of live-action shorts, with Bozzetto serving also as one of the actors. Those were mostly humorous caper movies, featuring chases, slapstick antics, and over-the-top disguises: *I ladri che mascalzoni* (*Thieves Are Such Troublemakers*) was shot in 1954, and so was *Il cerchio si stringe* (*The Net Is Closing In*). A later, unfinished instance of Bozzetto's trial run on live-action was *Due ragni nel piatto* (*Two Spiders on a Plate*, 1958). Bozzetto enjoyed a lot making those films with the collaboration of his classmates; he still believes that, if he were to continue down that path, he might have become a "pure" live-action filmmaker. However, the many difficulties he encountered (too few money, too much stress when covering simultaneously the roles of director, cinematographer, makeup artist, actor, etc.)[41] tempted him to soothe his desire for film with the lonelier and more accessible ways of the amateur animator.

Insects Matter

Then, however, there were also the aforementioned "scientific" documentaries. They were a rethinking of yet another Disney model, the "True-Life Adventures," a series of live-action documentaries (1948–60) that dramatized edited footage of wild animals with a narrating voice and songs. While the narrative shorts prefigured the half-whimsical, half-grotesque tone that Bozzetto's live-action works would have always retained since their return in the director's filmography in the 1970s—with the interstitials of *Allegro non troppo* being a foremost example of them—the documentaries were an outlet to Bozzetto's conceptual and literal interest in using minuscule players on a vast stage. His entomological stance on mankind (see the Introduction) was born from his experiences with real insects; it was a matter of practical cinematography (how to shoot a mass of small creatures, while making them appealing and communicative),[42] before than a metaphor of the relative irrelevance of mankind in respect to the vastity of nature. The trademark long shot of Bozzetto (Figure 1), which makes the proudest warrior look just as a meager ant (as seen in *I due castelli, The Two Castles*, 1963), has its roots there. The approach of the director to the animated anthropomorphic animal is also defined by this metaphor. The American "funny animal," exemplified by "stars" like Felix the Cat, Bugs Bunny, or Mickey Mouse, has almost no equivalent in Bozzetto's animation;

---

[41]Boscarino, *L'estetica di Bruno Bozzetto*, 129.
[42]Bozzetto remembers that, among the many inventions of his father, there was a miniature hand-operated treadmill for insects, made to allow a fixed-focus macro shooting of a walking ant. Bozzetto during a class for the History of Animation course at the Department of Cultural Heritage, University of Padova, Italy, November 25, 2014.

FIGURE 1 *A man leaves his cave and builds his own shack in the plain, from the Slavonic Dance no. 7 segment of* Allegro non troppo. *The "entomological" distance from the action and the essential drawing style make the shack feel like a lonely anthill, while the caves in the background seem some sort of bigger nest, teeming with crawling critters that are actually little men.*

the few exceptions are characters for commercials (Kuko, or Pildo, Poldo, and Baffoblù) or for children films, like Gastone, the talking dog that became Mr. Rossi's sidekick in the 1970s full-length features (and that was never really liked by Bozzetto). There are indeed other animals with human semblances and behavior in his works, but they are mostly insects. Among those that have main roles in Bozzetto's animations there are the bee of *Allegro non Troppo*'s *Concerto in C Major RV 559* episode, the mosquitoes of *Self Service* (1974), the whole cast of the TV serial "Lilliput-put" (1980), and the bug that loves a woman in *Baeus* (1987). It is as if Bozzetto, after having "zoomed out" on humans, revealing how much they look like insects from a distance, finds them turned into "real" insects when "zooming in"; after all, the 1967 short *L'uomo e il suo mondo* (*Man and His World*) is a single, continuous zoom out that ultimately reveals how the entire universe is just a colored spot on a butterfly wing. The human-insect allegory reaches an apex in the Oscar-nominated *Grasshoppers* (1990); notwithstanding its title, there are no grasshoppers among the insects that keep peacefully proliferating in the growing grass, after the umpteenth meaningless mutual annihilation of human factions. They are stylized representations of the real animals and of the resilience of nature, and not human caricatures; it is instead implied that the "grasshoppers" are the humans themselves, whose fury periodically destroys the landscape that always regenerates, totally oblivious of their belligerent motives. The allegory of human vices through animals stays thus implicit in the title and in the destructive habits of the animated men.

Tapum! The Professional Debut

In the late 1950s, Bozzetto started to hear encouragements to consider a professional debut in animation. They did not primarily come from his family, which was actually more concerned with Bozzetto's university choice. He pursued a scientific career. He wanted to study biology, but he was puzzlingly and not-so-tastefully told by someone that it was a "faculty for women";[43] so, he decided for geology. He later changed his mind and went for a law degree.[44] As the first exam sessions of geology came, though, Bozzetto was already dedicating more time to *Tapum!* on the ironing board than to studying for his tests. He did not have a specific ambition yet; he set a clearer goal for himself when some enlightened words of advice came into play. They were from Walter Alberti, head of the Milan Cinematheque and author of the very first Italian book on the history of animation, *Il cinema d'animazione, 1832–1956*, which was recently published at the time. Alberti, an acquaintance of Bozzetto, saw *Tapum!* and told to the young filmmaker about the Rencontres Internationals du Film d'Animation, a parallel branch of the Cannes Film Festival. He esteemed the film worthy of a submission; Bozzetto followed his advice. Not everyone had been as supportive as Alberti, anyway. For example, in the same period Bozzetto met with Nino Pagot, who energetically tried to dispel any dream of his about making animation into a real job: "For goodness sake, no way! At most it can be a pastime, but do something else!"[45]

The events that unfolded in Cannes gave Bozzetto a real career chance. First of all, he met and made his work known to several animators who were already among his artistic models: Norman McLaren, Dušan Vukotić together with nine other directors from the Zagreb School,[46] and John

---

[43]Di Stefano, "Bruno Bozzetto."
[44]Bozzetto in the documentary *L'arte è un delfino. Intervista a Bruno Bozzetto.*
[45]"Per carità, neanche per idea! Al massimo può essere un modo per passare il tempo, ma fai qualcos'altro!" Nino Pagot in Bozzetto, "Adagio, accelerando," 80.
[46]Enrico Azzano and Raffaele Meale, "Intervista a Bruno Bozzetto—Parte Seconda," *Quinlan. Rivista di critica cinematografica* (April 4, 2014), https://quinlan.it/2014/04/04/intervista-bruno-bozzetto-parte-seconda/ (accessed July 24, 2019).

Halas.[47] Bozzetto remained in contact with Vukotić, who later advised him on how to make animated commercials; Halas became an esteemed friend of Bozzetto, who paid him several visits in London. The Italian filmmaker was even to spend a training period under his guidance, which resulted in Bozzetto's second short film, *La storia delle invenzioni* (*The History of Inventions*, 1959). Halas and Bob Privett's *How to Cartoon for Amateur Films* (1951) was Bozzetto's textbook in his self-teaching efforts, in a curious parallel with Disney's biography: the young American cartoonist educated himself on an animation manual too, Edwin Lutz's *Animated Cartoons: How They Are made, Their Origin and Development* (1920). The fourth Italian edition of Halas and Privett's book, in 1972, sported Mr. Rossi on its cover. In Cannes, Bozzetto understood that he needed a direct and personal contact with the artists he admired the most. In the following years, he would have cultivated friendly relationships with John Hubley, Yōji Kuri, Břetislav Pojar, and Jiří Brdečka:[48] all of them have been major stylistic references for the Italian author.

A major boost to Bozzetto's career was going to come from a film critic, though. Pietro Bianchi, a journalist of the newspaper *Il Giorno*, walked out in the middle of the screening of *Desire under the Elms* (Delbert Mann, 1958), a film part of the main Cannes competition, featuring Sophia Loren, Burt Ives, and Anthony Perkins. He heard some bouncy music and laughs coming from a smaller room nearby; *Tapum!* was playing there. The day after, *Il Giorno* published an enthusiastic review of the animated short; the title stated that Bozzetto was better than Sophia Loren. By complete chance, one of the editors of *Il Giorno* was a friend of Bozzetto; he was the one who decided to put Bozzetto's name in the title of Bianchi's review.[49]

In hindsight, *Tapum!* was the best possible way to voice Bozzetto's distinct poetics of cinema for the first time, as it summed up some of its core characteristics. Humorous animated documentaries had appeared before (the film was made with *Toot, Plunk, Whistle and Boom* in mind, after all), and the use of flat, angular designs for characters and backgrounds, together with unrealistic color choices that fitted the mood of the scene, was barely a novelty; a part from the already-mentioned Zagreb School and UPA films, also Tex Avery, and the Warner Brother cartoons of Chuck Jones with eerily geometric landscapes by Maurice Noble were going down that path. However, it was the first time that such extreme stylization found its

---

[47]Marina Paoletti, "Nota Biografica," in Giannalberto Bendazzi and R. De Berti, *La fabbrica dell'animazione. Bruno Bozzetto nell'industria culturale italiana* (Milano: Editrice Il Castoro, 2003), 151.

[48]Bozzetto in Bendazzi, "Intervista a Bruno Bozzetto," in Tirapelle, *Il cinema di Bruno Bozzetto*, 58.

[49]Bozzetto during a class for the History of Animation course at the Department of Cultural Heritage, University of Padova, Italy, November 25, 2014.

way to Italian animation. Bozzetto elaborated on those design references by means of storytelling and thematic choices. The humor of *Tapum!*, quite expectedly, mostly stems from the contrast between the solemn, educational tone of the voice-over, and the ridiculous pantomimic misadventures of the characters; as such, it is founded on irony and on a game played with the expectations of the audience. Along the lines of this, there is also the setup of a formally strict chronological progression from the stone age to present days to tell the history of weapons, which gets regularly disrupted by blatant and surreal anachronisms, like the beard of a medieval monk turning into a machine gun. However, Bozzetto gives new life to this comedy routine with a personal retooling of the idea of variation on a theme. In this, his comedy dynamics are similar to those of Tex Avery, which often sprung from a narrative archetype (a chase or a renowned fairy tale like *Little Red Riding Hood*) disrupted by a breathless sequence of absurdist and metareferential gags. Bozzetto took history, instead, as his main archetype—or, better, the historical results of the human behavior. His source is anthropological, more than fictional; the final result, anyway, does not have any pretense of scientific accuracy.

In *Tapum!*, the weapons are exaggerated and caricatured; the claim to be showing their actual evolution is just an excuse to introduce new characters and situations so that while the topic remains the same throughout, the screen action changes continuously. It also increases in absurdity and violence: the single visual ideas of Bozzetto are mostly unprecedented, unpredictable, but always visually clear and cleverly devised. For example, the long beard of the monk sprouts little walking legs when it touches the ground. The effectiveness of those touches of absurdity comes also from the fact that they are fueled by the two-dimensional design. Bozzetto does not try to hide the simplicity (and the shortcomings) of his drawing style, nor the very limited animation he is using, but boldly plays with it, making it an integral part of the comedy. This is the case of the medieval armor, which is vertically subdivided in two halves and worn by simply pushing those together over the silhouette of the knight. In this, the surrealism of Bozzetto differed from that of Avery, who, especially during his MGM years, used full animation and three-dimensional character designs.

In the end, the argument stays inexorably focused and monolithic, but the narration is made of separated fragments; within each one of them, anything could happen, from the aforementioned beard-gun to a caveman playing with a yo-yo. The underlying anthropological theme gives thus the audience a rational and relatable ground; after such premise has been presented in a way that is clear enough, the visual gags freely unfold. In fact, the longest- and slowest-paced fragment of *Tapum!* is the opening one, about prehistory. The pacing of the variations on the theme becomes exhilarating faster as the film goes on, but the acceleration pattern gets varied as well: Bozzetto, in fact, never reaches the speed extremes of Bob Clampett or Avery but instead breaks down the apparently inexorable progression with long shots that usually offer pensive panoramic views, with no action. In those moments, *Tapum!* instates a figurative staple of Bozzetto's vocabulary: the contemplation of a landscape. Such views are sometimes populated by ancient and degraded artifacts that are not presented as things to marvel at but as a tragic testament to the dissipating fury of man's violence—or, alternatively, as enigmatic and accusatory remains of a tasteless invasion of the natural environment. They might have a positive value only when they signify a door to nostalgia, as in the *Valse triste* segment of *Allegro non troppo*; but also the concluding shots of the prehistoric segment of *Tapum!* are subtly tinged by this sentiment, as they mysteriously indulge in showing the peace of a lost world.[50]

After each pause, anyway, the gag variations resume their *crescendo*, up to the merciless climax: civilization gets wiped out by a single drop of liquid explosive, which brings humanity back to the stone age, ready to reignite its self-destructive pulsion. The voice-over suddenly seems to break the fourth wall, as the film closes with a remark that suddenly uses a disconcerted tone and implicitly addresses Bozzetto: "Mamma mia che pessimista," "My goodness, what a pessimist." In addition to the anthropologic themes, the pacing variations, and the good intuition for surreal visual gags, pessimism is another distinguishing trait of Bozzetto's storytelling. Several of his works end with the defeat or even the death of the protagonists, who have often no redeeming qualities. The director, in the following years, would have quite frequently received criticism over this choice: he accepted it, though.[51] As stated by *Tapum!*'s ending, Bozzetto is self-aware of his lack of faith in humanity and society. His films intend to present this opinion in a humorous way, without any kind of moral stance; this is why he refrains from indulging in idealized happy ends. His exposure of the contradictions and derangements of human life might hide, anyway, a secret hope for a listening and understanding ear; so, there could be a tasteful hint of optimistic moralism in his bleak apologues. In Anna Antonini's words, "Bozzetto bridges together Disney's dream of a better world, Avery's belief that such a thing does not exist and Cannon's wishful thinking that we may make it on Earth."[52]

Tapum!, however, lacked one important feature that would have contributed to define the mature style of the director: a meaningful interrelation between music and animation. The music by Mario Coppola

---

[50]Similarly, wondrous dream visions of multicolored trees and plants temporarily relieve the tribulation of the little man trapped in the inescapable repetitiveness of everyday live, in *Una vita in scatola* (*A Life in a Tin*, 1967).
[51]Bozzetto in the video *L'intervista di Enzo De Bernardis, 7 gennaio 1977*, https://www.swissinfo.ch/ita/compie-50-anni--west-and-soda-/42645310 (accessed July 24, 2019), 6:23.
[52]Anna Antonini, "Bruno Bozzetto: Wit and Wisdom," *Animation Journal* 25 (2017): 38.

was not fitted to the action in any way (Bozzetto's official filmography refers to it as "repertoire" music)[53] and keeps getting repeated in cycles, like impassive muzak.

After Cannes, Bozzetto did not quit the university, but he invested a growing amount of time in animation, nonetheless. The decision of accepting John Halas's invitation to do a one-year training period in London, at the Halas and Batchelor Studio, tells a lot not only about Bozzetto's commitment but also about the surprisingly mature self-awareness that the young author already had about his own style, as Bozzetto did not refrain to clash with his mentor in respect to comedy strategies and storytelling. Halas, in fact, did not understand at all the anachronistic absurdities that Bozzetto used as variations to his narrative themes. While coproducing *The History of Inventions*, the second short by Bozzetto, Halas rejected several gags, including one that showed a primitive man falling in a river and saving himself by climbing over a floating tree trunk. The man then pulled an outboard motor from the water, started it, and rode the speeding trunk until a traffic policeman stopped him and fined him for speeding. Halas objected that there were no motors and policemen in that age; Bozzetto felt like his "arms, teeth, hair and the rest"[54] fell out of disappointment. *The History of Inventions*, another mockumentary[55] in the fashion of *Tapum!*, ultimately became Bozzetto's least favorite film;[56] he even refrained from uploading it on his YouTube channel. Anyway, Bozzetto and Halas remained on good terms and their reciprocal esteem never wavered. Halas defined his former student as "one of the outstanding creators of satirical and humorous animation"[57] in his 1987 book *Masters of Animation*.

---

[53] https://www.bozzetto.com/pdf/synopsis_shorts.pdf (accessed July 24, 2019).
[54] "Le braccia, i denti, i capelli e il resto." Boscarino, *L'estetica di Bruno Bozzetto*, 132.
[55] The term "mockumentary" applies here, according with the definition of mockumentaries given by Jane Roscoe and Craig Hight: "fictional texts which, by varying degrees, represent a commentary on, or confusion or subversion of, factual discourse" (Jane Roscoe and Craig Hight, *Faking It. Mock-Documentary and the Subversion of Factuality* [Manchester: Manchester University Press, 2001], 1). The referenced film are not documentaries: they purposely introduce anachronisms and imaginary devices. Their aim is not to educate, as they provide the viewer with wrong information. The comedy springs from the contrast between the notions the spectator is supposed to have (about the history of humanity) and the absurdities shown by Bozzetto. They use the documentary modes of representation (like a serious-sounding voice-over) only to play with the expectations of the audience, by providing content that is plainly unreliable. See Craig Hight, "Mockumentary: A Call To Play," in *Rethinking Documentary: New Perspectives, New Practices*, ed. Thomas Austin and Wilma de Jong (Berkshire: Open University Press), 205.
[56] Bozzetto in Bendazzi, "Intervista a Bruno Bozzetto," in Tirapelle, *Il cinema di Bruno Bozzetto*, 64.
[57] John Halas, *Masters of Animation* (London: BBC, 1987), 90.

Enter Mr. Rossi

The positive effects that *Tapum!* had on Bozzetto's career were not over yet. In 1960, the director submitted the film to a festival in Bergamo, the Festival internazionale del film d'arte e sull'arte (International Festival of Art Films and Films on Art), but its president, Nino Zucchelli, rejected it. Bozzetto reacted by creating his more famous character, Mr. Rossi. The 1960 short film *Un Oscar per il signor Rossi* (*An Award for Mr. Rossi*) was a creative and pacific "vengeance" over Zucchelli, who was caricatured as Rossi. There was however also a bit of Bozzetto in him, as the story introduced Rossi as an average man who develops a burning passion for filmmaking. He shoots a film in his living room and brings it to a festival, only to get almost immediately kicked out from it. In a fit of rage, he devastates the reel by stomping, scratching, and tearing it. The festival sees by chance the "new" version of the film and acclaims as art its jumbled editing and random imagery. This is how Rossi earns an Academy Award. The storyline was suggested to Bozzetto by the films he actually saw at the Bergamo festival, after his rejection; Rossi's film is a satire of those.

The protagonist is a middle-aged married man, stylized as to convey the impression of an insignificant average fellow. His name is telling, in this respect, as Rossi is the most common Italian surname. His geometric and stumpy build is in continuity with the character design seen in Bozzetto's previous film; his big head, with a large round nose and both eyes always visible from either side, apparently elaborates on two-dimensional graphic solutions already seen in the UPA films or in works by Vukotić, like *Piccolo* (1959), whose protagonists (especially the short one) look like two proto-Rossi, even in the way they dress (e.g., the papillon tie of the taller one). A similar character model would have reappeared in many international limited animations of the 1960s, like the De Patie-Freleng Enterprises series of theatrical cartoons "The Inspector" (1965–9), inspired by the inspector Clouseau from the live-action feature *The Pink Panther* (Blake Edwards, 1963). Mr. Rossi's design was slightly altered in the 1970s, in order to make him feel more three-dimensional, by means of solid drawing. Bozzetto, however, says that the main source of graphic inspiration for Mr. Rossi was the animated commercials he saw on TV during his stay in London.[58] An example of the style of such late 1950s–early 1960s commercials might be found in the advertisement by Richard Williams "Guinness at the Albert Hall" (1962).

Far from a lovable or role-model figure, Rossi is presented as an everyman who dreams big, but whose efforts to stand out are constantly frustrated by the merciless and homogenizing constraints of modern society.

---

[58]Bozzetto in the documentary *L'arte è un delfino. Intervista a Bruno Bozzetto.*

However, Rossi is not really better than the crowd and its ruthless race to hedonism; he himself embraces the vacuous ideals of mass consumerism and can behave in questionable ways in order to achieve his goals. Personality-wise, he could be compared to a more pessimistic and unrulier version of Donald Duck. *An Award for Mr. Rossi*, for example, shows the character tyrannizing his wife to act in his amateur film. In later shorts, a frustration-maddened Rossi will reach extremes like whipping an old lady who he had previously run over at a zebra crossing (*Il signor Rossi compra l'automobile, Mr. Rossi Buys a Car*, 1966) or killing dozens of safari hunters in order to take a picture of wild animals (*Il signor Rossi al fotosafari, Mr. Rossi Goes to a Photo Safari*, 1972). Rossi was not going to retain those violent personality traits forever, anyway; he became quieter and more "politically correct" in the children TV series stemmed from three feature films during the 1970s, which adhere to the genre of the animated musical. According to Renato Candia,[59] there are at least three incarnations of Mr. Rossi: the first one is the more frustrated, wrathful, and mischievous, and pertains to the first seven theatrical shorts, but Bozzetto kept it alive also in the Mr. Rossi books and newspaper cartoons; the second tamer one, paired with the talking dog Gastone, is that of the TV serial, mostly depending on ideas from two of Bozzetto's close collaborators, Maurizio Nichetti and Guido Manuli; the last animated iteration of the character, which appeared in some TV commercials of the 1990s, returns under the control of Bozzetto and borrows traits from both the first and second versions. There is only one Mr. Rossi, though, in the perception of the general Italian audience; he is just a cartoon distillate of the worst traits of the Italian man, or better, of its archetype in the popular culture of postwar Italy. Characters of this kind started to populate the Italian mass entertainment, and especially cinema, on the wake of the so-called economic miracle, or economic boom: a period of growth spurt in market competitiveness, monetary strength, social security, and quality of life from the 1950s to the late 1960s. Its main reasons were the generous postwar reconstruction aids that came from the Marshall Plan (1948–52), the 1957 opening of the European Common Market, and the availability of low-cost labor force. The "miracle" increased the average income, and the Italian market capitalized on this by means of a broadened offer of commodities, as well as of aggressive communicative strategies intended to create new material needs and desires. "Carosello" was born out of those communicative and economic urgencies. A culture of leisure started to develop, also because, for the first time, Italians were granted the right to an annual paid leave from work, sanctioned by the article 36 of the 1948 Republican constitution. The summer holidays became a social ritual, whose

---

[59]Renato Candia, "L'italiano senza qualità: il signor Rossi," in Bendazzi and De Berti, *La fabbrica dell'animazione*, 109–10.

peak celebration was (and still is) August 15, a day known as *Ferragosto*, from the name of an ancient Roman holiday (*Feriae Augusti*, "Holidays of the Emperor Augustus"). Around that date, large masses of Italians reached for holiday resorts (mostly beaches) to spend their free time, while shops and offices closed down. Such national vacation became the annual goal of the average Italian man, and social success seemed to be proportional to the amount of owned goods that enhanced the fun during the breaks from work. However, some intellectuals saw a dead end approaching. Dino Risi's *Il sorpasso* (*The Easy Life*), a 1962 live-action film that is among the best examples of the *Commedia all'italiana* genre (Italian-style comedy), was precisely set on the day of Ferragosto. A reckless young man, Bruno (Vittorio Gassman), forces a meek law student (Jean-Louis Trintignant) to join him on his convertible car. They keep speeding between beaches and unlikely carefree adventures, until, after Bruno's favorite maneuver—an aggressive overtaking of other cars on the road—they end their ride over a rocky cliff. Pier Paolo Pasolini also argued that this easy ideal of success, while it momentarily appeased the self-esteem, was actually based on models that came from outside the individual, having been inculcated into the people by television and industry.[60] The film historian Gian Piero Brunetta said,

> The most important thing was to show off: the cinema of the 1960 tells about the staging of an illusory wealth, built on quicksand. The low-class Italian, the petite and average bourgeoisie conceals more and more their poor origins and dashes into the consumer culture. The new status does not prevent them to be aware that the change was too fast, that the road behind them is strewn with sentimental ruins and the economic well-being is achieved at the cost of an emotional wasteland and the sacrifice of not few ideals and values.[61]

The Italian cinema translated this situation into a number of bitter comedies, whose lead characters were antiheroic average men, often

---

[60]Pier Paolo Pasolini, "Una sfida ai dirigenti di Viale Mazzini," *Corriere della Sera*, December 9, 1973.

[61]
> Importante diviene l'apparire: il cinema degli anni Sessanta racconta la messa in scena di un'opulenza illusoria, costruita sulle sabbie mobili. L'italiano popolare, il piccolo e medio borghese, mimetizza sempre più le proprie povere origini ed entra di slancio nella civiltà dei consumi. Il nuovo status non gli impedisce di accorgersi che la rapidità del mutamento è stata eccessiva, il cammino alle sue spalle è disseminato di rovine sentimentali e il benessere economico è raggiunto al prezzo del deserto affettivo e alla rinuncia di non pochi ideali e valori.

Gian Piero Brunetta, "Il cinema italiano dal boom agli anni di piombo," in *Storia del cinema mondiale*, ed. Gian Piero Brunetta, vol. III, 2 (Torino: Einaudi, 2000), 946.

confronted with a clash between their grandiosity and their ultimate ineptitude at life; they were mostly interpreted by Alberto Sordi (*Il boom, The Boom*, Vittorio De Sica, 1963), Ugo Tognazzi (*I mostri, The Monsters*, Dino Risi, 1963), or Nino Manfredi (*Il padre di famiglia, The Head of the Family*, Nanni Loy, 1967).

Mr. Rossi is a cartoon satire of that grotesque and sad archetype, and as such in perfect tune with the cultural sensibility of his times; he is also a forerunner to the film character that would have cemented the archetype of the inept, uncouth but resilient average man in the Italian popular culture, Ugo Fantozzi, played by Paolo Villaggio in a live-action film series that started with *Fantozzi* (Luciano Salce, 1975). The resemblances between the types of Rossi and Fantozzi are heightened in the TV series, as Rossi is given a humiliating job and a tyrannical boss.

Pasolini's warning about the conditioning power of consumerism finds a comedic counterpart in almost all of the Rossi shorts, as the misadventures of the protagonist usually start from the deceptive words of some sly seller, which fuel the flames of Rossi's ambitions. In *An Award for Mr. Rossi*, the desire to make films started as an innocent curiosity is dramatically implanted in Rossi's head by the rhetoric of a shop clerk (rendered as unintelligible gibberish from a mouth that even morphs into a record, to signify meaningless repetitiveness); this makes the camera grow in Rossi's imagination, until it resembles a marvelous hi-tech contraption. In the next Mr. Rossi films, Bozzetto subjected the character to several entertainment obligations of the average Italian citizen. Rossi will always end up enraged, disillusioned, or defeated: the first destination is a skiing resort (*Il signor Rossi va a sciare, Mr. Rossi Goes Skiing*, 1963) and then a beach (*Il signor Rossi al mare, Mr. Rossi Goes to the Beach*, 1964); in the 1966 short he has to buy a car, while 1970 is the time for camping (*Il signor Rossi al campeggio, Mr. Rossi Goes Camping*). He even indulges in an elite leisurely activity like a photo safari (*Il signor Rossi al fotosafari, Mr. Rossi Goes to a Photo Safari*, 1972), before reaching Venice, one of the standard tourist destinations in Italy (*Il signor Rossi a Venezia, Mr. Rossi Goes to Venice*, 1974), concluding the first stage of his existence and then mutating into a positive adventurer for the TV series.

The reasons of Mr. Rossi's success are multiple; the appealing character design and the clever visual gags contributed to their solid foundations. On top of that, as remarked by Bendazzi, there is the universality and relative innocuity of Mr. Rossi's satire. Even though the average Italian is portrayed as petty, violent, and ultimately a loser, Mr. Rossi is just too flawed to be relatable; so, the spectator ends up laughing at him without feeling personally attacked, but just enjoying the comic relief.[62] It might be argued

---

[62] Bendazzi, *Animazione primo amore*, 21.

that the director's aim was to entertain with an exaggerated view of reality, and not to accuse anyone; his tales are at most cautionary, without a moral purpose. Bendazzi again suggested that Bozzetto points out the symptoms but never really talks about the illness;[63] after all, Bozzetto's onlook to society came from the privileged point of view of the only child of a well-to-do and supportive family. Moreover, it was a family from Northern Italy, the richest area of the country. Implicitly, this is also the social-geographic territory satirically targeted in the Mr. Rossi shorts that never take into account the economical divide—and the difference in the quality of life—between the north and the south of the peninsula. This is one of the few questionable points in Bozzetto's aesthetics, which however does not hinder the sharpness of his observations of reality and their transfiguration into material that is tailored to his animation style. The only other sensible issue, in term of content, concerns the use of an insistently male and patriarchal gaze in his storytelling. Again, this is usually played for laughs, with no intention to advocate for a gender discrimination. Anyway, since his first film, Mr. Rossi himself is presented as a man who just "uses" his wife as an actress to reach his purposes; when, at the end, the woman manifests the intention to shoot her own film, Mr. Rossi just flees. In *Mr. Rossi Goes to the Beach*, the character leers at the girls on the beach, just like the old satyr—who resembles a senescent Mr. Rossi—does to the nymphs of the *Prélude à l'après-midi d'un faune* from *Allegro non troppo*. In the same film, the bee of the *Concerto in C Major RV 559* is the caricature of a housewife. There are several instances of "damsels in distress" who need a prince charming to be saved; such is the (literal) case of the live-action cleaning girl at the end of *Allegro non troppo*, who flies away from her humiliating job when the animator (Maurizio Nichetti) turns her and himself into a fairy-tale cartoon couple, or of Clementina, the strong-willed but ultimately passive female lead of *West and Soda*. Lisa and Nervustrella from *Vip, My Brother Superman* fit into the same narrative trope. Women with an active role are a rarity in Bozzetto's stories; one of them is Eve, from the *Allegro non troppo* segment on the *Firebird Suite*, who, contrarily to her biblical counterpart, refuses to eat the apple. The others are no flattering testaments to female agency, as they are grotesque villains: Happy Betty in *Vip* and Sua Fertilità ("Her Fertility"), a giant overbearing monster from the sequel to *Vip*, the comic book *Minivip & Supervip: il mistero del viavai* (*Minivip & Supervip: The Mystery of the Come-and-Go*, 2018). In the same comic, though, Lisa, Supervip's girlfriend, is given the chance to voice her dissatisfaction with the overprotective attitude of her partner, which suffocates her career ambitions. The male-centric gaze in Bozzetto and Mr. Rossi is definitely a bias, but also a direct consequence of the society he

---

[63]Ibid., 33.

was satirizing: the patriarchal and catholic Northern Italy of the economic boom years. Even though the story is seen from a point of view that is unmistakably male, the masculine stereotypes are often exposed as vain and laughable. Mr. Rossi is far from being a model of volitional masculinity. Just like many other Bozzetto's characters who reserve to women unwanted attentions, he gets chastised and ridiculed: the topic is developed further in the comic book *Il signor Rossi e le donne* (*Mr. Rossi and Women*, 1970).[64] Other characters with the same fate are Il Cattivissimo ("The baddest one") of *West and Soda* or the abusive husband of *Baeus*. *Ego* (1969), probably Bozzetto's most provocative and harsh film, elaborates on the violent and sexist dreams that at night populate the subconscious of the average "model husband," condemned to a repetitive and empty life.

The lack of a strictly circumscribed and accusatory satirical stance in the Mr. Rossi films had a strategically positive result on the character, as it made it funny also outside of Italy. For his theatrical shorts, Bozzetto has always envisioned an international audience—that of the animation festivals—as he knew that the circulation of animated shorts in Italian cinemas was marginal and subjected to the prejudice that animation should be exclusively for children; such misleading belief is still deep rooted in the Italian cinema industry, as proves one of the first questions Bozzetto hears whenever he proposes a new project to a production company in the present days: "How old is your target children audience?"[65] Mr. Rossi's shorts often enjoyed an Italian distribution only after they were acclaimed abroad, just like it happened to *Allegro non troppo*. The films had the potential to stay effective everywhere, as they were in pantomime (the character "spoke" in a farcical gibberish), and the character type of the inept but perseverant Rossi was prone to be promptly understood by anyone, because it was conveniently formulaic but not boringly predictable. He seemed a descendant of many serial characters of the American cartoons of the 1930s and 1940s, which in turn were building on the world-famous comedy routines of Charlie Chaplin, Buster Keaton, and Harold Lloyd. However, Mr. Rossi has in its humor also deep traces of the music hall, *café-chantant*, *café-konzert*, *teatro di varietà*, and so on: the European light theater (which was also the point of origin of Chaplin, after all), with its pungent attitude to social satire. Bozzetto himself noticed how versatile was his creation when he decided to reuse it after *An Award for Mr. Rossi*, which was supposed to be the

---

[64]From the 1970s, Bozzetto started to draw cartoon series collected in books; the others were *Viva gli abominevoli sciatori* (*All Hail the Abominable Skiers* [Milano: Sperling & Kupfer, 1970]), *Mille piccoli cretini* (*One Thousand Little Cretins* [Milano: Sperling & Kupfer, 1971]). and *Le avventure di Ventun Din Fotoamatore* (*The Adventures of Twenty-One Din, Amateur Photographer* [Milano: Il Castello, 1972]).
[65]Bozzetto during a class for the History of Animation course at the Department of Cultural Heritage, University of Padova, Italy, November 25, 2014.

only appearance of the character; the director's choice gave to Rossi another relevant quality, that is, being the protagonist of the first animated theatrical serial of Italy.

In 1972, before the three full-length features later broadcasted on TV, Bendazzi foresaw for Rossi "a fast evolution, or his abandonment."[66] Bozzetto in fact decided to "kill" Rossi in one of the live-action interstitials of *Allegro non troppo*: the sheet where the character is drawn catches fire, and a desperate Rossi dramatically turns to ashes (Figure 2). His last appearance before his apparent demise was *Il signor Rossi e lo sport* (*Mr. Rossi and Sport*, 1975), a series of mini TV episodes of two minutes each, with a narrating voice by Walter Valdi—and also a few apparitions in the program "Gulp!", which proposed new stories of famous cartoon or comic characters narrated with still images, with no animation. But then, during the production of *Allegro*, the three films for children happened, even if it was more an involution than an evolution, in many respects. However, three features and its derived TV series explored a side of the character that was never seen before: the lyrical and contemplative one. Mr. Rossi is probably Bozzetto's more personal and pondered creation; the short film that features him might be considered a compendium and a measure of the director's potential. The extremes of sadism and absurdity that Bozzetto sometimes reaches in other films are never as lucid and well-timed as in the Mr. Rossi universe; however, until the TV series from the three features, Mr. Rossi had never ventured into the slow-paced lyricism that is integral to Bozzetto's directing style, and that was going to be expressed at best in the *Valse triste* segment of *Allegro non troppo*. The TV series smoothened Mr. Rossi's rough edges, added to him a great deal of childish naivety, and also made him less universal by providing him with a speaking voice. But the character was also given the chance to finally indulge in the peaceful admiration of the beauty of nature, something that, in truth, had always been among the character's primary motives when looking for entertainment. This proved that Rossi was able to express the whole of Bozzetto's poetics; he brought this newly discovered potential to his 1990s third version of the character, which mixed together the first two. Mr. Rossi, in the end, seems destined to stay alive: from 1993 to 2015, he was a constant presence among the cartoons printed in a column of the newspaper *Corriere della Sera*. As of 2021, Bozzetto and his studio are preparing a new TV series, the intention of which is to bring back something of the early personality of the character and to make him interact with the new technologies. The project has been conceived with the collaboration of Bozzetto's son Andrea and of Maurizio Nichetti.[67] A 1977 children book based on the feature film *Mr. Rossi's Dreams* was reprinted in 2018.

---

[66] "Una rapida evoluzione, o il suo abbandono." Bendazzi, *Animazione primo amore*, 21.
[67] Bozzetto in the documentary *L'arte è un delfino. Intervista a Bruno Bozzetto*. Also, Nichetti in a personal e-mail to the author, September 6, 2020; he reported that Bozzetto's prompt for

FIGURE 2 *Mr. Rossi on a food sneaking mission in* Allegro non troppo, *a few seconds before meeting the fate that awaits any cartoon creature exposed to fire. However, the "killing" of Mr. Rossi was just an inside joke of the film crew, which at the time was just quite fed up with the character. Mr. Rossi remained alive and well after that; Bozzetto and his studio are planning for him an animated comeback, as a follow-up to the celebrations for his sixtieth anniversary.*

The Bruno Bozzetto Film and the "Carosello" Years

Between the success of *Tapum!* and its festival misadventures that brought to the debut of Mr. Rossi, Bozzetto's career experienced another poignant development. The opening titles of *An Award for Mr. Rossi* reveal that Bozzetto was no longer working alone: the animation is credited to Sergio Chesani and Giancarlo Bassi, the backgrounds are by Giancarlo Cereda, Roberto Scarpa and Luciano Marzetti are the camera operators, and the music is by Pier Emilio Bassi. It is possible to see several of them at work

---

the development of the series was the question "How would Mr. Rossi behave today, in such a technological society?" ("Il signor Rossi oggi come si comporterebbe in una società così tecnologica?").

on the Mr. Rossi film in Bozzetto's documentary live-action short *Come si realizza un cartone animato* (*How to Make an Animated Cartoon*, 1961). That was the earliest production crew that Bozzetto gathered by searching among his friends and acquaintances (e.g., Cereda was the cousin of a former classmate of Bozzetto, Carlo Re);[68] when the young director accepted to do commercials for "Carosello" and for cinema, they worked at Bozzetto's studio in his parents' house. Other key artists who joined this early team, and who were destined to have a profound impact on Bozzetto's films, were Guido Manuli (1939), a lavishly creative animator and gagman, and the scenographer Giovanni Mulazzani (1941–2011), one of the most notable Italian illustrators.

In August 1958, in one of his first interviews, Bozzetto claimed that he absolutely did not want to work for the advertising industry.[69] As anticipated in the Introduction, he changed his mind by following the advice of a friend. The animated and live-action commercials he produced for "Carosello" and for theaters finally allowed him to make a living out of his hobby; when Bozzetto's advertisements got the first prize at a 1961 national competition in Trieste, his father suggested him to quit the university for good.[70]

During the adventurous homemade production of his first five animated "carosellos" for the Innocenti firm, drawings and other production materials literally invaded all the rooms and available spaces. Bozzetto's work conditions decidedly improved when he opened a proper studio in Via Melchiorre Gioia, which is still in use today as one of the headquarters of his company. It never became a large facility, though: all the other Italian studios specialized in animated commercials remained bigger than the Bruno Bozzetto Film. Also, a formal pipeline for animation production was never implemented before the 1990s: Bozzetto was more at ease with a freely creative environment and no rigidly established roles. There were of course specialists, but anyone could provide a gag or an idea and have a say on general decisions; the only rule was that Bozzetto had final word on everything. Such an apparently dispersive strategy was made efficient by the fact that Bozzetto always worked with people he closely knew and completely trusted. He rarely did formal public selections for new collaborators; one of those cases was when he hired Maurizio Nichetti, who soon after became a friend of him. Some artists spontaneously applied to join the studio; some others were brought there by sheer coincidence. Giovanni Mulazzani, for example, came to Milan with the intention to pursue a career as illustrator.

---

[68] Carlo Re is among the artists at work seen in the documentary *Come si realizza un cartone animato*; however, he was just acting, because he was not trained in drawing (he later became a lawyer). Nonetheless, Re contributed to several of Bozzetto's early productions, in various roles, including that of voice actor.
[69] Bozzetto in Tirapelle, in Tirapelle, *Il cinema di Bruno Bozzetto*, 16.
[70] Di Stefano, "Bruno Bozzetto."

He stayed at a guesthouse where another young man, who had tried to get a job as scenographer from Bozzetto but had not received a reply yet, was renting a room. Tired of waiting, he left after a few days; soon after that, Bozzetto called the landlady and inquired if that applicant was still there. The landlady said that he had gone away and, on her own initiative, recommended instead Mulazzani to the director.[71]

"Carosello" brought Bozzetto on new ground. He had to further hone his aptitude to concision in humor and storytelling, and also to develop an animated character: a protagonist fit to return in several different films—it is maybe not by chance that Mr. Rossi was born in 1960, the same year when Bozzetto was prompted to this task. Also, the smaller and low-definition black-and-white TV image did not allow for Bozzetto's favorite "entomological" long shots but asked for close-ups and clean designs. The director answered to these requirements with the creation of Kuko, a "funny animal": a crossover between a lion and a rodent, with a hat and a tie that are identical to those of Mr. Rossi. Kuko was animated in a rush, as the first proposal by Bozzetto did not pass the RAI evaluation.[72] The shorts had quite naïve plots: Kuko looks for peace but keeps being disturbed by other talking animals; they are actually little men in disguise who, when finally exposed by Kuko, declare themselves "not guilty." The Italian word for that is "innocenti"; at that point, Kuko disagrees, saying that Innocenti is instead the name of the advertised firm. The final payoff proceeds to introduce some of its products.

Bozzetto's production of commercials proceeded with no interruptions up to the end of Carosello, in 1977, and beyond. He was aware that the format limitations did not allow any character development or meaningful artistic exploration. Nonetheless, he created a gallery of protagonists that regularly encountered the favor of the audience, and that received numerous awards at festivals for film advertisements. For example, he returned to funny animals with Pildo, Poldo, and Baffoblù (1963) and Magno and Baffo (1972–3); he played with staple roles of popular narrative by inventing a magician (Guglielmone, 1964) and a ghost (Buc the Buccaneer, 1968–9). He even animated Zorry Kid, a famous character by one of the most renowned Italian comic artists, Benito Jacovitti (1923–1997). The foremost player in the cast of Bozzetto's "carosellos" was, however, Unca Dunca, an unlikely American Indian, quite stubborn and dimwitted, but of good nature. He did not have much to do with the goods he advertised—the Riello boilers—as was usual for many of the "Carosello" commercials that invested more in

---

[71]Giovanni Mulazzani in "I segreti di West & Soda," a documentary in the *West & Soda* DVD (Roma: Multimedia San Paolo, 2005).
[72]Gianni Rondolino, *Bruno Bozzetto Pubblicitario* (Torino: STIP, 1969); reprinted in Bastiancich, *Bruno Bozzetto*, 43.

character or verbal appeal than in actual consistency between the narration and the final claim.[73] Unca Dunca's cluelessness and indolence were personality traits that paved the way to a big comedic potential, explored by Bozzetto in eight series and forty episodes, between 1961 and 1968. The 1965 series "Fantasia" stood out because it did not feature narration but free variations on lines and shapes that, according to film historian Gianni Rondolino, were redolent of the films by the animation pioneer Émile Cohl.[74] The name "Fantasia," however, probably hinted also at the 1940 Disney feature, as the visual rhythms were synchronized with music. The Bruno Bozzetto Film studio had invested since its beginning in sound and music production. Notwithstanding its small dimensions, it was the only Italian animation facility to have an in-house recording stage. After *Tico-Tico*, the Unca Dunca commercials were probably the second step along the path that was to bring Bozzetto to *Allegro non troppo*; the music was not classical, though. It was provided by a famous pop, jazz, and rock songwriter, Enzo Jannacci (1935–2013), who, together with the composer and saxophonist Paolo Tomelleri (1938), scored also several theatrical shorts by Bozzetto (like *Alfa Omega* [*Alpha Omega*] 1961, and the Mr. Rossi films of 1963 and 1964). Franco Godi took over from Jannacci from 1966 to 1968; before that, Jannacci even sung for the Unca Dunca shorts,[75] while the character delivered his farcical lines in a broken Italian,[76] intermingled with stereotyped expressions ("augh") associated with the comedic representation of American Indians in those years. Even if such verbal gags are questionable by today's standards, because of their racist implications, they contributed a big deal to bring Unca Dunca alive and to make it easy to remember between his many equivalents from other "Carosello" serials.

In the 1960s, Bozzetto and his collaborators pursued a continuous technical development by means of trial and error, while their stylistic approach remained consistently focused on geometrical and flat designs, limited animation, and communicative straightforwardness. In the shorts of Bozzetto from those years, a peculiar visual storytelling device emerged and the "entomological" feeling of the camerawork was perfected. Not only characters were seen from a distance, but the camera also became essentially

---

[73]This was an imprint of the initial Carosello production rules. No reference to the advertised goods was supposed to appear in the opening short film (known as "pezzo," "piece"); the ending section, the "codino" ("small ending"), was the actual advertisement. See Piero Dorfles, *Carosello* (Bologna: Il Mulino, 1998), 16–17.
[74]Rondolino, *Bruno Bozzetto Pubblicitario*, 52.
[75]Francesco Riccardi, "La musica di Jannacci per i cartoni di 'Carosello'," *Linkiesta*, April 2, 2013, https://www.linkiesta.it/it/article/2013/04/02/la-musica-di-jannacci-per-i-cartoni-di-carosello/12650/ (accessed July 26, 2019).
[76]Carlo Re, a former classmate of Bozzetto, was the first to play Unca Dunca for "Carosello" (Carlo Re in a personal telephone conversation with the author, October 31, 2019).

still (except a few zoom-ins for emphasis), and editing tended to disappear, in favor of a single long take. The gaze of the spectator was firmly distanced from the action, as if the only possible role of the viewer was that of a passive witness. At the same time, however, it required an active viewership. The screen action occurred in selected portions of the screen, which changed throughout the film. The eye was thus invited to wander over a continuous comedic variation on the pristine fixed shot. In the 1969 short *Ego*, the relevant screen portions were inscribed into rectangles, while the rest of the screen went black; the encasing of the action into the small shape was also a visual commentary on the suffocating life routine of the protagonist, as opposed to the full-screen unleashing of his perverted night dreams. So, Bozzetto took the concept of variation that he used to propel the humor of his early shorts and made it essential to his directing style, which now rested strongly on persistent images subjected to some kind of mutation. He also created a rhythmic device: the gazes guided across the screen became a pulsation that articulated the timing of the story in a way that involved not only the perception but also the physical body of the spectator. The eyes needed to physically turn toward a certain region of the projected frame; such effect is of course rendered possible only by the generous dimensions of a cinema screen. Bozzetto's animation is intrinsically cinematographic; this is another reason why his style never found an ideal outlet in the "Carosello" commercials, notwithstanding their effectiveness in advertising.

Bozzetto probably took inspiration from Yōji Kuri, who also liked to use visual variations of a fixed shot (*Ningen Dōbutsuen*, *Clap Vocalism*, 1962); however, while Kuri mostly used this device to achieve a surreal image progression with no plot, Bozzetto adapted it to a linear narration. *Alfa Omega*, in 1961, is precisely an apparent fixed-camera long take of metaphoric incidents that happen to a naively drawn character, which stays still in the middle of the frame; it elaborates on the conditioning that society imposes on the individual from birth to death and Bozzetto animated it all on his own. The black and white *I due castelli* (1963) consolidated this idea. Two very stylized castles lie atop of two hills, on the two sides of the screen. Repeatedly, one or more warriors exit from the left castle and try to conquer the right one, but they get constantly wiped out. The back-and-forth visual motion continues until a giant head emerges from the right hill and reveals that the castle was just his crown.

"Why Don't You Make a Full-Length Animated Feature?"

During this age of his professional affirmation, Bozzetto had never thought about making a full-length animated film. The fixed-camera style he was exploring was very far from being exploitable in a work of one hour and a half; but, above all, he believed than he was not even remotely close to having the artistic and monetary resources to make a feature that could meet the Disney standards. However, as it happened for his Cannes debut, a well-thought advice from a respected person made him reconsider his position. It came from Attilio Giovannini,[77] a film history professor at the University of Milan, but also a director and screenwriter: he cowrote *The Dynamite Brothers*, the first and, in the early 1960s, only full-length animated feature that Italy had produced since 1949, together with *The Rose of Bagdad*. He was a close friend to Bozzetto and his family; during a seaside holiday in a city near Taranto, while they were having a walk on the beach, he said to the director, "Why don't you make a full-length animated feature?"

After an initial resistance, Bozzetto considered Giovannini's authoritative opinion. There were two major breakthroughs in the line of thought that convinced him of the feasibility of the project. First, he realized that, in order to follow Disney's example, while finding an original perspective, he needed a story that was not only as universal as the narrative sources of the American features (namely, fairy tales) but also substantially different from them. It occurred to him that the Western films, a genre he was particularly into, could constitute a modern equivalent of fairy tales and myths, because of their epic and compelling storylines, their deep penetration into international popular culture, and their use of highly stereotyped narrative roles that make immediately evident to the spectator who is the good guy, who is the bad one, who is going to die, and so on.[78] The second turning point was his appreciation of Mulazzani's artworks. In the first half of the 1960s, Bozzetto mostly assigned the scenography job to Giancarlo Cereda, who had a very graphic and clean approach, considered by the director close to that of the UPA films. Cereda would have provided with art several of Bozzetto's films; however, the director's sensibility found his drawings too flat and "cold" to stand a 90-minute character action with dialogues. Mulazzani's approach was flat and stylized as well, but it relied on the creation of calculated "imperfections" in the color palettes and the perspectival construction, which gave to Bozzetto the feeling of a wholesome atmosphere. In the director's view, Mulazzani's backgrounds looked as believable dwelling places for two-dimensional characters.[79] From the technical point of view, Mulazzani created palette modulations by washing the half-dried paint under running water, so as to cause random darker areas. He also painted with tempera over surfaces colored with India ink and engraved with patterns, drawn

---

[77]Bozzetto, "Adagio, accelerando," 84.

[78]Bozzetto during a class for the History of Animation course at the Department of Cultural Heritage, University of Padova, Italy, November 25, 2014.

[79]Bozzetto in "I segreti di West & Soda," a documentary in the West & Soda DVD (Roma: Multimedia San Paolo, 2005).

by scratching the half-dried tempera with a steel nail; he then washed the artwork, and the water partially removed the water-soluble paint but left unscathed the scratched areas where the India ink emerged.[80]

The extent of Bozzetto's confidence in the expressive value of Mulazzani's work is evident from the shape that the feature, *West & Soda*, finally took. Bozzetto clearly doted on his experience in the short format and fitted it into a wider story arc. This Western parody is replete with small separate gags. For example, there is an extended fight between the protagonist, Johnny, and his nemesis, Il Cattivissimo, rendered through an insistent long shot and a back-and-forth rhythmical orientation of the gaze, derived from *I due castelli*. That film is also referenced in a series of gags that see Johnny buried in the ground up to his shoulders, while a multitude of ants tries to attack his head; the scene was animated by one of the most influential artists who joined Bozzetto's studio in that period, Giuseppe Laganà (1944–2016), who previously worked at Gamma Film. The abundance of visual gags in *West & Soda* is preeminently due to Guido Manuli, who besides his animator duties had a fluvial talent for absurdist comedy; Bozzetto had often to limit his creativity in order to keep the film storyline in check. One of Manuli's gags was actually an attempt at bridging together the film scenes: the recurrent and showstopping appearance of a maddening chase between a stagecoach, a tribe of Indians, and a cavalry regiment.[81] However, even though that chase actually interacts with the plot (the return of it overwhelms the bad guys and helps Johnny rescue Clementina), this idea actually feels like one of the many clever "accents" that stand out individually over the rest of the story.

Notwithstanding being gag-ridden, and its inheritance of a great deal of Bozzetto's short film language, *West & Soda* remains the more satisfyingly unitary of all the animated full-length features by the director. The production strategy chosen by Bozzetto contributed to this outcome, too, as for the one year and a half when the film was in the making the studio did not take commissions for advertisements; the downside of this was that, after the film release, almost all the contacts with their customers had to be rebuilt from scratch. This did not happen for *Vip* and *Allegro*, as the animators alternated between the work on film sequences and on advertisements. While *Allegro* was not affected by this production strategy, being subdivided into independent episodes by definition, *Vip*'s storyline ended up being quite discontinuous.

---

[80]Mulazzani in "I segreti di West & Soda," a documentary in the West & Soda DVD (Roma: Multimedia San Paolo, 2005).
[81]Manuli was likely taking inspiration from similar recurring gags of Tex Avery's films, as the apparently incongruous appearances of the whistling Eggman, which periodically disrupted the story of *Little Red Walking Hood* (1937).

What unified *West & Soda* seems to be the attention that Bozzetto reserved to atmosphere, by taking inspiration from Mulazzani's backgrounds. The feeling of a scene, even when the events were farcical or absurd, was more important than the gags. The contemplative side of Bozzetto's storytelling guided his approach to directing: the landscapes were intended as vehicles for emotions. To bring out the "atmospheric" quality of the art, Bozzetto tried as much as possible to make his characters "live" in the backgrounds, in a follow-up to the intuition that made him choose Mulazzani over Cereda. To achieve this, he cared about using, for the first time in his animated productions, an editing that sometimes replicated that of live-action films. In particular, he rendered dialogues with a shot-reverse shot syntaxis, something that he learnt from Giovannini (who cowrote the screenplay). He also relied on the voice acting and the content of the dialogues themselves, which were not prerecorded but actually finalized in their writing and fitted to the moving mouths of the characters after the film was finished. The protagonists received a distinct vitality because of the contrast between the parodistic stereotypes that defined the roles (the bad guy's name means plainly "the very bad guy"; Clementina takes her name from the canon Western ballad *Oh My Darling, Clementine*; Johnny is inspired by Alan Ladd and his role in *Shane*, George Stevens, 1953; the good guy has a white hat, while the bad guys have a black one, and so on) and the original vocal characterization of each one of them, by professional actors with a long-standing experience in live-action dubbing (like Nando Gazzolo and Carlo Romano). Bozzetto also used camera movements in a more comprehensive way, in contrast with his fixed-camera trend. In respect to animation, he tried to assign each scene to the animator who was more in tune with its emotional tinge; for example, he gave a night exchange between Johnny and Clementine to Sergio Chesani, an expert RAI operator, who was able to create smoother and subtler slow movements.

The major unifier of *West & Soda*'s atmosphere is however the sequence Bozzetto considered the most important of all: the evening storm. He devoted several months to its animation, while the rest of the production proceeded. It does not contain gags or dialogue: it only depicts the slow approaching of menacing dark clouds, while the editing shows the environment and the characters. It makes an abundant use of sound effects and optical in-camera tricks (by Luciano Marzetti) that simulate lightning and color changes in the backgrounds. Bozzetto invested time and energies to make sure that the sequence had an enhanced atmospheric value: he also decided early about the music he wanted to hear during the buildup of the storm. His reference was a piece by Nino Rota for Federico Fellini's *8 ½* (1963), which played while Guido Anselmi dreamt about his dead parents. Bozzetto asked the composer Giampiero Boneschi to create new music inspired by the Rota piece; the result retained the same mysterious melancholy of its model. In the rest of the score, however, Boneschi mixed references to classic Western films with original inventions that underscored the action with humor; the use of a vocal choir and a long melodic arc in the main theme, which plays during the opening titles, sound like a nod to the music Ennio Morricone had freshly written for *Per un pugno di dollari* (*A Fistful of Dollars*, Sergio Leone, 1964), the film that defined the "Spaghetti Western" genre. Bozzetto often remarks that *West & Soda* could have been the first in this new film genre, but it missed the record by a whisker:[82] even if it started its production before Leone's film, it was released later, as animation requires more time than live-action filmmaking.

All in all, Bozzetto's solution to the problem of the long format resided in a marked detour from the Disney model, barely softened by a few concessions to it, mostly in the use of a cinematic language borrowed from live-action features (shot and reverse shot, camera movements, etc.). The absence of songs, the limited animation, the synthetic design, and the frequent visual gags repositioned the expectations of the viewers within a radically different aesthetics—a familiar one, given that it had a lot in common with the "Carosello" visual appeal, but also one that transcended the model of the comedic short film. The short film material was unified thanks to a quality work in the creation of atmospheres, mostly evoked by the backgrounds and the interaction of the characters with them. In *West & Soda*, all the characters are rigidly stereotyped: they are as limited as they should be in appearance and behavior, because their purposes are exactly those of spoofing the Western genre conventions and making each role immediately recognizable. What is vibrant with believable life is the landscape, which amalgamates the fragmentation of the plot and grounds the otherwise flat figurines into a consistent space. Conceptually, *West & Soda*—and the solution of the animated feature film dilemma—might be an elaboration on a recurring theme of Bozzetto, namely the insignificance of humans, and the destructivity inherent to their actions, in respect to the wholesome complexity of the events and emotions pertaining the environment, which could never be encased within the easy labels of a narrative genre.

Vip: Not-So-Super Man

Bozzetto decided to start the production of his second feature, *Vip, My Brother Superman*, a few months after the premiere of *West & Soda*. The intent was to capitalize on the extended crew of animation professionals formed during the previous production, and on the technical competences matured over about two year of work. The initial plan of the director was

---

[82]Bozzetto during a class for the History of Animation course at the Department of Cultural Heritage, University of Padova, Italy, November 25, 2014.

to make another parody, this time of a popular comic: Lee Falk and Ray Moore's *The Phantom*. He invented Minivip, a short and neurotic version of *The Phantom*, who imitated him down to his typical disguise: a trench coat with a hat and glasses, worn over his red[83] skintight costume. He was not far from Mr. Rossi, as a character type, but his need for psychotherapy spoofed a different set of malaises of the contemporary man.[84] By chance, in the feature film Minivip was voiced by Oreste Lionello, who later became the official Italian voice actor of Woody Allen; however, at the time Allen was just beginning his career, so the association between Minivip and the neurotic characters by the American director largely happened in retrospect.

Bozzetto wanted to confront Minivip with a story that mocked the advertisement market and its strategies. The director was not bitter against his work for "Carosello";[85] he just decided to talk about a topic he was a specialist of. Through his comical satire, however, he wished to present publicity as a product of malicious conspiracies and violent attacks on unaware people.

The film ultimately took a different direction because of interferences from American coproducers, who came in contact with Bozzetto thanks to the international circulation of *West & Soda*. Among them there was Lady Stearn Robinson, a quite obscure figure, author of the book *The Dreamer's Dictionary* (1975) and screenwriter of the Halas and Batchelor TV series in limited animation "DoDo, the Kid from Outer Space" (1965). Halfway into the production of *Vip*, she urged Bozzetto to steer the story toward a superhero parody, and to add another character: Supervip, Minivip's brother, endowed with "traditional" superpowers. She also demanded to paint in green the faces of the many little Chinese men devotedly serving the villain, Happy Betty, in order to avoid racial jokes that could have been ill-received in the Asian market. Finally, she wanted the film to be a musical; while Bozzetto enjoyed the songs that mocked the jingles of "Carosello" (they were by the most prolific "Carosello" composer himself, Franco Godi, who had also already provided music to several of Bozzetto's shorts), he was dissatisfied by the musical numbers that did not add to the plot, like the song of the lion on the island.

Vip, My Brother Superman was more successfully received than *West & Soda*, both by critics and audience. The production troubles, and the necessity to regularly detour the film crew to the animation of "Carosello"

---

[83] Bozzetto did not know that the original costume of *The Phantom* was purple; in Italian comic books it was always red.

[84] A later animated work featuring the character, the 2009 TV series in 3D computer graphic animation "PsicoVip" ("PsychoVip"), based each episode on the stories told by Minivip in a therapy session.

[85] Bozzetto in "Behind the Scenes," a documentary in the *Vip, My Brother Superman* DVD (Roma: Multimedia San Paolo, 2005).

commercials, gave however way to a less cohesive narration. Well aware of that, Bozzetto even let the animators indulge in a few sequences in a different and oversimplified style, as if they were independent experimental shorts; one of them is the visualization of Happy Betty's evil masterplan. In part by necessity, in part by his own will, in *Vip* Bozzetto embraced the possibility of an episodic structure within a full-length animated feature with a single continuing storyline; *Allegro non troppo* could be seen as a mature development of this constructive strategy.

After "Carosello": A Twilight and a New Dawn

The 1970s were an eventful decade for Bruno Bozzetto Film. Apart from the huge effort of *Allegro non troppo*, the end of "Carosello" required a rapid repurposing of the creative goals, also because, from February 1977, color TV broadcasts officially started.[86] The production team specialized in commercials was regrouped into a separate facility (Bruno Bozzetto Film 2) and, apart from a lesser amount of advertisements, it found an ideal outlet to its skills in animated intros for TV programs as well as in TV series, like the Mr. Rossi one (that became especially popular in Germany) and "Stripy," made from 1973 to 1984 for the Swiss broadcaster RTSI (now RSI: Radiotelevisione svizzera di lingua italiana). Other TV works for RTSI were "Lilliput-put" (1980) and "Mr. Hiccup" (1983). However, the revenues from the sales of those products were less substantial than the "Carosello" ones; moreover, they were sold to RTSI because the Italian market was saturated with cheaper animated series bought from abroad. The 103/1975 law, but more relevantly the Constitutional Court Resolution no. 202 of 1976, allowed private broadcasters, operating on a local level, to open their own TV stations. Private televisions proliferated to an impressive figure by the end of the decade; they were already 246 in 1977.[87] In 1980, the entrepreneur Silvio Berlusconi aggressively created the first national private broadcaster, Canale 5, by syndicating twenty-four local channels.[88] The private broadcasters filled their afternoon programming slots, destined to children, with animation bought from Japan, because of the favorable exchange rate between the Yen and the Italian Lira. In this scenario, Italian animated TV series were hardly competitive. In 1985, the RAI rejected Bozzetto's pilot for the projected series "Il Corsaro nero" ("The Black

---

[86]Dorfles, *Carosello*, 112.
[87]Gian Luigi Falabrino, *Storia della pubblicità in Italia dal 1945 a oggi* (Roma: Carocci, 2007), 74.
[88]Dorfles, *Carosello*, 113.

Pirate"), a humorous version of an adventure novel by Emilio Salgari. The first series that Bozzetto could produce for the Italian television came only in the late 1990s, when Italian animation enjoyed a relative renaissance after a prolonged crisis in the 1980s;[89] in that period, not even a single animated feature film was produced in the country. The good results of the full-length musicals by Enzo D'Alò, and the international affirmation of new studios whose series precisely targeted children ("Cuccioli," "Pet Pals," 2002–12, by the Gruppo Alcuni)[90] or teenagers ("Winx Club," 2004–ongoing, by Rainbow), encouraged domestic financial investments in animation. However, the target of such successful works reinforced the Italian stereotypes about animation being a "genre" for children. Anyway, Bozzetto benefited from this situation and had RAI produce the 1996 "La famiglia spaghetti" ("The Spaghetti Family") and the 2009 "PsichoVip." In 2008 he directed "Bruno the Great" for Disney Channel: the stick figure-like Bruno is a kind of new Mr. Rossi, unvaryingly inconclusive in his effort to impress his peers.

The main division of the Bruno Bozzetto Film remained devoted to the sole theatrical works of Bozzetto; however, at the end of the 1970s it suffered from two important defections as Guido Manuli and Maurizio Nichetti left the studio to pursue their own careers as directors. They always remained on good terms with Bozzetto, anyway.[91]

Nichetti was also instrumental to Bozzetto's return to live-action films. He was hired as a screenwriter (see Chapter 3) but was also resourceful as an actor. He convinced Bozzetto to make a short comedy in just a weekend, *Oppio per oppio* (*The Household Drug*, 1972), which was soon after followed by *La cabina* (*The Cabin*, 1973). After the live-action sequences of *Allegro*, Bozzetto made this thread of his filmography peak in the 1980s, with a few more shorts (most notably the 1984 series "Sandwich," made of twelve films of six minutes each) and, above all, a feature film, his fourth and last: *Sotto il ristorante cinese* (*Under the Chinese Restaurant*, 1987), which anyway included also sequences that mixed animated drawings with photographic footage. Bozzetto had plans for more animated feature films, but the self-production, with capitals from the sales of advertisements, was

---

[89]See Bruno Di Marino, "Integrati e apocalittici. Appunti per una storia dell'animazione italiana prima del 2000," in *Il mouse e la matita. L'animazione italiana contemporanea*, ed. Bruno Di Marino and Giovanni Spagnoletti (Venezia: Marsilio, 2014), 33–7; also Sabrina Perucca, *Il cinema d'animazione italiano oggi* (Roma: Bulzoni, 2008), 24–30.
[90]Marco Bellano, "Il Veneto e l'animazione dopo il 2000: botteghe al centro del mondo," in *Veneto 2000: il cinema. Identità e globalizzazione a Nordest*, eds. Antonio Costa, Giulia Lavarone, and Farah Polato (Venezia: Marsilio, 2018), 113.
[91]Nichetti in Roberto Tirapelle, "Conversazione con Maurizio Nichetti," in Tirapelle, *Il cinema di Bruno Bozzetto*, 50. Also Nichetti in a private e-mail to the author, September 6, 2020.

no more a feasible option. He applied for state cinema funds, but even if his projects sometimes received positive evaluations from the commissions in charge of the film grants,[92] they were never greenlighted. Right after *Allegro*, Bozzetto developed another film with the same architecture, a live-action frame, and a compilation of animated episodes; each one would have been an adaptation of a science-fiction short story, watched by live-action characters from a distant future on an old TV. Bozzetto had already acquired the rights to works by Isaac Asimov, Ray Bradbury (the short story "There Will Come Soft Rains," 1950), and Robert Silverberg ("Neighbor," 1964), and selected other stories by Fredric Brown and Robert Sheckley.[93] However, the release of *Heavy Metal* (Gerald Potterton, 1981) stopped the development of the film, because of the similarities between the Canadian feature and Bozzetto's concept.[94] Another unachieved feature project, from the early 2000s, was *Mammuk*. The plot revolved around a mountain split in half; one side of it collapsed, isolating a tribe of cavemen, who were stuck there with no chance of technological progress. On top of the mountain they see Mammuk, a huge mammoth-like creature, who they desperately try to reach and use as food. Finally, the screenplay of the 2018 graphic novel *The Mystery of the Come-and-Go*, drawn by Gregory Panaccione, was originally intended for a full-length feature starring new characters: the grand-grandchildren of Supervip and Minivip.

In the same years, though, Bozzetto was saluted with the highest honors of his whole career. In 1995, for example, Bruno Bozzetto Film was chosen by Hanna and Barbera to contribute with a short film (*Help!*) to the TV serial "What A Cartoon" (1995–7); in 2007, Bozzetto received an honorary master's degree in theory, technique, and management of arts and entertainment, from the University of Bergamo.[95] Above all, though, he got international accolades such as the Golden Bear for the Best Short Film at the 1990 Berlin International Film Festival and an Academy Award Nomination for Best Animated Short Film in 1991. The films that received such recognition were foremost examples of Bozzetto's mature style in the short format; in particular, *Mistertao*, the Golden Bear winner, was just three minutes long. Its simple tale of perseverance, inspired by the mountain walks Bozzetto used to take in his youth with his father, is condensed into

---

[92]Bozzetto during a class for the History of Animation course at the Department of Cultural Heritage, University of Padova, Italy, November 25, 2014.
[93]Bozzetto in Bendazzi, "Intervista a Bruno Bozzetto," in Tirapelle, *Il cinema di Bruno Bozzetto*, 65. Also in Mario Querin, *Bruno Bozzetto* (Trento: Centro di Documentazione Visiva, 1992), 10.
[94]Bozzetto in Alberto Crespi, "*Sandwich* e *Il Corsaro Nero*: e chissà che la tv non smantelli il ghetto ...," in Tirapelle, *Il cinema di Bruno Bozzetto*, 73.
[95]https://www.unibg.it/sites/default/files/documenti/26-05-2015/lhbozzetto.pdf (accessed July 30, 2019).

the figure of a little hiker who climbs a mountain, slowly but relentlessly. After the summit, he keeps walking in the sky, until he reaches God in the heavens. He has a short chat with him (in the usual gibberish of Bozzetto's short films), and then he leaves, peacefully climbing even higher than God. The whole film is based on the typical variations on a persisting image (the hiker) that stays at the center of the frame; the final twist is underlined by the sole derogation to this pattern, since the hiker goes off-screen while the spectator sees God's incredulous disconcertment. The drawings are of extreme simplicity and are done by Bozzetto himself, who animated the short film on his own: the "idea with a line around it" motto found there one of its best concretizations. The close-knitted music was by Roberto Frattini,[96] a composer of academic training and vast musical culture, with a special talent for comedic timing and creative quotations of classical pieces; he scored all of Bozzetto's productions after 1985.

The consolidation and maturation of Bozzetto's take on short films in the 1980s was furtherly favored by a collaboration he started with Italy's most authoritative journalist of popular science, Piero Angela (1928).[97] Bozzetto has always been an eager reader of popular science books, like those of Desmond Morris and Konrad Lorenz. He noticed that the ones by Angela had a special "visual" quality and stimulated his knack for impromptu book illustrations like no other. The director approached Angela to see if he was interested in making a film with him: their encounter resulted in three illustrated books[98] and about two hundred animated clips spanning from thirty seconds to ten minutes (1981–8), which amounted to a total of about seven hours of animation. They explained in a humorous but scientifically rigorous way facts and figures pertaining to one of the topics of the day, during Angela's TV program "Quark." Their brevity and essential character design make those works very close to *Mistertao*, which in fact was released in 1988, when Bozzetto's contribution for "Quark" came to an end; the clips for Angela had surely been a major exercise in concision and visual appeal through stylization, as well as a confirmation that, in documentaries, "much factual information is communicated more efficiently via animation than the spoken word,"[99] as Annabelle Honess Roe noticed.

In 1999 Bozzetto released another very successful short film, which even surpassed *Mistertao* in graphic simplification, while reinstating again the "theme and variation" structure so typical of his works. The characters

---

[96] http://www.robertofrattini.it (accessed July 30, 2019).

[97] On this collaboration, see Fabio Toninelli, ed., *Bruno Bozzetto. La linea intorno all'idea* (Cremona: Tapirulan, 2019), 74; also Piero Angela, *Il mio lungo viaggio. 90 anni di storie vissute* (Milano: Mondadori, 2017), 173–6.

[98] Piero Angela and Bruno Bozzetto, *Noi e la paura* (Milano: Garzanti, 1987); *Noi e la gelosia* (Milano: Garzanti, 1987); *Noi e la collera* (Milano: Garzanti, 1987).

[99] Annabelle Honess Roe, *Animated Documentary* (London: Palgrave Macmillan, 2013), 8.

of *Europe & Italy* are neither humans nor animals: they are circles and squares, filled with the patterns and colors of the European or Italian flag. The short is segmented into binary episodes; each one compares how Italian and European citizens deal with common aspect of social life. The comedic effects spur from a playful exaggeration of the worst stereotypes on Italians, contrasted with the calm and proper demeanor of the people from the rest of the continent. The short is remarkable not only for its powerful visual synthesis but also for its distribution strategy and animation technique. *Europe & Italy* won several prizes at short film festivals (Lovere, 1999; I Castelli Animati, Genzano di Roma, 1999; Tehran, 2001; Anima Mundi, 2001), but it was released on the internet; and, for the first time, Bozzetto used 2D computer animation. The popularity of *Europe & Italy* steadily grew and peaked in the social network age; as of early January 2021, its official 2012 YouTube upload on BrunoBozzettoChannel has more than 1.9 million views. Bozzetto, in fact, elected YouTube and the social networks (mostly Facebook) as the preferred destination for his new short films. This happened gradually, after a long transition. In 2000, Bruno Bozzetto Film and Bruno Bozzetto Film 2 ceased their activities; the director moved back to Bergamo. However, Bozzetto was at the time learning how to make the most of software animation tools like Adobe Flash: he was delighted by the fact that it allowed him to animate an entire short film all on his own, like he did when he was very young. So, he entered a new stage in his career, now centered around self-produced 2D computer animation. During this period, Bozzetto cultivated also an interest in 3D animation, expressed, for example, in the conclusive short released by the Bruno Bozzetto Film: *I cosi* (*The Things*, 2000). He soon realized that, just like in the 1960s the Disney features were the benchmark for full-length hand-drawn animated films, in the early 2000s the expectations of the market and the audience were set on the quality of the Pixar Animation Studios works. He joked on this unfair competition in a 2004 3D computer animated short, *Looo*, which featured an unlikely muscular superhero auditioning for a role in a 3D film with "Pixar quality." In that case, he joined forces with other artists, including Panaccione, who was later going to draw the comic sequel to *Vip, My Brother Superman*.[100] *Looo* was also a likely reference to *The Incredibles* (Brad Bird, 2004), a film that might have been loosely inspired by *Vip*. Also, in 2004, a hand-drawn Disney feature, *Home on the Range* (Will Finn, John Sanford), had a trio of cows as leading characters, which loosely resembled the three cows at Clementina's farm in *West & Soda*. Bozzetto, anyway, was flattered by the coincidences and never found any conclusive evidence about those homages or borrowings; he just noticed, with grateful surprise, that John Lasseter had a very precise knowledge of his filmography,

---

[100] Bozzetto and Panaccione later created another graphic novel, *Toajêne* (Paris: Delcourt, 2020).

during a 2012 honorary visit to the Emeryville establishment.[101] Bozzetto's efforts in 3D computer graphics found their more convincing expression in *Rapsodeus* (2013), which mixed 3D rendered models (and spectacular camera movements, which partly disconfirmed the "fixed image" aesthetics) with a 2D hand-drawn feeling. It was a new take on his trademark satires about the worst aspects to the human civilization; this time, it showed the history of how people vainly massacred each other to get hold of the "light" of mystic truth. The use of classical music (Franz Liszt's second *Hungarian Rhapsody*, a staple of cartoon music at least since *The Cat Concerto* by Joseph Barbera and William Hanna, 1947) connected the film also with *Allegro non troppo*; however, while its predecessor mostly relied on unaltered original scores, the music of *Rapsodeus* was comedically manipulated by Roberto Frattini to follow the animation, as it happened to classical music in Disney's "Silly Symphonies."

When *Rapsodeus* was made, though, Bozzetto's studio had already reopened. It happened in 2007, thanks to two former freelance 3D animators: Piero Pinetti and one of Bozzetto's sons, Andrea. The latter had initially pursued psychology studies;[102] however, in 2006 he helped in the production of a TV series derived from the 2000 short *The Things*, which Bozzetto outsourced to a 3D studio (The Animation Band) where Pinetti was working. In 2007, Andrea Bozzetto and Pinetti associated with and took the lead of the new Studio Bozzetto & Co.[103] The studio became soon competitive in the fields of TV series for children, commercials, corporate identity, video mappings, motion graphics, and augmented reality. Among their works, some of the most relevant are the preschool series "Topo Tip" ("Tip the Mouse," 2014 and 2018) and the animations for the Expo Milano 2015, in partnership with Disney. Bozzetto has never retired and still supervises all the projects of the Studio, but also leaves substantial creative autonomy to the young artists.

The main outlet to Bozzetto's most personal creations became the internet. Apart from the aforementioned YouTube channel, he posts videos and drawings on his Facebook profile, where the audience can also enjoy a few details that the artist occasionally spares about his private life. Bozzetto has finally settled back in Bergamo, a place he had never really left for good, anyway: when he lived in Milan, his family kept a house there and he regularly visited it in the weekends. His Facebook posts, however, are never indiscreet: the privacy of his wife Valeria "Wally" Ongaro, their

---

[101] Bozzetto during a class for the History of Animation course at the Department of Cultural Heritage, University of Padova, Italy, November 25, 2014.
[102] "Quelli dello Studio Bozzetto. Vale a dire: la Disney bergamasca," *Bergamopost*, December 14, 2014, http://www.bergamopost.it/vivabergamo/studio-bozzetto-disney-bergamasca/ (accessed July 30, 2019).
[103] https://studiobozzetto.com (accessed July 30, 2019).

sons Andrea and Fabio (a videomaker and digital artist),[104] and their twin daughters Anita and Irene is always respected. The protagonists of his Facebook posts are instead mostly the pets and wild animals around his house. Bozzetto's advocacy for animal rights became stronger over the years; he mostly entrusted his ecological views to pictures and cartoons dedicated to Beeella,[105] a sheep that strayed from her herd and was adopted by Bozzetto. Even though Beeella's antics are told with the usual knack for satire, Bozzetto never tries to humanize her; she is by no means a "funny animal" but an aloof and dignified witness of man's maddening race toward self-annihilation. As a Bozzetto character, she is maybe the ultimate one: not a stylized creation but a real creature in casual resonance with an intimate creative desire, who Bozzetto sensibly found in the living environment his foremost source of inspiration.

---

[104]http://www.fabiobozzetto.com (accessed July 30, 2019).
[105]The name is a pun on the Italian onomatopoeia for the bleating of sheep, "beee," and the word "bella," which means "beautiful."

2

Allegro non troppo at a Glance

"A Film Full of Fantasia!"

"A film that will let you ... see the music and listen to drawings; in a word, a film full of *Fantasia*!"[1] Within the very first minutes of *Allegro non troppo*, when the actor Maurizio Micheli addresses the film audience as a sleazy and mellifluous host, the gamble the film is going to take is revealed straightaway. In Italian, the word *fantasia*, accented on the *i*, means "imagination," but it also identifies a kind of musical composition for instruments only, "whose form and invention spring 'solely from the fantasy and skill of the author who created it'."[2] This double entendre is easily perceivable also by English speakers (who however prefer to accent the word on the second "a"), and it is precisely because of this that Walt Disney and Leopold Stokowski chose it to name their "concert feature," which was destined to use animation to freely visualize images inspired by a miscellaneous selection of classical music pieces.[3] In Bozzetto's film, though, that word becomes a *triple* entendre: while in Micheli's line it seems to mean just "imagination," its shout-out to the Disney film works also as a metaphorical wink to the spectator. The implicit meaning is that, disregarding the pompous claims of originality and creativity of the host, the author knows exactly what he is doing: the film that has just begun is an unashamed and provocative parody of *Fantasia* itself. The joke gets reinforced by the almost literal quote of

---

[1] "Un film dove potrete ... vedere la musica e ascoltare i disegni, in una parola un film pieno di fantasia."
[2] Christopher D. S. Field, E. Eugene Helm, and William Drabkin, "Fantasia," in the New Grove Dictionary of Music and Musicians, Grove Online, https://www.oxfordmusiconline.com/grovemusic/view/10.1093/gmo/9781561592630.001.0001/omo-9781561592630-e-0000040048?rskey=x541Fd (accessed August 1, 2019), quoting in turn Luis de Milán, *El maestro* (Valencia, 1536), ed. Charles Jacobs (University Park, PA, 1971), 6.
[3] John Culhane, *Walt Disney's Fantasia* (New York: Harry N. Abrams, 1987), 18.

Disney's famous tagline for *Fantasia* ("you will be able to SEE the music and HEAR the picture"),[4] but also by the phone call that Micheli takes right after he has dropped the name of the Disney feature. From his reactions, we get that someone from Hollywood is complaining about this blatant case of plagiarism. Micheli gets angry, hangs up the phone, and then says while looking into the camera: "They are crazy. ... They claim that this film ... had already been done, many years ago, by a certain ... Frisney, Prisney, Grisney ... An American guy, in short."[5] Those jokes would have missed the point altogether if someone in the audience had never heard of Disney or *Fantasia*. However, those references were taken for granted, and reasonably so: Bozzetto and his collaborators experienced firsthand how deeply the Disney features had rooted into the expectations of the Italian audience and film market, to the point that any animated feature project by an Italian studio needed to choose between two mutually exclusive alternatives: do as Disney, or reject that aesthetics altogether (see the Introduction and Chapter 1). So, it was a sure bet that the jokes would have been understood by the vast majority of the audience. Moreover, in the mid-1970s *Fantasia* had finally gained its status of "cult" film, after its disappointing 1940–1 box-office performance in the United States, paired with mixed reviews; as Robin Allan wrote, "The critical reception was muddled and the public puzzled by the film."[6] *Fantasia* earned back its $2.28 million budget and started to make a profit only after its third reissue in 1963.[7] The film was gradually repositioned as a "classic," a forerunner to the psychedelic vogue, which granted it a circulation in arthouses and colleges. In Italy, the film had theatrical reruns in November 1973 and November 1975;[8] Bozzetto could thus securely assume that many cinemagoers had fresh memories of it, while also taking a chance to watch the film again himself and bear it in mind during the production of *Allegro non troppo*.

The *Allegro non troppo–Fantasia* Connection: A Premise

Allegro non troppo is not a copycat of *Fantasia*, though; but it could not be understood without having first watched that Disney feature. It is a film

---

[4]Ibid., 36.
[5]"Sono dei pazzi. ... Sostengono che questo film ... l'avrebbe già fatto, parecchi anni fa, un certo ... Frisney, Prisney, Grisney ... Un americano, insomma."
[6]Robin Allan, *Walt Disney and Europe* (London: John Libbey, 1999), 105.
[7]Amy Davis, "The Fall and Rise of *Fantasia*," in *Hollywood Spectatorship. Changing Perceptions of Cinema Audiences*, ed. Melvyn Stokes and Richard Maltby (London: BFI, 2001), 72.
[8]Nunziante Valoroso, "Stagioni cinematografiche Walt Disney Italia 1938–2000," *Cabiria* 171 (2012): 57.

whose meaning depends completely on another film: in a word, *Allegro non troppo* is a parody. In their 1993 article on Bruno Bozzetto and parody, Raffaele De Berti and Elena Mosconi try to define parody as a binary relationship where "the parodying one exists thanks to the parodied, of which it reveals its constituting principles, its inner workings, by separating from it."[9] Then, they elaborate on four modes of generic transformation posited by John G. Cawelti—humorous burlesque, evocation of nostalgia, demythologization of generic myth, and affirmation of myth as myth[10]— holding that Bozzetto uses only the last two to "propose ... self-reflective criticism on mass culture and obtain an amusing and beneficial effect of estrangement."[11] The two authors, however, do not take into account *Allegro non troppo* and just refer to Bozzetto's first two animated feature films, which they consider more similar in tone and style (and closer in term of release date). If *Allegro non troppo* was to be compared with those modes of generic transformation, it could be argued that all the four of them are in fact exploited; the parodistic discourse changes between episodes, and delves indeed into nostalgia; as for burlesque, the whole of the live-action interstitials is a grotesque exaggeration of the introductions to each one of the animated shorts of *Fantasia*.

Bendazzi, however, differed on this point. He agreed on the fact that the first two animated features by Bozzetto are parodies: "Tradition serves as a connecting device; by using it as a support, Bozzetto can operate at ease, without narrative or explanatory constrictions. ... The choice of a tradition, one the audience is as familiar with as a physical place, allows for the exploitation of all the situations it offers."[12] In his view, instead, *Allegro non troppo* is not a parody at all. He reasoned that "the reviewers and the audience never hesitated to consider (and praise) it as an autonomous work, with values of its own. It is rather an example of a cinematographic postmodern: a deliberate and claimed use of fragments of mass culture for

---

[9] "Il parodiante esiste grazie al parodiato del quale svela, distaccandosene, i principi costitutivi, i meccanismi di funzionamento." Raffaele De Berti and Elena Mosconi, "Il mondo alla rovescia. Bruno Bozzetto e la parodia," in *Il movimento creato. Studi e documenti di ventisei saggisti sul cinema d'animazione*, ed. Giannalberto Bendazzi and Guido Michelone (Torino: Edizioni Pluriverso, 1993), 46.

[10] John G. Cawelti, "Chinatown and Generic Transformation in Recent American Films," in *Film Theory and Criticism: Introductory Readings*, ed. Gerald Mast, Marshall Cohen, and Leo Braudy (Oxford: Oxford University Press, 1992), 508.

[11] "Proponendo ... delle riflessioni autocritiche sulla cultura di massa e conducendolo ad un divertito e benefico effetto di straniamento." De Berti and Mosconi, "Il mondo alla rovescia," 48.

[12] "La tradizione serve da connettivo; usando di essa come di un supporto, Bozzetto è in grado di operare a suo agio, non costretto da impegni narrativi o espositivi. ... Siamo alla scelta di una tradizione, ben presente al pubblico quanto un ambiente fisico, ed allo sfruttamento di tutte le situazioni che essa offre." Giannalberto Bendazzi, *Bruno Bozzetto: animazione primo amore* (Milano: ISCA, 1972), 22.

the sake of citation, in order to compose a new work."[13] The considerations by Bendazzi and De Berti-Mosconi might possibly be mutually balanced if seen through the definition of modern parody as proposed by Linda Hutcheon in 1985.[14]

After advancing that "there are no transhistorical definitions of parody. The vast literature on parody in different ages and places makes clear that its meaning changes."[15] Hutcheon suggests that modern art forms might specifically activate a neglected secondary meaning of the ancient Greek prefix *para*, the etymological root of the first half of the word "parody": "*para* in Greek can also mean 'beside', and therefore there is a suggestion of an accord or intimacy instead of a contrast."[16] Still, "a critical distance is implied between the backgrounded text being parodied and the new incorporating work."[17] So, the modern parody can keep a close relationship with the original text while remaining substantially independent from it. In this view, the perceivable reference to a parodied text does not hinder the autonomy of the parodying work.

On top of that, what *Allegro non troppo* parodies is not the visual or narrative content of *Fantasia*, but its overall structure and audiovisual premise. More in general, it could be said that the target of the parodistic discourse in *Allegro* is the logonomic system of *Fantasia*—that is to say, the features that are pertinent to the genre or textual mode of the film. In his study on film parody, Dan Harries elaborated on the semiotic concept of logonomic system of a text after Robert Hodge and Gunther Kress;[18] he held that, in a parody, the reference to a logonomic system "helps to guide the viewer by evoking particular textual norms and conventions."[19] In *Allegro*, the overall reference to the audiovisual model of *Fantasia* gives to the spectator enough ground to compare the two works, while providing the director with ample space to innovate, content wise.

At the time of Bozzetto's film, the logonomic system of *Fantasia* was still unique: no other film had ever used it again. A compilation of animated

---

[13]"La critica e il pubblico non hanno mai avuto dubbi nel considerarlo (e lodarlo) come opera autonoma, dotata di valori suoi propri. Esso è piuttosto un esempio di postmoderno cinematografico: un deliberato, rivendicato uso citazionistico di frammenti di cultura diffusa, allo scopo di comporre un'opera nuova." Giannalberto Bendazzi, "La maturità del ragazzo d'oro," in *Bruno Bozzetto. Cinquant'anni di cartoni animati*, ed. Dino Aloi (Torino: Edizioni Il Pennino, 2005), 33-4.
[14]Linda Hutcheon, *A Theory of Parody: The Teachings of Twentieth Century Art Forms* (New York: Routledge, 1985).
[15]Ibid., 32.
[16]Ibid.
[17]Ibid.
[18]Robert Hodge and Gunther Kress. *Social Semiotics* (Ithaca, NY: Cornell University Press, 1988).
[19]Dan Harries, *Film Parody* (London: British Film Institute, 2000), 104.

pantomimes, whose rhythms were closely knitted to classical music, was an unmistakable reference to *Fantasia*, even without any shout-out to famous moments in the Disney feature. That is to say, *Allegro* does not need to use any of what Harries calls "intertextual disruption":[20] an explicit sign of the referenced text, which conspicuously emerges as an extraneous item in the parodistic work. There is a shout-out in *Allegro*, though, but only to the title of *Fantasia* and to the name of Disney, during the opening monologue of Maurizio Micheli, who also informs the audience about the film structure. However, that moment seems to be there exactly because of how the *Fantasia-Allegro* parodistic connection works. As the object of parody is a large-scale formal structure, without that shout-out the spectator would not be able to clearly see the *Fantasia* reference at least until the beginning of the first animated episode. That shout-out moment is the only overt intertextual intromission in the parodistic stance of *Allegro*, but it does not contradict it, as it is functional to let the spectator see the *Fantasia* reference straightaway, while waiting for the rest of the film structure to unfold. It sets their expectations right, in a sense. After that shout-out, nothing in *Allegro* can be directly linked to a precise moment in *Fantasia*. There are a few visual allusions indeed, for example, in scene layouts; however, those feel more like homages than parodies.

The concept of homage is actually tangent to that of parody in many points. In her discussion of modern parody, Hutcheon finds that homage can be a consequence of a particular take on irony.

For Hutcheon, irony is a spontaneous consequence of the friction between the two texts involved in the modern parodistic process. While, as mentioned above, they are texts with an affinity—signified by the *para* prefix in "parody"—such affinity is (ironically?) what allows the audience to notice the differences between the old and new work. Irony is born from the rhetoric use of the gap between two texts with a strong mutual affinity. It does not necessarily mean mockery, though, as, by following Hutcheon again, "there is nothing in *parodia* that necessitates the inclusion of a concept of ridicule, as there is, for instance, in the joke or *burla* of burlesque. Parody, then, in its ironic 'trans-contextualization' and inversion, is repetition with difference."[21] *Allegro non troppo* is indeed a "repetition with difference" of Disney's *Fantasia*, but not a plain mockery of it. Hutcheon noticed that the ironic intertextual device in modern parody does not always have a negative ethos, which is ridicule.[22] There is also a kind of ironic parody of a "reverential variety ... [that] would be closer to homage than to attack." This is where the more "intimate" meaning of *para* gets activated, as

---

[20]Ibid., 113.
[21]Hutcheon, *Theory of Parody*, 32.
[22]Ibid., 56.

a signifier of closeness between texts, more than opposition. It could be argued, then, that this kind of ironic parody is pertinent to the animated episodes of *Allegro non troppo*, or the parts of the film that try to break new grounds in Italian animation while demonstrating an affectionate respect for Disney's achievement. The live-action interstitials, instead, are marked by an irony with a negative ethos, as they take their *Fantasia* counterparts and desecrate their educational intent by twisting the whole concert-hall narrative into a grotesque farce. Even with this dual ethos, the ironic stance of *Allegro non troppo* seems endowed with that "power to renew"[23] that Hutcheon attributes to modern parodies.

The presence of such complex intertextuality leads to another deduction about the film: *Allegro non troppo* does not include very young children in its ideal target audience. This is actually one of the reasons behind the troubles the film had with Italian distributors (see Chapter 3); in all, it is a film that requires the cognitive resources of at least an average teenager. Apart from that, some of its themes and imagery would not be suitable for preschool children; in fact, it includes violent visualizations of the perverse effects of consumerism and sexual innuendo, especially in the opening and closing episodes. As a matter of fact, those two episodes were completely removed from the film in occasion of the 2003 and 2005 Milan "concert" screenings with a live orchestra, which were open to a general audience; they were a case of forced targeting, which is a symptom of the persisting Italian prejudice about animation being an expressive form for children only.[24]

Outside of Italy, the quirky nature of *Allegro non troppo* did not prevent it from having a very satisfying circulation. Among Bozzetto's features, it was the one with the best international results;[25] its first wide release was in the United States; the film then opened in Germany and received a full Italian distribution only on December 22, 1977 (see Chapter 3). Its pervasive use of pantomime, the fame of its model, the technical quality of the animation, and the effectiveness of the visual gags made the film universally enjoyable. However, *Allegro non troppo* remains a film that

---

[23]Ibid., 115.
[24]On December 20, 2003, the film was accompanied by the Orchestra Sinfonica Giuseppe Verdi di Milano, conducted by Marcello Bufalini at the Auditorium di Milano (Luigi Di Fronzo, "I cartoon di Disney e Bozzetto. Questa sì che è buona musica," *La Repubblica*, December 20, 2003, https://ricerca.repubblica.it/repubblica/archivio/repubblica/2003/12/20/cartoon-di-disney-bozzetto-questa-si.html?ref=search (accessed August 2, 2019); on April 16, 2005, the same orchestra, in the same place, was conducted by Ruben Jais and the show also featured two actors: Nicola Olivieri and Marco Calabrese (Luigi Di Fronzo, "Allegro non troppo. Il film di Bozzetto musicato dalla Verdi," *La Repubblica*, April 16, 2005, https://ricerca.repubblica.it/repubblica/archivio/repubblica/2005/04/16/allegro-non-troppo-il-film-di-bozzetto.html?ref=search (accessed August 2, 2019).
[25]Bozzetto during a class for the History of Animation course at the Department of Cultural Heritage, University of Padova, Italy, November 25, 2014.

works only within a specific context: its reference needs to be kept in mind, in order to appreciate at best its communicative intent. The intertextuality, or the cross-dependence between a text and its sources, is a trait of all kind of narrations and it is so emphasized and celebrated in Bozzetto's film that it becomes its defining feature. As such, *Allegro non troppo* is an outstanding case of a "lazy machine," an expression that Umberto Eco used to define a narrative text in respect to what it requires to its audience: "It demands the reader to contribute a considerable amount of effort in order, so to speak, to fill in the empty spaces that have been left blank, the spaces where what has not been said and what has already been said belong."[26] The "empty spaces" of *Allegro non troppo* cannot be filled just by remembering *Fantasia*; as explained before, its status of a modern parody implies a great deal of autonomy and innovation. First of all, the parodied feature was not seen from a neutral point of view, but it was filtered by the sensibility of a mature director with a style and a technical approach very different from those of *Fantasia* or Disney in general. The author respected greatly the legacy he was referencing, but he wanted also to make comedy out of it: hence the dual ethos of the irony featured in the film. Then, Bozzetto's point of view was immersed in a sociocultural environment that was separated a great deal from that of the Disney artists from the 1940s: Bozzetto revisited *Fantasia* in the Italy of the second half of the 1970s. Such points are integral to the poetics of *Allegro non troppo* and constitute a necessary premise to its appreciation and analysis. The next pages will thus provide an introduction to the film, opened by an overview to its content (in general; summaries of the single episodes can be found in Part Two); its context will then be outlined, first by means of a panorama on the Italian history and popular culture in the 1970s. The discourse will then move on to a comparison between *Allegro non troppo* and *Fantasia*; the aim will be to not only explain the communicative strategy of the film but also show that the intertextual relationship between the two films is biunivocal: it is not just *Fantasia* that explains *Allegro*, but *Allegro* might also work as a commentary on *Fantasia*.

The Tales of *Allegro non troppo*

Allegro non troppo is a collection of animated episodes joined together by a live-action continuing story. The episodes are varied in style and content, while the live-action frame is homogeneous: it is photographed in an

---

[26] "Il testo è una macchina pigra che esige dal lettore un fiero lavoro cooperativo per riempire spazi di non-detto o di già-detto rimasti per così dire in bianco." Umberto Eco, *Lector in fabula. La cooperazione interpretativa nei testi narrativi* (Milano: Bompiani, 1979), 24–5.

"expressionist"[27] black and white, intended to create a stark visual contrast with the colorful animated shorts. Sometimes, however, animated characters or effects (in color) interact with the live-action parts.

The encasing storyline is a deranged version of its equivalent in *Fantasia*: the performance of a symphonic concert program by an orchestra, explained by a commentator. Nothing of the solemn authoritativeness of the Disney film remains; the situation is surreal from the start. The host (Maurizio Micheli) reads from notes and seems to dissimulate his musical ignorance and indifference under excessive emphasis and fake enthusiasm. He talks to an empty theater (the Donizetti, in Bergamo) where a young cleaning girl (Marialuisa Giovannini) keeps doing her job, with no seeming interest in what is going on. The conductor (Nestor Garay) is a vulgar and violent Argentinian man, who kidnaps a bunch of old ladies to make them pose as his orchestra; they then sit on stage in vintage party dresses and in a seating setup nothing like that of a professional ensemble. They get often scolded and comedically brutalized during the performance. Next to the orchestra, there is a figure in charge of creating impromptu translation of the sounds into images and stories: an animator (Maurizio Nichetti) chained to his animation desk who is treated as a slave by the conductor. The host incompetently introduces each one of the pieces, with no concern about providing serious details about the music; the tales that unfold, even though replete with tongue-in-cheek humor, are however untouched by the cultural degradation of the host and conductor. They implicitly indicate the oppressed animator as the only person in possession of commendable professional skills. The animated episodes start from a mythological world, where an old satyr, obsessed by sex and the female body, courts wood nymphs in vain, until he hallucinates and sees feminine body parts everywhere (Debussy). The second episode introduces a community of people that obsessively copycat one member of them, who ultimately tries to kill everyone else by taking advantage of their compulsion to imitate his actions (Dvořák). The next story is about the birth and evolution of life on a faraway planet (but it might also be the Earth itself)[28] from a drop of carbonated drink inside a Coca-Cola bottle littered by astronauts, which sprouts a procession of wondrous beasts, destined to be dramatically interrupted by the sudden outbreak of human civilization (Ravel). Then comes the sad stroll of a stray cat in the ruins of the house where he used to live with his owners; the place is now empty but still full of memories that vividly come alive (Sibelius). The misadventures of an anthropomorphic bee, who gets ready to feast on

---

[27] Bozzetto defined it as such, in "Ricordando *Allegro non troppo*," a documentary in the *Allegro non troppo* DVD (Roma: Multimedia San Paolo, 2005).

[28] Bozzetto voluntarily refrained from clarifying this point; he prefers to leave open all the possible interpretations about the pictured planet. Personal communication to the author via Skype, January 20, 2019.

a flower, come next; she risks to be squished by a couple of human lovers, who roll on the grass and almost sit on her, until she decides to use her sting (Vivaldi). The last piece is a quirky take on the biblical tale of Adam and Eve: the apple gets refused by both of them and the snake decides to eat it himself, only to be caught in a dizzying assault of commercials, power, and wealth symbols that make him regret his decision (Stravinsky). The live-action plot interwoven to those episodes focuses on the contrast between the animator and the conductor; the younger and smaller man tries to rebel to the arrogance of the bigger one, sometimes by using his drawing skills, sometimes by recurring to brute force (to no avail); finally, he turns himself and the cleaning girl into a cartoon prince and princess, free to fly away from the theater. The host and the conductor are thus left without a conclusion for their show; so, they call Franceschini, the protagonist of an extra-animated episode of *Allegro non troppo*, but one that is not set to a single piece of classical music. He is a farcical hunchback, possibly inspired by Igor (Marty Feldman) from *Young Frankenstein* (Mel Brooks, 1974; "Franceschini" might be a pun on "Frankenstein"),[29] and the keeper of a cellar in the theater where stock finales are kept; he needs to choose one and so reviews some of them (one more absurd than the others), but no one seems useful. Fragments from majestic conclusions of classical compositions (not from the previous animated episodes) are heard during the unlikely finales that Franceschini checks. The distraught host and conductor start to conjure up a new feature, a love story between a tall woman and seven small men. While they casually drop the title *Snow White and the Seven Dwarfs*, a zoom-out reveals that such events are parts of the finales that Franceschini is still reviewing; he approves and closes the curtain. From the little theater he was looking at, the snake from the Stravinsky episode pops out; he bites Franceschini's nose. The hunchback runs away until a "happy end" written in bulky letters smashes onto his head.

Notwithstanding its wildly heterogeneous selection of stories, *Allegro non troppo* has a lingering narrative continuity. All its constituents are variations on the theme of the struggle against overwhelming forces that secretly superintend to the everyday life of the characters. The satyr is subjugated by the impairments of old age and by the desire for the feminine sensuality, from which he cannot escape because the very world he lives in is the naked body of a giant woman; in the Dvořák segment, the little clever

---

[29]Bozzetto agrees that this could be the case, but he does not remember if this pun was actually discussed or mentioned during the production. Bozzetto in a meeting with the author, Bergamo, July 5, 2019. Giuliana Nuvoli, instead, argued that the name could have a darker undertone, as it could be a reference to Alberto Franceschini, a member of the Red Brigades who participated in the kidnapping of the judge Mario Sossi in 1974. Giuliana Nuvoli, "Allegro oggi," in *Allegro non troppo. Un tesoro dell'arte italiana*, ed. Chiara Cereda, Shirin Chehayed, Priscilla Mancini, and Andrijana Ružić (Milano: Agema, 2016), 6.

man cannot escape from being obsessively imitated by a mindless crowd; in the *Boléro*, the long and relentless march of creatures is wiped away in a few instants by the violent outburst of a civilization that seemingly came out from nowhere; the cat of the *Valse triste* chases happy memories of his old place, but the wasted rooms of his half-collapsed house are ready to be demolished by a wrecking ball; in Vivaldi's *Concerto*, the picnic of the bee is ruined by the arrival of two humans, who are unaware of the disasters they cause to the small world of insects while carelessly indulging in amorous play; the snake of the *Firebird Suite* is buffeted by the rapturous lures of consumerism, which transform him into a caricature of a bourgeoisie man. In the live-action interstitials, the animator tries to evade from the clutches of the conductor; even the finale, which plays with the impossibility to find a proper conclusion to the film, celebrates a defeat–not of a character but of a narrative trope (the necessity of an ending). In few occasions, the struggle is actually victorious: the bee stings the male human and the animator flees with the cleaning girl into a world of fantasy. However, the latter event seems to imply that no real victory can be achieved against the forces that dominate reality: the only way out seems that of escapism into dreams and imagination.

Another continuing thread is that of a landscape affected by changes that spiral out of control. In all of the animated episodes, the characters have to deal with an environment that dangerously changes against their own will, as a consequence of the superior forces they try to fight. The satyr, the little clever man, the Boléro monsters, the cat, the bee, and the snake all long for the pristine form of their world, and sometimes they find it in nostalgia and contemplation: those give birth, however, only to short-lived illusions.

These unifying themes elaborate on Bozzetto's recurring pessimism on the human–environment relationship; however, there could be a link between those and the events that changed the sociohistorical circumstances of Italian citizens during the 1970s and that made the whole country feel under the control of unescapable hidden forces.

Italy in the 1970s: Liberation and Violence

Allegro non troppo, as already anticipated, came into being at the twilight of "Carosello." A daily creative fostering of spending desires was going to be forever withdrawn from the lives of the Italian spectators. Its void was anyway going to be soon filled by the aggressive marketing strategies of the private broadcasters, which introduced commercial breaks in Italian television. Without knowing about this impending far more pervasive form of conditioning, which the scholar of publicity Gian Luigi Falabrino called "an indigestion of TV commercials, unthinkable in other European countries,"[30] around 1976 several intellectuals and commentators saluted the end of "Carosello" with relief. The journalist Enzo Biagi called the program "a transmission that showed a world that does not exist, a fantasy Italian";[31] Pasolini, instead, labeled it "the factory of cretinism."[32] On the magazine *La civiltà cattolica* was stated that "Carosello" ignored social problems and conflicts and implicitly affirmed that the only valid values were those of consumers.[33]

It is not true, however, that "Carosello" and commercials in general did not take into account the problems of their age. They surely kept an escapist and overtly optimistic stance on life, but the issues of their time and the new voice of previously silent members of society sept into their language and representational practices. As the 1970s approached, Italy entered one of the most tumultuous periods in its recent history. The economic boom was over; in 1973–4 a new word defined the life of Italian consumers, *austerity*. Following the 1973 international oil crisis, the Italian government had to limit the energy consumption by means of restrictive norms. Social issues arose, with unprecedented vehemence: the patriarchal primacy of the average male man was starting to be questioned by young people and women. The European student agitations of 1968 reached Italy and mixed with an upraise of factory workers in demand of better employment conditions, together with a radicalization of subversive strategies from far-right and far-left organizations. The period of strikes and demonstrations of 1969 was called the "Hot Autumn"; according to the journalists Indro Montanelli and Mario Cervi, the uprise was not due to poverty (the salaries of Italian factory workers were still among the lowest in Western Europe, but the quality of life had significantly improved over time) but to an identification with the ideological turmoil of that age.[34] The tensions were exasperated by the ineffectiveness of the Italian government in promulgating social reforms, due to the fragility of the alliances between the parties dominated by Christian Democracy, a centrist political force that guided Italy, with few interruptions, from 1944 to 1994. Between 1968 and 1970, the cabinet in charge changed for five times; the far-left PCI (Italian Communist Party) became the second biggest political force and from 1972, when Enrico

---

[30] "Un'indigestione pubblicitaria televisiva, impensabile negli altri paesi europei." Gian Luigi Falabrino, *Storia della pubblicità in Italia dal 1945 a oggi* (Roma: Carocci, 2007), 46.
[31] "Una trasmissione che mostrava un mondo che non esiste, un italiano fantastico." Enzo Biagi in Marcello Zane, *Scatola a sorpresa. La Gamma Film di Roberto Gavioli e la comunicazione audiovisiva in Italia da Carosello a oggi* (Milano: Jaca Book, 1998), 198.
[32] "La fabbrica del cretinismo." Pier Paolo Pasolini in Zane, *Scatola a sorpresa*, 198.
[33] Enrico Baragli, "Requiem per Carosello," *La civiltà cattolica* 3036 (December 18, 1976): 580–7.
[34] Indro Montanelli and Mario Cervi, *L' Italia degli anni di piombo, 1965–1978* (Milano: BUR Rizzoli, 2018), 65.

Berlinguer took its leadership, it sought a "historic compromise" with Christian Democracy, in order to shift the political axis of Italy to center-left. However, the 1970s opened with a shift to the right, because of a reaction to the tumults of 1968 and a need of stability from middle-class people. A movement called Silent Majority, in Milan, gave voice to those claims. The filo-fascist MSI (Italian Social Movement) became a driving force of the new cabinets; in 1970 an ex-fascist and former member of the MSI, the prince Junio Valerio Borghese, almost perpetrated a fascist golpe intended to occupy the Ministry of the Interior, the Ministry of Defense, the RAI, and the main offices of telecommunications, while kidnapping the president of the Republic, Giuseppe Saragat, and killing the head of police Angelo Vicari; Borghese and his political party, Fronte Nazionale, called the golpe off at the last minute for unclear reasons. Anyway, the votes of the MSI, in 1971, had a relevant weight in the election of the new president of the Republic, Giovanni Leone.

Several extraparliamentary associations, both from far-right and far-left, arose in those year and started to contrast the sociopolitical establishment with terrorist attacks. Such violent actions were not always claimed, so their purpose remained sometimes unclear: however, it was suggested[35] that the neofascist terrorism operated in accordance with a "Strategy of Tension"[36] devised in collaboration with secret services and people from the government to create chaos and render democracy ineffective, so as to undermine institutions and contrast the growth of anti-fascist movements and the leftist shift of the Italian government, which was gradually responding to the pressures from students and workers during the "Hot Autumn." The neofascist attacks mostly consisted in random bombings of public places. The far-left terrorism, instead, was marked by the initiatives of the Brigate Rosse (Red Brigades), a subversive communist group established in 1970; they elected kidnappings and killings of institutional figures as their preferred line of action. The virulent escalation of political violence was the most outstanding and tragic characteristic of the Italian 1970s, which were later remembered by journalists and historians as the "Years of Lead."[37] The massacres started in 1969: after two minor bombings at the FIAT pavilion at the Milan Fair (April 25), and on several trains (August 8–9), which resulted in a number of severely injured people but no casualties, on 12 December an explosion in the Piazza Fontana branch of the Banca Nazionale dell'Agricoltura (National Bank of Agriculture) killed seventeen and left eighty-eight injured. The next fascist terrorist attacks

---

[35]Pier Paolo Pasolini, "Che cos'è questo golpe?" *Corriere della Sera*, November 14, 1974; now in Pasolini, *Scritti corsari* (Milano: Garzanti, 2008), 88.

[36]Paul Ginsborg, *Storia d'Italia dal dopoguerra a oggi*, trans. Marcello Flores and Sandro Perini (Torino: Einaudi, 2006), 450.

[37]Ibid., 511.

and political assassinations by far-left extremists followed up at a frantic pace: among the most relevant events, on March 26, 1971, Alessandro Floris, a security guard, was killed by far-left terrorists during a robbery in Genova; on May 17, 1972, terrorists from the far-left association Lotta Continua (Continuous Struggle) killed police officer Luigi Calabresi; on May 31, 1972, neofascists killed three Carabinieri with a bomb in Peteano; on April 16, 1973, the radical left-wing group Potere Operaio (Power of the Workers) attacked the MSI militant Mario Matteo by setting fire to his house in Rome, killing his two sons; on May 17, 1973, an anarchist threw a bomb during a ceremony in honor of Calabresi at the Milan Police Command, killing four and injuring forty-five; eight were killed and 102 wounded in a new bombing that made casualties among civilians, during an anti-fascist demonstration in Piazza della Loggia, Brescia, on May 28, 1974. The first murders by the Red Brigades happened on June 17, 1974, in Padova, where two MSI members were killed; in the following years, the assassinations by the group continued, targeting policemen, judges, lawyers, and journalists.[38] The most historically relevant of their crimes was the abduction (March 16, 1978) and then the assassination (May 9, 1978), after a failed negotiation with the Italian government, of Aldo Moro, former prime minister and then president of Christian Democracy. The fascist bombings continued, too: on August 4, 1974, 12 died and 105 were injured on the Italicus Rome-Brennero express train, at San Benedetto Val di Sambro. The most severe terrorist attack occurred on August 2, 1980, at the railway station of Bologna: the bomb destroyed a large portion of the building, killing eighty-five and leaving more than two hundred injured. The subversive aggressions became then less frequent but continued well into the next decade.

Notwithstanding the turmoil, however, the social progress of Italy did not stop. Several laws granted more rights and freedom of expression to minorities and disadvantaged groups: apart from the improvement of the work conditions, equality between women and men started to be promoted; Italian regions were given more autonomy from the central state (1970); divorce became legal (1970) and was later confirmed as such by a popular referendum (1974); abortion also was similarly legalized (1978; referendum in 1981). In 1971, the Sentence no. 49 of the constitutional court decriminalized the promotion of contraceptive practices; in 1976, the Ministry of Health authorized the free sale of the contraceptive pill in pharmacies.[39] All those new norms participated in giving more agency to women in respect to life choices; even though a perfect equality with men was (and still is in 2021) far from being achieved, the voice of women,

---

[38]Ibid., 517.
[39]Bozzetto later celebrated the pill in an educational short film (*La pillola*, The Pill, 1983).

thanks to the multiplication of demonstrations and initiatives by feminist associations, became heard at a national level after 1975.[40]

"Carosello" and other forms of communication indirectly acknowledged the ongoing transformations in social life. In general, the advertisements started to be more daring in content and language, especially as far as the representation of women is concerned. However, the cases of alignment with the feminist ideals were rare and not well-received: in 1966, for example, a live-action "Carosello" for the SuperShell gasoline presented two fighting armies of young and strong girls; the "good" ones, in white robes, were served by men scientists. At the time, the advertised product was mostly targeted to men, so the sales results were far from encouraging.[41] The narrative on freedom and self-determination of women occasionally reappeared in advertisement about sanitary pads, shampoos, or clothes: in 1978, the clothing brand Cori promoted a woman model that was "neither witch, nor Madonna," and as such beyond stereotypes.[42] In most cases, though, the discourses on the sexual liberation of women became just an excuse for the insertion of higher rates of innuendo centered on the female body, and mostly directed to heterosexual males. A 1971 "Carosello" featured the blonde actress Solvi Stubing and advertised a brand of beer, with the claim "call me Peroni, I will be your beer," "for men that are used to get the best";[43] in the same years, printed advertisement for a liquor (Fior di Vite Ramazzotti) played with a double entendre related with the "blonde" color of the product, sometimes reinforced by an apparently naked girl partly hidden behind a bottle: the text exhorted the reader to have "two blondes," "if you think you are enough of a man to have one."[44] Naked women appeared in several advertisements for bras or jeans of 1973 and 1974;[45] a couple of outstanding cases were the printed advertisements for the jeans brand Jesus, which sought (and obtained) scandalized reactions by proposing erotic pictures (by Oliviero Toscani) of the waist or rear of a female model wearing skimpy jeans, with a quotation from the Bible (or one that sounded like that) printed over them. Notwithstanding those advertisements seemed to challenge restrictive moral codes, they actually perpetuated the patriarchal status quo, only conceding more explicit appeasements to its hidden desires and reinforcing ideas as women being commodities for "true" men. The sex-obsessed old satyr in *Allegro non troppo* seems to be an elaboration on this toxic masculinity that shows how sad and trapping the latter could become for men themselves. In the *Firebird*

---

[40] Ginsborg, *Storia d'Italia dal dopoguerra a oggi*, 495.
[41] Falabrino, *Storia della pubblicità in Italia dal 1945 a oggi*, 79.
[42] "Né strega, né Madonna."
[43] "Chiamami Peroni, sarò la tua birra," "per uomini abituati al meglio."
[44] "Se pensi di essere uomo abbastanza da farti una bionda."
[45] Falabrino, *Storia della pubblicità in Italia dal 1945 a oggi*, 81.

episode, moreover, there could be a direct reference to the exploitation of sexual imagery of women in ads for alcoholic beverages: some blonde and naked female figures emerge from beer cans (Figure 3). In 1977, Bozzetto referenced the commodification of the body of women also in *Strip Tease*, a short film that mixed animation with live-action footage of a showgirl; in a theater, a crowd of little men—whose design is close to the typical rendering of the "average man" by Bozzetto, like Mr. Rossi or the satyr in *Allegro*—indulges in exaggerate cartoon reaction to a striptease (a likely reference to the wolf in Tex Avery's classic *Red Hot Riding Hood*, 1943). At the end of the dance, the naked lady brings the whole theater down; its ruins drop out as crumbles from the undone fly of the pants worn by a man, who walks away nonchalantly.

In parallel to the far-from-flattering direction Italian advertising was taking, other examples of social communication gained new ground. In 1970, Guido Mengacci (president of the TP association of advertising professionals) and Vittorio Orsini (president of OtiPi, the association of advertising agencies) were introduced by David Campbell Harris to the USA Advertising Council, an institution that made fundraising campaign to sustain the army during the Second World War and later converted itself into an organism devoted to the promotion of charity, health, and

FIGURE 3 *A production cel and background from the* Firebird *episode of* Allegro non troppo. *Two naked blonde girls gush out from beer cans and try to seduce the discombobulated snake, lost in a nightmarish visual trip about the worst sides of consumerism. The image satirizes the sexist vocabulary and imagery that many Italian TV ads of the 1970s adopted after the "sexual revolution" of the late 1960s; the main reference here is the advertisement copy of a beer brand that played on a double entendre of the word "blonde." This production cel was on display as part of the special exhibition on Bozzetto included in "Super," the 15th Mostra internazionale di illustratori contemporanei (International Exhibition of Contemporary Illustrators; Cremona, Italy, November 30, 2019–January 26, 2020).*

social assistance. Mengacci, Orsini, and Giorgio Fiaschi saw the creation of an Italian version of the Advertising Council as an occasion to reconcile journalists, sociologists, consumer organizations, and left-wing politicians with advertisements.[46] Even with this opportunist motivation, the Pubblicità Progresso (Progress Advertising) committee (later made into a foundation) introduced a new trend in Italian commercials; the resulting ads did not invite to buy goods, but to help less fortunate people, promote health care, and protect the environment. The visual and verbal language of those commercials embraced the "sensationalist" vogue of the advertising of the 1970s, but with completely different content, tone, and purpose; the language did not shy away from direct and imperative appeals to awaken the sense of responsibility of the target, as in the first campaign (1971–2), "Donate sangue" ("Donate Blood"), whose claim was: "C'è bisogno di sangue. Ora lo sai" ("There is a need for blood. Now you know it").[47] The supporting images were often shocking, in order to solicit a strong emotional reaction in the viewer: the TV ad of "Donate Blood" opened with the staged ending of a successful heart surgery on a 8-year-old child, with no sounds but those of gas from oxygen tanks and blood drops in the intravenous feeding.

In the 1970s, commercials could still be considered Bozzetto's area of greater expertise, as he himself acknowledged in the late 1960s, when he commented about the thematic choice of his feature *Vip, My Brother Superman* (see Chapter 1). However, Bozzetto gradually decreased his output in this field and substituted it with animated intros to TV programs, such as "Scacciapensieri" (1973) for the RTSI, or the RAI shows "Tante scuse" (1974), "Spaccaquindici" (1975), and "Portobello" (1978): this peaked in 1977, with nine different shows featuring openings by Bozzetto and his studio. The production of commercials did not completely end, though, as the studio kept producing "Carosellos" until 1976; they were mostly shot in live-action and directed by people other than Bozzetto (Emilio Uberti, Francesco Carnelutti, Franco Taviani, Maurizio Nichetti). Bozzetto and his collaborators contributed thus to the advertising trends until the late 1970s; just like in *Vip, My Brother Superman*, in the previous decade, this situation favored a cross-pollination between the commercials and the theatrical works. *Allegro non troppo* is connected with the sociopolitical climate of the Years of Lead by its recurring theme of overruling hidden menaces. In the *Firebird* sequence, the aggressions to the snake by symbols of police forces, like clubs and blue flashing lights, might be a reference to urban riots and their repression. Such theme is generally avoided by commercials; it is specific to *Allegro*. However, the film seems also to be under the influence of

---

[46]Ibid., 59.
[47]https://www.pubblicitaprogresso.org/it/campagne/campagne/c-e-bisogno-di-sangue (accessed August 12, 2019).

the tales about social equality, defense of the environment, and freedom of expression that audiovisual communication was spreading in Italy. A little nod to the issues of factory workers (but also a cutting remark on the vacuous ways of the people who dealt with them) appears at the very end, when Micheli and the conductor discuss about remaking *Snow White*; the host wants the film to star "seven workers, got it? Workers. We add in the social side, too."[48] The environmental topic, as suggested before, is inherent to the use of natural or urban landscapes as "lost paradises" that fuel the desires of the characters. It is also evident in the event that gives birth to the march of uncanny creatures in the *Boléro* segment: the disrespectful littering of a Coca-Cola glass bottle impacts a deserted planet in a cataclysmic way, by bringing to it life and the destructive fury of human civilization. In commercials, the theme of landscape and pollution had already been tackled by Bozzetto and his studio in a series of mixed-technique "Carosellos" titled "Sapore di Città" ("The Taste of the City," Guido Manuli and Maurizio Nichetti, 1972–6). In them, a live-action man is confronted with the living buildings and cars of a city, which suffocate him with smog. The use of nuanced shadows on the animated characters prefigured the visual style of the *Boléro*.

Another link between *Allegro* and the Italian audiovisual trends of the 1970s could be found in the so-called psychedelic vogue. The term "psychedelic" was invented by the English psychiatrist Humphry Fortescue Osmond in 1956;[49] it is made of two ancient Greek words that mean "mind-manifesting," in reference to some of the effect that LSD and other substances had on perception: "enriching the mind and enlarging the vision."[50] The youth counterculture of the 1960s and 1970s celebrated the effects of LSD in a large array of artistic products; as the scholar David S. Rubin explained, "Something about the LSD trip—marked by super-saturated colors, psychic disjunctions, and surrealist juxtapositions—influenced the entire epoch, spilling over from avant-garde culture to mainstream advertising, as psychedelia became pop cliché and common vernacular."[51] Animation was a preferred vehicle for psychedelia; its visual freedom, in comparison to the "realism" of photographic live-action, allowed to create close equivalents to the lysergic hallucinations. The foremost example of psychedelic animation was saluted in *Yellow Submarine* (George Dunning, 1968), the full-length feature based on songs by the Beatles; the press

---

[48] "Sette lavoratori, capito? Lavoratori. Noi ci mettiamo anche il risvolto sociale."
[49] Humphry Fortescue Osmond, "A Review of the Clinical Effects of Psychotomimetic Agents," *Annals of the New York Academy of Sciences* 66, no. 3 (1957): 429.
[50] Ibid.
[51] David S. Rubin, *Psychedelic: Optical and Visionary Art since the 1960s* (Cambridge, MA: MIT Press, 2010), 51.

called it "the ultimate trip,"⁵² and the designs by Heinz Edelmann, marked by sinuous and concentric lines, flat surfaces, radical color contrasts, and unlikely settings and characters, were "so powerful that stills from the movie today serve as iconic representations of that hippy era,"⁵³ as John Grant commented. Other films that gained (retrospective) consensus as champions of the psychedelia were the Disney ones, and especially *Alice in Wonderland* (Clyde Geronimi et al., 1951) and, as already said, *Fantasia*. *Allegro non troppo* was not explicitly intended to be a psychedelic piece; however, its use of metamorphoses, flat designs, and bright and unrealistic colors, with lack of dialogue, evidenced a connection with the trending manners of visual psychedelia. Bozzetto actually made subtle references to Edelmann's designs for *Yellow Submarine* in the streamlined and ever-changing backgrounds of at least two animated "Carosello" series: "Los Prinziamo" (1969) and "Supermano" (1971). No reference to radical color palettes was possible, as they were in black and white, just like all the "Carosellos." Traces of the psychedelic style can be seen also in the mixed-technique "Carosellos" for the Zucchi bed linens (Giulio Cingoli, Guido Manuli, 1971–3), which have a real girl on a black background interact with shape-shifting flat drawings, while an obsessive jingle by Franco Godi, based on whispered gibberish, creates an oneiric and vaguely disturbing atmosphere.

Allegro non troppo and *Fantasia:* A Comparison

The work that had the biggest impact on *Allegro non troppo*, and that constitutes the main source of its intertextual communication and humor, remains however *Fantasia*. If compared, the two films display a remarkable amount of deliberate similarities; but it is the departures from the model that consolidate *Allegro non troppo* as an original work, with a status of modern parody. Those differences are a consequence of how Bozzetto filtered and interpreted the Disney film according to his own directorial approach, but also of the deep distance between the two in terms of geography, historical period, culture, production method, technology, artistic skills, and budget. The cultural specificities of the Italian feature have been already addressed in the previous paragraphs; so, in order to understand how and why *Allegro non troppo* took after *Fantasia*, a comparison between the two can be made in respect to the following areas: Bozzetto's interpretation of the Disney film; the overall structure of the feature; the musical selection; the use and presentation of music; the visual styles; and the animation techniques.

---

⁵²John Grant, *Masters of Animation* (New York: Watson-Guptill, 2001), 78.
⁵³Ibid.

The most direct source on Bozzetto's view of *Fantasia* is a pair of notebooks he kept in the early 1970s (the date on the first page is December 23, 1972), plus a few extra pages collected in a binder; they contain mostly one-page memorandums of stories he imagined while listening to classical music pieces. They also include a series of notes about *Fantasia*,[54] distributed over four pages. They neither confirm nor disprove the fervent admiration that Bozzetto has always expressed for the Disney film (see Chapter 1); they are just short and functional lists of keywords and brief thoughts about each episode in the film program. The episodes are in a random order; the notes were maybe not taken after a screening of the film, but on the basis of memories.

Fantasia is structured as follows: a live-action sequence, subdivided into sections intercalated to the animated shorts, shows the musicians of the Philadelphia Orchestra as backlit silhouettes, seated around the equally backlit Leopold Stokowski on his podium; the space has a two-dimensional feeling and there is no establishing shot of the whole orchestra; the spatial disposition of the instruments is sometimes hinted, but usually the camera shows only the shadows nearest to the podium, or it singles out soloists or small groups of players, without any clear description of their position in the orchestra and in respect to the audience. The music critic Deems Taylor gives short introductory speeches to each episode, standing between two harp players. There is no live-action conclusion; the film ends right after the last animated short. The first episode is the *Toccata and Fugue in D minor BWV 565* by Johann Sebastian Bach (originally for organ, orchestrated by Stokowski); the *Toccata* is visualized with a montage of shots featuring the silhouettes of the musicians, embellished by colored effects; the *Fugue* introduces an animated abstract landscape populated with shapes inspired by parts of musical instruments. The next number is a selection from Pëtr Il'ič Čajkovskij's *The Nutcracker Suite Op. 71a*, arranged in a different order than the original; the animation illustrates the seasonal changes in a wood, caused by little fairies; meanwhile, mushrooms, fishes, and flowers dance. The third episode is the most famous one: *The Sorcerer's Apprentice*, based on Paul Dukas's homonymous tone poem. It generated the whole *Fantasia* project; it was born as a stand-alone musical short, with a concept similar to that of the "Silly Symphonies" films: a pantomimic action synchronized to "a unique form of musical pastiche," as Russell Merritt and J. B. Kaufman said.[55] *The Sorcerer's Apprentice* differed in that it used a single musical piece and did not feature a one-shot main character: it starred Mickey Mouse with a new design by Fred Moore. When

---

[54]Select scans from the notebooks are featured as an extra, called the "Quaderni di *Allegro*" ("*Allegro* notebooks"), in the Italian DVD edition of the film (2005); on their cover, Bozzetto wrote "Diario. Allegro non troppo" ("Diary. Allegro non troppo").

[55]Russell Merritt and J. B. Kaufman, *Walt Disney's Silly Symphonies. A Companion to the Classic Cartoon Series* (Gemona: La Cineteca del Friuli, 2006), 8.

the film exceeded by three or four times the series' usual production budget, Disney and Stokowski decided to write off the expenses by creating a whole feature film around it.[56] The story tells about how Mickey loses control of the broom he brought to life with the magic hat of his master, an old and powerful sorcerer. After the short, the live-action interstitial shows a handshake between the silhouettes of Stokowski and Mickey Mouse, which "art historian Robert Hugues calls a defining moment in popular culture."[57] The fourth episode is based on excerpts from Igor Stravinsky's ballet *The Rite of Spring* and reconstructs, with a documentary-like attitude, the birth and evolution of life on Earth up to the extinction of the dinosaurs. Then comes an intermission: the musicians indulge in a jam session on fragments from the third movement of Ludwig van Beethoven's *Symphony no. 6 Op. 68 "Pastoral,"* followed by Taylor interacting with an imaginary animated visualization of the soundtrack, which translates the timbres of different instruments into vivid graphic patterns. The *"Pastoral"* ensues; its five movements, drastically shortened, are associated to characters and settings that make up an idealized and decorative version of ancient Greek mythology. The subsequent *Dance of the Hours*, from the opera *La Gioconda* by Amilcare Ponchielli, is a ridiculous ballet of quasi-anthropomorphic animals, ending in a catastrophic chase between alligators, hippopotamuses, elephants, and ostriches. The ending number is made up of two adjoined musical pieces: the tone poem *Night on Bald Mountain* by Modest Petrovič Musorgskij and Stokowski's orchestration of Franz Schubert's *Ave Maria*. The first piece shows a witches' sabbath presided by the enormous demon Chernabog; in the *Ave Maria*, chiming bells dispel the evil forces and a procession of pilgrims slowly walks through the pillar-like trees of a forest, toward the rising sun.

Bozzetto's notes start from the *"Pastoral" Symphony*, commented by the keywords "Country life—Classicism—Poetry—Cupids—Gods."[58] There is no mention of ancient Greece, or of the more sumptuous imagery that populates the short, like the flock of winged horses or the goddess Artemis that fires an arrow by using a moon crescent as a bow. Instead, he singled out the naked cupids—probably the weakest and kitschiest characters in the whole film, which Christopher Finch compared to *passé* ornamental tropes for restaurant murals of the 1930s[59]—and the "country life," which is something that Bozzetto probably caught in the open-air setting, the rustic festival with dances and wine celebrated around a chubby and tipsy version of the god Dionysus and the little flute-playing

---

[56]Culhane, *Walt Disney's Fantasia*, 17–18.
[57]Merritt and Kaufman, *Walt Disney's Silly Symphonies*, 8.
[58]"Vita campestre—Classicismo—Poesia—Amorini—Dei."
[59]Christopher Finch, *L'arte di Walt Disney. Da Mickey Mouse ai Magic Kingdoms*, trans. Marta Fornasier (Milano: Rizzoli, 2001), 71.

satyrs. It seems that Bozzetto was more intrigued by the weakest figurative elements of *Fantasia*'s "*Pastoral*," the ones that were actually conceived for a different piece of music, the ballet *Cydalise et le chèvre-pied* (*Cydalise and the satyr*) by Gabriel Pierné, and that were only later fitted to the more solemn music by Beethoven.[60] The reason for this becomes quite clear when reading a small annotation by Bozzetto near to the title of the *"Pastoral" Symphony*: "Fauno," which means "satyr." Bozzetto was evidently thinking about his take on Debussy's *Prélude à l'après-midi d'un faune* and thus delving into the *Cydalise* side of Disney's episode, more than in its dignified moments in tune with Beethoven's language, to find inspiration for the inept, displeasing, and small satyr he was to use as a protagonist. This explains why the "Pastorale" comes first in Bozzetto's notes: the satyr episode is the one that opens *Allegro*.

Similarly, "*Boléro*" is written in small letters near to the title of the second *Fantasia* section considered by Bozzetto, *The Rite of Spring*. The keywords are "Birth of life—Prehistoric Age—Struggle for existence—Extinction of the Dinosaurs—Earthquakes."[61] The keyword "struggle for existence" is revealing about Bozzetto's knowledge of scientific literature: the expression was used by Charles Darwin to title the third chapter of *The Origin of Species*. With this, Bozzetto implicitly acknowledged the scientific value of *The Rite of Spring* (even though it was already more than thirty years old, in the 1970s); his *Boléro* would later take a more imaginative and free direction. The theme of struggle would remain, anyway, just like the extinction and the earthquakes. Such catastrophes, in *Allegro*, are however not natural phenomena but consequences of skyscrapers sprouting from the ground, to symbolize the advent of man.

Bozzetto seems to have been less intrigued by the next two episodes he listed, which have a lesser number of keywords. *The Nutcracker* is defined as "Little portraits on nature and animals. Dances—Romanticism";[62] *The Sorcerer's Apprentice* is appreciated as the only part of *Fantasia* that features a storyline, as the keywords point out that it is a "Tale—Dream of a young person."[63]

The *Night on Bald Mountain* is then considered separately from the *Ave Maria*. Bozzetto wrote "Faust" near the title: an *Allegro non troppo* musical project that was never developed (see Chapter 3). From this point onward, the director starts taking notes with a different strategy: he first synthesizes with an adjective the tone of the whole episode at issue and then highlights some elements that caught his attention. For the *Night on Bald Mountain*, the

---

[60] Culhane, *Walt Disney's Fantasia*, 134.
[61] "Nascita della vita—Era preistorica—Lotta per l'esistenza—Estinzione dei Dinosauri—Terremoti."
[62] "Quadretti su natura e animali. Danze—Romanticismo."
[63] "Racconto—Sogno d'un giovane."

text is: "Dramatic. From a graveyard, souls soar to the Bald mountain that turns into a devil. The bells defeat evil. At morning everything goes back to normal."[64] It is a minimal summary of the main events. The adjective choice ("dramatic," for an episode replete with horrific and sometimes grotesque imagery), together with the lack of mention of the bold designs of monsters and witches, or the powerful acting of Chernabog, animated by Bill Tytla, suggest that Bozzetto was not interested in taking inspiration from the visuals, but to figure out how the Disney artists created a narrative arc over the musical structure of a composition. In fact, the preproduction diaries of *Allegro non troppo* are almost devoid of character design or directorial ideas; they are mostly made of schematic breakdowns of short storylines inspired by classical music pieces. Bozzetto thought that the most difficult challenge in approaching the *Fantasia* model was to find a story that had a satisfying dramatic pacing while following a given musical architecture. He discarded several compositions he enjoyed because the mood shifts of the music were unfit to the storyline he had in mind (see Chapter 3).[65]

The *Dance of the Hours* is defined by the words: "Satirical. Mockery of classical dances. Female hippopotamus courted by an alligator."[66] In this case, Bozzetto considered preeminent the spoofing of dance routines, probably because of the relevance of satire to his own animation style. The *Toccata and Fugue* is instead just "Surrealistic—Striped dunes that chase each other."[67] The brevity of the commentary is understandable: there is no "abstract" episode in *Allegro non troppo* and, given Bozzetto's preoccupation for finding storylines, the director was probably not much into this purely visual segment. The "dunes" that intrigued Bozzetto, however, might have inspired some of the monsters in the *Boléro*, which have sometimes gibbous shapes that move over their back. The same "dunes" perhaps influenced also the voluptuous landscape at the end of the *Prélude à l'après-midi d'un faune*. In another page of the notes on *Fantasia*, Bozzetto redacted a comment that said: "Tracking shot over the body of a woman (plasticine?). Toccata and Fugue."[68] The woman-landscape of the *Prélude* is hand-drawn (and rotoscoped: see Chapter 3), though; Bozzetto would have used plasticine (claymation), instead, at the beginning of the *Firebird*.

The *Ave Maria* is then paired with the *Valse triste*. Also in this case, the interest of the director seems to have not been piqued: the essential commentary is "Religious—Procession of women in the woods."[69] There are

---

[64] "Drammatico. Da un cimitero le anime volano sul monte Calvo che diviene un diavolo. Le campane sconfiggono il male. Al mattino tutto torna normale."
[65] Bozzetto during a meeting with the author in Bergamo, Italy, on January 4, 2019.
[66] "Satirico. Presa in giro danze classiche. Ippopotama corteggiata da alligatore." Bozzetto uses an unexisting (and funny) female form of the noun "ippopotamo" (hippopotamus).
[67] "Surreale—Dune rigate che si inseguono."
[68] "Carrellata su corpo di donna (plastilina?) Toccata e fuga."
[69] "Religioso—Processione di donne nel bosco."

not much correspondences between the slow, steady pace of the *Ave Maria* animation and the swinging moods of Bozzetto's more vivid *Valse triste*; they are both suffused with a melancholic tinge, though. The only remaining part of *Fantasia* annotated by Bozzetto, the soundtrack performance in the intermission, was positively commented as "Several sounds interpreted by the track. Poetic presentation of a technical phenomenon."[70] The transformation of a technological item into a character apparently appeased Bozzetto's penchant for popular science, later expressed in his collaboration with Piero Angela and the TV program "Quark" (see Chapter 1). In *Allegro non troppo*, however, there is nothing that corresponds to the intermission of *Fantasia*. There is also nothing like the meeting between Mickey and Stokowski, even though some animated characters (including Mr. Rossi) interact with the live-action world. Bozzetto had in mind to make something out of that famous moment of the Disney film, anyway, as it is mentioned twice (with no commentary)[71] in the *Fantasia* pages of the *Allegro* notebooks.

Bozzetto's reading of *Fantasia* was functional not only to his film project but also to his will to imprint *Allegro* with traces of the Disney feature; he extracted from the animated episodes the characteristics that served both to help him shape up his ideas and to retain some of the key feelings evoked by the 1940 film. In parallel to this, Bozzetto's analysis of *Fantasia* was a quest for cleverly paced storytelling, more than being an appreciation of bravura pieces in animation technique and unbridled imagination. In fact, this story-oriented approach governed the whole structure of *Allegro non troppo*.

The structural comparison between *Allegro* and *Fantasia* shows how the different importance that Bozzetto and the Disney studio reserved to narration impacted the final shape of their features. *Fantasia* did not envelop its animated parts within a goal-oriented plot because of its premises. First, *Fantasia* was not conceived as any feature film but as a new form of entertainment intended to enhance a concert-going experience by visualizing the "design and pictures and stories that music inspired in the minds and imaginations of a group of artists," as Deems Taylor says in his introductory speech. It foregrounded outstanding technological innovations, like a precursor of the stereophonic sound, the Fantasound. It was a landmark in the exploration of three-dimensional soundscapes for entertainment purposes. Its distinct feature was a combination between the rendering of variable aural depth and the possibility to isolate the instruments by groups, and project their sound anywhere in the space, without adhering to a realistic reconstruction of the orchestra setup, in order to achieve expressive

---

[70] "Vari suoni interpretati dalla colonna. Present. poetica d'un fenomeno tecnico."
[71] "Topolino e Stokowsky" ("Mickey and Stokowsky"); "Topolino appare tra gli orchestrali e parla con Stokowsky" ("Mickey appears among the orchestra players and talks with Stokowsky").

effects in relation with film scenes; it "required the largest outlay of sound equipment that has been used commercially in the theater to date," as its inventor William E. Garity and Watson Jones reported in 1942.[72] Other proposed experimentations, which were never actualized, included a 3D sequence (the *Toccata and Fugue*) to be watched with cardboard Polaroid glasses and wafting flower scents through the audience during the *Nutcracker Suite*.[73] All those novelties were to be forwarded to the audience through the simulation of a familiar context: the "ritual" of a classical music concert.[74] The live-action segments are set in a place that, notwithstanding the creative display of lights and colors, bears the fundamental marks of a concert hall. The opening of a curtain at the beginning of the film, and to mark the fifteen-minute intermission, reinforced in the audience concert-going memories. The curtain idea was even mentioned in the marketing campaign of the film, which reinforced the concert "highbrow" aura of the picture by letting the spectators know that if they were to treat *Fantasia* like a conventional picture, and thus expecting to have time to get seated during the opening titles, they would have not enjoyed the show at best: the audience was supposed to behave just like in a concert hall.[75] As Maureen Furniss put it, "The idea was to present a film-viewing experience that would rival that of a live symphony."[76] *Fantasia* did not thus need a strong narration to keep its different sections together: it was to be understood as a symphonic concert, a public event based on performances of orchestral musical pieces. So, there is no continuing story in the intercalated live-action parts, but just shots of the silhouettes of the musicians and of Taylor speaking.

The nonnarrative premise of *Fantasia* was also functional to what the future of the film was initially intended to be. Disney wanted "to make a new version of *Fantasia* every year. ... Its pattern is very flexible and fun to work with—not really a concert, not a vaudeville or a revue, but a grand mixture of comedy, fantasy, ballet, drama, impressionism, color, sound, and epic fury."[77] *Fantasia* had to be "loose" from the narrative point of view from the start, as it was to be partly renovated at each new release, by keeping old favorites and mixing them with new animated shorts. This did

---

[72]William E. Garity and Watson Jones, "Experiences in Road-Showing Walt Disney's *Fantasia*," *Journal of the Society of Motion Picture Engineers* 39 (1942): 6.
[73]Culhane, *Walt Disney's Fantasia*, 10.
[74]It also simulated the aura of authority of a classical concert: see Marco Bellano, "Painted Orchestras. Orchestration and Musical Adaptation in Fantasia and Fantasia 2000," in *Relaciones Música e Imagen en los Medios Audiovisuales*, ed. Teresa Fraile and Eduardo Viñuela (Oviedo: Ediciones de la Universidad de Oviedo, 2015), 277–87.
[75]Irene Kletschke, *Klangbilder. Walt Disneys "Fantasia" (1940)* (Stuttgart: Franz Steiner Verlag, 2011), 76.
[76]Maureen Furniss, *Animation: The Global History* (London: Thames & Hudson, 2017), 107.
[77]Walt Disney in John Culhane, *Fantasia/2000: Visions of Hope* (New York: Disney Editions, 1999), 10.

not happen during Disney's lifetime, due to the financial failure of the film; the later *Fantasia/2000* (Don Hahn and others, 1999) was based on Disney's wish, but the program was completely different, except for *The Sorcerer's Apprentice*.

The final shape of *Fantasia* was that of an about 125-minute[78] "concert feature" subdivided into two parts; the interval splits it almost perfectly in half, as the "curtain" reopens at about sixty-seven minutes. The eight animated episodes are distributed into two groups of four; the second part also has the "soundtrack" divertissement. The running time of the animated parts (including the Mickey-Stokowski handshake and the end of the *Fugue*, where Stokowski is superimposed to the animation) is largely preponderant: about 104 minutes against 21 minutes of live-action interstitials. *Allegro non troppo* is shorter, at about eighty-five minutes. The animated episodes are just six, plus a few mixed-technique moments and Franceschini's search for a finale. There is an intermission, which was however removed in the home video version: it consists of about one minute of live-action footage that ends with an old lady who states, "I really think that part one ends here,"[79] plus the title cards that signal the end and beginning of reel one and reel two. This intermission divides *Allegro* in two almost equal halves like *Fantasia*, each one with three animated shorts. The second part features also the Franceschini sequence. The proportion between animation and live-action is however very different than that of *Fantasia*. The Disney feature was about 83 percent animation, with just a 17 percent of live-action; *Allegro* has instead about fifty-four minutes of animation (including the mixed-technique parts and the end titles) against thirty-one minutes of live-action, making the corresponding percentages about 64 percent and 36 percent. In comparison, there is much more live-action in *Allegro* than in *Fantasia*. The lower production costs of those parts might of course be accounted responsible for this choice; however, the interstitials required more screen time also because, unlikely those of *Fantasia*, they had a progressively unfolding storyline, filled with gags and incidents (see Part Two for details on the storyline). *Allegro* did not want to mimic a concert experience, nor it was due to be released again with variations in its program: so, its structure could be cohesive and oriented by a unitary narration. The animated and live-action parts are even interwoven by visual gags that make them interact with each other; for example, the Coca-Cola bottle of the *Boléro* is thrown by the conductor, who is later stung by the bee

---

[78]This is the running time of the current home video releases. The 1940 "roadshow" version of Fantasia was about one minute longer, because of a series of scenes from the "*Pastorale*" featuring racially stereotyped black centaurettes. Those had been censored since the 1969 rerelease of the film. The film also circulated in shortened versions, which expunged all the interventions by Taylor.

[79]"Mi sa tanto che qui finisce il primo tempo."

from Vivaldi's *Concerto*; the smoke from the conductor's cigar provides the *Valse triste* with its misty atmosphere; and so on. In addition to that, each one of the animated shorts in *Allegro* has a clear narrative backbone, while in *Fantasia* this is true for the *Sorcerer's Apprentice* alone.

If narration is the major feature that structurally distinguishes *Allegro* from *Fantasia*, in respect to the musical selection the two films are conceptually close. In fact, both of them stray from the requirements of a conventional symphonic concert. A symphonic program usually presents pieces arranged to create an emotional arc that is both well-varied and quite consistent in terms of style and involved players. *Fantasia* and *Allegro* only embrace the idea of the alternance of moods, but for the rest they take a detour from that tradition. In the symphonic concert model that consolidated throughout the twentieth century, a standard structure in the programs was required: as synthesized by William Weber, "by 1900 concert programmes had reached a form that was to be basic in many respects for the 20th century. With recitals, chamber music concerts and orchestral concerts increasingly separated, orchestras now performed shorter programmes of fewer works than before, in the most generic form, an overture, a concerto and a symphony."[80] *Fantasia* avoided altogether such conventional lineup, likely because the length and form of classical concertos and symphonies would have been ill-fitted to a feature made of short films of about ten or twenty minutes each. Classical concertos and symphonies have in fact a length of about twenty to thirty minutes; during the Romantic age, they expanded to forty minutes and more. They were made of multiple movements (the norm was three for concertos and four for symphonies) that build up a dramatic progression: two fast-paced movement encased a slower one and (in symphonies) a dance (minuet) or a rhythmically connotated scherzo. By using both a whole concerto and a symphony, *Fantasia* would have featured an almost identical dramatic structure twice. Also, giving a different and unrelated animation to each one of the ten-minute movements would not have been feasible, because of the conceptual unity of those classical compositions. There is actually a symphony in *Fantasia*, the *"Pastorale,"* a famous but slightly unusual item from the late classic symphonic repertoire, in that it had five movements and a descriptive program related with impressions from country life. The animation was made to present five different episodes taking place in the same setting; however, what Stokowski recorded can hardly be called Beethoven's *"Pastorale."* It is instead a "miniature" version of it, which summarizes in about twenty-two minutes a work whose performances

---

[80] William Weber, "Concert (ii)," *New Grove Dictionary of Music and Musicians*, Grove Online, https://www.oxfordmusiconline.com/grovemusic/view/10.1093/gmo/9781561592630.001.0001/omo-9781561592630-e-0000006240 (accessed August 16, 2019).

could reach thirty-nine minutes[81] and beyond. Apart from this somehow "forced" presentation of a symphony, *Fantasia*'s program takes a completely different route from a standard concert program. It also does not seek any chronological or stylistic coherence. The selection encompasses pieces that are singularly renowned (and sometimes even widely popular, like the *Toccata and Fugue* or the *Ave Maria*), but that do not usually appear side to side in concert programs. The film starts from a twentieth-century arrangement of a late Baroque piece, Bach's *Toccata and Fugue*; it serves Disney's intention to open *Fantasia* with quasi-abstract animations, in that it provides music of "absolute" nature ("music that exists simply for its own sake," as Taylor advances). This resonates with ideals from the late-nineteenth-century musical aesthetics: Eduard Hanslick commented, in respect to Bach, that "older music affords still more unmistakable proof that it aims at nothing beyond itself."[82] The selection continues with excerpts from a late Romantic ballet, the *Nutcracker*. The ensuing *Sorcerer's Apprentice* is from the same age, but it is a tone poem: an orchestral piece with a narrative program. Then there is again a ballet, but of a completely different style: the rhythmic and harmonic asperities of *The Rite of Spring*, in 1940, sounded as brutal as they did during the May 29, 1913, premiere in Paris, Théâtre des Champs-Elysées, where a riot broke out among the audience. The decidedly less aggressive *"Pastorale"* goes then back in time, to the early nineteenth century; the *Dance of the Hours* is instead a lively ballet excerpt from an Italian opera of 1876. The final diptych joins together another late-Romantic tone poem, the *Night on Bald Mountain*, with a new arrangement of Schubert's 1825 *Ave Maria*; notwithstanding its popular title, however, it is not a setting of the Catholic prayer with the same name, but *Ellens dritter Gesang (Ellen's Third Song)*, the third part of the song cycle *Liederzyklus vom Fräulein vom See*, from Walter Scott's *The Lady of the Lake*. *Fantasia* ends thus on a quiet note. While this was functional to the evil versus good theme inherent to the animated finale, it was yet another transgression to the canonical concert model, that, by ending with the fourth movement of a symphony, it is usually wrapped up more assertively.

The music of *Allegro non troppo* is equally far from the canon of symphonic events; in this case, however, the film is not trying at all to simulate a concert hall context. While in *Fantasia* there is at least a coincidence between the authoritativeness of the featured performers and that of the recorded music, which is really played by Stokowski and the Philadelphia Orchestra, in *Allegro* there is no relation at all between the laughable "orchestra" of old

---

[81]David Daniels, *Orchestral Music: A Handbook*, 4th ed. (Lanham, MD: Scarecrow Press, 2005), 48.
[82]Eduard Hanslick, *The Beautiful in Music: A Contribution to the Revisal of Musical Aesthetics*, trans. Gustav Cohen (London: Novello, 1891), 43.

ladies and the quality performances selected by Bozzetto. In fact, differently from *Fantasia*, no music was especially recorded for *Allegro*, apart from the "light" music heard during the interstitials and the end titles, by Franco Godi. Bozzetto acquired the rights to some Deutsche Grammophon[83] recordings by the Berliner Phiharmoniker conducted by Herbert Von Karajan (Debussy, Dvořák, Ravel, and Sibelius), the Münchener Kammerorchester conducted by Hans Stadlmair (Vivaldi), and the Rundfunk-Symphonieorchester Berlin conducted by Lorin Maazel (Stravinsky).[84] Curiously, while those are all stereo recordings,[85] the finished film used a monaural mix: another marked difference from *Fantasia*, which brings *Allegro* very well away from the Fantasound aesthetics of its precursor and even farther from a concert simulation of any kind. On top of that, while *Fantasia* relied on the suggestions of Stokowski and Taylor, *Allegro* did not have any music consultant at all; Bozzetto and his collaborators were not musicians and made their choices out of a combination of sheer intuition and a demanding trial-and-error routine (see Chapter 3). However, even with its distance from concert standards, the musical program of *Allegro non troppo* eventually turned out more plausible than the *Fantasia* one. This has to do with the duration of the selected pieces; while *Fantasia*, as it will be detailed soon, opted for reduced versions of long pieces that would have been unlikely to fit into the same concert evening, *Allegro non troppo* went for short pieces to be heard in full, except for the *Firebird*. By taking out Stravinsky's ballet, the program would make sense at least in respect to length and dramatic alternance of moods. The six pieces, in fact, seem to be arranged in couples that contrast opposite emotional ranges: The dreamy *Faune* clashes with the ebullient *Slavonic Dance*, while the majestic *Boléro* is followed by the nostalgic spleen of the *Valse triste*. The gaiety of Vivaldi is then toned down by the gentle *Ronde des princesses* from the *Firebird*, and the *Danse infernale du roi Kastchei* gives to the film a fiery finale.

The anthology is quite consistent also from the stylistic point of view. The starting point is a tone poem by Debussy, with a sensual atmosphere—an eminent example of the so-called musical French "impressionism" of late nineteenth to early twentieth century. It is followed by a *Slavonic Dance* (a *Skočná* in C minor) from the sixteen Dvořák orchestrated, originally collected in two sets (1878 and 1886) for piano four hands. The *Boléro* is another French composition, but by Maurice Ravel; its date of composition (1928) makes it the most recent piece in the whole program. However, it

---

[83]Deutsche Grammophon later collected Bozzetto's selection in a stand-alone LP dedicated to *Allegro non troppo* (DG 2535 400).

[84]After the release of *Allegro non troppo*, Bozzetto met Maazel by chance at a dinner; he recognized him because his name was written on his eyeglasses. Personal communication to the author via Skype, March 14, 2019.

[85]They are featured as such in the Deutsche Grammophon *Allegro non troppo* soundtrack LP.

does not introduce any stylistic rupture as that of *The Rite of Spring* in *Fantasia*. The stylistic homogeneity of *Allegro*'s program stays strong at least up to the *Valse triste*, from the incidental music written by the Finnish composer Jean Sibelius for Arvid Järnefelt's 1903 play *Kuolema* (*Death*). All the first four pieces pertain to the transition to post-Romantic tonal languages, which reacted to the grandiloquence and wandering harmonies of late-nineteenth-century music by seeking simplicity and expressivity through refined combinations of sounds. The use of the first movement from a Vivaldi *Concerto*, though, makes a sudden move to Italian Baroque; the final number returns to the twentieth century, as it uses two parts (*Ronde des princesses* and *Danse infernale du roi Kastchei*) from the 1919 version of the ballet suite *The Firebird*, a major example of Strankinskij's rhythmic and sumptuous style of his "Russian" period (but nowhere as aggressive and dissonant as *The Rite of Spring*).[86] Bozzetto initially considered some pieces that would have brought some transgressive "modernism" to the selection, but he ultimately was not able to pursue that choice (see Chapter 3).

From the comparison of the musical programs, *Fantasia* appears more varied and daring than *Allegro*. In terms of adherence to the shared motto "see the music and hear the picture," however, the use and presentation of music in *Allegro* actually came closer to the ideal of "visual music" than *Fantasia* did. While *Allegro* considered the musical performance an almost unmodifiable guide to the animation (hence Bozzetto's preproduction tribulations in finding stories that could perfectly fit the structure of the musical pieces), *Fantasia* allowed for major alterations of the scores in order to meet the necessities of animation. That was something that was customary in the other theatrical productions by Disney, where music responded to animation, and not vice versa; this often gave way to the so-called mickey-mousing, a pattern of close synchronization that Michel Chion defined as "following the visual action in synchrony with musical trajectories."[87]

Fantasia does not feature any piece of music in its original version, as immediately noticed by the music critics who almost unanimously condemned the film at the time of its first release.[88] Each composition was rearranged and reshaped with two concurrent goals: to follow more closely

---

[86]*Fantasia 2000*, the 1999 *Fantasia* sequel/remake, was concluded by an episode on a selection from the 1919 *Fireburd Suite* as well: it used the two parts featured *in Allegro non troppo*, plus the *Berceuse* and the *Finale*. It might be a coincidence, as John Culhane reports that "it was one of the first selectons that Walt Disney and his associates considered in 1938" (*Fantasia/2000: Visions of Hope* (New York: Disney Editions, 1999), 151–2). However, given Bozzetto's reputation among the Disney artists, the possibility of an unacknowledged homage to *Allegro non troppo* is not to be entirely discarded.
[87]Michel Chion, *Audio-Vision: Sound on Screen*, trans. Claudia Gorbman. (New York: Columbia University Press, 2017), 54.
[88]Moya Luckett, "Fantasia: Cultural Constructions of Disney's 'Masterpiece'," in *Disney Discourse: Producing the Magic Kingdom*, ed. Eric Smoodin (London: Routledge, 1994), 224.

the entertainment needs of the animation, while keeping the impression of a legitimate artistic authoritativeness, reinforced by the presence of Stokowski himself and certified by Taylor, who introduced each number without mentioning any shortening or manipulation. The changes appear to be concerned with keeping a feeling of integrity to the music, anyway. Stokowski is credited with all the interventions on the music, and it is certainly because of his competence as an orchestrator that in most of the film episodes the compositions manage to retain a clear trace of their original form. There seems to be three main strategies of intervention on the music in *Fantasia*. One is the alteration of the *pacing* of the music; then it's possible to talk of modifications in the *form* of the composition; finally, there are changes in the *orchestral palette*. The category of the pacing alterations includes all the cuts or iterations that transform the length and phrasing of the original music but do not modify its structure. On the contrary, the interventions on form reshape the inner architecture of the music. The use of a new orchestral palette modifies instead the timbre of the sound and is generally aimed to provide a piece with a more grandiose impact on the audience: it always works in the sense of an expansion of the orchestra.

The *Toccata and Fugue* is presented in Stokowski's orchestral version, which however was not realized specifically for *Fantasia*, but dates back to 1926. The orchestration does not alter the structure of the composition, which is actually the same of Bach's original for organ. It surely alters its sound palette, though, offering to the ear of the spectator an interpretation of Bach's music where each episode has its own acoustic "color." Moreover, the *Fugue* features a little cut of four bars, so a pacing alteration that slightly condensates the discourse occurs. Compared with the far vaster cuts and rearrangements in the other episodes, it is a quite minor modification, but it is still there, as to remember, implicitly, that what we are hearing is no more Bach, nor Stokowski, but an "authoritative" playground for the creativity of Disney's artists.[89]

The *Nutcracker Suite* is more explicit in distancing itself from Čajkovskij, as it is evident how two movements are missing, and the others are played in a wrong order. However, the individual compositions actually maintain their basic integrity: the *Dance of the Plum Fairy* and the *Chinese Dance* are presented in full, and the remaining dances are deprived only of repeated phrases or reprises of episodes. Actually, in some moments is even possible to listen to something that was not part of the original *Suite*. Stokowski added

---

[89]On a side note, it is interesting how this "simulated" authorship probably contains yet another problem about authorship itself. In fact, Stokowski rewrote the *Toccata and Fugue* just by writing down notes on the margins of a copy of the organ score: the actual orchestration was probably done by one of his collaborators, Lucien Cailliet. See Marjorie Hassen, ed., *Bach-Stokowski Toccata and Fugue for Organ, d Minor*, http://www.library.upenn.edu/exhibits/rbm/stokowski/bach.html (accessed August 17, 2019).

a few touches to the orchestration, for example, making the harp reinforce the sforzatos in the *Dance of the Plum Fairy* and requesting glissandos of the trombones in the *Russian Dance*.

The *Sorcerer's Apprentice* simulates the integrity of Paul Dukas's tone poem in the same way that was exploited in the *Nutcracker*: the key is, again, the systematic suppression of binary repetitions. So, the form remains virtually intact, while the summarization of the phrasing is actually strong, and it gives to the score a completely different dynamism. The animation is also aided by the onomatopoeic (mickey-mousing) addition of cymbal crashes in moments like the off-screen "killing" of the first broom.

The approach to *The Rite of Spring* is instead sensibly different: this is the first case, in *Fantasia*'s program, of an evident alteration on the form of the composition. Notwithstanding contradictory accounts about Stravinsky's opinion on this segment of *Fantasia*,[90] it is easy to understand how an author would be troubled in witnessing such a radical rearrangement of his creation. The opening high-pitched bassoon solo is repeated at the end of the sequence (with omissions in the orchestration of the accompaniment), transforming the *Rite* in a sort of cyclic composition while offering an interesting subtext to the images of the extinction of the dinosaurs, hinting to the rebirth of life after the catastrophe. But more importantly, the First Part of the composition is truncated right before the section named *Spring Grounds*, jumping directly to the Second Part. And then, to provide an appropriated musical lead to the conclusive visions of earthquakes and erupting volcanoes, the music returns to the episode *The Kiss of the Earth (The Oldest and Wisest One)*, from the First Part. Behind such a drastic manipulation of the original source lies maybe an unspoken assumption by Disney and Stokowski about their supposed audience: their ideal spectator was someone who was not familiar with Stravinsky's *Rite*, and who would be positively surprised in discovering its harsh dissonances joined with powerful images of primitive life. More than on preserving the authorship of the form, *Fantasia*'s *Rite* seems concerned about keeping a sensation of authorship in the language: that is to say, exhibiting the disruptive expressive force of the music while controlling and somehow justifying it with the animated reconstruction of a wild and lost world. Following Nicholas Cook, who noticed how in this episode of the film "explosions appear to take place in strict synchronization with the strings' sixteenth notes (though the effect of rhythmic precision disappears if you look at the film without the music)" and "the pizzicati in the lower strings bring out the balletic quality of the jogging dinosaurs,"[91] it is possible to argue how dissonances are here managed by an underlying mickey-mousing approach that, thanks

---

[90] Allan, *Walt Disney and Europe*, 128.
[91] Nicholas Cook, *Analysing Musical Multimedia* (Oxford: Clarendon Press, 1998), 179–82.

to the creation of fictitious cause–effect relationships, transforms them in accompaniments and onomatopoeias.

Stokowski's presentation of Beethoven's *"Pastoral"* managed to bring to *Fantasia* the *Symphony*'s structure in five movements. Notwithstanding the preservation of the fundamental outline of Beethoven's work, the musical editing actually affected its form in a crucial way. Apart from the customary suppression of many binary phrases, Stokowski systematically expunged from the movements all the development sections. So, Beethoven loses the dramatic drive of his dialectic style, and only the pretexts to his musical thinking, the themes, are heard. Without development, they remain as objects of a rather hedonistic listening: they sound as melodies for the sake of melodies and nothing more. This is the place of the least successful simulation of authorship in *Fantasia*.

On the contrary, Amilcare Ponchielli's *Dance of the Hours* is performed in a more than complete way: the *Dance of the Hours of the Day* is in fact played twice, and the second time it features original variations conceived by Stokowski. The new orchestration is here not just trying to make the score more original or spectacular, but it is actually providing comical support to the animation. In fact, the repeat of the first dance marks the ironic debut on screen of the hippo Hyacinth and her fellow ballerinas: her rather serious attempts at being graceful are here not a consequence but the cause of Stokowski's variation, which transformed the airy motive played originally by the woodwinds in a heavy and mockingly staid statement from the bass clarinet and the double basses.

Night on Bald Mountain and the *Ave Maria* are a large celebration of the third kind of approach to musical adaptation in *Fantasia*, namely the change of the orchestral palette in order to achieve better emphasis. The connection between the two pieces is actually the less daring invention by Stokowski, as it was sufficient to omit the last ten measures from Musorgskij's piece, which ends in D major, and to start right away with a G major transposition of the *Ave Maria* (which was originally in B flat major): the transition sounds like a perfect cadence from a dominant to its tonic. But, besides this, both the compositions are largely reworked: in the case of the *Ave Maria*, the orchestration is completely new and features also a humming choir, before the entry of the soloist singing Rachel Field's English version of the song. *Night on Bald Mountain* is instead based on Nikolaj Rimsky-Korsakov's revision of the tone poem, with a series of novelties mainly consisting in a different management of brass instruments and percussions, and the addition of the xylophone, a traditional evoker of the macabre since Camille Saint-Saëns's *Danse Macabre*, but well known with this role also in popular culture: Walt Disney's first Silly Symphony, *The Skeleton Dance* (1929), can serve as an example. However, apart from a few cuts of repeated periods in Musorgskij's composition, both *Night on Bald Mountain* and the *Ave Maria* are not altered in their formal structure.

Allegro non troppo does not need to simulate musical authorship, because its images do not try to convey any in the first place. In the animated episodes, though, Bozzetto took literally Disney's claim about the music–image relationship in *Fantasia* and adhered to it as strictly as he could. He has never been aware of the cuts and manipulations in the Disney feature: he has always believed that the film was based on unadulterated performances of original scores.[92] Anyway, *Allegro* took a few musical licenses, too, the only ones that the use of preexisting recordings allowed: they mostly consisted in selection of single movements from larger works or in the expunction of bars at the beginning or ending of a piece. Debussy's *Prélude* is left untouched; the *Slavonic Dance* is used in full, too, but it is just one out of sixteen. The *Boléro*, instead, does not start from the beginning: the music fades in four bars before rehearsal number four, when the soloist is the E flat clarinet. This episode, however, features also the only case of sound quality manipulation in *Allegro non troppo*: when the marching creatures fall into a ravine, the recording of the *Boléro* performance gets muffled, as if heard through an obstacle of some sort, until the animals resurface. It was probably intended to create a diegetic effect, as if the music went "underground" with the characters. The *Valse triste* does not have cuts, but the music starts on a sound bridge with the live-action interstitials: the coughs of the animator are heard for a few seconds after the episode has begun. In Vivaldi, only one movement out of three is used (but with no alterations); in Stravinsky, the selected movements are two (out of six); the *Ronde des princesses* is however cut at the beginning, as it starts from the bar before the rehearsal number 5. Bozzetto made himself respect the concept of basing animation on classical music much more than Disney and his artists. Paradoxically, it could be said that *Fantasia* only simulated the transposition of a true concert-listening experience into animation; this ideal became real only with a film that (respectfully) spoofed that model, *Allegro non troppo*.

Visual styles and animation techniques are the areas where *Fantasia* and *Allegro non troppo* depart the most from each other. As he did in his whole career, Bozzetto never tried to imitate the Disney aesthetics, partly because of his own integrity as an author, partly as a consequence of the budgetary, technical, and artistic limitations. For the animation of *Allegro*, Bozzetto pursued the approach he consistently adopted since the beginning of his career: making the most of the available resources by using simplification and stylistic variety in accordance with strong story ideas. In respect to this, the story-oriented structure of *Allegro* might even be read as a way to even out the otherwise unfair comparison with *Fantasia*, which had masterful animation but was lacking in narrative prowess. Bozzetto explicitly stated that the creation of a good story is the ground where he believes to be on par

---

[92] So he said in a conversation with the author in Bergamo, on October 16, 2017.

with the greatest animation studios in the world, like Disney or Pixar: the only needed equipment for that is a pencil, a sheet of paper to write on, and ideas.[93] For the *Allegro* stories, Bozzetto sought many different animation styles; each one depended on a different animation director (see Chapter 3) and had to mirror the mood of the plot as much as possible. The visuals of the film might as well be considered variations on a unitary storytelling style (all the episodes have similar themes and they are kindred in their writing and humor), in accordance with Bozzetto's recurring use of a theme-and-variation structure as a scaffolding to hold together his films (see Chapter 1). The *Prélude à l'après-midi d'un faune* uses suffused and unrealistic colors, soft designs, slow movements, and rotoscoped characters; the *Slavonic Dance* was animated by Bozzetto alone, so it is rough and sketchy in all its aspects, to reinforce the pungent satire on populistic power and conformism; on the contrary, the *Boléro* is lush, detailed, and technically elaborated. It is the *Allegro* segment that sets up the most a three-dimensional space: the illusion is achieved by the use of chiaroscuro on the solid-drawn bodies of the characters and dramatic camera movements that require multiplane parallaxes effects. The animation is also fluid and the movements are organic and believable; it is maybe the closest Bozzetto ever got to the Disney standard of the so-called "illusion of life," as the animators Thomas and Johnston called it in a seminal monograph.[94] The character designs by Giorgio Valentini are however far from the typical Disney standards, as they are neither somber and grave like the dinosaurs of the *Rite of Spring* nor "appealing" as most of the animals that appear in Disney features; the only Disney characters they resemble (probably by coincidence) are Maleficent's Goons in *Sleeping Beauty* (Clyde Geronimi and others, 1959). A convergence with *Fantasia* however emerges in the camerawork: the whole episode is built around an unceasing panoramic shot from left to right,[95] to convey the idea of the unstoppable march of evolution. The *Ave Maria* from *Fantasia* used a prolonged panoramic shot from left to right too, even if it was decidedly slower and with a different expressive goal (giving a sense of direction and pace to the religious walk of the pilgrims toward the rising sun). A shot from the *Boléro* seems actually to quote the *Ave Maria*: the creatures, seen from the side, walk behind a curtain of trees while

---

[93]Bozzetto during a class for the History of Animation course at the Department of Cultural Heritage, University of Padova, Italy, November 25, 2014.
[94]Frank Thomas and Ollie Johnston, *The Illusion of Life: Disney Animation* (New York: Disney Editions, 1981).
[95]This kind of panoramic shot is also largely featured in the segment about the evolution of life of the animated documentary *Of Stars and Men* (1964), by John and Faith Hubley. That segment might have influenced the Italian director: the topic of evolution is close to that of the *Boléro*, the animation in the documentary is choreographed to classical music, and Bozzetto knew and admired the films by the Hubleys.

the camera follows them, just like the candle-bearing pilgrims in the Disney film. In fact, the *Boléro* contains other likely visual reference to Fantasia: a shot of the creatures heading toward a desert is staged just like an equivalent moment in the *Rite of Spring*, and the towering statue that appears at the end, because of its pose, size, lighting, and shooting angle, is remindful of Chernabog from *Night on Bald Mountain*.[96] The cat of the *Valse triste* is instead akin to the skinny felines (like Sergeant Tibbs from *One Hundred and One Dalmatians*, Wolfgang Reitherman and others, 1961) featured in some of the Disney films of the Xerox years, when a "pencil" feeling appeared in the contour lines due to the time- and cost-saving use of xerography to print the drawings of the animators directly on transparent cels. However, the *Valse triste* aesthetics is more three-dimensional than the average Xerox film by Disney, thanks—again—to a volumetric use of colors on the character, paired with daring animations of the whole background in dream sequences, where the wrecked house literally "sprouts" its former rooms back in place, popping them up toward the viewing point. The sequence also mixes in some live-action footage. The style changes yet again in the Vivaldi episode; the watercolor backgrounds become vivid and flat, and the character design cartoony; the rotoscoping of the human couple adds in a contrasting three-dimensional flavor to the rest of the setting. The final piece, the *Firebird*, has a claymation introduction, with ever-changing monochromatic hues; this latter trait, in particular, might have been inspired by the *Toccata* from *Fantasia* and its changes in the backlighting color. In fact, as stated before, in his notes on *Fantasia* Bozzetto mentioned "plasticine" while referring to the *Toccata and Fugue*; the color changes in the plasticine sequence of the *Firebird* might thus have been borrowed from there. The rest of the episode turns back to flat surfaces and stylized designs that however border with the comedic grotesque (especially the giant devils) and interact with live-action elements. A strong vein of grotesque also returns in the Franceschini conclusion; but such film episode also restores a volumetric feel, thanks to shadows drawn on the characters and full animations of objects moving in a three-dimensional space. Each one of the "finales" that Franceschini evaluates actually introduces a slight stylistic variation: the most daring one features a kiss between Humphrey Bogart and Audrey Hepburn. The heads of the two actors are portrayed in a realistic chiaroscuro pencilwork by Mirna Masina; the animation is limited (it feels like a sequence of stills more than a fluid movement). After the kiss, their mouths keep stuck together; as the two faces move away from each other, the drawings become caricatural and exaggerated. The eyes pop out and the skin stretches until it rips off,

---

[96]The similarity between the evil statue in Bozzetto's film and Chernabog was mentioned before by Massimo Maisetti in "Il cinema d'animazione a Milano," *Ciemme* no. 98 (Oct.–Dec. 1991): 25–6.

revealing bare teeth. This idea might have influenced later similar renditions of absurdist kisses by the US animator Bill Plympton (*How to Kiss*, 1988, and *H Is for Head Game*, 2014), as Bozzetto himself conceded;[97] the strong resemblance in expression and animation with the grotesque masks on tortoises that move close together in Walt Disney and Salvador Dalì's short *Destino* (1946, unfinished; later completed in 2003 by Dominique Monfery) is instead entirely coincidental.

Fantasia is much more homogeneous in its approach to design and animation. It is true that it has moments when the character designs stray away from the round, appealing shapes of the Disney norm, like in the almost abstract *Toccata and Fugue*,[98] in the blocky and quasi-expressionist prehistoric animals of the *Rite of Spring*, and the horrid legion of demons from the *Night on Bald Mountain*. In general, however, the animation style is a consistent testament to what Chris Pallant called Disney-Formalism, an artistic paradigm that Disney artists fully embraced after *Snow White* and that was dominated by hyperrealism: "The most significant element of Disney-Formalist hyperrealism is the lifelike movement—or motor function—of the animation, which reflects both the actual movements of live-action models and the skill of the animator."[99] *Fantasia* exhibits a great deal of powerful animated acting and three-dimensional use of the scenic space to convey a sense of solid presence; it is however much more "formalist" than *Allegro* in respect to stylistic variation. Even in the use of colors, *Fantasia* is more moderate than the Italian film in straying too much from believability. It is clear that the palette is scripted so to accentuate the emotional content of the scenes; for example, in the *Rite of Spring*, "red is used to underline brute force. ... Brown is the palette of the earth, of bodies and of mud, black that of space, the depths of the sea. Yellow is harsh, a burning sun, desert, sand, bones. Greens and blues are dark, misty, rain swept ... The colors echo the raw quality of the film, its geographical location in America's West."[100] However, the colors dare to completely detach from reality and pursue pure emotional values only in a few moments: in the interstitials planned by the color stylist Lee Blair, when the lights behind the orchestra mutate according to the musical moods (in a further likely connection with the legacy of Fischinger and other specialist of visual music), and in the aftermath of Mickey's "killing" of the first broom in *The Sorcerer's Apprentice*, as the palette gets radically desaturated to convey feelings of failure and emotional

---

[97]Bozzetto in a meeting with the author, Bergamo, July 5, 2019.
[98]The *Toccata and Fugue* retained something of the visual patterns typical of a European master of abstract animation that Disney hired, only to see him later leave the *Fantasia* production out of creative divergences: Oskar Fischinger.
[99]Chris Pallant, *Demystifying Disney: A History of Disney Feature Animation* (London: Bloomsbury, 2013), 41.
[100]Allan, *Walt Disney and Europe*, 131.

low after a moment of panic. By contrast, the colors of *Allegro* have almost always no verisimilitude; "psychedelia" is the word that comes to mind in respect to them, especially when thinking about the sociocultural context of the film discussed above.

Other than being a consequence of the consolidation of the Disney style at the beginning of the 1940s, the "formalism" of *Fantasia* is also to be seen in light of Disney's preoccupation in dealing with high culture. To justify the use of classical music with animation Bozzetto could safely rely on the knowledge his audience had of the *Fantasia* model; it had already been done before, and that was the whole point of *Allegro non troppo*. Disney, instead, was breaking new ground: he did not just want to make comedy out of classical music but also wanted to create a new form of entertainment, bringing animation to the same level of highbrow art. He needed to give to his film an authoritative and dignified feeling, to play it "safe" but also to come to terms with his own discomfort with the classical repertoire, which he did not fully understand; the director and animator Wilfred Jackson once said that "Walt was a person with no musical background at all."[101] By means of the union between classical music and film graphics, Disney wanted to carry "the animated film beyond its roots in comic strips and slapstick film shorts,"[102] as Culhane noticed. Bozzetto, who also had no musical training, had no such intention; on the contrary, he reveled in slapstick and cartoon antics, to the point that some of the gags of *Allegro non troppo* are direct quotations of slapstick classics: the fights between Nichetti and Garay are modeled after those of Stan Laurel and Oliver Hardy.[103] Also the gag with the pencil sharpener falling down the tilted table, with Nichetti repeatedly catching it on the fly, comes from a film of the famous comedy duo: *The Music Box* (James Parrott, 1932).

In conclusion, *Allegro non troppo* is an Italian film with an international vocation. Constructed as a modern parody (in Hutcheon's sense, as discussed before), the film straightforwardly foregrounds its ties with *Fantasia*, but at the same time it uses them as a springboard to innovate. The reference to the Disney feature sets up the expectations of the audience about the structure and audiovisual strategy of the film. At the same time, the ironic distancing and the stylistic differences make it detour from *Fantasia* and reveal a remarkable degree of artistic autonomy. The visual and narrative content is very distant from that of the 1940 film, also because of the different place and time of its production. *Allegro* is influenced by some of the crucial sociocultural issues that shook Italy during 1970s, from terrorism

---

[101]Michael Barrier, *Vita di Walt Disney. Uomo, sognatore, genio*, trans. Marco Pellitteri (Latina: Tunué, 2009), 115.
[102]Culhane, *Walt Disney's Fantasia*, 10.
[103]Nichetti in the documentary "Ricordando *Allegro non troppo*."

to feminism, to the right of workers to the ethics of advertising; it is by no means a film essay on those topics, though, and it is not intended to talk to a strictly Italian audience. Its pantomimic approach to film animation speaks a universal language, which however also departs from *Fantasia*, as it favors a story-driven structure and a wide stylistic variety, whereas the model was more focused on imposing visual virtuosity and relative aesthetic homogeneity. There is then a strong difference in tone: while *Allegro* is satiric, caricatural, and sometimes aggressive, *Fantasia* is mostly solemn and seeking a grandiose kind of appeal. The comparison with *Fantasia* reveals however that the use of classical music in *Allegro* was more respectful of the integrity of the original repertoire. It would be unfair to say that *Allegro* perfected the *Fantasia* model, though, as Bozzetto's feature was nowhere as ambitious and technically advanced as the Disney one. Instead, the essence of *Allegro*'s relationship with *Fantasia* might be summed up as a rendition of Bozzetto's own ideas on the Disney film. The late-1960s theatrical revival of *Fantasia* favored its slow transition from a bizarre commercial failure to a mythical achievement in animated features; Bozzetto was under this impression, when he worked on *Allegro non troppo*. The idealization of the model, paired with a humble attitude with no wish of emulation and a strong creative desire, brought to *Allegro non troppo* some of the best traits of *Fantasia* (or those that Bozzetto figured in his mind as such, like the use of untouched classical music) while letting the director's authorial voice come through, as the artists he coordinated were free to pursue their own styles, devising original storytelling and visual solutions to make up for the lack of budget and resources.

3

The Path to *Allegro non troppo*

No canonic animation pipeline or production process could be compared to how *Allegro non troppo* came into being. *Fantasia* itself was an atypical item, in this respect; it was not just a full-length animated feature but an anthology of short animated films interwoven with live-action sequences that used a stylized cinematography, dominated by colored background lights and dark silhouettes. The production started from the short *The Sorcerer's Apprentice* and was later converted and widened in scope, to allow the creation of the other shorts. However, even the productive setting of the animated omnibus film, which can optimize time and costs by splitting the crew into smaller units, each one working in parallel on a different short, does not apply to *Allegro non troppo*. Even though there were indeed separate units (and even separate studios) simultaneously at work on the project, the process was not linear and favored instead free-flowing creativity and trial-and-error approaches. A careful planning was needed anyway, especially to meet one of Bozzetto's main concerns: obtaining a convincing synchronization between screen action and preexisting music. However, during the production the artists had to experiment with new techniques and learn from direct experience, with no preparation for the task. Each subproduction unit advanced at a different speed; the crews had to occasionally disband and regroup to produce animated TV intros or commercials, the main source of income for the Bruno Bozzetto Film; moreover, such crews were not strictly separated, as an artist could contribute to more than one short; Bozzetto directed them all (whereas each *Fantasia* short had a different director). Apparently, *Allegro non troppo* was made in a counterproductive way; Bozzetto's approach seems far away from the ideal mindset behind an efficient animation production, summed up by Hannes Rall as: "to utilize one's creative resources for the optimal communication of content, whether they be linear/narrative or abstract/experimental in nature."[1] However, what Bozzetto did was precisely optimal—not necessarily to save time and money but to achieve the best artistic results in respect to the challenging productive setting, the continuity with his usual creative routines, and his own expressive needs, which favor immediacy and fresh improvisation over strict planification. This last point is something he clung to with proud tenacity; in 2019, for example, he lamented the overdetailed preparation of character designs and storyboards that the Studio Bozzetto & Co. had to comply with in the making of a new Mr. Rossi series, while he would have preferred a more instinctual and free attitude.[2]

The intricate production history of *Allegro non troppo* can be untangled by pointing out the main events and people who influenced the decision-making. First of all, Bozzetto's creative strategy will be introduced, with an overview of the several ideas that never reached the final film: the episodes of an alternate *Allegro non troppo* that never was. Then, the artistic profiles of the main creatives who contributed to it will be detailed and commented.

The Origin of *Allegro non troppo*

In Bozzetto's memories,[3] the inspiration to make *Allegro non troppo* came to him in the early 1970s while he was about to enjoy a weekend in Bergamo. In that period, he used to visit his hometown once a week, while in the other days he worked in Milan. While he was packing, he was listening to classical music broadcasted by a cable radio network. A performance of Ravel's *Boléro* caught his attention. The *Boléro* is an atypical symphonic ballet piece (see Part Two); it is based on two unchanging melodies that get repeated nine times each, with no development. At each repetition, the themes are assigned to different instruments and sounds more majestic and richer in orchestral color. Bozzetto already knew the composition, but at that time he was awestruck by the inexorable progression of musical inventiveness and sonic power; in his imagination, the listening experience activated memories of his popular science readings about the evolution of life on Earth. He keenly caught a key detail of Ravel's musical architecture and merged it with a typical trope of educational narrations about evolution: as the music reaches the eighteenth repetition of the thematic material and prepares the

---

[1] Hannes Rall, *Animation from Concept to Production* (Boca Raton, FL: CRC Press, 2018), 3, ePub.
[2] Bozzetto in a meeting with the author, Bergamo, July 5, 2019. This is no longer possible today, if the Studio needs to stay competitive in the animation market; Bozzetto now adopts his peculiar strategy only for the short films he creates all on his own, for his YouTube channel.
[3] Bozzetto during a class for the History of Animation course at the Department of Cultural Heritage, University of Padova, Italy, November 25, 2014.

listener to the conclusive coda, Ravel changes for the first and only time the tonality of the piece. The *Boléro* is obstinately in C major, but for a few bars it turns to E major; the change uplifts the music, with an exhilarating emotional effect. Bozzetto felt a natural parallel between Ravel's short modulation and the twenty-four-hour clock analogy, a visual scheme shaped like a clock analog dial used to visualize all of the history of the Earth as having taken place in just one day. It is basically a pie chart that shows the different geologic eras and their main events as proportional sectors on the dial, as if the 4.55 billion years since the formation of Earth were condensed in a single day starting at 0:00 a.m., with the present moment coinciding with 24:00 p.m.. In this analogy, the most impactful event of all, the advent of human beings, takes place at the very last moment: a few tens of seconds before midnight.[4] Bozzetto felt like that Ravel's bold shift to E major was just the same: a last-minute twist with a tremendous effect. It provided the perfect conclusion to the evolutionary fantasy he was having, and it left a long-standing impression on him.

The *Boléro* was to become the *Sorcerer's Apprentice* of *Allegro non troppo*: it was the first short film to be conceived, and the one around which the whole project developed. When he started to share with his collaborators the idea he got while listening to the cable radio broadcast, though, Bozzetto was not thinking at all about making a feature film, or even some parody of *Fantasia*. After all, pantomimic animated films synchronized to recordings of orchestral music had already appeared in Italy by then, the ones by Gianini and Luzzati being the most renowned efforts in this field (see the Introduction), and they did not need to make any direct reference to *Fantasia*. Bozzetto just believed to have stumbled upon some good concept for a short film that would have allowed him to pour into it his love for classical music.[5]

The enthusiastic interest Bozzetto had for classical music was another trait he inherited from his father. As a child, he actually disliked the records his father avidly listened to. They were all of instrumental pieces (no operas—those stayed out from Bozzetto's later musical preferences, too), which the future director scornfully addressed as «"music for the dead."[6] However, he slowly changed his opinion on the supposed boringness of that repertoire, and he developed a habit of listening so many times to the performances he liked that he ended up knowing them by heart, an ability that proved strategic during the making of *Allegro non troppo*.

---

[4]A commented instance of that diagram can be found in J. William Schopf, *Cradle of Life: The Discovery of Earth's Early Fossils* (Princeton, NJ; Princeton University Press, 1999), 11.
[5]Personal communication to the author via Skype, March 14, 2019.
[6]"Musica da morti." Personal communication to the author via Skype, January 20, 2019.

Bozzetto does not exactly recall when and how the *Boléro*, after it had been positively received by his collaborators and entered an early stage of development, evolved into *Allegro non troppo*. Since the 1968 release of *Vip, My Brother Superman*, Bozzetto had often been invited to consider making a new feature-length picture. However, he stayed true to his attitude of having ideas determine the shape and scope of his film projects, and not vice versa. So, he was determined to develop a new animated feature only when in possession of an idea that called for that effort.

When it became clear that the *Boléro* was going to be part of an omnibus animated film based on classical music, Bozzetto took his first decisions about the production and artistic content of the work. He initially focused on the animated parts, with no concern about the live-action interstitials; in fact, at that stage he was not planning any form of direct reference to *Fantasia*.[7] He looked up to the Disney model for inspiration, but the film he initially devised did not have to replicate its structure and throw parodistic references at the spectator. The parodical intent slowly came into being during the preproduction, when it felt instrumental to the narrative cohesion of the picture; as such, it was mostly entrusted to the live-action segments, whose content was decided only halfway into the production of the animation.

The earliest step Bozzetto took was the choice of the title and of the musical repertoire. He worked completely on his own and took track of his efforts in the *Allegro non troppo* diaries (see Chapter 2). However, the dates on the diaries show that the production of the animation started when Bozzetto was still going on with his listening and decision-making routines: so, the preproduction and actual production intermingled and were not consequential. For example, a note dated May 22, 1975 says that the completed part were the *Boléro*, the *Faune*, Vivaldi, and Sibelius; the music for the remaining two shorts was still to be chosen among the *Firebird*, an unspecified piece by Rossini (probably the *Guillaume Tell Ouverture*; see Appendix 1), the *Slavonic Dance*, and the *Ouverture* from Giuseppe Verdi's opera *Un giorno di regno* (*King for a Day*).

The title page of the second notebook from the *Allegro* diaries documents what seems a brainstorming on the title of the feature. Right in the center, among two preprinted horizontal lines intended to be compiled with the personal information of the notebook owner, stays the final title *Allegro non troppo*, without any kind of special mark or emphasis. All around it, the page is scattered with puns on the music vocabulary. The position of this page at the beginning of the second notebook tells that the title decision happened in the course of the preproduction, and possibly when the production of some of the shorts had already started; the director at that point had already

---

[7]Personal communication to the author via Skype, January 20, 2019.

embraced the *Fantasia* reference. In fact, all the considered titles are based on the same wordplay strategy used in the naming of the Disney feature (Italian terms from the musical lexicon that also have a second meaning as a mood description) and most of them add some ironic or diminishing attribute to the word "fantasia." Such are the titles prevalently grouped in the upper half of the page: "Senza Fantasia" ("Without Fantasia"), "Fantasia Bacata" ("Bug-ridden Fantasia"), "Poca Fantasia" ("Not Much Fantasia"), "Fantasia dei Poveri Diavoli" ("Fantasia of the Poor Devils"), "Fantasia Senza Soldi" ("No-Money Fantasia"), "Piccola Fantasia" ("Little Fantasia"), "Fantasia in La Minore" ("Fantasia in A Minor"), "Fantasia Moderata" ("A Moderate Fantasia"), and "Fantasia Allegra" ("Cheerful Fantasia"). All those titles could also be fit for actual musical pieces: they are variations on "fantasia," a name that, apart from the blatant reference to the Disney feature, traditionally identifies a kind of musical composition (see Chapter 2). Bozzetto explored further this naming rule by playing around with other typical titles of classical compositions, in the lower half the page: "Follia n. 3 in La Maggiore" ("Follia no. 3 in A Major"; "follia" or "folia" is the denomination of an ancient Portuguese theme often used in the Baroque age for songs, dances, and sets of variations;[8] in Italian it also means "madness"). There might be there, coincidental or not, a subtle Disney reference: *Snow White and the Seven Dwarfs* was famously known as "Disney's folly" among film industry insiders. "Capriccio Italiano" ("Italian Caprice") continues with the wordplays on music titles, and Bozzetto actually wrote it down twice, underlining one of its instances. It might be that this was his early title choice; it was close to the name of a composition by Čajkovskij, the *Capriccio Italien Op. 45* for orchestra. However, it was probably discarded because of being nearly identical to the title of a previous Italian live-action omnibus film, *Capriccio all'italiana* (Mauro Bolognini, Mario Monicelli, Pier Paolo Pasolini, Steno, Pino Zac, Franco Rossi, 1968).

Bozzetto then contemplated original titles with no reference to the formal musical jargon, like "Musicanimata" (written down also in English, "Musicanimation") and "La Macchina della Musica" ("The Music Machine"). However, the last group of titles recorded in the notebook returns to the musical vocabulary, and in particular to a subset of words referring to dynamics or performance indications;[9] they tell the musician how to play the piece. Bozzetto singled out one of them on the opposite

---

[8] Giuseppe Gerbino and Alexander Silbiger, "Folia," in the New Grove Dictionary of Music and Musicians, Grove Online, https://www.oxfordmusiconline.com/grovemusic/view/10.1093/gmo/9781561592630.001.0001/omo-9781561592630-e-0000009929#0000009929.3 (accessed September 21, 2019).
[9] A few composers, though, have used such indications as titles, too; see Chopin's *Allegro de concert*, Op. 46, or Bartók's *Allegro barbaro*, BB 63, SZ 49.

page, all in upper-case letters, "FORTISSIMO." On the title page there is one more attempt of this kind ("Allegro spiritoso," "Humorous Allegro"), and then the conclusive *Allegro non troppo*, which in Italian means "Cheerful, not too much." Most of the titles seem to respond to two alternate communicative urges: signaling that the film was to be a "minor" or derivative version of *Fantasia* and revealing that its mood was going to be boldly vivacious, although occasionally tinged by introspective tones.

Structuring *Allegro non troppo*: Repertoire Scouting and Discarded Ideas

Bozzetto's preparation to the film production mostly consisted in a tireless listening routine. He went through his massive collection of records (mostly Deutsche Grammophon ones) multiple times, in search of compositions that inspired him a definite storyline, and that as such responded to the primacy he intended to give to narration in the film (see Chapter 2). His notes in the diaries present two kinds of picks from the records: those he merely considered interesting, whose titles were just written down (with rare short comments hinting to keywords or story ideas), and the ones he deemed worthy of the elaboration of a one-page plot outline.

The repertoire selected by Bozzetto has been collated from the several lists of the diaries and reproduced here in Appendix 1. When available, short story ideas or keywords by Bozzetto have been included. Some of the listed pieces ended up in the film; some others were elaborated into one-page plots but were ultimately discarded. There are also cases of alternate and abandoned plots for the final film pieces.

The list testifies a deep and eclectic knowledge of the symphonic repertoire, far beyond that of an average amateur. While it comprises several items that would qualify as staples of worldwide easy-listening habits, like the first movement of Beethoven's "Moonlight" *Sonata*, *In the Hall of the Mountain King* by Edvard Grieg or Jacques Offenbach's *Barcarole*, there are many others that probe less popular recesses of the production of famous composers, such as the *Benedictus sit Deus K. 117* by Wolfgang Amadeus Mozart and *Jeu de cartes* by Stravinsky, or that are even by composers whose names are still virtually unknown to mass culture, like Aleksandr Mosolov or Darius Milhaud. The rationale behind the choices, anyway, had never been educational; Bozzetto just took note of what stimulated his own narrative imagination the most. He did not even restrict himself to the so-called "classical" or "high" repertoire: the list in fact features also the names of Jimi Hendrix and Tijuana Brasses. Those forays outside the "classical" precinct would have strayed *Allegro* even farther from *Fantasia*; Bozzetto considered them for the finale of the film, which he envisioned as endowed with some "extremely modern"[10] music, as he repeatedly wrote in the diaries and confirmed in conversation with the author.[11] Bozzetto remembers that his first preference in this respect went to some daringly dissonant electronic song by a rock or pop German band; he was awestruck by the aural chaos that it stirred, and so he contacted the group to ask for permission to use it. It was denied,[12] reportedly because they suspected that the use of their song in an animated feature would have been incongruent with their band identity.[13] Bozzetto was not expecting that, considered that he had already plotted the storyline of the Biblical snake that eats Adam and Eve's apple and gets overwhelmed by the worst sides of human progress. The *Allegro* diaries sometimes label that story idea as "hell."[14] The "hell" tag appears also near a mention of *Kontakte* by Karlheinz Stockhausen and of an unspecified piece for two pianists by Sylvano Bussotti, which is likely to be *Tableaux vivants (avant La Passion selon Sade)*. So, it seems that before adapting the storyline to two movements from *The Firebird*, Bozzetto's search for the "modernism" he desired had a very wide range. As for the band Bozzetto initially wanted to involve, it remains uncertain; he could only recall that the album that contained the song had a completely black cover and that the musician dressed in black too. When showed some examples of rock groups that could fit his description, Bozzetto said that the closest match would be the Faust band, a krautrock ensemble (a kind of electronic art-rock) that in 1972 released an album with an all-black cover, titled *So Far*. The song Bozzetto wanted to use had the same title of the LP.[15] In the diaries, there are two instances of the name Faust (not referring to the homonymous opera by Charles Gounod, mentioned by Bozzetto in other pages) that could confirm this identification; one is next to Bozzetto's commentary of *Night on Bald Mountain* from *Fantasia*, which had a plain connection with the "infernal" undertones sought by the director (see Chapter 2); the other one is just above the redacted name of Stockhausen's *Kontakte*, suggesting that there Bozzetto was indeed thinking about the aggressive hypermodern soundscape he desired for the end of the film.

---

[10] "Modernissima."
[11] Personal communication to the author via Skype, March 14, 2019.
[12] Other cases of permission denial (from the heirs of the composers) occurred to Bozzetto in respect to *Till Eulenspiegel's Merry Pranks, Op. 28*, by Richard Strauss and the first movement from Gustav Mahler's *Symphony No. 3 in D minor*. Personal communication to the author via Skype, March 14, 2019. The denials were usually justified with the suspect that the music was going to be mocked in the film (Chiara Cereda, "La nascita di un capolavoro," in *Allegro non troppo. Un Tesoro dell'arte italiana*, ed. Chiara Cereda, Shirin Chehayed, Priscilla Mancini, and Andrijana Ružić (Milano: Agema, 2016), 17.
[13] Personal communication to the author via Skype, March 14, 2019.
[14] "Inferno."
[15] Personal communication to the author via email, September 18, 2019.

Even though Bozzetto holds that the second piece he picked after the *Boléro* was the *Slavonic Dance Op. 46 No. 7* by Dvořák,[16] it is evident from the diaries that its animated short was among the last ones to be produced, together with *The Firebird*. It was not even developed into a one-page plot, unlike other pieces of the final program; the only one that was similarly neglected was Vivaldi's *Concerto*. However, the concept for the *Slavonic Dance* story is present as a short annotation (see Appendix 1); and, in general, the final film fluidly borrowed ideas from the one-page plots, even reallocating other music stories originally conceived for different pieces. The plots have been here translated and collected in Appendix 2.

For example, the theme of degenerated military power in the hand of ill-fit commanders, akin to the story of the *Slavonic Dance* little man who takes advantage of the crowd that mindlessly imitates him, recurred in the plot sketches for Johannes Brahms's *Hungarian Dance* No. 1, for *Uranus*, from *The Planets* by Gustav Holst, and for the *King for a Day* overture by Giuseppe Verdi. This theme overlaps with that of vanity, to which two more plots, inspired by Grieg's *In the Hall of the Mountain King* and Weber's *Invitation to the Dance*, are dedicated. In the story on Grieg's piece, the image of the ugly larvae that inflate, become as beautiful as kings, and then explode might have influenced the story arc of the gigantic and bug-like alien queen known as Her Fertility, from the 2018 graphic novel *The Mystery of the Come-and-Go*. The sad vanity of the old satyr in the *Faune* is not featured in the diaries, though, since the *Faune* plot sketch just talks of him as someone who leaves behind a ugly wife to have a stroll in the woods with his flute. This early iteration of the character connects instead with another theme that recurs in the one-page plots, and that would have become one of the major narrative cores of *Allegro* (see Chapter 2): the search for freedom. The musical repertoire that made Bozzetto think about it included Ravel's *Daphnis et Chloé*, Antonio Vivaldi's *Gloria*, and the *Dance of the Comedians*, from Smetana's opera *The Bartered Bride*. The latter was supposed to be a satiric ballet about the relationship between office workers and their chief; in a note (see Appendix 1), Bozzetto pondered the use of a multitude of Mr. Rossi. The image of the exploited crowd might be, once again, a prefiguration of the *Slavonic Dance*. On the other hand, there is no doubt that the ecological narrative that threads together several *Allegro* shorts was repeatedly anticipated in the diaries, and in particular by the plot idea for the first movement of the *Symphony No. 3 in D minor* by Gustav Mahler, which imagined a lethal monster made of wasted cars forming on its own from polluted water. Such monster alone ended up in the finished film, and precisely in the *Firebird* episode: it rises like a cobra ready to spit its poison. The concept of spontaneous generation of life from waste might

---

[16] Personal communication to the author via Skype, January 20, 2019.

have inspired also the polymorphic offspring of a Coca-Cola drop at the beginning of the *Boléro*, though. Moreover, the idea is surprisingly featured in a comic written and storyboarded by one of Bozzetto's favorite Disney artists, Carl Barks (see the Introduction): *Be Leery of Lake Eerie*. It was unlikely that Bozzetto could know it was by Barks, as the art was by Kay Wright and, at the time, there were no credits in the Italian editions of Disney comics; nonetheless, he could have read the story, as it was published in the issue 931 of the magazine *Topolino*,[17] in September 1973. This might be just a curious coincidence, anyway, as the director has no memory of having read that comic.[18] Another horrific by-product of human progress appears in the story on *Daphnis et Chloé*, as a sentient monster city; this image was going to be echoed by the city violently springing from the ground in the *Boléro* ending. Catastrophes are in fact another recurring motif of the one-page plots, which in at least four cases foresee the annihilation of the entire Earth by means of an implosion into a dark void: the already-mentioned *Hungarian Dance* No. 1, but also the *Guillaume Tell* ouverture by Gioachino Rossini, Mahler's *Symphony No. 3*, and the *Hungarian Rhapsody No. 2 in C-sharp minor* by Franz Liszt. Bozzetto wanted the *Rhapsody* by Liszt, a staple of classic cartoon music, in its piano and orchestra version; however, such version does not exist, but it is precisely a consequence of the cartoon heritage of the *Rhapsody*. A piano and orchestra (partial) arrangement by Scott Bradley was in fact featured in one of the most famous shorts that used the piece, *The Cat Concerto* (William Hanna, Joseph Barbera, 1947); it is likely that Bozzetto unconsciously held it as a legitimate alternate score by Liszt. Anyway, his prospected *Rhapsody* had a totally different storyline, featuring a chase between a witch and a hunchback; while the latter was probably foreshadowing Franceschini from the *Allegro* finale, the subtheme of malicious masculine lust inserted here was reshaped into the inane sex obsession of the satyr in the *Faune*. The plot for the *Pizzicato Polka*, from Léo Delibes's *Sylvia*, stroke a similar chord, with a girl-pinching pervert (*pizzicato* means "pinched," in Italian) who could have ended up played by Mr. Rossi, as Bozzetto wrote in his notes—so, by a character whose design is not far from that of the *Allegro* satyr.

The one-page plots deal also with consumerism and advertising, as in the *Danse des petits cygnes* from Čajkovskij's *The Swan Lake*. Advertisements,

---

[17]*Topolino* is one of the longest-running and most famous weekly comic magazines in Italy. Its name is Italian for Mickey Mouse; it publishes Disney comics, almost exclusively written and drawn by Italian authors. Over the years, it has become a major part of the Italian popular culture. The weekly demand for new comics favored the consolidation of a renowned Italian school of Disney comics; at a global scale, about half of such comics come from Italy. *Topolino* had its first run as a newspaper-sized magazine, from 1932 to 1949; in 1949, it became digest-sized and restarted from number one. It is now published by Panini Comics.
[18]Personal email to the author, December 12, 2019.

in *Allegro*, appear as live-action inserts in the *Firebird*; they try to lure the snake toward them, just like a TV does to a chicken in the *Danse des petits cygnes* plot. The *Firebird* has however its own preliminary plot, not far from the one in the film (just like the *Boléro*); it is attributed to Stockhausen's *Kontakte*, though, as explained before. The visual theme of Adam and Eve's apple was also explored by Bozzetto in the story for *Guillaume Tell*.

The only moment for melancholia in the whole collection of preproduction notes is the *Valse triste*, just like in *Allegro*; during this stage the cat was not in the story yet, though, as the main role was given to an old man who sees his whole life again. Anyway, a lyrical kind of mood was also established in the bird-like flight toward freedom of the characters imagined for *Daphnis et Chloé*, as well as in a Christmas-time story variant for the *Dance of the Comedians*.

As in the case of the live-action sequences, the final decisions on the program of *Allegro non troppo* came well into the production. In the diaries, on June 20, 1974, Bozzetto marked as "done"[19] the *Boléro*, the *Faune*, the *Valse triste*, and the "hell" (the *Firebird*, presumably); he listed two more shorts as still missing, the *Slavonic Dance* and Smetana (a likely reference to the *Dance of the Comedians*). On May 22, 1975, however, Bozzetto tagged as "approved"[20] the *Boléro*, the *Faune*, *Vivaldi*, and the *Valse triste*, while a "not sure"[21] list mentioned Rossini (possibly the *Guillaume Tell* ouverture), the *Slavonic Dance*, the "Finales" conclusive sequence, and even the *Firebird*; it is thus unclear whether that last short was completed in 1974 or 1975. In any case, from those lists it seems that Bozzetto initially intended to use the *Boléro* as an opening piece; he later decided that having the *Faune* come first was more effective.[22] With its calm pace and suffused atmosphere, the *Faune* made a good contrast with the hectic live-action debut of the feature. It also enhanced the impact of the *Boléro* in the middle of the film, by instating a crescendo of visual engagement. The spectator gets to that lavishly animated march of metamorphic creatures through simpler approaches to animation: a subdued and lyrical one in the *Faune* and an abstract and frenetic one in the *Slavonic Dance*.

During the making of *Allegro*, Bozzetto remained the sole responsible of the musical choices and of their narrative elaboration. He firmly pursued his vision; for example, he rejected a suggestion that came up at his studio about inserting dialogues and sound effects in the animated shorts, in order to make them more appealing to a general audience.[23] No music consultant

---

[19]"Fatti."
[20]"Approvati."
[21]"In dubbio."
[22]Personal communication to the author via Skype, March 14, 2019.
[23]Personal communication to the author via Skype, January 20, 2019. Bozzetto cannot remember who made this suggestion.

was ever hired; a major music professional almost joined the production during the planning of the live-action interstitials, though: Claudio Abbado (1933–2014). Bozzetto considered to assign him the role of the orchestra conductor and had some early agreement with him, in this respect;[24] the idea was later abandoned, when that role became a parodistic one (see below).

Screenplay and Storyboard

Bozzetto started to share his film project and to involve more people in the creative process when he entered the screenplay and storyboard stages. Just like the previous preproduction activities, both those phases were neither clearly separated nor strictly consequential; the whole preproduction process was fluid, driven by a friendly and open dialogue between the director and the other artists; while keeping his authority and reserving for himself the right to have final word on any production issue, he remained very open to suggestions, changes, and second thoughts. Bozzetto's crew reportedly worked in an enjoyable and amusing context.[25]

The screenplay was written by Bozzetto with the animator Guido Manuli and the actor and assistant director Maurizio Nichetti. While Manuli had joined Bozzetto's studio almost since its establishment (see Chapter 1), Nichetti was a fairly fresh addition to the team, who contributed in reviving Bozzetto's interest in live-action during the 1970s (see Chapter 1). The collaboration of the three was positive and very productive; Bozzetto only remembers a few details about the work on the screenplay, and mostly that he had to continuously restrain Manuli from inserting continuous surreal gags,[26] especially in respect to the shorts where comedy would have been out of place, like the *Boléro* and the *Valse triste*.[27]

The storyboard was developed mostly at Giuseppe Laganà's studio. Bozzetto, Manuli, and the key animators of each episode (see below) worked there by continuously listening to the selected musical pieces. The individuation of the synchronies was done by ear, with no technical aid; this is why the storyboard panels were subject to continuous revisions, as the familiarity of the artists with the music and the stories increased over time. A huge load of movable paper patches and corrections rendered the storyboard very rough-looking. This became particularly evident for the

---

[24]Bozzetto in "Ricordando *Allegro non troppo*," a documentary in the *Allegro non troppo* DVD, part of the DVD collection "Tutto Bozzetto (o quasi)" (Roma: Multimedia San Paolo, 2005).
[25]Ibid.
[26]Bozzetto in Mario Querin, ed., *Bruno Bozzetto* (Trento: Centro di Documentazione Visiva, 1992), 9.
[27]Personal communication to the author via Skype, January 20, 2019.

Boléro, whose storyboard was ridden with emendations and was seven meters long and two meters tall.[28]

The Animation Crew

There are very few stylistic or design indications, in the plot outlines; once again, it is evident that, during his intensive scouting for musical repertoire, narrative effectiveness was the primary need of the author. Nonetheless, Bozzetto affirmed[29] that he actually had instinctive thoughts about the visual style he wanted for each one of the stories, even though he did not take notes about that; in those thoughts he also identified who, among his collaborators, was the fittest to bring a particular story to the screen.

The end titles of *Allegro non troppo* do not specify the production team for each episode; they just list the whole film crew according with their creative mansion, in alphabetical order. The identification of the leading roles in the short film units is anyway possible through Bozzetto's own recollections, a few essays and interviews,[30] and the documentaries that complement the Italian DVD edition of the film. The final cast and crew amounted to less than one hundred people, including Bozzetto.

When the artistic goals for each one of the prospected animated shorts became more defined, with a particularly high one set for the *Boléro*, Bozzetto resorted to a decision he had never taken before: to outsource some of the animation to other studios. He did so not only to improve the potential of his own studio but also to let his collaborators keep on with the jobs from their usual clients in the advertisement and TV industry, which constituted their main income source; in fact, during the production of *Allegro*, Bozzetto Film kept accepting commissions for ads and TV program intros, unlike it did for *West & Soda* (see Chapter 1). The studios that joined forces with Bozzetto were all in Milan: Master Programmi Audiovisivi S.r.l. that, however, only animated the claymation intro to the *Firebird*; Giuseppe Laganà's own freelance studio; and RDA 70 (also known as Erredia 70), whose name stands for "Reparto di Animazione" ("Animation Division"). It was in fact born as the animation division of the Gamma Film studio

---

[28]Personal communication to the author via Skype, March 14, 2019; documentary "Ricordando *Allegro non troppo*."
[29]Personal communication to the author via Skype, March 14, 2019.
[30]Andrijana Ružić, "Un romanzo corale," in *Allegro non troppo. Un tesoro dell'arte italiana*, ed. Chiara Cereda, Shirin Chehayed, Priscilla Mancini, and Andrijana Ružić (Milano: Agema, 2016), 21–4; Valerio Sbravatti, "Colloquio tra Valerio Sbravatti e Bruno Bozzetto su *Allegro non troppo*," in Sbravatti, *Allegro non troppo. Vedere la musica e ascoltare i disegni* (Roma: Il glifo, 2015), Kindle; Mario Verger, "Addio Walter Cavazzuti," *Note di tecnica cinematografica*, April 2003–January 2004, 28–9.

of the Gavioli brothers (see the Introduction), which eventually branched out into an independent facility by initiative of Walter Cavazzuti, Angelo Beretta, Giorgio Forlani, Riccardo Denti, Giovanni Ferrari, and others.[31] They brought to *Allegro non troppo* a technical level that went far beyond that of Bozzetto Film, which was specialized in a highly stylized approach based almost completely on self-taught skills. Bozzetto acknowledged[32] that the crew at RDA 70 was proficient in a more lifelike and three-dimensional hand-drawn style of animation, along the lines of the Disney one, because they learned directly from American artists while at Gamma Films: in the 1960s, the studio of the Gaviolis was visited several times by Marc Davis (1913–2000), one of the Nine Old Men, the core animators and directors who consolidated and refined the Disney style; other foreign guests included Chuck Jones (1912–2002), one of the foremost animators and directors at Warner Bros. Cartoons, and an unidentified Disney artist who worked on the film *The Jungle Book* (Wolfgang Reitherman, 1967).[33] A remarkable chance of training in a Disney-like animation style was also *The Night the Animals Talked*, a 1970 internationally coproduced animated short for the ABC network, directed by James "Shamus" Culhane (1908–1996), an animator and director especially renowned for his work at Disney, and in particular for the direction of the "Heigh-Ho" song sequence in *Snow White and the Seven Dwarfs* (David Hand and others, 1937). The Gamma Film artists who were directed by Culhane in *The Night the Animals Talked* included the future *Allegro non troppo* crew members Paolo Albicocco and Giovanni Ferrari.

The artists with lead creative responsibilities in *Allegro non troppo*, besides Bozzetto himself, were Guido Manuli, Maurizio Nichetti, Giuseppe Laganà, Giovanni Ferrari, Walter Cavazzuti, Giorgio Valentini, Giancarlo Cereda, Giorgio Forlani, and Paolo Albicocco. Their specific contributions will be discussed during the analysis of the film episodes in Part Two, in the paragraphs titled "Program Notes." As to provide basic reference information to identify the artists, succinct bio details of each one of them will be provided in the next paragraphs; their roles in the *Allegro non troppo* production will be listed below their names.

---

[31] Verger, "Addio Walter Cavazzuti," 28.
[32] Personal communication to the author via Skype, January 20, 2019.
[33] Marcello Zane, *Scatola a sorpresa. La Gamma Film di Roberto Gavioli e la comunicazione audiovisiva in Italia da Carosello a oggi* (Milano: Jaca Book, 1998), 116, 153. Zane credits the *Jungle Book* crew member just as "Klim"; he mentions that "many of the *Jungle Book* characters were created by him" ("gran parte dei personaggi del *Libro della Jungla* sono stati creati da lui"). There is no "Klim" among the character designers or animators of that film; Zane adds only that he drew a caricature of himself laying at the feet of Davis's self-caricature on the wall of a reserved room in the Gamma Film canteen. He might have been Bill Keil (1916–2003), an uncredited *Jungle Book* animator who also had a long-standing collaboration with the Hanna-Barbera Productions.

- *Guido Manuli* (1939)
  Screenplay
  Concerto in C Major RV 559: character design
  The Firebird: character design
  Finale(s): character design, key animation

A native of Cervia, a seaside city in the Romagna territory, Manuli became one of the driving forces of Bruno Bozzetto Film since 1961:[34] the first production he contributed to was *Il signor Rossi va a sciare*, 1963.[35] He soon distinguished himself as a prolific provider of anarchic and extreme gags, which he visualized with hand-drawn animations prone to high dynamism, visual excess, and risqué humor. Bozzetto felt that Manuli's eccentric extroversion was a much-needed antidote to his own penchant for pessimism.[36] As Alberto Rigoni and Giovanni Russo argued, Manuli's approach was a "sensual" manifestation of his "contagious love of the medium, even when his collections of gags are not strongly cohesive."[37] He was inspired not only by Tex Avery but also by Disney: desecrations of the character of Snow White are among Manuli's favorite visual themes, not to be understood as a unabashed panning of the Disney heritage, but instead as a desperate love letter to an unattainable animation ideal. As his internationally awarded[38] 1983 short film *Soltanto un bacio (Just a Kiss)* shows, Manuli's violent desire for Snow White is bound to be chastised and ridiculed: it is a metaphor of the technical and budgetary limits of Italian animators, who frustratingly work for a domestic audience whose benchmark is the foreign Disney style.

Manuli had his directorial debut in 1973 with *Opera*, a short film he cocreated with Bozzetto (who directed the second half of the film). The first film he fully directed was *Fantabiblical* (1977); after he left the Bozzetto Film in the late 1970s, he joined forces with Maurizio Nichetti, instating a collaboration that started with the short film *S.O.S.* (1979) and peaked with *Volere volare (To Want to Fly*, 1991), a mixed-technique full-length feature directed by Nichetti, marketed as "the Italian response to *Who Framed Roger Rabbit*"[39] and that brought to Manuli and Nichetti a Davide of Donatello Award for Best Screenplay.

---

[34]Sabrina Perucca, *Il cinema d'animazione italiano oggi* (Roma: Bulzoni, 2008), 241.
[35]Carlo Chatrian, "La giusta idea. Incontro con Guido Manuli," in *Maurizio Nichetti. I film, il cinema e …*, ed. Massimo Causo and Carlo Chatrian (Cantalupa, TO: Effatà Editrice, 2005), 133.
[36]Documentary *Gente di Milano—I mondi di Bruno Bozzetto*.
[37]Alberto Rigoni and Giovanni Russo, "All Roads Lead to Animation: Gianini, Luzzati, Cavandoli, and Manuli," *Animation Journal* 25 (2017): 58.
[38]It won the International Critics' Award at the 1983 Annecy Festival.
[39]Rigoni and Russo, "All Roads Lead to Animation," 59.

Manuli also directed three feature-length, hand-drawn animated films: *L'eroe dei due mondi* (*The Hero of the Two Worlds*, 1994), on Italy's national hero Giuseppe Garibaldi, with the participation of the renowned painter-animator Manfredo Manfredi; *Chi ha paura ...?* (*Monster Mash*, 1999), a TV film coproduced with overseas partners; and *Aida degli Alberi* (*Aida of the Trees*, 2001), a musical fantasy adventure loosely based on Antonio Ghislanzoni's libretto for Giuseppe Verdi's opera *Aida*, with a score by Ennio Morricone. It was an attempt to create an Italian equivalent to the animated Disney musicals of the 1990s; however, the final result was not on par with its model. In the 2000s, Manuli went on to produce Adobe Flash animated shorts he released through his YouTube channel Guido Manuli Animation, similarly to Bozzetto. He currently resides in Annecy, France.

According to Bozzetto,[40] the satyr in the *Prélude à l'après-midi d'un faune* short of *Allegro non troppo* ended up being a caricature of Manuli, even though that was not his initial intention.

- *Maurizio Nichetti* (**1948**)
  Screenplay
  Actor (the animator)

On April 30, 1970,[41] a 22-year-old Maurizio Nichetti brought an acting portfolio to the Bruno Bozzetto Film. He was a Milanese student of architecture at the Politecnico (he was going to graduate in 1975); he had a little experience in advertising, as he had already gotten a few freelance jobs as copywriter, and he was now applying for an acting job in a "Carosello" production. As he made acquaintance with Bozzetto and his young crew, Nichetti cast a glance over the other portfolios that had already came in; he felt discouraged,[42] as he believed that his competitors were all more handsome than him; he was more the funny type, with a big moustache and round glasses. When he took his leave, anticipating a rejection, he suggested, "In case my application will not go well ..., please consider that I can also write stories and gags ... for advertisements."[43] Bozzetto took his remark seriously; Nichetti noticed that and added that he would have preferred writing comedy scripts, as they were his specialty. By chance, Bozzetto was having an emergency meeting with his collaborators, because one of his scriptwriters had quit his job just the day before. He asked Nichetti to wait as he went inside the meeting room; he came back after five minutes

---

[40]Personal communication to the author via Skype, March 14, 2019.
[41]Nichetti, personal communication to the author via email, September 6, 2020.
[42]Nichetti in the documentary *Gente di Milano—I mondi di Bruno Bozzetto*.
[43]"Se per caso andasse male il provino ..., tenete presente che io posso anche scrivere le storie, le gag ... per la pubblicità." Nichetti in the documentary *Gente di Milano—I mondi di Bruno Bozzetto*.

and asked Nichetti to return the next morning, to start a three-month trial period[44] in the story department. He was going to stay for almost nine years. Since his first day, he sat next to Guido Manuli, who took an interest in improving the gags provided by the new member of the crew. After a while, Nichetti was able to do the same to Manuli's gags; that was the start of their long-standing mutual collaboration, and of their friendship.[45]

Bozzetto's bet on Nichetti was going to be a winning one: he went on to build a solid career as an actor, scriptwriter, and director. His humor was akin to that of Bozzetto, who gladly accepted Nichetti's prompts to return to live-action filmmaking (see Chapter 1). Meanwhile, Nichetti took acting courses at the Piccolo Teatro of Milan, including one in mimic acting taught by Marise Flach, a former pupil of Étienne Decroux, the foremost modern French mime. In 1974, he founded with fellow alumni of the Piccolo a theatrical company and acting school called "QuellidiGrock" ("TheGrockBunch"), in honor of the stage name of the Swiss clown Charles Adrien Wettach (1880–1959); the first members included Gero Caldarelli, Osvaldo Salvi, and Angela Finocchiaro. "QuellidiGrock" and Flach contributed to *Allegro non troppo*: the former ones were acting extras, the latter provided mimic consulting.

Nichetti's duties at the Bozzetto studio included also roles as assistant director to live-action productions, which helped him gain an expertise that proved crucial when he decided to venture on his own and start a career as a film director with *Ratataplan* (1979), his first full-length feature. He wrote and directed twelve more, both for the TV and the theater; his acting and comedy style was sometimes compared with that of Jacques Tati.[46] Other than for *Volere Volare*, with Guido Manuli, he received accolades for *Ladri di saponette* (*The Icicle Thief*, 1989), which won the Golden St. George at the 16th Moscow International Film Festival. He was in the jury of the 1998 Berlin Film Festival and of the 1999 Cannes Film Festival.

While continuously engaged in acting and directing for the theatrical stage, during the 1980s Nichetti also hosted TV shows ("Quo Vadiz?", 1984–5; "Pista!", 1985–6). In 2006, he wrote and directed the TV animated series "Le avventure di Neve & Gliz" ("The Adventures of Neve and Gliz"), starring the mascots of the 2006 Winter Olympics in Turin and animated by the Lanterna Magica Studio.

After 2000, Nichetti took also teaching duties at the Centro Sperimentale di Cinematografia (the animation department in Turin), the Civic Cinema School in Milan, the Catholic University in Milan, and the IULM University.

---

[44]Nichetti, personal communication to the author via email, September 6, 2020.
[45]Maurizio Nichetti, *Autobiografia involontaria* (Milano: Bietti, 2015), 27.
[46]Roberto Manassero, "Escaping Reality," in *Infinity Festival 2005*, ed. Roberto Manassero (Cantalupa, TO: Effatà Editrice, 2005), 107.

- *Giuseppe Laganà* (1944–2016)
  Prélude à l'après-midi d'un faune: storyboard, layout, character design, backgrounds, key animation
  Boléro: artistic direction, storyboard, layout

Giuseppe Laganà was one of the most respected Italian animators of the second half of the twentieth century. Bozzetto entrusted him with the artistic direction of the *Boléro*, the most complex of all the *Allegro non troppo* parts, because of his remarkable skills and strong artistic background. He was also in charge of all the main creative roles for the *Prélude à l'après-midi d'un faune*, which he endowed with a nuanced style, mostly achieved through the use of watercolor and Ecoline paintwork in the backgrounds.

He studied at the Brera Academy of Fine Arts in Milan, the city where he was born. He entered the Italian animation market in the early "Carosello" age, at the Cartoon Film studio of Pierluigi De Mas; there, he had a chance to perfect his skills under UPA artists like Harry Hess and Jimmy Teru Murakami, who were in Italy to participate in the making of some advertisements.[47]

He then worked at the Gamma Film studio, where he met more international artists (see above); his advertisement series "Sul ritmo di ogni spiritual" ("To the Rhythm of Every Spiritual," 1963),[48] for the Comitato Italiano Cotone ("Italian Cotton Committee"), received an award at the Advertising Film International Festival in Cannes.

He began his collaboration with Bozzetto with *West & Soda*; he regularly contributed to the output of the studio until *Vip, My Brother Superman*, often together with Manuli. Then, he opted for a freelance position, accepting thus jobs also from other clients (like the cartoonist and director Marco Biassoni). It is in this independent role that he was later hired back by Bozzetto to work on more "Unca Dunca" carosellos and, of course, on *Allegro non troppo*.

Laganà consolidated his reputation as an animation filmmaker by authoring a huge variety of products, from music videos to TV series; he is also remembered as the first director to make an Italian computer-animated short, *Pixnocchio* (1982).[49] In 1991 he founded his own company, the Animation Studio, later converted into the Animation Band (1996); among the works he directed, there are the TV series "Tiramolla Adventures"

---

[47]"Addio al regista e animatore Giuseppe Laganà," *Il Blog di Fumodichina*, January 5, 2016, https://ilblogdifumodichina.blogspot.com/2016/01/addio-al-regista-e-animatore-giuseppe.html (accessed October 17, 2019).

[48]Guido Michelone and Giuseppe Valenzise, *Bibidi bobidi bu: la musica nei cartoni animati da Betty Boop a Peter Gabriel* (Roma: Castelvecchi, 1998), 97.

[49]Maya Quaianni, "È morto Giuseppe Maurizio Laganà," *Lo Spazio Bianco*, January 5, 2016, https://www.lospaziobianco.it/morto-giuseppe-maurizio-lagana (accessed October 17, 2019).

(1992), "Lupo Alberto" (1997–2001), "The Last of the Mohicans" (2004), "Kim" (2008), and "Treasure Island" (2016). He also directed two full-length features coproduced with German studios: *Felix—Ein Hase auf Weltreise* (*Felix—All Around the World*, 2005) and *Felix 2—Der Hase und die verflixte Zeitmaschine* (*Felix 2—The Mechanical Rabbit and the Time Machine*, 2006). In 2003 he renovated his collaboration with Bozzetto by directing a TV series he ideated, "La famiglia Spaghetti" ("The Spaghetti Family").

He also provided cartoons to magazines and newspapers like *Il Corriere dei Piccoli*, *Linus*, *Il Corriere della Sera*, *Playboy*, *Cosmopolitan*, and more. In 2004–7, he taught at the course in Performing Arts (DAMS) of the University of Udine in Gorizia.

- *Giovanni Ferrari* (1937–2017)
  Boléro: key animation
  Valse triste: key animation
  Concerto in C Major RV 559: key animation
  The Firebird: key animation

Giovanni Ferrari was an artist whose works influenced a great deal the Italian pop culture from the 1960s to the 1990s. Apart from *Allegro non troppo* and the other works he animated for Bozzetto—the "Carosello" character Mammut, Babbut, and Figliut, the hysterically laughing Stripy mascot from the intro of the Swiss TV program "Scacciapensieri," and the cat in the Bozzetto/Hanna and Barbera short *Help!* (1995)—he was the creator of several famous characters from commercials, like the dwarfs advertising the Loacker wafer brand, the genie of the Mastro Lindo cleaning supplies, and the anthropomorphic egg of the Kinder chocolate. More importantly, he animated the protagonists of *Lucky and Zorba* by Enzo D'Alò, the 1998 full-length animated feature that made Italy competitive again in the animation market. He also animated the characters of Nichetti's *Volere volare*.

Ferrari was born in Stienta, near Rovigo and the river Po. He attended the civic art school Dosso Dossi in Ferrara and graduated from the Venturi art institute in Modena.[50] He moved to Milan in the early 1960s, where he joined the Gamma Film Studio, and later the RDA 70.

He spent his late years in Villasanta, near Monza, where he kept painting and teaching fine arts.

- *Walter Cavazzuti* (1946–2004)
  Boléro: key animation
  The Firebird: key animation

---

[50] Riccardo Rosa, "Dai film di Nichetti a Mastro Lindo: addio a Giovanni Ferrari, l'uomo capace di disegnare i sogni," *Corriere della Sera*, December 27, 2017.

Like Ferrari, Cavazzuti was one of the most talented animators of the Gamma Film Studio, and later a driving force of the RDA 70. However, Cavazzuti considered himself a character designer, above all.[51] In fact, Cavazzuti designed the main cast of some of the most successful Italian animated features between the 1990s and the early 2000s, those directed by Enzo D'Alò: *La freccia azzurra* (*How the Toys Saved Christmas*, 1996), *Lucky and Zorba*, *Momo alla conquista del tempo* (*Momo*, 2001), and *Opopomoz* (2003). His expertise in animation went well beyond that, though: the experience he matured at Gamma Film had Bozzetto entrust him with the complex character animation required for the *Boléro*, where the marching creatures had intricate shadow patterns on their bodies. Cavazzuti attended to the painstaking work of defining the shadows for each pose, together with Ferrari: they drew them in pencil and then printed the poses on the transparent cels by using xerography, a process that was imported to Italian animation production by Gamma Film, Cavazzuti, and Ferrari's former studio, around the mid-1960s.[52]

Cavazzuti also directed a few animated independent short films, starting from *Il gatto nero* (*The Black Cat*, 1972; lost), inspired by the stylized animation of the Zagreb school.[53] In 1987 he directed *Tunnel*, which featured a visual experimentation based on the use of Ecoline colors and chemical diluent on cels. His interest in design was reaffirmed in *The End* (1989), his last directorial work: a black-and-white character runs away from a "killer" who wants to paint it in color; he finally gets caught, but the splash of paint leaves a blank silhouette on the wall behind him; the chase is thus not over.

Another important contribution of Cavazzuti was the direction of the animation of Nichetti's *Volere volare*; moreover, in 1980 he had established his own advertising and animation studio, Quick Sand Production, with a fellow animator and a former colleague at RDA 70: Michel Fuzellier.

- *Giorgio Valentini* (1948)
  Boléro: character design
  Valse triste: character design

Giorgio Valentini approached Bozzetto in 1972, after he spent several years working as a goldsmith. In fact, his education included goldsmith courses at art institutes in Fano (his native city) and Venice.[54] Because of his interest in cinema and animation, he then attended the "Scuola del Libro"

---

[51] "Walter Cavazzuti," Girodivite.it, https://www.girodivite.it/antenati/xx3sec/_cavazzuti.htm (accessed October 18, 2019).
[52] Zane, *Scatola a sorpresa*, 109.
[53] Verger, "Addio Walter Cavazzuti," 28.
[54] "Giorgio Valentini," Motusfilm.com, http://www.motusfilm.com/SitoItalia/CvGiorgio.htm (accessed October 18, 2019).

("Book School"), the art institute of Urbino, which had an animation department; other two members of the main *Allegro* crew came from this same school, Giorgio Forlani and Paolo Albicocco (see below).

Valentini aroused Bozzetto's interest by showing him an animated short film of his own. He first contributed to *Il Signor Rossi a Venezia* (1974); he then worked to all the principal productions of the Bozzetto Film until the late 1980s. In the 1990s, he joined the animation crew of D'Alo's features, codirecting the animation of *Lucky and Zorba* and providing storyboards, layouts, and animation to *Momo*.

Valentini proved to be a versatile professional: a part from the designs of some of the key characters of *Allegro non troppo* (the *Boléro* monsters and the *Valse triste* cat), and of the animated creatures populating the parallel world in Bozzetto's fantasy live-action film *Under the Chinese Restaurant*, he was able to serve as storyboarder, screenwriter, and animator for animated advertisements, TV series, and live-action films. He also directed several shorts, like *Lo scrittore* (*The Writer*, live-action, 1981), *È questione di vita o di morte* (*It's a Matter of Life or Death*, live-action, 1983), *DNA* (animated, 1996), *Cafè l'Amour* (animated, 2005), and *Le nuvole sono solo nuvole* (*Clouds Are Just Clouds*, live-action, 2007). In 2000, he established with Silvio Pautasso the production company Motus Film.

- *Giancarlo Cereda* (1929–2004)
  Boléro: backgrounds

Giancarlo Cereda received from Bozzetto a precise request about how to visualize the primeval world of the *Boléro*: he was asked to paint the backgrounds by using an airbrush, in order to convey a nuanced and layered impression of depth.[55]

Cereda was one of the very first artists to join Bozzetto's studio: he was among the ones the director selected among his acquaintances as a student (as already pointed out, he was the cousin of one of Bozzetto's classmates, Carlo Re). He consistently kept his role as background artist.

His family initially wanted him to pursue a career in accounting, so he could join the business company of his uncle; after two years of studies in that field, though, Cereda decided to take instead art courses at the fine art academy of Brera, in Milan. He sometimes involved Re in his life painting exercises; for example, Re posed for a Jesus Christ oil painting Cereda did in the atelier he established in a large, windowed pavilion of a mansion owned by a well-to-do fellow art student, in Corso Italia.

---

[55]Ružić, "Un romanzo corale," 23.

Other than being a background artist for animation, Cereda also worked as a book illustrator (e.g., in Marino Giuffrida, *Come nasce l'automobile*, "How the Car Is Born," Milan: AMZ, 1969). In his late years, before his premature death due to a leukemia, he put to new use his academic training: he took commissions for portraits that perfectly imitated the style and appearance of famous paintings. In each one of those, the original subject was given the face of Cereda's client. The idea, however, was not so successful: he only did about six paintings of this kind. One of them was for Bozzetto.[56]

- **Giorgio Forlani (1934)**
  Concerto in C Major RV 559: backgrounds

Giorgio Forlani graduated in 1958 from the design course at the "Scuola del Libro" art institute of Urbino. He worked for several years at the Gamma Film studio.[57]

- **Paolo Albicocco (1936–2011)**
  Valse triste: backgrounds

Albicocco was another graduate (in 1958) of the "Scuola del Libro" of Urbino, where he studied lithography.[58] He moved to Milan in the early 1960s to join the Gamma Film studio; he later participated in the foundation of the RDA 70.

In animation, he became a background specialist, even for international productions. As background supervisor, he was in fact part of the crew of *The Night the Animals Talked*, directed by Shamus Culhane. Culhane also hired Albicocco to do the backgrounds of his 1980 TV animated special *Last of the Red-Hot Dragons*. Albicocco's backgrounds were also featured in *Maria d'Oro und Bello Blue* (*Once Upon a Time*, 1973), a German-Italian coproduction directed by Rolf Kauka.

Albicocco was a book illustrator as well:[59] he created the cover art for the RDA 70 children's book *Il gigante orripilante* (*The Hair-Rising Giant*, text by Italo Calvino), for Nilde Cima's *Un uomo e una volpe* (*A Man and a Fox*, 1971), for Elisa Franzoni Zane's *Partigiani in casa mia* (*Partisans in My House*, 1984), and for the repertory of literature from the Friuli region *Il Tesaur de Leteradure Pai Fruts* (Gianni Nazzi, 1987).

---

[56] Carlo Re in a personal telephone conversation with the author, October 31, 2019.
[57] "Cento anni di vita dell'Istituto d'Arte di Urbino. Capitolo Quarto," https://www.prourbino.it/ScuolaDelLibro/StoriaCarnevali_cap4.htm (accessed October 18, 2019).
[58] "Cento anni di vita dell'Istituto d'Arte di Urbino. Capitolo Quarto," https://www.prourbino.it/ScuolaDelLibro/StoriaCarnevali_cap4.htm (accessed October 18, 2019).
[59] "Addio ad Albicocco, grande cartoonist," *Il Resto del Carlino*, April 15, 2011, 27.

- Other crew members

Other notable members of the *Allegro non troppo* crew were Luciano Marzetti, Ugo Micheli, and Franco Godi. Marzetti, who was a regular collaborator of Bozzetto, was in charge of the visual effects. For example, he created the light refraction effect on the curved glass of the Coca-Cola bottle at the beginning of the *Boléro*: he did so by modeling the bottle in relief on the transparent cel, by applying spirit gum on the plain surface. The animation of that effect required one month, and it had to be reshot six times, because of the precision that was required to make the light reflection feel natural.[60]

Ugo Micheli, instead, was an editor; he would have kept this role in many of the later films by Bozzetto. In *Allegro*, though, he was assigned a different task: he was responsible for the musical synchrony. His job consisted in making chalk marks on a 35 mm magnetic tape recording of the music, to evidence the moments when Bozzetto or the animators wanted to achieve a synchrony with the screen action, producing thus not only a visual guide for the animation[61] but also a reference to set up the exposure sheet (x-sheet), which had a dedicated column for all the musical downbeats relevant to the animation, similar to a lip synch x-sheet routine, but much more complicated.[62] The exact frame number corresponding to a certain chalk mark on the tape was deduced by having the tape, which was as wide as a film strip (35 mm), run in a moviola.[63] The synchronies were identified during the storyboarding and animation; finding their exact place on the tapes by mere listening was a difficult task, also because the slow-motion advancement of the tape, required to precision-search for a certain musical moment, heavily distorted the sound and rendered the musical instruments unrecognizable.

Franco Godi, the most important "Carosello" composer and former author of the music of *Vip, My Brother Superman*, completed the *Allegro* soundtrack with light ballroom music that plays during the live-action interstitials, the finale, and the end titles. In particular, the end title track is based on a medley of the main themes from some of the classical pieces used in the animated shorts (*Boléro, Valse triste, Slavonic Dance*).

Preproduction of the Live-Action Scenes

The development of the live-action frame of *Allegro non troppo* took place when the production of the animation had already begun, as previously

---

[60]Bozzetto in the documentary "Ricordando *Allegro non troppo*."
[61]Bozzetto, personal communication to the author via Skype, March 14, 2019, and also during a meeting with the author in Bergamo, Italy, on July 5, 2019.
[62]Bozzetto, personal communication to the author via Skype, March 14, 2019.
[63]Bozzetto during a class for the History of Animation course at the Department of Cultural Heritage, University of Padova, Italy, November 25, 2014.

mentioned; this did not prevent Bozzetto from collecting notes about it in the *Allegro* diaries.

The initial concept was fairly close to that of *Fantasia*. It had to be serious in tone and to involve a real orchestra with a renowned conductor (Abbado). What Bozzetto wrote about the visual treatment reveals an even deeper connection with *Fantasia*: he borrowed from the previous film ideas like showing the players as shadow silhouettes and having the instruments change color according to the music. He also made a little sketch (the only one in the *Allegro* diaries) showing how he wanted to arrange the silhouettes of the musicians: the similarity with the unrealistic orchestral seating seen in *Fantasia* is evident.

The diaries however also testify the next step in Bozzetto's approach to the live-action parts, which drastically steered the content toward grotesque comedy. The notes show that the director intended to make the musicians into quirky characters, prone to anarchically disrupt the performance: he mentioned a "dwarf"[64] and a "pleasure-seeking woman at the harp."[65] There is a note about having "jazz at the beginning,"[66] and then, in unspecified moments, "someone falls behind cubes (Indian face)? They bring him out in pieces on a stretcher. / Someone makes out with the harpist. / One brings down a player to take his place. / The pianist gets stabbed after a solo. He asks: who did that?"[67] While this is consistent with the later full-blown slapstick style of the *Allegro non troppo* live-action scenes, in this preproduction outline the humor was maybe more inspired to the musical antics of the Marx Brothers in *A Night at the Opera* (Sam Wood, 1935) than to Laurel and Hardy, who later became the main reference for Nichetti and Garay's interactions in the film. It is also peculiar how much Bozzetto's concept foreshadowed the dysfunctional orchestral players of Federico Fellini's *Prova d'orchestra* (*Orchestra Rehearsal*, 1979); at the end of the *Valse triste*, moreover, a wrecking ball demolishes a wall, just like in the finale of Fellini's film. Later, in the early 1980s, Fellini actually called Bozzetto with the intention to commission him the opening titles for *Ginger e Fred* (*Ginger and Fred*, 1986); Bozzetto however refused the job, as he believed that Fellini's ability to transform live-action actors in something completely unforeseeable was stronger than any cartoon creation.[68]

---

[64]"Nano."
[65]"Godereccia all'arpa."
[66]"Jazz all'inizio."
[67]"Uno cade dietro cubi (faccia indiano?). Lo portano via a pezzi su barella. / Uno limona con arpista. / Uno getta giù orchestrale per prenderne il posto. / Pianista pugnalato dopo a solo. Dice: chi è stato?"
[68]Bozzetto in the documentary *L'arte è un delfino. Intervista a Bruno Bozzetto*.

A further unforeseen Fellini connection,[69] even though it was likely a coincidental one, is revealed by other pages of the diaries about the director's plans about the narrator, the equivalent to Deems Taylor in *Fantasia*. Bozzetto hoped to cast Marcello Mastroianni, the quintessential Fellinian protagonist, in that role; he was supposed to speak about classical music while holding a portable stereophonic system that did not work. After repeatedly hitting it, he would have had the music started; however, the recording would have failed, repeating over and over the same passage. The action on screen would have been similarly replayed many times, in synch with the music.

Other ideas penned down by Bozzetto included a mention of animators on-screen; this clearly led to the later development of Nichetti's character. The original project, though, was to joke about animating music to match the musical experience of a mentally disordered person, as cartoon artists were supposed to be "all have some mental disorder."[70] Bozzetto wanted to illustrate this with shots of animators at work, dressed in absurd ways and surrounded by drawings and signs hanging from the walls.

The diary notes on the live-action included also a project for a sequence dedicated to solo instruments. Their sounds were supposed to be visualized as animated patterns, in evident homage to the "soundtrack" intermission from *Fantasia*. There is also a short plot that introduces a character close to the satyr from the *Faune* animation (and to its early incarnation in the preproduction materials; see Appendix 2), but more vicious and aggressive: "A sex addicted on a beach dreams about killing his ugly wife; a beautiful girl undresses and throws herself at him; when they meet there is an explosion. Or else: a guy sees women everywhere / they come out from his eyes, head, ears / cartoon."[71] The last remark might suggest that the effects on this live-action sequence would have been animated.

When the time to plan the production of the live-action parts came, Bozzetto returned to the idea of staging up a believable concert setting; he took advantage of a maintenance closure of the Donizetti Theatre in Bergamo (Figure 4) to ask the municipality permission to shoot in that location, including the ancient underground foundations where the animator/Nichetti was going to be imprisoned, for about four days (that

---

[69]Bozzetto actually reported that the first American reviewers of *Allegro non troppo* often called the live-action parts "Fellinian," in a negative sense; the director did not like the comparison and said that they just did not get his grotesque humor. Bozzetto in Sbravatti, *Allegro non troppo*, 91.

[70]"Sono un po' tutti dei malati mentali."

[71]"Maniaco sessuale su spiaggia sogna di uccidere moglie brutta e bella ragazza si spoglia e gli si getta addosso. Esplosione quando si incontrano. Oppure tipo che vede donne dappertutto / gli escono da occhi, testa, orecchie / cartone."

FIGURE 4 *The inside of the Donizetti Theater in 1977. The live-action sequences of* Allegro non troppo *were all shot inside this historical building, which was inaugurated in 1791 and then rebuilt in 1801, after a fire destroyed it.*

was the overall duration of the live-action photography, according to Nichetti).[72] He still wanted the orchestra scenes to be funny, so he considered hiring actors instead of real musicians; however, he was struggling to find out how to make that idea into something convincing.[73] The first draft of the screenplay was just a collection of variations on typical gags on the theme of the orchestra, including a scene with a hairpiece blown away by a trombone.[74] The game-changing inspiration arrived on a day[75] when Bozzetto, Nichetti, and Manuli had scheduled an inspection of the theater. While Bozzetto was waiting for them in Bergamo, Nichetti and Manuli were traveling together by car from Milan. They discussed some possible options to save on the live-action budget while making the scenes interesting, and they come up with the idea of an orchestra of spunky old ladies, led by a brute. As they told Bozzetto about this, the director had an immediate

---

[72]Sbravatti, *Allegro non troppo*, 12; confirmed also by Nichetti in a personal email to the author, September 6, 2020.
[73]Personal communication to the author via Skype, January 20, 2019.
[74]Nichetti in Massimo Causo and Carlo Chatrian, eds., *Maurizio Nichetti. I film, il cinema e …* (Cantalupa, TO: Effatà Editrice, 2005), 24.
[75]For a reconstruction of that day, see Nichetti, *Autobiografia involontaria*, 115–16.

positive reaction:[76] this would have avoided them a lot of problems about musical synchrony and research about orchestras, while providing to the film the cheeky comic relief they needed to contrast and counterbalance the more abstract animated shorts.

This decision sped up the casting operations, too. The old ladies were found among acquaintances, families, or locals: Bozzetto involved also caretakers, ladies from retirement homes, as well as his mother-in-law and her friends.[77] Among the extras there were Jolanda Cappi and Osvaldo Salvi, who played the gorilla that attacks Nichetti after the *Boléro*. Another extra was a member of the "QuellidiGrock" acting company: Angela Finocchiaro (who would have later built a remarkable career in Italian cinema). She played among the old ladies, in disguise: she is the one who falls down and breaks up in pieces, bringing thus to the screen one of the gags featured in the *Allegro* diaries. Nichetti helped also in the casting of the main roles, because of his connections with theater actors. For example Maurizio Micheli, the host, was an alumnus of the Piccolo Teatro, like Nichetti; he was also to have a successful career in theater and cinema. The Argentinian Nestor Garay, instead, was cast as the conductor because, in Nichetti's view, he was able to bring forth some Laurel and Hardy vibes. First of all, his imposing body type was a perfect contrast with Nichetti's slim and short appearance; moreover, according to Nichetti, Garay resembled Eric Campbell,[78] a silent film actor who had supporting roles in films starring Charlie Chaplin, as well as James Finlayson in the Laurel and Hardy short film *Big Business* (James W. Horne, Leo McCarey, 1929).[79] In the mid-1970s, Garay had already a career in Italian cinema, mostly in comedies and B-movies; Maria Luisa Giovannini, who played the cleaning lady, was instead a newcomer to acting, and that of *Allegro non troppo* remained her only film role. According to Nichetti, she was a painter and a marathon runner who later relocated to Portugal.[80]

Bozzetto codirected the live-action sequences with Nichetti with the precise intention to make them narratively and visually distinguishable from the animated shorts. As already remarked (see Chapter 2), he sought an "expressionist"[81] black and white style, full of light and shadow contrasts, which however hid the colorful attires of the old ladies (that had a purposely kitsch "Charleston" fashion, to joke about how they were indeed old-timers,

---

[76]Personal communication to the author via Skype, January 20, 2019.
[77]Bozzetto in Sbravatti, *Allegro non troppo*, 110–11.
[78]Nichetti in a personal email to the author, September 6, 2020.
[79]Nichetti in the documentary "Ricordando *Allegro non troppo*." He actually does not mention Finlaynson by name, but he references him as the cross-eyed sidekick to Laurel and Hardy; he then confirmed this in a personal email to the author, September 6, 2020.
[80]Nichetti in the documentary "Ricordando *Allegro non troppo*."
[81]In another instance (personal communication to the author via Skype, March 14, 2019), Bozzetto called this black-and-white cinematography "neorealist."

but still full of the energy of the "Roaring Twenties"), created by the costume designer Lia Morandini. The cinematography was by Mario Masini, a renowned collaborator of esteemed directors like Carmelo Bene and the Taviani brothers.

The live-action footage that appeared in some of the animated shorts (*Valse triste*, *The Firebird*) was instead personally shot by Bozzetto with his 16mm Bolex Paillard camera; in the *Valse triste*, the characters featured in the memories of the cat are Bozzetto himself (on the rocking chair, with a dog nearby), his wife, and children, and also some acquaintances of him;[82] in *The Firebird*, the billboards and advertisements were shot by Bozzetto in the Duomo square in Milan. Bozzetto also shot some reference footage for the wrecked house of the *Valse triste*, in Milan, too.

The End of the Path: *Allegro non troppo* in Theaters

Production on the film ended in 1976: Bozzetto annotated in the *Allegro* diaries that the finished print was ready in July that year. A celebrative early screening had anyway been organized earlier, on March 12, 1976, at the Arcobaleno Cinema in Milan. It was attended just by forty people: thirty crew members, five journalists, and five casual cinemagoers.[83]

For the distribution in Italian cinemas, the director contacted the Cineriz company in Rome, as he had done for his previous two feature films. Bozzetto's proposed deal was only about the cost of the prints and of their distribution in cinemas, with no production attachments.[84] However, Cineriz refused the deal. The alleged motives confronted Bozzetto with the worst consequences of the Italian prejudice about animation being for children only (see Chapter 1). The objections focused on the target of the film: the work was appreciated per se, but it was deemed "not for children"[85] and as such not marketable as "animation." On the other hand, they argued that it could not fit into the category of underground "adult" animation, which at the time, in Italy, was identified with films like *Fritz the Cat* (Ralph Bakshi, 1972), which had been released in Italian cinemas by Medusa Film two times, in 1972 and 1973. Consequently, in this respect, they dismissed *Allegro non troppo* as not "pornographic" enough.

---

[82]Bozzetto in the documentary "Ricordando *Allegro non troppo*."
[83]Bozzetto in the documentary *Gente di Milano—I mondi di Bruno Bozzetto*.
[84]Bozzetto in Sbravatti, *Allegro non troppo*, 106, and also during a class for the History of Animation course at the Department of Cultural Heritage, University of Padova, Italy, November 25, 2014.
[85]"Non è per bambini." Bozzetto in Sbravatti, *Allegro non troppo*, 106.

The film was at risk of remaining unreleased; however, a former collaborator of Bozzetto, Giuliana Nicodemi, offered her help to set up a distribution in the United States. She had been the sales manager of Bozzetto Film since 1972;[86] she made a deal with Pat Finley's company Specialty Film. After being in competition at the Chicago International Film Festival (November 1976), the film had a US release on July 27, 1977, to mostly positive reviews, which only objected about the grotesque tone of the live-action sequences.[87] In 1978, Nicodemi moved to New York to establish, on January 11, Italtoons, her own production and distribution company, which would have later become a gateway to an English-speaking audience for the later works of Bozzetto, Nichetti, and Manuli; she also distributed works by non-Italian artists, like Bill Plympton. Nicodemi had also the merit to terminate the contract between Bozzetto and Specialty Films when the company was facing dire financial problems, on the verge of bankruptcy. That move saved the film from sinking into oblivion; it was instead resold first to New Line, and then (1981) to Don Krim's Kino International, until 1987. The distribution was both theatrical and nontheatrical. In 1990, Nicodemi favored a new American theatrical run of *Allegro non troppo*, thanks to a new contract with Expanded Entertainment, a Los Angeles company managed by Terry Thoren, who was an admirer of Bozzetto. The film was relaunched with the support of a relevant advertising campaign; some scenes that had been partially expunged in occasion of the first American release were reintegrated to promote the film as a director's cut. Later, the RCA Corporation bought the rights to produce and sell videotapes and videodiscs of *Allegro*, but technical difficulties prevented this; so, in 1994 the home video rights were passed on to the Public Media of Chicago (later Home Vision). *Allegro* had also a parallel American circulation in campuses and universities, through 16 mm prints; in 1982, Bozzetto personally attended several campus screenings in the East and West Coast.[88]

The overseas success of *Allegro non troppo* acted as a springboard for its Italian release. In 1977, Bozzetto got a call from the United States: a representative of Roxy International asked if the film had already an Italian distributor and advanced a proposal that brought *Allegro* in Italian cinemas on December 22, 1977.

The worries of Cineriz about the lack of a target audience did not prove true: the ticket sales were satisfactory, because of a kind of audience that no Italian distributor would have considered as a target for an animated film, at the time. As a cinema manager once told to Bozzetto, "Those who

---

[86]Giuliana Nicodemi in Alessandra Raengo, "L'amica americana. Intervista con Giuliana Nicodemi," in Bendazzi and De Berti, *La fabbrica dell'animazione*, 136.
[87]Bozzetto in Sbravatti, *Allegro non troppo*, 107–8.
[88]Nicodemi in Raengo, "L'amica americana," 138.

come to the cinema look like as if they are from the same mold: they are all young, around 18–20, wearing blue jeans, shirts and maybe with long hair."[89] By appealing to young adults with much more than just sexual undertones, *Allegro non troppo* became also a groundbreaking achievement in the Italian popular perception of animated films, and a confirmation of Bozzetto's ability to intercept and interpret the spirit of his age.

---

[89]"Le persone che vengono al cinema sembrano fatte con lo stampino: sono tutti giovani, sui 18–20 anni, coi blue-jeans, con le camicie e magari con i capelli lunghi." Bozzetto in Sbravatti, *Allegro non troppo*, 106–7.

PART TWO

The Episodes and Their Frame

Premise

Audiovisual Analysis, *non troppo*

Allegro non troppo was not made by musicians or musicologists. No one was hired to play its soundtrack, which mostly consisted of prerecorded tracks (except for the interstitial and end titles "ballet" music by Franco Godi); no music consultant provided advice to the director and the animators. Nothing like the rearrangement and repurposing of the music to animation seen in *Fantasia* was ever done. Bozzetto and his crew, instead, approached the repertoire as creative but respectful listeners. They tried to figure out by ear only what were the features that would have been fitter to underscore a screen action, on the basis of their competence in filmmaking and what they believed were the expectations of an audience in respect to the relationship between music and moving image. They looked for the musical episodes that would have worked as synchronic accompaniments of movements, rhythmic reinforcements of visual dynamics, onomatopoeias, and emotional commentaries; then, they created animation to bring out the audiovisual potential they saw in that music.

This strategy posits that Bozzetto and the production team acted as an audience to the music of *Allegro non troppo*. Not any audience, though, but an active one: the record of their reactions to the listening experience are the episodes of the film. Nichetti as the enchained animator, in the live-action sequences, is a parodical embodiment of such creative listening role, as he has to draw animation while inspired on the spot by the music played by the orchestra. It is not clear how his drawings could ever be enjoyed as finished animations by the conductor, the orchestra, and the host. However, according to their reactions, it is evident that all the characters are poetically enabled to see Nichetti's work; sometimes the animation even interacts with them.

It could be said, then, that *Allegro non troppo* is particularly strong in the representation of its narratee. In literary theory, this is a stand-in for the audience situated within the narrative world. It is the concept of the receiver, as embedded in a text: it could be explicitly incarnated in a character, or it could just stay implicit: in a film, it identifies "not the real viewer, nor the 'implied viewer', but a pickup agent at the other end of the narrator's communiqués,"[1] as David Bordwell explained. Seymour Chatman evidenced that a text can invoke a narratee in different degrees,[2] from being totally oblivious of it to making it a key player in the story. *Allegro non troppo* seems to firmly reside in the second half of this spectrum.

However, what audience are Nichetti, Garay, Micheli, and the other actors representing? Are they a film version of the production team as the listening entity that visually interpreted the music? Or are they a projection of the cinema audience itself? In a strict sense, Nichetti would symbolize the film crew, being an animator; Micheli, the host, reacts instead both to music and images, just like the audience in the theater. In this regard, Garay would thus not identify with anyone, being in a role with no correspondence in reality: someone who performs the music and watches the images that result from it. Bozzetto has surely never thought out this metaphor in detail, as his priority was the setup of a funny variant of the scenes framing the *Fantasia* shorts and a context for slapstick gags, in contrast with the flair of the musical animated shorts. Moreover, if the roles of the live-action characters really hide a metaphor within them, that might more likely be that of a cheap TV cast, making fun of many popular Italian shows from the 1970s (see Chapter 4). Anyhow, multiple narratees converge in them and reinforce this narrative function, whose strong presence foregrounds that the whole audiovisual setting of *Allegro non troppo* is audience-oriented: the animated shorts are the result of a peculiar listening activity by a restricted creative audience, which is in turn offering to a larger theatrical audience an audiovisual listening guide to a concert program.

If *Allegro non troppo* must be analyzed and explained, an audiovisual point of view needs to be also taken into account. For this purpose, it might be better to use a methodology that takes into account the audience and its perspective. A particularly profitable one, in this respect, seems to be the film/music analytic method recently advanced by Emilio Audissino in the book *Film/Music Analysis. A Film Studies Approach* (2017). Audissino's intent was that of superseding past models of audiovisual analysis that appeared too "separatist"[3] (strictly separating music analysis from film theory), too focused on communication models (fixated on discerning "who is the sender of the musical message"),[4] or relying too much on a

---

[1] David Bordwell, *Poetics of Cinema* (New York: Routledge, 2012), 129.
[2] Seymour Chatman, *Story and Discourse: Narrative Structure in Fiction and Film* (Ithaca, NY: Cornell University Press, 1978), 254.
[3] Emilio Audissino, *Film/Music: A Film Studies Approach* (London: Palgrave Macmillan, 2017), 54.
[4] Ibid.

"top-down, theory-driven approach,"[5] too abstract and complicated to be practical. A typical example of a highly detailed analytical model for audiovisual analysis would be that of Sergio Miceli, as described in his 2009 book *Musica per film*. However, while his system of audiovisual functions and minute subcategories is a strong descriptive tool, it has a low grade of adaptability: the detailed schematization offers little room for exceptions. For example, it is quite difficult to use Miceli's system to describe the incessant engagement and disengagement of the music from the film diegesis that often occurs in some silent film scenes.[6] Moreover, even though Miceli's descriptive method has the merit to equally address the specific features of film and of music, it does not consider the audience reception in order to verify how the audiovisual functions influence spectatorship. To bridge the gap between the different methods and bring the analysis of music in film closer to cinema studies, Audissino chose instead a neoformalist approach, as defined in the writings by David Bordwell and, more prominently, by Kristin Thompson.[7] It draws its conceptual framework from the literary theories of Russian Formalism, mainly defined by the works of Yury Tynjanov, Viktor Šklovskij, and Boris Ėjchenbaum; they were centered on the refusal of the form/content split ("subject matter and abstract ideas all enter into the total system of the artwork"),[8] and the emphasis on the act of perception of the artwork by the audience: "the viewer's activity and how the formal qualities of the film interact with her/him is the central concern. To account for the viewer's activity, Constructivism and Cognitivism replace Psychoanalysis. ... Cognitivism sees the viewer as an active constructor of the film's form and meaning, applying rational procedures."[9] In respect to film music analysis, this approach points toward the individuation and discussion of music–image relations that create audiovisual wholes with a recognizable meaning that orientate the reaction of the audience by playing with their expectations. Such expectations, in Audissino's words (which refer to music but are easily applicable to any artistic experience), "are formulated from our previous knowledge and experience of the ... conventions of a given style and period, and also on innate structures of our sensory and cognitive systems."[10] The innate structures that respond to the audiovisual wholes are explained by Audissino in terms of Gestalt qualities. Gestalt means,

---

[5] Ibid., 53.
[6] See Bellano, "Silent Strategies: Audiovisual Functions of the Music for Silent Cinema," *Kieler Beiträge zur Filmmusikforschung*, 9, 2013, http://www.filmmusik.uni-kiel.de/KB9/KB9-Bellano.pdf (accessed October 22, 2020).
[7] David Bordwell and Kristin Thompson, *Film Art: An Introduction*, 10th ed. (New York: McGraw-Hill, 2012).
[8] Ibid., 58.
[9] Audissino, *Film/Music*, 72.
[10] Ibid., 96.

approximately, "configuration": the word defines a school of thought in psychology, established in early twentieth century by Max Wertheimer, Wolfgang Köhler, and Kurt Koffka. A Gestalt is a perceptual configuration that is dynamically understood as a meaningful whole by our cognitive system. In music, a melody is a Gestalt, as it remains recognizable even when it starts from a different note (being transposed to a different tonality); from a visual point of view, the perceived separation between a bright figure and its background in a two-dimensional art piece is another result of a Gestalt activity. In film music, a good example of a Gestalt is that of audiovisual synchronization:[11] a sound and a visual event get entangled in a cause–effect relationship they do not necessarily have, thanks to a temporal coincidence.

It could be argued that Bozzetto's deciphering of the narrative potential in the musical program of *Allegro non troppo* was an unaware search for Gestalt audiovisual qualities. In pieces that had not been conceived for animation, he looked for musical features that could play with the expectations of the audience and take new meanings when arranged together with synchronic movements, narrative moods, and features of the film language like the camerawork, the editing, and the lighting. The film/music neoformalist approach by Audissino seems thus an appropriate way to analyze the final audiovisual result while being respectful of the creative process of the author, so heavily informed by a cognitive labor from the point of view of a listener, which is to say the audience of a music composition.

The audiovisual commentaries of the next chapters will be based on the film/music approach. As such, they will use a terminology introduced by Audissino, which explains the effects of the audiovisual configurations on the cognitive expectations of the audience in terms of *motivations* and *functions*.

The motivations are four:[12] *realistic, compositional, transtextual,* and *artistic*.[13] The *realistic* one appears when music is used to make a scene believable in respect to our knowledge of comparable situations in the real world; for example, the sound of loud pop music is expected in a scene set in a disco. The *compositional* motivation helps instead holding together the narrative structure of the film: the leitmotiv, or the recurring theme associated with an important character or situation, is a typical instance of this. The motivation is *transtextual* when it harks back to film genre conventions, like abrupt orchestral "stingers" in horror movies; it can also be played for laughs, when the genre reference is inconsistent with the tone of the film (as the Alfred Hitchcock's *Psycho* shower theme playing when the "terrible"

---

[11] Ibid., 104.
[12] Audissino argues that a fifth motivation, an "economical" one, might come into play in the case of musical elements whose presence is dictated by marketing strategies only, like songs by best-selling performers and the like. Audissino, *Film/Music*, 127.
[13] Ibid., 125.

girl Darla makes her screen debut in *Finding Nemo*, Andrew Stanton, 2003). The *artistic* motivation, instead, relies solely on the sensibility of the author and seeks an innovative aesthetic effect.

As for the functions, they are subdivided into three sets, pertaining to the area of activity in film-viewing: *perception*, *emotion*, and *cognition*. The *emotive* function is aimed at creating sustained moods in the film scenes, and in general at creating the distinct tone of a whole picture. As such, it can be subdivided into a *macro-emotive* and *micro-emotive* function: the former refers to the whole emotional scaffolding of the film, while the latter operates within a single scene. The *perceptive* function is instead mostly evidenced by temporal patterns. It becomes a *spatial perceptive function* when it pinpoints, by analogy, some meaningful visual pattern—like a trajectory—by means of similar qualities: for example, a descending scale could connect with a character falling down. A *temporal perceptive function* has instead more to do with rhythm: for example, a recognizable musical feature (a downbeat, an accent, or a distinguishable melodic pattern) could happen in synchrony with a visual event (the steps of a character or a dramatic cut in the editing) to merge with it and become its apparent consequence.

Finally, *cognitive* functions facilitate the understanding of the film meaning. There are two subcategories: first of all, the *denotative cognitive function* points to relationships between narrative elements, clarifying or stressing their connections. It is the kind of function that foreshadows developments, or that communicates something that happens off-screen; however, there are many possible instances of it, based on the general purpose of creating structural narrative links in the film. For example, a denotative cognitive function is at work in the scene from *C'era una volta il West* (*Once Upon a Time in the West*, Sergio Leone, 1968) when the reason behind Harmonica's resolution to kill Frank is revealed: in the past, Frank had stuffed a harmonica in the boy's mouth while he was tied and supporting on his shoulders his older brother, who had a noose around his neck, strung from an arch. This cruel game ended with the death of Harmonica's brother; right before that, with the instrument stuck in his mouth, the boy involuntarily panted three obsessive notes through it, over and over. Those three notes are the main motif in the theme Ennio Morricone assigned to Harmonica through the whole film; by showing the reason of their obsessiveness, the scene gives consistency in hindsight to the leitmotiv choice and to the otherwise gratuitous association between the character and that specific musical instrument.

A *connotative cognitive function* appears instead when there is no self-evident connection between the music and the scene, and the cause of their simultaneous occurrence needs a work of interpretation. This particular function does not appear in *Allegro non troppo*, because of the premises of Bozzetto's interpretative activity. His goal was to align a musical material that was not made for cinema with animations that, in turn, were made to feel convincingly connected with it: they were supposed to illustrate the music, and not to clash with it, in order to achieve the utopia of the "see the music and hear the picture" motto, which implies a total cohesion between music and images, pointing toward a synesthetic experience.

The episode commentaries of the next chapters will be not only about audiovisual analyses, though. There will also be historical information about the compositions, as well as observations on the artistic and directorial choices. The purpose of each commentary might thus not seem distant from that of "program notes" to a concert; while this is surely an intended parallel, given the nature of *Allegro non troppo*, the "program notes" commentaries will also build upon the information of Part One, in order to confirm and expand the previous discussion.

4

The Live-Action Frame

Description

The opening titles appear over a black-and-white shot of the foyer of the Donizetti Theatre in Bergamo. The place is empty, except for a girl (Maria Luisa Giovannini) who is silently intent in cleaning. She enters the equally deserted parterre; she is later seen sweeping a carpet from a dais. A host (Maurizio Micheli) starts talking off-screen; while the girl keeps working, he glorifies the film that is about to begin, claiming its absolute originality and historic value in putting together animation and classical music. He is finally shown, sitting in a dais, in a suit with a flashy decorative pattern; when he realizes that he is being filmed, he stutters and turns toward the camera, looking into it. He stutters again as he forgets his lines and reads from some notes. When he announces that the film will be full of fantasy, with the Italian word "fantasia," a telephone rings. He takes the call: someone from Hollywood protests that the film has already been done. The host feigns surprise and disbelief, reporting that the supposed author of the previous film was a "Frisney, Prisney, Grisney"; he dismisses the call as the act of a lunatic.

The film cuts to a new scene that seems actually quite lunatic itself. In a warehouse, a bunch of caged old ladies wave their hands and loudly ask for help. A brutish, huge, cigar-smoking man in his undershirt (Nestor Garay) is their keeper; he opens the cage and urges them to hurry, because "the film has already started."[1] He loads them on a truck and implies that they had been taken care of, while imprisoned, for some purpose; they ask for their instruments, and the man says they are already on the way, with their stage clothes. The host is sitting on the truck: he looks in the camera and mischievously asks if "Pisney" has ever done something like that.

---

[1] "Il film è già cominciato."

The host's voice then goes on to celebrate the artist who will provide the film with animation, and his distinct freedom. However, the images, once again with dark irony, show the brutal keeper in the dungeons of the Donizetti Theatre, who unlocks yet another cage: the animator (Maurizio Nichetti) is detained there, half-unconscious, hanging from the ceiling. The keeper mentions that he had been in chains for five years. The animator awakens with puppet-like moves and stumbles around; so, the keeper lifts him and carries him upstage on his shoulder.

In the theater, the curtain goes up. The sound of an orchestra tuning is heard. The old ladies are the players, now dressed in vintage party clothes and sitting in four parallel rows at decreasing height. They casually chat about frivolous matters, while the animator is pushed onstage, and the host makes sure he does not leave. As the animator sets up his table and equipment, the host reprises his grand announcements about the film, looking into the camera; but the angle changes after a cut, so the animator prompts the host (with gestures only; he is a silent character) to turn toward the right direction. The host announces the conductor; an old lady blows into a postal horn (until she drops to the floor, out of breath), while the cleaning girl unrolls a ceremonial carpet. The brutal keeper makes his entrance as a rude and bossy maestro. He greets the old ladies and announces that they will play Debussy's *Prélude à l'après-midi d'un faune*. The host cornily magnifies the piece choice; he then makes excited comments on what the animator is about to draw with his pencil, while the latter is plainly in trouble and keeps crumpling his sketches. After a gag involving a falling pencil sharpener, borrowed from the Laurel and Hardy film *The Music Box*, the performance is ready to begin: the host pretends to cue the music with a cheeky count off "one, a-two, a-one, a-two, a-three, a-four," which has nothing to do with orchestral conducting and with the actual tempo of the *Prélude*.

After the animated short, the host is caught by the camera with a bored and uninterested expression; he starts clapping and praising the performance, nonetheless. The animator stands up to bow, but the conductor makes him sit down, angrily whispering that he was not amused. The cleaning girl, who is ironing nearby, casts a worried gaze to the animator. Then, she brings a bottle of champagne to the host, who is humming the main melody of the *Prélude*. He pops the bottle open and he purposely fires the cork at one of the old ladies, who falls down from her seat and literally breaks into pieces. The cleaning girl picks her remains up and carries her offstage on a cart, while the conductor mellifluously makes sure that the other ladies are fine, by starting an absurd reflex-testing routine that makes them sit and stand at increasing speed. However, one of the women is not following his directions and stays seated; so, the conductor goes with her offstage, behind a black tent. While screams and sounds of a wild beating are heard, the host compliantly says that it is hard to maintain a level of discipline in an orchestra. When the conductor comes back, he announces *the Slavonic*

Dance No. 7 by Dvořák and violently slaps the animator's back, reminding him that now the music is going to be funny, and so he needs to be. As the animator crawls back to his seat and the orchestra tunes, the conductor menacingly whistles toward him the main theme of the *Dance*, to prod his inspiration.

The *Slavonic Dance* delights the conductor, who bursts into laughter. The orchestra laughs too, but because of the chamber pot that appeared on the head of the conductor: it is as if it came from the animated drawings, where it was previously seen. Annoyed, the conductor calls a break. The cleaning lady brings in a cart and serves an unpleasing-looking soup to the noisy ladies, while the host and the conductor enjoy chicken and potatoes at an expensively laid-out table. They discuss the next piece, Ravel's *Boléro*: the host plainly does not know anything about the author, and yet keeps emphatically talking about him, inventing also a story about Ravel's Umbrian origins. Meanwhile, the girl serves the soup to the animator, and a silent understanding arises among them. However, the soup drops on the floor; so, the hungry animator resorts to his art to steal some food from the conductor. He draws Mr. Rossi and he sends him for the chicken; the conductor lights a cigar and inadvertently puts the burning match near to the character, who goes up in flames. The girl passes a Coca-Cola bottle to the animator to console him, but the conductor snatches it from him. He goes to the podium with it and he mistakenly brandish it in place of his baton, so the soda flows out and wets his arm. Furious, the conductor throws the bottle away. The animator, inspired, draws it and makes it land inside the next animation.

After the end of the first part of the film (and a remark from an old lady that breaks the fourth wall, by calling out the intermission), a big gorilla (Osvaldo Sappi) from the universe of the *Boléro* wreaks havoc on stage, while a contrabassoon plays the theme from Ravel's piece, followed by a restless percussion passage. The gorilla snaps the support of the animation table and a gush of animated water springs out of it. It triggers a snowfall inside the theater, commented by a dreamy melody played by a synthesizer, which soon changes in a Russian-like folk tune: it follows the movements of the animator and the gorilla that seem to be doing a Cossack social dance. They are cheered by the old ladies and encouraged to do a second dance, now a funny swing with piano and brass flourishes. The conductor and the host are angry and clueless; the cleaning lady keeps working; one of the ladies from the orchestra, instead, wildly joins the dance and leaves with the gorilla. The conductor then steps in front of the animator and the music slows down in synch with Nichetti's change of attitude. Back to his table, the animator learns that the next number will be the *Valse triste*. The smoke from the conductor's cigar becomes the mist at the beginning of the animated episode.

The whole orchestra weeps, after the sad story of the *Valse triste*. The conductor is displeased again by the somber mood; he confers with the host, and they decide to cheer up the animator by buying him a hooker, unaware of the budding romance between him and the cleaning lady. They stuff him inside the piano and invite the prostitute to join him there. As they keep the piano shut, the host mentions that Vivaldi's *Concerto* will come next. The keys of the instrument frenetically go up and down, with a dissonant synth sound; the piano is now stuck close, and the host makes excuses while looking in the camera, saying that old pianos sometimes have issues like that. A blow from the conductor's fist breaks the piano open; the animator is now urged to produce something really funny. The host waits for the beginning of the music, but he is once again startled by the position of the camera. He finally looks into it as usual and, with a fake smile, says "curtain."[2]

The final shout from the character in the animation overlaps with that of the conductor: he has just been stung by the same bee who starred in the Vivaldi episode, and who now flies around him in a mixed-technique moment. The bee, in color, returns to the animator's papers; the conductor notices it, and even though the animator is fast at crumpling the sheet with the character, he prepares to take his vengeance. A slapstick fight ensues, with the two taking turns in hurting the other, while the old ladies are cheering. When Nichetti makes Garay put his hand on his own head in a finger gun gesture, and then fire a cartoon shot, the conductor loses it and tries to throw the pianist at the animator. The host tries to dissimulate the incident with empty excuses and directly addresses the operator, asking to move the camera away from the riot. He starts to talk about the *Firebird*, the conclusive piece of the film, but the noises of the fight muffle his voice. Nichetti is saved by the intervention of the gorilla, who smashes the conductor through the floor of the stage. The host covers the resulting hole (in the shape of Garay's silhouette) with a carpet, angrily looks for the camera, and then goes on to attribute the *Firebird* to Fëdor Dostoevskij, while a man in the prompter's box prepares a gramophone. The last episode will be accompanied by a record, in a nod to the actual music production strategy Bozzetto used for the film.

As the *Firebird* ends, the animated snake from the short appears in color on the stage, scaring away the whole orchestra. Meanwhile, the animator and the cleaning girl court each other by using noises and squeaks from their respective tools of the trade. While the host desperately tries to give some kind of explanation to the out-of-control situation, the animator turns himself and the girl into a cartoon prince and princess; they fly away, finally free. Failing to flee with them, the host is left with the task

---

[2] "Sipario."

of finding a proper finale to the film. He then gives a phone call to the archive, seeking the help of Franceschini to search among a collection of stock conclusions.

The search for a finale is unsuccessful. Or is it? As the conductor reemerges from the stage, completely covered in bandages, the host conjures up with him a new feature: a retelling of *Snow White and the Seven Dwarfs*. It turns out that this very moment is one of the finales perused by Franceschini, who at first seems to be delighted by it; however, the *Firebird* snake appears and bites his nose, just before a huge "happy end" sign falls on his head from above. The end titles roll on a circus fanfare that soon becomes a "ballroom" medley of themes from some of the *Allegro non troppo* program pieces.

Program Notes

The live-action frame of *Allegro non troppo* was the last part of the film conceived by Bozzetto, who initially wanted it to be a "serious" representation of an orchestral performance, with just a few creative extra touches in lighting and design, which would have drawn it nearer to the stylized appearance of the live-action interstitials of *Fantasia* (see Chapter 3). Notwithstanding its last-minute production, which took place in a mere four days, this "frame" went on to become the most important narrative tool of the work. It defines the onlook the spectator is supposed to have in respect to the whole picture: a laughable attempt at putting the daunting task of remaking *Fantasia* in the hand of some shady and ignorant Italian showmen.

The relationship between *Allegro* and *Fantasia* seems to be the ultimate reason of the virulent satirical stance of the live-action frame. Bozzetto did not originally want to assert a relationship between his feature and the Disney one; their parallel nature, however, proved unconcealable as the production progressed (see Chapter 2 and 3). When it became evident that the idea of hiring a real orchestra was too expensive and dangerously prone to make *Allegro* look like a passive imitation of the "concert feature," Bozzetto accepted Manuli and Nichetti's suggestion to avoid and subvert it altogether, by conjuring up an unlikely orchestra of old ladies. The goal of the live-action part thus became a blatant exhibition of the similarity between *Allegro* and *Fantasia*, while exasperating the distance between the solemn tone of the original and the fictional grotesque cheapness of the Italian production. The *Fantasia-Allegro* connection was turned into a running joke, founded on a familiar narrative of Italian popular culture: after having witnessed their power and efficiency at the end of the Second World War, Italians dreamt to be on par with Americans, but they could only steal their ideas and shamelessly make them into something cheap. In cinema, such a narrative was popularized, for example, by *Un americano a Roma* (*An*

American in Rome, Steno 1954),[3] which staged the laughable effects of the postwar American dream on an Italian young guy, Nando Moriconi (Alberto Sordi), who uses pseudo-English expressions and gaudy imitations of the American lifestyle to assert his predestination to find success overseas.[4] It could be argued that Bozzetto and Italian animators in general have always been especially familiar with this narrative, given their constant struggle with the audience preference for Disney films; the only way out of this was either a passive imitation or a sharp refusal of the model. In *Allegro non troppo*, Bozzetto opted for the second option, but he disguised his choice behind a mocking context story that instead feigned a full-scale and self-important plagiarism.

The exaggerated tone of the live-action frame averts also all the expectations the audience can have about a realistic visual rendering of a musical performance. A film/music analysis is here not needed, as the music has a decidedly secondary role in these interstitials. Unlike *Fantasia*, *Allegro* never shows anyone conducting or playing music (except for a few comical instances, like the lady blowing into a postal horn). The interactions between the actors make soon clear that the show is set in a slapstick universe, informed with a cartoon logic: people can break into pieces after taking a fall, or they can be smashed through a wooden stage leaving a silhouette-shaped hole, and then reemerging covered in bandages like a mummy. Some characters also embody stereotypes that hark back to the cartoon or fairy-tale heritage. The barefoot cleaning girl is a kind of Cinderella; her final transformation into a cartoon princess, with Nichetti waving his pencil as a magic wand, resonates of the scene from Disney's *Cinderella* (Wilfred Jackson and others, 1950) where the heroine is given a sumptuous dress by the Fairy Godmother. The conductor is the typical ogre-brute that antagonizes a smaller but smarter hero (Nichetti), as in the Peg Leg Pete-Mickey Mouse case. Moreover, cartoon characters (Mr. Rossi, the bee, and the snake) interact with the live-action performers. The audience is thus invited to suspend their disbelief and accept the impossible for the sake of laughs: there is no way that the flawless musical performances heard in the soundtrack could come from that conductor and that makeshift orchestra (whose musical instruments also look fake), but the comedy setting makes this an irrelevant issue. Moreover, Bozzetto even hints at the truth behind the music performance in the scene when the *Firebird* gets played from a record, as the orchestra is unavailable because of a riot. In other instances, we see the characters dancing to the "ballet" music by Franco Godi: the ensemble

---

[3] See David W. Ellwood, "Containing Modernity, Domesticating America in Italy," in *The Americanization of Europe: Culture, Diplomacy, and Anti-Americanism after 1945*, ed. Alexander Stephan (New York: Berghahn Books, 2006), 262.
[4] Bozzetto himself would have made fun again of the unfavorable comparison between Italian and foreign mores in his 1999 short *Europe & Italy*.

playing it is nowhere to be seen, but this does not hinder the scene in any way; similarly, the piano inside which Nichetti meets the hooker sounds like a synth. The black-and-white "expressionist" cinematography contributes to the suspension of disbelief. The heavy light and shadow contrasts create a parody of horror movies (with a potential model in Mel Brooks's *Young Frankenstein*), mostly intended to ridiculously overstate the malevolent and abusive nature of the conductor and the tortures of his captives; at the same time, they make the whole live-action frame quite abstract in appearance, and as such more prone to depict surreal events, while creating a visual fault with the colorful animated sequences. The fast-paced editing, some overemphatic angles, and the frequent use of the handheld camera give to the whole live-action frame a frenetic pacing, well in tune with the slapstick comedy-cartoon heritage Bozzetto is drawing upon.

The whole set of characters and situations that populate the live-action frame could actually include another layer of satirical deprecation. As explained above, *Allegro* is presented as a lazy Italian-style spoof of an American original; the orchestra is so ridiculous that no one expects it to perform in a realistic way. The underlying theme seems to be *incompetence*, which is to say undertaking a task without being qualified to do it. The epitome of it is arguably the host: Micheli's character is constantly forcing buoyancy and enthusiasm, while he is clearly not interested at all in classical music. In contrast with his role of master of ceremonies, he makes a lot of embarrassing mistakes, like forgetting his lines, reading from notes, and, most of all, failing to speak to the camera. The characterization of the host seems to hint that the incompetence Bozzetto wants to focus on is of a very specific kind. In fact, notwithstanding the constant playful diminution of *Allegro* in respect to *Fantasia*, the live-action frame never really advances that the film is a bad attempt at making animation. In the story, the animator's talent is often applauded and praised; he is a positive, humble, and resilient hero,[5] destined to meet a true happy ending with the cleaning girl, who is equally hard-working and dignified. The over-the-top harassment they receive from the conductor and the host is a quite evident metaphor. It refers to the questionable work and social conditions that Italy was still imposing to artists and women during the 1970s (see Chapter 2), and a general shout-out to the hardships that Italian animators had to face at the time. The metaphor inherent to the incompetent characters, instead, seems to be that of the main crew from a TV variety show: the host, the conductor, the orchestra. Such was the typical set of performers appearing

---

[5]Nichetti revealed to the author in a personal email (September 6, 2020) that his character in *Allegro* is intended to be an exaggerated self-portrait. At the time, the Studio was simultaneously working on this film, the three Mr. Rossi features, and several commercials. So, it was not unusual to work overnight, and even on weekends. Hence the idea of a chained and beaten animator.

in the most successful Italian variety show of the 1970s. It was a musical live event, based on the performance of pop songs, which took place in a theatrical stage (the Teatro delle Vittorie in Rome): "Canzonissima" (1956–75).[6] Another pertinent example would be the broadcast of the most famous song competition in Italy, the annual San Remo Festival (since 1951). The TV reference seems mostly evoked by the attitude of the host: even though his presence could be justified by the necessity of an equivalent to Deems Taylor in *Fantasia*, his constant resorting to a script, his live reactions to unforeseen accidents, and, most of all, his mistakes in looking into the camera and his appeals to invisible cameramen allude to a live TV show much more than to the shooting of a film. With his usual critical stance against television and commercial broadcasts, Bozzetto implicitly takes a jab at the supposed fakeness and incompetence inherent to the musical TV entertainment of his country. It was not the first time that such a satirical content appeared in Italian animation: for example, in *The Magic Bird*, a Gamma Film production, Lola Falena (Lola Moth), a parody of the showgirl Lola Falana, conceals her repulsive appearance by wearing ridiculously heavy makeup, and then she playback sings by using a record player hidden inside her wig. Similarly, the orchestra and the conductor of *Allegro non troppo* mock the musical professionals of Italian TV, if the reference to "Canzonissima" and the like is correct. More than to specific musicians, though, Bozzetto's satire could be addressing a more general cultural problem underlying those shows. In the 1970s, Italian TV was progressively losing its pedagogic role, previously founded on a solid offering of cultural and educational programs, in favor of a larger investment on entertainment.[7] The music popularized by the TV shows was very far from the classic repertoire Bozzetto cared about; the audience had fewer and fewer chances to be introduced to it. It is not by coincidence, maybe, that the Donizetti Theatre where *Allegro non troppo* gets "performed" is desolately empty. In fact, the communication strategy of entertainment was increasingly verging on lowering the cultural quality of the content, in order to meet a "national-popular" average, accessible without effort by anyone. According to the semiologists Giancarlo Bettetini, Paolo Braga, and Armando Fumagalli, the champion of this "national-popular" trend, in TV variety shows, was the host. They argued that this figure was

---

[6] See Aldo Grasso, *Storia della televisione italiana* (Milano: Garzanti, 2004), 235–6; also Damiano Garofalo, *Storia sociale della televisione in Italia, 1954–1969* (Venezia: Marsilio, 2018); and Aldo Grasso, Luca Barra, and Cecilia Penati, eds., *Storia critica della televisione italiana* (Milano: Il Saggiatore, 2019).

[7] Fausto Colombo spoke of an educational "strategy of the cricket" ("strategia del grillo"), which he opposes to an entertainment-heavy "strategy of the crow" ("strategia del corvo"), that precisely included "variety TV shows from the origins to the Seventies" ("televisione cabarettistica dalle origini agli anni Settanta"). Fausto Colombo, *La cultura sottile. Media e industria culturale in Italia dall'ottocento agli anni novanta* (Milano: Bompiani, 1998), 19.

supposed to hold together the show as a whole, by "tying together parts otherwise disconnected, declaring their meanings. ... The interpretative key of the Italian variety show, especially in respect to its 'national-popular' trait, stays also in the ability of the host to foreground, according to his personality, the national community."[8] By staging an incompetent host, Bozzetto might have not only expressed his doubts about the quality of TV entertainment but also about the cultural trend of Italy as a national community in the 1970s. Doing so within a parody of *Fantasia* especially made sense, since the Disney feature attempted to bridge together high and low culture, with an educational and authoritative attitude. *Allegro non troppo* provided a bleak follow-up to this utopia, by totally surrendering its pristine goal; it acknowledged, instead, a dramatic gap between art and entertainment, embodied by brutish stand-ins of TV performers abusing a couple of dreamers. Notwithstanding the poetic flight of the two lovers and the humorous setting of the rest, Bozzetto's pessimism about the Italian culture and entertainment industry (that, as a matter of fact, initially denied *Allegro non troppo* a theatrical distribution) lingers over the whole live-action frame.

---

[8] "Dovrebbe saper legare parti che risulterebbero altrimenti indipendenti tra loro, dichiarandone i significati. ... La chiave di lettura del genere del varietà italiano, soprattutto rispetto alla sua caratteristica di 'nazional popolare', sta anche nella capacità del conduttore di dare risalto, secondo la sua personalità, alla comunità nazionale." Giancarlo Bettetini, Paolo Braga, and Armando Fumagalli, *Le logiche della televisione* (Milano: FrancoAngeli, 2004), 94.

5
Prélude à l'après-midi d'un faune

Description

The first animated short of *Allegro non troppo* takes place in a fictitious arcadian world, vaguely connected with the imagery and stories from ancient Greek myths. As the music by Debussy starts, a panoramic shot from left to right reveals a quiet woodland landscape: on a patch of grass, several nymphs are shown in amorous attitude with satyrs. The colors are bright and nuanced: there is no realism in them. The characters have even green or purple skins and hair. The synthetic but subtly restless line style, together with the bold color contrasts, could contain a reference to Henry Matisse and the fauve artists from the early twentieth century.

The camera movement ends on the revelation of a big birthday cake on a table, an item that, despite looking quite out of context, is actually of major narrative importance: the many candles on it, in fact, tell that the little onlooking satyr in front of it is very old. Secondarily, this detail could also signify that the whole situation takes place after a birthday party. A close-up shot, moreover, reveals that the candles are sculpted in the shape of headless bodies of naked woman. This serves as a visual introduction to the sorrow that is consuming the satyr, a burning physical desire for women that cannot be appeased anymore, as the youthful charms of the old guy are gone forever.

What happens next elaborates on the frustration of his sexual obsession: the satyr is startled by the sight of a naked green nymph in a field of flowers. He sneakily approaches her with an expression of greedy anticipation on his face. He then stands on a rock and tries to show off with athletic poses and a handstand. While doing so, however, his body fat collapses on his shoulder and face. The nymph, who was initially courteously curious, now leaves disconcerted.

The sad satyr looks at his own reflection in a pond; he himself is surprised at how aged his face looks. He inanely tries to stretch it, probably to hide the wrinkles. Then, he sits under a tree and fantasizes about his young self that materializes from a hazy cloud, initially working as a comic balloon on the character's head. The satyr in there looks strong, fit, and enjoys the company of beautiful girls. The memories soon dissipate in thin air; the satyr walks back toward the pond and now worries about his few and floppy hair. By looking again into his reflection, he tries to straighten and comb them, but they unrulily pop back in their previous state. However, a flock of birds suddenly approaches him: they each take a strand of hair in their beak and twist it around until the satyr's hairdo gets more elegant. Then, they apply paint on them and on his beard, and powder on his face; with this makeup, the satyr regains some of his confidence. A group of small wood "funny animals" watches him as he leaves behind the trees.

The satyr prowls around the shadows and the strange vegetation of the forest. His jerky and fast movements make him bump against a branch, disturbing a couple of funny-looking birds. The male one addresses to the satyr a typical Italian gesture, waving a hand with all the fingertips brought together, to mean a disapproving disbelief about someone else's actions. The satyr restarts his quest: he pops out of a giant flower, using its outstretched stamens as an observation post to look around from above; he slides on swirly ivy vines, he jumps on top of boulders, until he trips and curls up in a rolling ball shape.

When he stands again, he sees yet another naked nymph under a waterfall. She runs behind the curtain of falling water. The satyr approaches and, bewildered, sees female body parts surface from different points of the waterfall. There is a whole group of nymphs there. They start to dance in the water. The satyr chases one with blue hair. He emerges in front of her, striking a pose that makes him look like a cheap fountain decoration (he even holds a fish that gushes water from its mouth, in form of a heart). The nymph playfully splashes him; however, this makes the satyr's makeup melt down. The nymph, surprised, runs away; the satyr sadly washes his face, while the fish laughs at him.

Back in the woods, two "funny animals" point to somewhere off-screen. The satyr reacts joyfully; a reverse shot reveals a girl leaning down on her left side, eating an apple. He takes confidence and, with a mischievous face, grabs some leaves and powder from plants nearby; he looks now more colored and with a blonde mane. He refuses some sudden advances from a weird female horse, with a face ironically resembling that of the satyr himself. The protagonist then crawls neat the nymph and proudly reveals himself; with a smile, the girl offers him her apple. He bites it and passes the apple back, but his false teeth remained stuck on the fruit. The face of the embarrassed satyr turns red, while the girl drops the apple and walks away. He puts the teeth back in place; two birds brush them with a string-like tree branch. While the nymph picks some more fruit, the satyr appears in between some plants that look just like his nose. He chases the girl, who unexplainably starts to grow taller and bigger. He tries to match her transformation by holding the breath and inflating himself, to no avail; he finally jumps and holds onto her leg for a while. Then, the satyr falls to the ground, back to his pristine color. The giant nymph, scornful, flicks his fake hair off his head with a finger.

A strange, tapir-like animal on two legs approaches the weeping satyr, playing a violin made out of a tree leaf. A female tapir appears near the satyr, too; she caresses the satyr's head, but when she notices the violin player goes to kiss and seduce him. They leave together.

Now alone, the satyr starts to hallucinate. To his eyes, a tree with a woman trunk and female breasts as leaves gradually appears; near to it there is a bush of waving female legs. The "leaves" of the tree float away before the old guy can reach them; the bush reacts after being grabbed by one "branch" and rolls away in the distance. A third apparition reveals a composition of large female hands, gently swaying as leaves in a breeze. Once again, when the satyr comes close, they flee; they divide into three couples, flapping like bird wings. In the sky, a cloud with woman-like features passes past the demoralized satyr and dissipates.

Alone in a land that has now dusky colors, the satyr cries and picks from the ground his scarf and cane. As he renounces to keep concealing his age, he notices a hill with a nipple. The aspect of other areas of the landscape worries him. Nonetheless, he tiredly walks away. A combination of crossfades and a zoom out finally reveal that the whole world of the satyr was an enormous naked girl, resting on her back. She slowly turns to her side, apparently asleep, while the night falls and the moon and the stars appear above her.

Program Notes

The short film is based on one of Claude Debussy's most famous works: a symphonic piece he minutely composed over two years (1892–4), inspired by the poem *L'après-midi d'un faune* (*The Afternoon of a Faun*). The author was Stéphane Mallarmé (1842–1898), a French poet and playwright whose work contributed a great deal to the aesthetics of Symbolism, a nineteenth-century art movement that aimed to reveal the hidden truth of the world with indirect allusions and hints: in Mallarmé's words, an artist should "paint, not the thing, but the effect it produces."[1] The first edition of the poem was illustrated by four wood engravings by Édouard Manet (1832–1883), printed in black and hand-tinted in pink. The work dealt with an ancient bucolic setting, perhaps the Sicily once chanted by the Greek poet

---

[1] Stéphane Mallarmé in Rosemary Lloyd, *Mallarmé: The Poet and His Circle* (Ithaca, NY: Cornell University Press, 2005), 48.

Theocritus, in the third century BCE.[2] Its story is about a satyr who wakes up in the afternoon and remembers that, in the morning, he came across two nymphs and tried to make love to both of them at once, to no avail. He then imagines embracing the goddess Venus, but he soon gets afraid of his own daring fantasy and decides to fall asleep again. According to the comparative literature scholar Steven F. Walker, the events in the poem could allude to a "comic deflation of the faun's male ego,"[3] being thus "pure sexual comedy."[4] The satyr seems to be "sexually inexperienced,"[5] and as such quite young.

Debussy's symphonic piece was apparently written with no intention to replicate the narrative plot of the poem in detail. In this regard, there are a few remarks by Debussy himself that sound quite telling: the first program notes to the piece, which Debussy apparently sanctioned,[6] reported,

> The music of this prelude is a very free illustration of Mallarmé's beautiful poem. By no means does it claim to be a synthesis of it. Rather there is a succession of scenes through which pass the desires and dreams of the faun in the heat of the afternoon. Then, tired of pursuing the timorous flight of nymphs and naiads, he succumbs to intoxicating sleep, in which he can finally realize his dreams of possession in universal Nature.[7]

Moreover, in an oft-quoted letter to the critic Henri Gauthier-Villars, aka Willy, Debussy added,

> The *Prélude à l'après-midi d'un faune*? Dear sir, might it be what has remained of the dream at the tip of the faun's flute? More precisely, it is the general impression of the poem, because in following it more closely, music would run out of breath as if a dray horse were competing for the Grand Prix with a thoroughbred. ... All the same, it follows the rising

---

[2]Steven F. Walker, "Mallarmé's Symbolist Eclogue: The 'Faune' as Pastoral," *PMLA* 93, no. 1 (January 1978): 106.
[3]Ibid.
[4]Ibid.
[5]Ibid.
[6]Marie Rolf, "Semantic and Structural Issues in Debussy's Mallarmé Songs," in *Debussy Studies*, ed. Richard Langham Smith (Cambridge: Cambridge University Press, 1997), 179.
[7]
> La musique de ce prélude est une illustration très libre du beau poème de Mallarmé; elle ne prétend pas en être une synthèse. Il s'agit plutôt de fonds successifs sur lesquels se meuvent les désirs et les rêves du faune dans la chaleur de cet après-midi. Enfin, las de poursuivre les nymphes et les naïades apeurées dans leur fuite, il s'abandonne à un sommeil enivrant, riche de songes enfin réalisés, de pleine possession dans l'universelle nature. (Quoted in Léon Vallas, *Claude Debussy et son temps* [Paris: Albin Michel 1958], 181)

motion of the poem, and it is the décor that is described so marvelously in the text.[8]

However, David J. Code[9] and Arthur Wenk argued that a precise connection exists between the structure of Debussy's *Prélude* and that of Mallarmé's work. It is anyway sure that Debussy conceived the *Prélude* just as an introductory piece to a longer score, as the name itself says: the poem was supposed to inspire two more movements, called *Interludes* and *Paraphrase finale*.[10] As a stand-alone piece, the *Prélude* remained a tribute to the musicality and eroticism of Mallarmé's poetry, and a landmark in the history of modern music: the composer and conductor Pierre Boulez (1925–2016) stated that "modern music was awakened by *L'Après-midi d'un faune*."[11]

Bozzetto was aware of the backstory of Debussy's piece. In good accordance with the composer's reported intentions, he did not pursue a literal illustration of Mallarmé's text, though. He retained the setting, a vague elsewhere with features that suggest ancient Greek myths and arcadian traditions. A further reason for keeping this scenery was likely also to instate a parallel with a *Fantasia* number, namely the *Pastoral* sequence, which had a similar taste in playing with mythologic and bucolic visual formulas. The woodland context and the amorous theme probably come from the *Pastoral* segment with the centaurs and centaurettes. This is likely confirmed by the short gag that shows the satyr courted by an ugly female horse with a caricatural human face; also, the birds and creatures helping the satyr to "dress up" have a role similar to the cupids in that same segment from the Disney film. Apart from that, some more connections with Debussy and Mallarmé remained: for example, the humorous contrast between the faun's grand sexual fantasies and his ineptitude at seducing, paired with the ridiculing of the stereotypes on masculine sexual power. In a clever subversion of the original sources, comedy gets spurred on by the faun being no more too young, but too old. By doing so, Bozzetto had also a chance to ridicule Italian popular entertainment of the 1970s, and in particular the

---

[8] Le *Prélude à l'après-midi d'un faune*? cher Monsieur, c'est peut-être ce qui est resté de rêve au fond de la flûte de faune? Plus précisément, c'est l'impression générale du poème, car à le suivre de plus près, la musique s'essoufflerait ainsi qu'un cheval de fiacre concourant pour le Grand prix avec un pur-sang. ... Maintenant cela suit tout de même le mouvement ascendant du poème, et c'est le décor merveilleusement décrit au texte. (Quoted in David J. Code, "Hearing Debussy Read Mallarmé," *Journal of the American Musicological Society* 54, no. 3 [2001]: 508).

[9] Code, "Hearing Debussy Read Mallarmé"; Arthur Wenk, *Claude Debussy and the Poets* (Berkeley, University of California Press, 1976).
[10] Wenk, *Claude Debussy and the Poets*, 151.
[11] Pierre Boulez, *Notes of an Apprenticeship* (New York: Alfred A. Knopf, 1968), 345.

promotion of the use of cosmetics to conceal one's age and align with the shallow beauty ideals seen on TV.

In *Allegro non troppo*, though, the satyr does not sleep or dream; he hallucinates, instead. A "dreamy" quality is however evident in the film, and this is mostly conveyed through the colors and the drawing style. Giuseppe Laganà was the main responsible for the design and animation (see Part One, Chapter 3); on Bozzetto's suggestion, he did an extensive airbrush job to create a nuanced atmosphere. This gets enhanced also by the use of semi-transparent layers in multiplane shots: it is sometimes possible to see through the scenery elements that pass over the characters. The phantasmagoric and warm color palette adds to the oneiric feeling of the episode: as mentioned in the description before, a French artistic movement of the age of Debussy and Mallarmé, the fauvism, could have been referenced by Laganà; on the other hand, there is no apparent connection with the artworks provided by Manet to the first edition of the poem, as they were monochromatic and much more synthetic in their style. The simple forms and bold, flat colors of Henri Matisse could instead be a good comparison in this respect. One of the most famous among Matisses's paintings, *La danse* (1910), might have been a direct source of inspiration, because of the unrealistic skin tones and the streamlined human figures. The *Prélude* in *Allegro non troppo*, in fact, uses also human characters: while the satyrs are cartoony (the protagonist, who loosely resembles Guido Manuli by coincidence, is the typical big-nosed "average man" by Bozzetto, like Mr. Rossi), the nymphs are drawn in a more naturalistic way. This is because they are actually rotoscoped: live footage of a model was traced, frame by frame, to create all the female characters. The nude modeling was done by a professional, chosen by Bozzetto and his collaborators from the catalogue of an agency; her straightforwardness at undressing and posing initially embarrassed the artists, as some of them (like the director) did not come from art academies and were not used to life drawing.[12] The contrast between the rotoscoped "realistic" movements of the nymphs and the caricatural clumsiness of the satyr creates a humorous disparity between the protagonist's fantasies and his actual appearance. Rotoscoping was in fact instrumental to Bozzetto's need for slower movements throughout the episode, to enhance its "dreamy" quality.[13] On top of that, the fact that all the nymphs come from one rotoscoped model could also be targeting again the growing standardization of beauty ideals in the 1970s: the "dreams" of the average heterosexual Italian man (the satyr), even in his old age, were conditioned to obsess over a fictitious female archetype, embodied by objectified TV soubrettes and actresses who all looked the same, as if they were "traced" from a single model. It is maybe

---

[12]Bozzetto in the documentary "Ricordando *Allegro non troppo*."
[13]Personal communication to the author via Skype, March 14, 2019.

not a mere coincidence that among the most successful TV showgirls of the time there was a couple of identical twin sisters: Alice and Ellen Kessler.

The audiovisual treatment of the *Prélude*, in accordance with its "dreamlike" stance, makes use of quite loose relationships between music and animation. The preferred function is in fact the *emotive* one, in the sense that the action connects mostly with the overall mood of the music, and not with single notes or chords. It does so both in a *macro-emotive* (the whole symphonic piece connects with the storyline and visual style of the animation) and *micro-emotive* fashion (the mood of a music episode reinforces that of a specific sequence). In this last respect, for example, a passage where a surge in the music dynamic and symphonic texture is followed by a diminuendo based on the doleful repetition of a melodic fragment is synchronized with the satyr showing off on a rock to the first nymph: during the crescendo he pulls off a few successful moves, but when the music goes "down" in emotional and aural intensity his body fat collapses and the nymph leaves. It is remarkable how the emotional articulation of Bozzetto's animation divides the episode in narrative segments that perfectly coincide with the main musical structures within Debussy's work, demonstrating how attentive and competent was the director's listening. For example, Debussy's *Prélude* can be subdivided into a first section, dominated by the opening flute theme, archaic and melodic; a second section, with a more agitated pace and a different set of themes; and finally, a conclusive section where the opening theme returns. Bozzetto's animation first introduces the satyr and his frustrated quest for sexual gratification; then, together with Debussy's "agitated" section, the satyr puts on a "youthful" makeup and hopes to fool the nymphs. The "reprise" section finds the protagonist back to his old self, now lost in a world of surreal sexual visions.

Even though they are few, there are also functions based on synchronizations between animations and musical events: *spatial* and *temporal perceptive functions*. An example of the first kind is the sudden "flourish" in the main flute melody, used together with the startled reaction of the satyr at seeing his own reflection in the water. In that way, the visual quality of the movement (a sudden jitter) connects with the "jittery" feeling evoked by the fast melodic detour; however, there are no punctual correspondences between notes and actions. Another instance of this function is in the third section; a diminuendo and ritardando repetition of a descending fragment by the flutes is conjoined with the image of the bush of legs rolling away in the distance. Several qualities of the music dote here at once on the spatial perception of the viewer: the diminuendo suggests something that is getting away, while the repeated fragment goes well with a cyclic movement like that of rolling.

The temporal perceptive functions usually get the most attention in music-based animation, because they create an illusory causal relationship between a visual event and a sound; it is the same function that allows lip-synch in animation, making the spectator believe that a character is actually talking beyond the screen. Such functions create a sense of presence and immediacy, and as such they get through very efficiently, from a cognitive point of view; it is not by chance that the film that made Mickey Mouse a sensation of sound cartoons, *Steamboat Willie* (1928), was preeminently based on those functions; and this is also why they are sometimes called mickey-mousing by film sound scholars (see Part One, Chapter 2).

Maybe because of the "dreamy" atmosphere of the short film, the *Prélude* makes a very limited use of temporal perceptive functions. Sometimes, they are even staged in a way that makes them barely recognizable; for example, it is not uncommon for the satyr to walk in synch with the rhythm of a certain melody; however, the moderate tempo and the lack of emphasis in the animated steps renders the existence of this detail almost inconspicuous. It participates, anyway, in making the music and the film more mutually cohesive. This kind of "hidden" synchs have been identified by Sergio Miceli as "implicit synchronies."[14] It must be said that Debussy's piece almost lacks any musical feature that would work as a spectacular point of synchronization, like a strong accent, a "stinger" chord, or the entrance of an instrument with an appealing and easily distinguishable sound (like a cymbal crash). There are only two instances of this in the *Prélude*. The first is the use of a solo violin; on screen, it gets synched with a little animal playing a weird leaf-violin, creating thus also a *realistic motivation* to the sound (we see a violin look-alike playing, which justifies the sound as situated in the narrative universe of the film). In truth, when the solo flute plays at the beginning of the piece, we see a satyr playing a Pan flute; however, the movements of his fingers are too fast for the music tempo, and also the panoramic camera movement leaves the character off-screen too soon to actually have a synchronic relevance. Instead, the second instance of an instrument sound used for the sake of perceptual synchrony is the delicate ringing of the so-called ancient cymbals in the finale. Bozzetto ignores their first presentation, but later he synchronizes their sound with a tear dropping from the eye of the satyr, and with the appearance of the stars in the sky. For the rest, Bozzetto and his crew made up temporal perceptive functions with subtler musical elements, like changes in the harmony or in the timbre. For example, the entrance of brasses is synchronized with the gesture of a group of small creatures that points toward a beautiful nymph off-screen, soon to be revealed by a reverse shot. Similarly, in a previous sequence, the satyr reacts to an off-screen nymph (the first one he courts) when a peculiar change in the harmony occurs.

---

[14] "Sincroni Impliciti." Sergio Miceli, *Musica per film. Storia, Estetica, Analisi, Tipologie* (Milano: Ricordi LIM, 2009), 638–41.

There is also a special subset of temporal perceptive synchronizations, which does not make use of unexpected changes in the musical discourse, but rests on the junctions between its phrases and periods. Quite often, an editing cut happens together with such musical articulations, when a phrase ends and another one starts. This kind of attention reveals how true Bozzetto and his team stayed to the nature of Debussy's composition, by choosing to devise a pervasive synchronic strategy that did not have any kind of spectacular immediacy to the lay viewer but created nonetheless a strong and respectful entanglement between the animation and the score. Bozzetto ironically played with the expected reaction of the audience in the following live-action interstitial, when Maurizio Micheli is caught by the camera bored and distracted; however, the *Prélude à l'après-midi d'un faune* is not dull in its exploration of the image–music relationship. Moreover, while demonstrating the level of detail reached by Bozzetto in the decoding of the music structure based on sole listening, the soft-spoken attitude of the short provided a good emotional prelude to the whole set of episodes, creating a much-needed starting point for an artistic crescendo destined to peak in the middle of the film with the *Boléro*.

6

Slavonic Dance Op. 46 No. 7

Description

From one of the many little caves excavated in the side of a terraced hill, a little man steps out and walks in the plain. He builds a straw house for himself. Amazed, all the hill people peek out from their cave dwellings; they rush to the plain and imitate the first man, building a whole city of straw houses.

Angered, the little character kicks down his house and builds a new and taller one, made of bricks. Soon, all the others do exactly the same; so, the man proceeds to add more stories to turn his house into a skyscraper. But the crowd keeps on imitating him.

Night falls. At his window, the angered little man ruminates about vengeance. In a comic balloon, we see how he wishes to kill his neighbors. Suddenly, a malevolent grin appears on his face.

He goes in the street and starts behaving in a foolish way: he jumps on two feet, on one foot, on his hands; he then makes a silly dance with an umbrella. He sits down and waits with a malicious face. Immediately, the crowd repeats all his pointless actions. So, he goes on with his plan. He does a somersault; he scratches himself and he hits his head with a hammer that he finally eats. All the people repeat this sequence. The man removes his head, while the others do the same; the imitation ensues also when he juggles his head. He then puts a chamber pot on his head; he takes a "standing at attention" military pose and does the roman salute. The imitation now includes three more gestures at the end (a military salute, a march-in-place step, and a victory sign made with the index and middle fingers), which the lead character maybe did while off-screen. Pleased, the man fixes a chin strap to his chamber pot; he puts on boots and pulls out a rifle from his jacket. The crowd proceeds to copycat him.

Now on a slope, the main character marches in place, making the goose step. The others start to follow him. He reaches the edge of the cliff and notices a branch sticking out from the rock wall, just a little bit below his feet. He malignantly laughs while looking behind him, anticipating the fate of his imitators; he then throws himself over the edge, promptly stopping his fall by grabbing onto the branch. At first, he wickedly cackles; however, as nothing happens, he gets perplexed and climbs back to the cliff top.

When he peeks from the edge, the imitators, who were standing still in wait, swiftly turn on their heels, pull down their trousers, and bend forward to flash at him their bare bottoms.

Program Notes

The *Slavonic Dance* is the only short in *Allegro non troppo* that Bozzetto completely designed and animated on his own. He says that, according to his own recollections, he might have received some help only for the inbetweening.[1] Consequently, the stylistic features of Bozzetto emerge here with distinct evidence, much more than in the rest of the film: the "entomologic" distance from the subject, the sketchy and flat line art, and the stylized and caricatural characters with big noses make the *Slavonic Dance* a close relative of shorts like *I due castelli*.

The symphonic score that inspired the animated piece is the seventh in an 1878 collection of eight dances by the Bohemian composer Antonín Dvořák (1841–1904). Originally composed for piano four hands, they were commissioned by the Bonn publisher Fritz Simrock, who asked for some folk pieces in the fashion of the highly successful *Hungarian Dances* by Johannes Brahms (1833–1897). Brahms was friend both with Simrock and Dvořák; he was the one who brought his younger colleague to the attention of the publisher, recommending a release of Dvořák's *Moravian Duets*, a collection of folk songs for two voices with piano accompaniment. The success of the *Duets* persuaded Simrock to advance a commission for the *Slavonic Dances*. In fact, at the time, the German music market was particularly receptive toward pieces that sounded "exotic."[2] Dvořák, as he did for the *Duets*, complied for free;[3] it was anyway a wise decision, as the *Dances* became his breakthrough to reach international fame and monetary success. There was nothing especially Bohemian in those pieces, though; they were modeled after Czech folk dance patterns, but the melodies were original creations by Dvořák (unlike Brahms's *Hungarian Dances* that used Magyar themes). A second set of eight *Dances*, which followed in 1886, was truer to its title,

---

[1] Personal communication to the author via Skype, March 14, 2019.
[2] Michael Beckerman, "The Master's Little Joke: Antonín Dvořák and the Mask of Nation," in *Dvořák and his World*, ed. Beckerman (Princeton, NJ: Princeton University Press, 2012), 145.
[3] Kurt Honolka, *Dvořák* (London: Haus, 2004), 44.

as it used also dances from other regions and countries of the Slavonic area; however, the melodies were still by Dvořák. The overall setting of the music, moreover, was very far from folk music; it was in a late Romantic rigorous idiom not far from that of Brahms. This became even more evident when the *Dances* got orchestrated soon after their release by the composer, because of the good audience response: the resulting symphonic sound was not in tune with the popular heritage of Bohemia or Moravia, just like it happened to Brahms's *Hungarian Dances*. According to Michael Beckerman, "Dvořák was no more familiar with the ethnographic or spiritual source of his materials than was Brahms."[4] So, when Dvořák identified as a *Skočná* his seventh *Dance Op. 46*, he just stated that the overall rhythmic pattern of the piece fits into a Czech tradition of duple-time fast dances that bore that name. The musicologist John Tyrrell noticed that the historical traits of the *Skočná* are actually so vaguely defined that the name is interchangeably used for many other duple-time dances from the same geographic area.[5] That indeterminacy (and the lack of the ethnomusicological scholarship that would have developed in the twentieth century) allowed Dvořák to create his own imaginative take at Czech musical folklore.

It is, however, curious how Bozzetto's interpretation of Dvořák's *Skočná* is respectful of some of the few known aspects historically attributed to this dance. In fact, Tyrrell stated that this dance rhythm, and the texts sometimes sung to it, had a "humorous nature," which Bozzetto perfectly caught. Moreover, "skočná" means "leaping," because the dancers were supposed to do jump-like moves. In the *Slavonic Dance* animation, the gags about jumps and leaps are abundant, up to the final one, which sees the protagonist faking a deathly leap into a ravine. There is even more, though: it seems that in the late nineteenth and twentieth centuries the term "skočná" identified a competitive dance, "in which the dancer attempts to jump higher than his rivals."[6] The episode in *Allegro non troppo* is precisely about a rivalry between a crowd and a man who tries to outwit everyone. There is even one moment when the protagonist tries to reach higher than his opponents, by building a skyscraper. It is likely that all these correspondences are the fruit of Bozzetto's own deciphering of the choreographic values embedded in the music discourse, rather than of a philological study on Czech dances; his conclusions were nonetheless strikingly accurate.

The theme of imitation that Bozzetto developed in the short also comes from other musical features of Dvořák's work. The *Dance* is in fact replete with imitations, on multiple levels. At a larger scale, its main

---

[4]Beckerman, "Master's Little Joke," 145.
[5]John Tyrrell, "Skočná," *Grove Music Online* (2001), https://www.oxfordmusiconline.com/grovemusic/view/10.1093/gmo/9781561592630.001.0001/omo-9781561592630-e-0000043852 (accessed November 17, 2019).
[6]Ibid.

theme is distinguished by couplets where the same thematic fragment gets immediately repeated. More in detail, there is a continuing contrapuntal imitation: the thematic fragment is echoed in the lower registers by other instruments. However, this latter kind of imitation does not give way to audiovisual functions; Bozzetto used only the phraseological imitations in the main melody, immediately evident to the lay listener and thus more widely effective, to construct the unnerving action symmetries between the protagonist and his copycats.

The attention Bozzetto reserved to the theme of imitation and the comic relief he wanted to introduce in *Allegro* with this short were the premise for a thorough use of temporal perceptive functions in the audiovisual treatment: basically, the music and the images stick together thanks to explicit synchronies. Those are immediately evident, as in the initial long shot where the character walks in the plain: his steps happen perfectly together with the notes of the main theme. The music provides plenty of incisive points of synchronizations; for example, during the malicious manipulation attempts, the hammer hits the character's own head in synch with a cymbal crash. This evens out the lack of temporal perceptive functions in the *Prélude à l'après-midi d'un faune*; however, just like that short, the *Slavonic Dance* also presents synchronies with camera movements, which remark the subdivision into phrases of the musical discourse; they are much more evident than in the previous number, as Bozzetto resorts here to fast zoom-ins and zoom-outs and to whip pans. There are also instances of a spatial perceptive function, for example, when the full-orchestra repetition of the main theme coincides with the multitude of cave dwellers invading the plain, suggesting a parallel between the massive presence of their movement in the shot and the powerful surge of a multilayered full orchestral sound. On the other hand, the humorousness of the whole story is in tune with the overall emotional content of the *Dance*, instating in this way a macro-emotional function.

Another quality of the *Slavonic Dance* animated short is that it manages to follow closely the musical structure while reprising all the staples of Bozzetto's style. The whole short fits into the tradition of Bozzetto's taste in humorous retellings of the history of life and evolution, as it starts from cavemen (dressed in what seem animal skin clothes) and ends with skyscrapers and modern weapons. The whole process is mostly observed from a distance, with "entomological" objectivity, except from the part when we have a zoom-in on the main character at the window, plotting his revenge (while wiggling his fingers together with the swirling motion of the music, in yet another temporal perceptive function). On top of that, the action is often seen from the side (also because of the flat character design that is not as much effective when frontal views are used), swinging back and forth from left to right. However, this does not happen within the same shot, like in *I due castelli*, but it is conveyed by the editing, alternating shots, and reverse shots. Thematically, the short is replete with Bozzetto's pessimism about mass-media communication. The first part of the short elaborates on the danger of the homologation of actions and desires. In the second part, instead, the focus becomes the concentration of communicative power in the hand of a single agent, who could manipulate the message in a malevolent way: it is an allegory of the perils inherent to gatekeeping in mass media, "the process of culling and crafting countless bits of information into the limited number of messages that reach people each day,"[7] in the words of Pamela J. Shoemaker and Tim P. Vos. The idea is not far from the brain-missile metaphor seen in *Vip, My Brother Superman*: a one-way message implanted in the head of a TV spectator by a malicious conspirator.

In conclusion, the *Slavonic Dance* achieves the difficult goal of staying pure Bozzetto while adhering to the choreographic needs of a musical piece with a completely different cultural background, by taking advantage of its bold, synchrony-prone sound events and its general playful spirit.

---

[7]Pamela J. Shoemaker and Tim P. Vos, *Gatekeeping Theory* (New York: Routledge, 2009), 9.

7

Boléro

Description

A Coca-Cola glass bottle, thrown away by the angry conductor, gets drawn on paper and used as an inspirational piece by the animator. As the short film begins, the bottle is now flying over an empty and eerie landscape, while high-pitched electronic sound effects accompany its trajectory. In the distance stays the silhouette of a landed space vehicle, with a shape not far from that of the command module of the Apollo Moon missions. The bottle seems to have come from there; with a loud thud, it plunges into the ground and leans to the left. Being very close to the point of view, it almost fills the screen transversally. It still contains a few drops of Coca-Cola. The spaceship takes off with a roar: the light from its engines outlines the profile of the bottle.

When the sound of the spaceship wanes away, the music of the *Boléro* slowly fades in. Inside the bottle, the liquid seems to be pulsating. It slowly and jerkily reaches the mouth of the bottle. It finally erupts from it and splashes into the ground beneath. Now seen in a close-up view, it looks like a weird dark amoeba, which soon sprouts a single round eye on a thin tentacle. The creature starts crawling around, from left to right.

The light changes. The amoeba now has a more definite shape: it seems to have grown a tubular mouth. It is attracted by a kind of vegetable growing on the top of a rock; it comes closer to it and sucks on it, pulling it from the ground and gradually revealing its long, slimy, and oddly ramified roots.

The creature grows bigger but loses its balance. It falls and hits stony asperities until it smashes onto the ground. A part of it outstretches and gives birth to another creature that soon finds a hot lake and goes underwater. Its position is revealed by air bubbles coming up from below; it apparently smashes onto a half-submerged rock and finally resurfaces. It seems to be struggling to move; it tenses up, until a bundle of vegetable-like and ever-growing tentacles erupts from its body. The camera frantically follows the expansion, until a limb forms from the branches and outstretches from above; it lands, immediately followed by a round body with a large mouth, two tusks, and an eye.

The whole looks like a new monocular monster, who immediately starts to jump on its single leg and chase small colored lights around it. It eventually melts down, giving birth to many smaller monsters of different shapes and colors, while volcanoes erupt in the background. The last to come out, yellow and with a very wide mouth, starts eating the others.

The last surviving prey climbs up a small volcanic cone to flee from the voracious monster; a sudden eruption propels it into the air. It starts to flap its limbs, like a bird. It makes a smug grin toward the predator that remained on the ground and then evolves into a much more complex flying creature. It frolics and spirals into the air, but then, during one of its stunts, it gets eaten by something that looks like a carnivorous plant.

This entity splits up into several multicolored worms. They crawl while intertwining; one of them, a pink one, tries to get away but is promptly caught and brought back into the bunch. A large egg appears among their spires. Many other similar bunches of worms are seen crawling and producing eggs in the same way.

The eggs simultaneously open and generate pulsating tree-like lifeforms. A forest is born. A procession of animals walks through it; some other join in climbing down the trees. A menacing ape lurks from above and observes the beasts on the march, always walking to the right of the screen. Now elaborate horns adorn the heads of the creatures, and they come in a lot of different sizes and colors. The horns of one of them get stuck in tree branches; scared to death, it stays unnoticed by three gigantic, dinosaur-like animals that are passing by.

The procession is now heading toward a canyon. The sky turns dark; lightning flashes come from the crack in the mountain. Inside the canyon, the flashes are insistent and ominous. The shapes and sizes of the beasts keep becoming more elaborate; one of them, with a globose large head, comes toward the camera. However, the spherical thing was a bunch of bats, perched on the horns of the creature. They flutter away and swirl into the sky. The rain starts to fall. A dinosaur-like mother, while walking, shelters her pups under her tail. An ape with her cub, though, violently chases them away and takes their place.

The camera shows the many leaps and levels of a huge waterfall. The procession gets across on top of it, but one of the monsters falls down. When it goes underwater, it turns into an aquatic creature and, quite relieved, it survives. However, it is soon threatened by other beings that try to eat it. The massive foot of an animal stomps onto one of such beings. The procession is now wading across the water. The malignant ape reappears; it pulls a shielded monster off-screen and soon after reappears, using the carapace as a boat and a club as a paddle. A smaller monster (perhaps the son of the previous owner of the shield) follows the ape in the water, only to be smashed on the head with the club.

An ice age seems to be beginning. Plateaus and hills of ice spread around, covering the animals. The ice momentarily seems a colored and flat graphic pattern, but then it mutates into a solid whole. A snowstorm breaks out; a flying monster cannot keep itself flying and lands on an elephant-like creature. The ape returns, as aggressive as ever. It chases a hairy white monster. A camera shake implies that the ape killed it off-screen with its club; in fact, when it returns it is wearing the fur of that animal. The procession cannot be stopped by the snow anyway, and the stomping steps of the larger beasts shake the ground and make the smaller ones rhythmically leap in the air. However, the soil cracks under the weight and many animals fall inside a ravine. Fire erupts from there: it goes up and surrounds the other creatures that try to escape from the flames. The ape is scared as well and covers its eyes with its hand; when it looks at its club, though, it sees it burning. At first puzzled, it soon discovers the destructive power of fire, which can turn other creatures to ashes. In eager anticipation of some malignant plot, it runs ahead of the procession and disappears in the distance.

The sun reappears. Now the landscape is a desert. New creatures join in, including a small, flightless bird who jumps around. The light changes: a solar eclipse is about to start. The animals are terrified. They bump into each other, they retract into their shields, they dig holes, and hide into them. The multitude stops and trembles, looking at the sky and at the eclipsed sun in fear. But then, they outstretch their neck in marvel at the returning light.

A fade in shows tornados raging around. Many of them surround the procession, engulfing it in sand. Notwithstanding the fear, the monsters keep walking and flying. And then, pyramids appear. Some creatures fly around their top; while most of the others ignore the monuments, one beast urinates on their stone walls.

Another unexpected object comes in the way: a few animals stop to contemplate an intimidating large cross that rises from a relief in the terrain. Other gloomy signs of civilization appear around them: a roman helmet and a spear, a line of gallows, an abandoned tank, open cans, and garbage. Suddenly, the animal cannot proceed anymore. The way is blocked by a multilevel road junction. The ground cracks open and skyscrapers start sprouting from it. The creatures are sent flying around; some of them turn into mechanical contraptions, like a building crane or an excavator. Finally, a whole city appears, as the *Boléro* ends. Skyscrapers are everywhere. A giant man looms above them. He seems a statue; the shadows on his face make him resemble a hangman. He is actually alive, because he malevolently smirks and looks down. However, the face breaks like concrete; it sonorously crumbles and reveals that he was empty inside. From the inner cavity the ape emerges. Without a word, it rests its head on its hand and looks into the camera. The image fades to black: only the evil red eyes of the ape remain visible, lingering in the dark.

Program Notes

Maurice Ravel's *Boléro* was the trigger to the whole *Allegro non troppo* project (see Part One, Chapter 3); it became its main showpiece and one of the most technically complex hand-drawn animated short films ever made in Italy. It reportedly stayed in production for more than two years; its storyboard, seven meters wide and two meters tall (see Part One, Chapter 3), was fine-tuned by many layers of emendations; its background artworks by Giancarlo Cereda, made to accommodate long horizontal panoramic takes, were about two meter long. The storyboard was accompanied by detailed notes on the color atmospheres to be used in each sequence: an idea not far from the device known as colorscript in contemporary animation pipelines. The organic transformations and movements of the grotesque fauna designed by Giorgio Valentini were rendered by some of the top creatives from the RDA 70 studio, who had previously learned animation from international artists when they worked for Gamma Film (see Part One, Chapter 3): Walter Cavazzuti and Giovanni Ferrari. The intricate shadow patterns on the characters were painstakingly defined in pencil on each pose and then transferred to the cels through a Xerox process. The ending of the episode features a lesser amount of shadows, because they were more synthetically rendered to speed up the production as the deadline approached.[1] Luciano Marzetti worked on the special effects: his most remarkable contribution was the opening sequence with the Coca-Cola bottle (see Part One, Chapter 3), which required about eight hundred drawings[2] and had to be reshot six times to achieve the desired result. The artistic direction of the whole was instead entrusted to one of Bozzetto's closest collaborators, Giuseppe Laganà. The short was made by Bozzetto with the *Rite of Spring* episode from *Fantasia* in mind; however, the two films bear no stylistic resemblance. The Disney one presented a reportedly "accurate" rendition of the history of life on Earth[3] from the beginning to the

---

[1] Bozzetto in "Ricordando *Allegro non troppo*," a documentary in the *Allegro non troppo* DVD, part of the DVD collection "Tutto Bozzetto (o quasi)" (Roma: Multimedia San Paolo, 2005).
[2] Ibid.
[3] It is actually replete with factual mistakes; e.g., *Tyrannosaurus* did not live in the same age of *Stegosaurus*, and yet they share screen time in a life-or-death battle. Moreover, *Tyrannosaurus* is represented with three fingers on each hand, while it had only two; even though at the time no specimen of a *Tyrannosaurus* hand had been discovered yet, and there had been early-twentieth-century museal reconstructions sporting three fingers, it had already been assumed it had two fingers in analogy with other members of the tyrannosaurids for which fossils of the hands were available, like *Gorgosaurus*.

extinction of non-avian dinosaurs, by using livid colors and blocky designs; Bozzetto's *Boléro*, instead, mused about an alternate history of evolution featuring unlikely rounded monsters, with bold, ever-changing colors. Even so, the *Boléro* is the one of the two parts of *Allegro non troppo* that features recognizable visual homages to *Fantasia* (the other one being the *Concerto RV 559*). In fact, as already mentioned before, a sequence with the monsters walking toward the desert, seen from behind at an angle, has an identical layout to a shot of the *Rite of Spring*, with dinosaurs in it; then, there is an image of a line of monsters seen from the side, walking behind a wall of trees in the depth of a forest. The feeling of the shot is not far from some moments from the *Ave Maria* in *Fantasia*, with the pilgrims in religious procession seen through the thin and tall trees designed by Kay Nielsen. Finally, the giant statue that rises over the skyscrapers feels not so distant from the menacing attitude of Chernabog, as he loomed over the landscape in *Night on Bald Mountain*. A minor reference to the Disney heritage might perhaps be traced back to *Dumbo* (Ben Sharpsteen et al., 1941), and specifically to the sequence set to the song *Pink Elephants on Parade*.[4] There are a few visual similarities between that scene and the *Boléro*: in *Dumbo*, the elephants are continuously morphing into weird creatures, and instead of originating from Coca-Cola, they are hallucinations born from the bubbles (and the alcohol) in the champagne inadvertently mixed with the water drunk by Dumbo.

Notwithstanding being the flagship segment of the film, comparable to what *The Sorcerer's Apprentice* is for *Fantasia*, the *Boléro* is the episode that detours the most from the music-image dynamics established by Bozzetto, who prescribed that the music should have stayed unaltered while the animation had to follow it. In fact, the *Boléro* makes a conspicuous use of sound effects at its beginning and at the ending, when no music plays; Ravel's score itself is not used in full, but fades in when it has already started (at the end of the second iteration of the second theme, when the theme is played by the E flat clarinet). A further alteration of the music recording is of a very peculiar kind: the sound gets muffled when the procession of beasts stomps on some unstable ground and falls down a deep ravine. The sound only gets clear again once the animals exit from the cave. This stands out as a remarkable exception in the audiovisual aesthetics of *Allegro non troppo*. In fact, apart from contravening to the general rule about not touching the original music, the sound quality manipulation also situates the music itself within the universe of the animated story, and not outside it, as it is implied by the live-action frame, from which the spectator learns that the music is being played by an orchestra and the animation is just being added to it by an artist. The "muffling," instead, seems to imply that the music happens

---

[4] I am grateful to one of my students, Stefano Santini, for coming up first with this observation.

in the same place of the fallen creatures, which is to say that it becomes diegetic: the sound momentarily cannot escape from the underground world, just like the animals. While in contrast with the rest of the music strategy in *Allegro non troppo*, this particular touch in the soundtrack is anyway clearly staged so that its meaning gets easily through to the audience.[5] It might be argued that this is the only place of *Allegro non troppo* that faintly recalls the Fantasound effects in *Fantasia*. The film by Bozzetto used a mono sound mix, so it had no chance to replicate the spectacular stereophonic spatialization that Disney, Stokowski, and their sound engineers concocted. However, the muffling has indeed a spatial significance; it tells the spectators about the aural quality of the place where the action is taking place. The audiovisual meaning comes here close to the music motivation that Audissino calls realistic, in that it conveys a "believable" sound event in relation to the situation depicted on screen; at the same time, a spatial perceptual function gets also activated there, because of the aforementioned link between the sound quality and the change of location of the action.

This kind of manipulation is anyway much less invasive than the ones used in *Fantasia*. In respect to the use of sound effects, they seem intended to heighten the dramatic impact of the beginning and finale, as to single out those moments. The fade-in is in fact much more suggestive of the slow appearance of life than a clear-cut entrance of the music would have been. More importantly, though, the opening and the ending coincide with the absence of wildlife as opposed to the devastating impact of mankind on the environment. By this choice, Bozzetto creates a consistent parallel between music and natural, free evolution, while silence and sound effects (synthetic ones, on top of that) are synonymous with extinction and pollution.

In this regard, the *Boléro* is a concentrate of all the themes and narrative strategies Bozzetto has cared about during the whole of his career: it elaborates on his pessimistic view of the relationship between mankind and nature, while playing with a "evolutionary" storyline[6] that however negates any educational or scientific value by showing plainly impossible events and creatures; its story gets told by means of a series of variations on a visual model, which in this case is a relentless march from left to right. The metaphors of the evolution as a march (or a relay race) and of the depiction of all the stages of evolution into a proportional artistic rendition (that inevitably makes mankind pop up at the very last minute) come from Bozzetto's beloved books of popular science (see Part One, Chapter 3).

---

[5]It was interpreted in a diegetic sense also by Valerio Sbravatti, *Allegro non troppo. Vedere la musica e ascoltare i disegni* (Roma: Il glifo, 2015), 48.

[6]In this case Bozzetto is not using the structure or enunciation mode of a popular science documentary, so the *Boléro* cannot be called a mockumentary, as it was instead the case of *Tapum!*. The model here is in fact *The Rite of Spring* from *Fantasia*, and not a documentary.

The variation-based narrative strategy that Bozzetto instated since his first short film, *Tapum! The History of Weapons*, is in good accordance with the formal structure of the *Boléro* score, which is a series of variations on the orchestration of just two thematic ideas, with no development whatsoever. The fact that such variations are incremental, in the sense that more instruments join in at each iteration (together with a constant crescendo), made Bozzetto think of an evolutionary growth, from extreme simplicity to complex and larger lifeforms (see Part One, Chapter 3). Actually, Ravel's music originally had a underlying storyline: the irresistible seductiveness of an indifferent and unattainable woman, sitting on a round hotel table among a group of desperate men.[7] As it is evident, it has nothing to do with Bozzetto's interpretation: it was a choreography invented by Bronislava Nijinska (1891–1972) for a performance by dancer Ida Rubinstein (1885–1960) who commissioned to Ravel in 1927 a "ballet of Spanish character."[8] Ravel initially aimed for an orchestral transcription of six piano pieces from the *Iberia* suite by Isaac Albéniz. A few copyright problems, though, had the composer change his plan and go for a more experimental project, which he envisioned as follows: "No form in a strict sense, no development, no or almost no modulation; a theme like a Padilla, rhythm and the orchestra."[9] For the rhythm, Ravel initially thought about a fandango but finally resorted to a bolero. The *Boléro* ballet was first performed on November 22, 1928, at the Paris Opera; the score was later adapted for symphonic concerts with no choreographic action.

It was not the first time that repetition rather than development was the foundation of the variation principle inherent to a musical piece. Ravel himself, before the *Boléro*, had already introduced repetitive rhythmic patterns in his *Habanera* (1895), in the bacchanal finale of the opera *Daphnis et Chloé* (1909–12) and in *La Valse* (1920). Iterative structures were actually common in ancient music: several compositional techniques used ostinato formulas as a scaffolding for the musical discourse (e.g., the isorhythm of French music from the thirteenth and fourteenth centuries or the dance models like the passamezzo, the folia, the romanesca, and many others). The music of late eighteenth and nineteenth centuries had largely superseded those procedures, preferring a musical syntax based on development rather than on repetition. The *Boléro*, however, was audacious in making repetition not only a scaffolding but also a pervasive feature of the whole symphonic composition: the alluring obsessiveness it achieved

---

[7]Willi Reich, "In Memoriam Maurice Ravel," *La Revue Musicale* 19, no. 187 (December 1938): 275.
[8]"Ballet de caractère espagnol." Quoted in Marcel Marnat, *Ravel* (Paris: Fayard, 1986), 627.
[9]"Pas de forme proprement dite, pas de développement, pas ou presque pas de modulation; un thème genre Padilla, du rythme et de l'orchestre." Quoted in Joaquín Nin, "Comment est né le Boléro de Ravel," *La Revue Musicale* 19, no. 187 (December 1938): 213.

was unprecedented in this repertoire. A few commentators[10] wondered if this quality of the *Boléro* could be an omen of the mental illness that would have impaired Ravel in his final years. Reportedly, a woman in the audience shouted, "You are crazy!"[11] to Ravel, during one of the first performances of the *Boléro*; the composer, later informed of this by his brother, nonchalantly commented, "That one, she figured it out."[12] In fact, after a few more works (the orchestration of the *Menuet antique*, 1929; the two *Piano concertos*, 1930–1; the three songs of the cycle *Don Quichotte à Dulcinée*, 1933), the composer found himself unable to create music. His writing and speaking abilities became heavily compromised by an unknown cerebral condition; he died in 1937, after an unsuccessful brain surgery.

The core materials that generate the structure of the *Boléro* amounts to just five elements: a first theme (a), a second theme (b), a rhythmic refrain (c), an eight-bar modulation (d) to E major (the rest of the composition stays in C major), and a very short conclusion (e). The modulation "d" spectacularly appears just before the finale, and it was the element that Bozzetto saw as an equivalent to the sudden appearance of mankind at the end of evolution (see Part One, Chapter 3). The "a" and "b" themes are composed of two musical phrases each. The *Boléro* arranges such themes in a nineteen-part structure (in the score, the first part is not numbered; so, there is an implied part 0 at the beginning, and the last one is part 18); one part usually starts with the presentation of the rhythmic refrain, followed by one of the themes: "ca" or "cb." In most cases (parts 0–16) the same theme appears in two adjacent parts ("ca-ca"; "cb-cb"; "ca-ca" ...); so, each theme is played twice alternately. Part 17, however, introduces a "cb" structure instead of an expected "ca"; after it, part 18 starts with the modulation ("d"), which is actually a mutation of "b," and continues with two repetitions of "c" and the conclusion "e": a dissonant chord and a descending scale. It must be noted that the rhythmic refrain "c" is not just an introductive feature to the "a" and "b" themes; instead, it steadily supports the whole piece, without any interruption until the last two bars. During "a" or "b" it just continues as an accompaniment. It is introduced and perpetuated by the snare drum, together with a very simple bass line (featuring only the notes C and G, the tonic, and dominant of C major), which marks the three beats of the ¾ time signature.

The perpetual rhythm that propels the *Boléro* is the most prominent musical feature that Bozzetto translated into an audiovisual function: a *temporal perceptive* one. Bozzetto's *Boléro* is first of all a matter of

---

[10] As André Suarès, "Ravel. Esquisse," *La Revue Musicale* 19, no. 187 (December 1938): 48–52.
[11] "Au fou." Quoted in Serge Gut, "Le phénomène répétitif chez Maurice Ravel. De l'obsession à l'annihilation incantatoire," *International Review of the Aesthetics and Sociology of Music* 21, no. 1 (June 1990): 44.
[12] "Celle-là, elle a compris." Gut, "Le phénomène répétitif chez Maurice Ravel," 44.

mickey-mousing. The bizarre creatures that march toward extinction always walk with a cadenced pace, in perfect synchrony with the notes in the bass line of the "c" rhythmic pattern: one-two-three, one-two-three. The animation is however far from being pedantic. Even though the beat is always kept on screen by some action, the movements are rendered in many different fashions: Valentini's monsters do not just walk, they pulsate, extend, roll, and mutate. In a way, the principle of variation is applied at several levels at once, becoming pervasive: not only the whole *Boléro* sequence is about a gradual evolution, but the creatures themselves are singularly transforming and offering multiple animation chances within the same shot, giving way to a feverish display of creativity. The initial visual theme (the bubbly soft drink) is brought to the extreme: each single creature is constantly boiling up so that the herd of monsters, from a distance, feels like an ever-changing evolutionary hotpot.

The music–image synchronizations are not limited to the movements of the characters. As in other episodes of *Allegro non troppo*, Bozzetto opts also for an audiovisual accentuation of his dynamic camerawork. Over the years, the director has consolidated a preference for whip pans and fast zoom-ins or zoom-outs. This might be a consequence of his early stylistic approach to animated drawing, which used flat designs with limited animation and long, fixed-camera takes on an unchanging background; *I due castelli* is a preeminent example of this. In that short, the scarce camerawork invites the eye of the spectator to turn toward the relevant action in the shot, alternatively to the left and to the right (see Part One, Chapter 1). In Bozzetto's later work, it is as if the eye movements implied in the earlier animations were ultimately embedded into the camerawork, which took a distinctive darting quality. In the *Boléro*, the "darting" of Bozzetto's camera is finely synchronized with the rhythmic accompaniment, making it even more evident and spectacular. The camerawork, anyway, has also a more macroscopic connection with the narrative of the *Boléro*: after the Coca-Cola "amoeba" has learnt how to move, the camera starts following it from left to right (Figure 5). This slow panning is a stylistic constant in the camerawork of the *Boléro* and responsible for the extraordinary width of some of the background artworks. Bozzetto conceived this camera movement as a visual equivalent to the concept of "evolution":[13] a steady, monodirectional shift that follows the rhythmic procession of bizarre creatures.

As in the *Prélude à l'après-midi d'un faune*, there is however also a close correspondence between the structure of the music and that of the story. Each one of the nineteen parts of the *Boléro* is translated into a relatively independent set of events in Bozzetto's short; it is possible to verify this in the above description of the episode, where each paragraph was arranged to

---

[13]Personal communication to the author via Skype, January 20, 2019.

FIGURE 5 *The march of evolution goes always from left to right, in the* Boléro *from* Allegro non troppo. *The layout and the camera movements relentlessly remark this, so as to reinforce a feeling of unstoppable growth that goes well with the obsessive crescendo of Ravel's music. The growth will be actually stopped by the last-minute advent of mankind (and by a modulation to E major in a music that obstinately stayed in C major up to that point). The image is a combination between a production cel and background that however come from two different shots of the* Boléro.

coincide with a part of Ravel's piece. As it is evident, the narrative content of the single paragraphs is fairly self-conclusive, but all the same contributing to the whole "evolutionary" thread. The articulations between the sections happen when the "c" rhythmic refrain is heard: to mark those separations and enhance the dramatic potential of that musical idea, Bozzetto consistently made plot twists happen in those moments. The rhythmic refrain is both the engine of Ravel's *Boléro* and of Bozzetto's evolutionary fantasy. In the film, the path of life waits for that musical item to take decisive turns. When the refrain plays, creatures get eaten (like the winged one that ends up into a sort of carnivorous plant) or tumble down a waterfall, or the ground suddenly collapses. The random quality of those dramatic developments suggests that Bozzetto developed his idea of evolution in close accordance with Charles Darwin's theory. The director's intention to reference the renowned British biologist was clearly signaled by the expression "struggle for existence" in the notes he took while reviewing the *Fantasia* episode, which is kindred to the *Boléro*, the *Rite of Spring* (see Part One, Chapter 3). In Darwin's book *The Origin of Species*, the chapter about that topic posits that "there must in every case be a struggle for existence, either one individual with another of the same species, or with the individuals of distinct species, or with the physical conditions of life."¹⁴ The winners of this struggle are usually the fittest to survive; however, commentators of Darwin noticed how also sheer chance plays a great role in this evolutionary model. For example, Grant Ramsey and Charles H. Pence observed that "Darwin uses the term *chance* sixty-seven times in the *Origin,* and most of these instances are in the context of either the origin of variation ... or survival and reproduction. ... And in some places Darwin seems to endow chance with causal powers of its own."¹⁵ So, Bozzetto seems to have used his knowledge of Darwin to visualize a metaphor of evolution dominated by struggle and chance. Also the idea of variation itself might come from *The Origin of Species*: in fact, the "Struggle for existence" chapter of the book is the one that also defines for the first time what the natural selection is, and establishes it as a principle "by which each slight variation, if useful, is preserved."¹⁶

Mankind, in the *Boléro*, is instead presented as a disturbance in the order of nature. The big apes, latecomers to the march of life, do not accept the catastrophes thrown by chance at the other creatures. They take shortcuts by stealing and killing, taking for themselves at once what the animals painstakingly conquered by going through eons of merciless evolution: protective shells, warm fur, safe shelter. Bozzetto's negative opinion on the human–nature relationship is based on a strong belief in the innocence of plants and animals—a position that might be seen as close to some philosophers of the Enlightenment, like David Hume (1771–6). In the *Boléro*, some animals are depicted while eating others; however, there is no character presented as markedly evil or good. The ones that feed on other animals seemingly do so out of instinct and necessity. As Hume once argued, if there is a deed that would be considered criminal among men, "the very same action, and the same relations in animals have not the smallest moral turpitude and deformity,"¹⁷ as there is no reasoning behind them, but just a natural behavior. On the other hand, the ape that foreshadows mankind is drawn with an evil grimace since its debut on-screen; its actions always exude malice, as they are staged to show a causal and opportunistic reasoning (in a freezing cold weather the ape kills an animal to wear its fur, for example).

---

[14] Charles Darwin, *The Origin of Species* (London: Wordsworth, 1998), 50–1.
[15] Grant Ramsey and Charles H. Pence, "Chance in Evolution from Darwin to Contemporary Biology," in *Chance in Evolution*, ed. Pence Ramsey (Chicago, IL: University of Chicago Press, 2016), 1.
[16] Darwin, *Origin of Species*, 49.
[17] David Hume, *Treatise Concerning Human Nature*, ed. Lewis Amherst Selby-Bigge (Oxford: Oxford University Press, 1888), 467.

Technology is the embodiment and the vehicle of mankind's egoistic plots, from the club to the buildings that invade the environment. Interestingly, this concept is not far from the take on man and technology expressed in the work of another major filmmaker: in the first part of *2001: A Space Odyssey* (1968), Stanley Kubrick had already suggested, with a memorable editing that paired a bone thrown in the air with a spaceship, that every technology is a distant relative of the first human tool, the club, that was used for killing. The ultimate outcome of the human/nature technological disparity, according to Bozzetto, is the end of evolution and the extinction of animals. In the short film, as already pointed out, Ravel's music stops when a modern metropolis appears, with a giant statue of a malevolent man overlooking it. The use of sound effects, as distant thunder or the cracking of the mask of the statue, creates a stark contrast with the lush aural quality of the symphonic piece by Ravel; in a similar way, the color palette becomes monochromatic and desaturated, as opposed to the quirky and luxuriant chromatic richness seen in the marching monsters, to communicate desolation and lifelessness. The idea that evolution has stopped altogether because of mankind is today debated;[18] when *Allegro non troppo* was made, it definitely circulated in scientific literature, but it was already questioned. For example, in 1969 the scholar Victor Ferkiss wrote that a harmonious technological development was hindered by the widespread assumption that "at a certain point in the distant past man became man and evolution stopped."[19] In fact, at a closer look, Bozzetto's *Boléro* is not entirely negative on the role of mankind. As noticed before, the structure of the short film is circular: there is no music at the beginning and at the end, and mankind is indirectly present even in the first sequence, with the spaceship and the Coca-Cola bottle. Bozzetto voluntarily left no explanations about the location where the *Boléro* is set. Is it the ancient Earth, which is being visited by aliens? But in that case, how come they drink Coca-Cola? And why are the prehistoric animals so different from those seen in textbooks? Are we on a distant planet that is being visited by humans, maybe? Bozzetto says[20] that no one has a final answer to those questions. By this reticence, the author is possibly implying that evolution, after all, notwithstanding his monodirectional left-to-right camerawork, is a cyclic process, and that chance (the propeller of evolution) could turn even the most damaging actions on the environment (littering an empty bottle) into a rebirth of life. This does not actually present mankind under a positive light; however, it instates the optimistic hope that nature might be stronger than technology and relentlessly take back what was stolen from it.

---

[18]See, e.g., Richard C. Francis, *Domesticated: Evolution in a Man-Made World* (New York: W.W. Norton, 2015).

[19]Victor C. Ferkiss, *Technological Man: The Myth and the Reality* (New York: Braziller, 1969), 19.

[20]Personal communication to the author via Skype, January 20, 2019.

8

Valse triste Op. 44 No. 1

Description

The smoke from the cigar of the conductor transitions into the landscape imagined by the animator, who keeps coughing for a few instants, while the music starts. Among the mist, a bird's-eye view of a city emerges. It is a grey expanse of squarely arranged blocks of flats, all identical. Among the dull parallelepipeds, however, there is a small free area. A wrecked house seems to be there, faintly glowing in the fog. A series of zoom-ins and cross dissolves reveals that it is a ruined tenement with communal balconies—a kind of popular housing typical of Italian urban areas in the first half of the twentieth century.[1] Only a single wall of the house still stands; the rest has collapsed.

There are broken toys in the inside of the house, as the camera slowly reveals; then, a dramatic shot shows the remaining wall from a low angle.

Two eyes peek from inside what once a fireplace was. They belong to a thin tabby cat. He stretches and licks his fur, then he starts looking around.

He wanders around the ruins. He jumps on a cornice, and he almost falls, but he is quick to regain his balance. Suddenly, he turns his head; his big eyes reflect something green. On a previously empty wall, a ghostly vision of a cage with a canary appears. It is not an animated drawing but a colored live-action picture, just like all the ghosts he will see in the remainder of the short film. The cat joyfully attempts to reach for the bird, but the image soon vanishes, leaving him alone and sad.

However, it happens again. The reflection in his eyes is now magenta; he sees a man on a rocking chair in mid-air, near to the wall. The cat is about

---

[1] It was Nichetti who suggested to Bozzetto this kind of old-style Italian house; Bozzetto in the documentary "Ricordando *Allegro non troppo*," in the *Allegro non troppo* DVD, part of the DVD collection "Tutto Bozzetto (o quasi)" (Roma: Multimedia San Paolo, 2005).

to approach him, but he sees a dog near to the chair. He reacts by ruffling his hair and running away to hide behind a corner. When he looks again, the ghosts fade away.

The visions are not over, though. Now looking toward the camera, the cat sports purple reflections in his eyes. A reverse shot shows that from the wrecked wall a whole room literally "pops up"; the furniture gradually takes its pristine colors. The cat goes to rub against the leg of a table. Next, a kitchen appears, in the same fashion of the previous room. The cat runs to three milk bottles, then he gets distracted by something off-screen: an open oven. He jumps over it and tries to peek inside.

Other rooms sprout from the wall. One by one, like jigsaw pieces, they fill up all the empty spaces in the house remains. What finally appears is a colorful section view of the three-story place, with six rooms full of life. The cat jumps on an armchair and curls up, but soon everything disappears again; the animal is left in mid-air. He barely makes it to the wall nearby, casting a worried glance to the vertiginous height below him.

After licking his fur, he sadly strolls around again. New ghosts come forward; announced by a reflection in shifting color in his eyes, a woman ironing clothes appears. She does not stay much though, to the cat's dismay. However, a few instants after, the cat sees the rooms popping up again. Each one of them gets populated by colorful spirits: two girls playing with toy boats near the bathtub, a man sitting on the armchair, a group of friends playing cards at a round table, a woman cooking in the kitchen.

The rest of the house appears; it is no more a section view. A threefold axial cut on the happy face of the cat introduces a montage of the merry activities now making the house a joyful and warm place. The woman keeps cooking and then serves something to the cat on a plate; the sudden arrival of a child on a tricycle gives the animal a fleeting start. Another triple axial cut, synchronized with the music, shows the girls with the toy boats; they sprinkle some water on the delighted cat. At an increasing pace, we see the guys playing cards, two children laughing together, and a girl who blows soap bubbles that the cat bursts with his paws. A happy couple spins around hugging, while the image of two hands clinking glasses during a toast superimposes over them. A birthday cake full of burning candles appears on a table, and the cat licks his lips in anticipation. But the candles get put out and the cake dissolves into thin air. Everything does the same: the children, the toasting hands, the cooking woman, the girl blowing bubbles, the friends. Only the table and the cards remain; while the light changes and colors fade away, they start to swirl around, spinning into a dark void.

The house is now just a wrecked wall and a bunch of ruins. The sad cat makes a few steps more, but then he vanishes, too: he was a ghost of times past as well.

The music ends. The wall is again shown from a low, ominous angle. With a clattering sound, a crane with a wrecking ball approaches. The ball is thrown at the wall by the machine: the action freezes one instant before the demolition; however, the roar from the collapsing building is heard.

Program Notes

The *Valse triste* is the *Allegro non troppo* episode that differs the most from the rest of the film. The contrast is chiefly provided by its mood. While it seconds the pattern of contrasting pairs that appears throughout the six musical shorts, being the low-key emotional counterpart to the flamboyant *Boléro* (and also complementary to it in its audiovisual functions, as the temporal perceptive function that dominated the *Boléro* is here scarcely present and substituted at large by the emotive function, relying on the musical atmosphere and not on the rhythmic synchronization), the *Valse triste* is the only short in the whole work that features no comedy whatsoever. After all, this is a "sad waltz," as the title literally says; so, Bozzetto wanted to stay as true as possible to that indication, even by restraining his co-screenwriter, Guido Manuli, who wanted to add in some of his typical absurdist gags. In fact, the episode is the one that most closely follows the narrative content of its source, maybe just on par with the *Prélude à l'après-midi d'un faune*, in this respect.

On several occasions,[2] Bozzetto reported that he was aware of the story that Jean Sibelius had in mind, when devising his short film. His recollections of that story, though, have always focused on a scene that is not in the original sources: a man "goes up to the attic and finds a trunk containing his dead wife's clothes, that come out of it and start to dance on their own."[3] Bozzetto might have based this image on a detail of the program notes that Rosa Newmarch, an English poet and music writer who was also a longtime correspondent of Sibelius, wrote for a 1904 edition of the *Valse triste* piano reduction: the mention of the long white garment of a bedridden woman that transforms into a ball dress in a dream vision.

> It is night. The son, who has been watching beside the bedside of his sick mother, has fallen asleep from sheer weariness. Gradually a ruddy light is diffused through the room; there is a sound of distant music; the glow and the music steal nearer until the strains of a valse melody float distantly to our ears. The sleeping mother awakens, rises from her bed and, in her long white garment, which takes the semblance of a ball dress, begins to

---

[2]For example in Valerio Sbravatti, *Allegro non troppo. Vedere la musica e ascoltare i disegni* (Roma: Il glifo, 2015), 100.
[3]"Lui sale in soffitta, trova un baule in cui ci sono i vestiti della moglie defunta che escono e ballano." Bozzetto in Sbravatti, *Allegro non troppo*, 101.

move silently and slowly to and fro. She waves her hands and beckons in time to the music, as though she were summoning a crowd of invisible guests. And now they appear, these strange visionary couples, turning and gliding to an unearthly valse rhythm. The dying woman mingles with the dancers; she strives to make them look into her eyes, but the shadowy guests one and all avoid her glance. Then she seems to sink exhausted on her bed and the music breaks off. Presently she gathers all her strength and invokes the dance once more, with more energetic gestures than before. Back come the shadowy dancers, gyrating in a wild, mad rhythm. The weird gaiety reaches a climax; there is a knock at the door, which flies wide open; the mother utters a despairing cry; the spectral guests vanish; the music dies away. Death stands on the threshold.[4]

There is anyway something else that Bozzetto took from this plot, and that ended up in the short film: ghosts from distant and happy memories. The director acknowledged that "this kind of music tells about something that awakens from the past and dances, and it is fascinating, as well as sad, but engaging."[5] In fact, Sibelius destined the *Valse triste* to be part of the incidental music he wrote in 1903 to the drama *Kuolema* (death), by his brother-in-law Arvid Järnefelt, a tragic story about Paavali, a young man who sees his mother die, gets married, and has a child, but ultimately perishes in the fire that destroys his house, while seeing ghosts from the past. The scene detailed by Newmarch pertains to the first of the three acts of the play. The presence of a ruined house in Bozzetto's film, just like in the third act of Järnefelt's play, might be coincidental. The setting of the short comes in fact from a second source that Bozzetto used for his story: memories of his own family.

Bozzetto mixed the backstory of Sibelius's *Valse triste* with the true story of his wife's cat, who returned to the ruins of the house where he used to live before the place was demolished to make room for a new building. He opted for this autobiographical touch to be more connected with the sadness he wanted to express, but also because it allowed him to have an animal character, and not a human one, which in his opinion would have posed much more acting problems.[6] The animated performance of the cat was entrusted to Giovanni Ferrari, who worked on a design by Giorgio Valentini. Ferrari kept the anthropomorphic behavior of the animal to a minimum; notwithstanding its loose resemblance to some cartoon cats from the Disney features of the 1960s, he has a very moderate facial expressivity.

---

[4]Rosa Newmarch, frontispiece notes to *Valse triste. From the Music to Arvid Järnefelt's Drama "Kuolema." By Jean Sibelius. From Op. 44. Arranged for Pianoforte Solo* (New York: Schirmer, 1904).
[5]"Questo tipo di musica racconta di qualcosa che si sveglia dal passato e balla, ed è affascinante nonché triste, ma coinvolgente." Bozzetto in Sbravatti, *Allegro non troppo*, 101.
[6]Ibid.

FIGURE 6 *The tabby cat from the* Valse triste *sequence in* Allegro non troppo *was designed by Giorgio Valentini and animated by Giovanni Ferrari. While the big eyes are clearly exaggerated (and they make for a very important visual and narrative device, as the ghostly apparitions are usually announced as reflections inside them), Ferrari animated the cat in a realistic way, on the basis of memories from his own pet.*

The exaggeratedly big, deep eyes alone convey a feeling of loss, while being also a reflective element, used in many instances to create visual tension by showing in them the colored light coming from the ghosts, before those appear on screen. Apart from the face, the cat is otherwise animated in a realistic way: the elasticity and subtleness of his movements, while being in accordance with the furtiveness of many passages in Sibelius's score, are the result of Ferrari's familiarity with his own pet (Figure 6). He did not use him as a life model, though, nor he used reference footage; he based his animation on memory and experience only.[7]

Some live-action footage, however, participated in the making of the *Valse triste*. The wrecked house where the cat dwells, as well as all the ghosts, is based on photographic references: the house was drawn and painted after some pictures Bozzetto found in the outskirts of Milan, while the ghosts are the director's friends, his four children, his wife, and himself, who appears on a rocking chair near to a dog. Such elements were supposed to invite the

---

[7]Bozzetto in a personal communication to the author via Skype, March 14, 2019.

spectator to feel a stronger empathy with the memories of the cat, being more lifelike and making thus the sad story more grounded in reality.[8] At the same time, it could be said that the photographic elements reinforce the unbridgeable gap between the present and the past. The sentiment of loss is the key theme of Bozzetto's *Valse triste*, and it gets tangibly paralleled by the aesthetic divide existing between animated drawings and live-action footage: they can coexist on screen, but their pertinence to separate visual domains cannot be hidden. Actually, the "ghosts" also get manipulated with visual effects that brightly tinge them with monochromatic hues. This makes them more "otherworldly," but at the same time it creates a positive contrast with the bleak palette of the wrecked house. The house itself gets revamped in vivacious colors as it is seen "sprouting" its old rooms back in place. The distance between a joyous past and the mournful emptiness of the present gets thus reinstated also with the color dynamics throughout the short film.

As in the previous episodes of *Allegro non troppo*, the narrative structure of the *Valse triste* directly translates the formal scheme of the music. The piece by Sibelius alternates between a brooding idea, mostly played in the low register, that does not concede anything to melody except a short, noble cadence at the end of each phrase. It is contrasted with a much more spirited episode, faster in its tempo and dominated by the high pitch of violin, with a rapturous melodic attitude. This second episode is alternated twice to the first one: in the film, it plays when the visions overwhelm the cat and the house returns back to its ancient appearance. This emotional alternance makes the music an agent of an emotive function, which works both at a macro level (the whole "sadness" Bozzetto aimed for) and a micro one, that operates within the single sequences. Basically, the doleful mood of the first idea of the Valse is the emotional confirmation of the melancholy of the cat in the present, while the second idea goes well with the satisfactory happiness of the colorful memories. The synchronies that create temporal perceptual functions are decidedly less important; there are several of them that almost go unnoticed. They are implicit, just like in the *Prélude à l'après-midi d'un faune*. The movements often are perfectly choreographed to the single notes of some passages, but the lack of strong accents and distinct musical timbres makes this accuracy almost inconspicuous; it anyway serves its purpose, which is to create a rhythmic tie-in between the timing of the animation and that of the music that has an organizational meaning (to elegantly fit the action within the phrasing of the music) more than a spectacular one.

There are, however, some moment where the spectator can perceive a functional link between single sounds and actions. The temporal perceptual function becomes evident when the cat starts strolling through the ruins for the first time: the music plays staccato, and as such with short, well-isolable

---

[8] Bozzetto in a personal communication to the author via Skype, March 14, 2019.

notes. The movement of the cat's leg is in visible synchrony with the staccato. Another instance, instead, reiterates Bozzetto's taste for making an expressive use of his camerawork: during the "happy" sections of the music, a rapidly flowing phrase gets introduced by three bold chords that are played rubato, which is to say by "holding back" the tempo for better emphasis and contrast with the fast passage that ensues. This happens twice; in both instances, the three chords are synched with a triple axial cut, the first one on the happy face of the cat, the second one on the "ghosts" of the little girls playing with her toy boats.

The *Valse triste* is thus the place of *Allegro non troppo* that mostly fuels its audiovisual strategy with the emotional link between images and music. The taming down of evident synchronies is a sensible choice, which implicitly acknowledges the long-standing connection that the cartoon practice has established between comedy and temporal perceptual functions, since the first Mickey Mouse cartoons.[9] The audience is accustomed to laugh at mickey-mousing: a wider use of that in a melancholic animated short could have elicited wrong emotive responses, hindering thus the pathos that the story intended to convey.

---

[9]Daniel Goldmark, *Tunes for 'Toons: Music and the Hollywood Cartoon* (Berkeley: University of California Press, 2005), 6.

9

Concerto in C Major RV 559

Description

The music begins. A red stage curtain opens on an idyllic summer landscape in the countryside. The slow panoramic shot transitions to the same landscape in autumn, with a curtain-shaped wipe effect. The same happens with a transition to winter, when all the leaves have fallen from the trees. Snow starts to fall and covers everything with white. Three transitions show different stages of the snow melting down; a new curtain wipe marks the arrival of the spring. Flowers appear on the tree branches; grass grows on the ground, stretching out in synch with the music chords in the slow introduction (Larghetto) of the first movement of Vivaldi's *Concerto*. One after one, all the trees get in full bloom at once. The flowers and their vivid colors appear on the ground. A swift zoom-in focuses on the flower that was the last to appear.

The Allegro section of the movement starts. From the foliage of a flower a funny bee-housewife comes, with a big nose and an apron. With an efficient and content air, she swiftly cleans everything in her reach with a little handheld duster. She takes her apron off and rests it on a petal of a big daisy; she extracts some cutlery from it and, after cleaning that as well, she rests it on another petal. Then she also extracts two glasses; she is actually setting the flower as a table.

A whip pan to the left reveals a car rapidly approaching. It parks on the grass; from a low angle the camera foregrounds a tire and a leg of a man coming out of the vehicle and stepping on a flower.

The bee keeps on with her preparation. She flits about and brings a stool to the flower, while continuing with her unstoppable dusting.

A man and a woman playfully run on the grass; we just see their legs. The man is pulling the arm of the woman, inviting her to come with him; she removes her shoes while the man impatiently taps his foot on the ground.

The bee prepares her meal. She grinds, shakes, grates, and slices: her side dish is now ready on a plate. She flutters toward the flower and decks it; she is not content with her first arrangement, though, so she changes it fast. Then, she goes to retrieve a small TV that she rests opposite to her sitting place at the "table." She dusts some more, and then she puts some seasoning on the yellow seeds of the flower. She licks her lips in anticipation; the seeds seem to release some kind of aroma.

However, a shadow appears over her. A black handkerchief covers the bee and the flower, soon followed by a foulard. The bee emerges from underneath, with a huffy countenance. She pulls the fabric away to reveal that her flower has gotten completely disarranged. She is angry, but then she gets a sudden scare; she sees that the man letting himself falling seated to the ground nearby. Everything gets shaken.

The bee puts on glasses and disconcertedly looks at the woman getting seated on the ground as well. The two humans rest their hands on the grass, side by side. The man moves his fingers in a walking motion toward the hand of the woman. He touches her; they hold hand under the horrified gaze of the bee. They get closer and embrace each other. Their shadows gradually fall over the bee and cover the sun. In the dark, the insect has to fetch an abat-jour and light it near the table, to be able to see again. She rearranges the table, checks a glass, and cleans it with a rag. She is ready to have lunch again; she prepares the cutlery and casts a worried glance to the humans. Everything seems quiet, though, so she takes a forkful of seeds from the flower. However, she cannot bring it to her mouth.

The humans, whose face profiles are now visible, exchange a kiss on the lips. They hug and lie down, right on the bee who barely manages to collect all her things and scramble to safety. Quite upset, she fixes her "hair" and sets a new flower up like a table. She puts some oil on the seed to season them and smugly grins toward the humans. However, in horror, she sees that they are now rolling on the grass toward her while embracing. She desperately picks up her things again, but she has to throw them away, as they are coming too fast. The human beings finally end up on top of her.

The music ends and the sound of bird singing fades in. The two lovers are now laying on the ground. But the peace gets violently broken: the man tenses up and jumps in the air, giving out a loud shout. The bee has stung him. The shout is still going on when the film cuts to the conductor from the live-action interstitial, who has just gotten stung by the same bee.

Program Notes

In popular culture, Antonio Vivaldi is synonym with *Le Quattro Stagioni* (*The Four Seasons*), the first four concertos for violin, solo strings, and basso continuo from the series of twelve *Il Cimento dell'Armonia e dell'Inventione*

(*The Contest between Harmony and Invention*, 1723–5). They are among the best-known pieces from the "classical" repertoire; their presence in the contemporary musical landscape is so pervasive that they have even reached the unflattering status of "an ever-present piece of muzak,"[1] as the composer Max Richter puts it. In the twentieth century, the reputation of Vivaldi's musical originality declined also because of an oft-quoted joke attributed to Luigi Dallapiccola (1904–1975) and Igor Stravinsky, according to which the only thing Vivaldi had ever accomplished was to write four hundred times the same concerto. However, it seems that neither Dallapiccola nor Stravinsky ever said that; the only documented remark that comes close to it appears in the book by Robert Craft, *Conversations with Igor Stravinsky*: "Vivaldi is greatly overrated—a dull fellow who could compose the same form so many times over."[2] Such opinions are not shared by the most recent scholarship on the author, which holds Vivaldi as one of the most creative authors who voiced the musical idiom of the late Italian Baroque: as the musicologist Bella Brover-Lubovsky wrote in 2008, for example, "Vivaldi regularly displays stunning imagination in creating shades of dramatic feeling through a masterful exploitation of major and minor keys within a single work."[3]

Bozzetto's interpretation of the first movement from the *Concerto in C Major RV 559* seems to acknowledge the common parlance on Vivaldi and his music, even though in a matter-of-fact way, far from being derisory. The point is made by using a "four seasons" visual theme on a concerto that is not part of those staples of Vivaldi's repertoire; this basically implies that Vivaldi cannot be separated from *The Four Seasons*, and that any music of his could stand in for those famous concertos. To be honest, a recurring motif from the *Allegro* section of the concerto movement picked by Bozzetto sounds identical in melody and rhythm to one of the hallmarks of the first movement of *The Spring* from *The Four Seasons*: the motif made up by the notes G-A-G, which insistently wraps up the first thematic idea. The parallel extends even slightly beyond that: in the *Concerto RV 559*, the notes that immediately precede the G-A-G clause are different in pitch from the equivalent ones in *The Spring*, but their harmonic function is identical to those in the other concert. The coincidence was perhaps noticed by Bozzetto, as he ostentatiously set the story on a spring day. The bee's

---

[1] Max Richter in uDiscover Team, "I Fell In Love With The Original Again": Max Richter on Recomposing Vivaldi's Four Seasons," uDiscovermusic, August 31, 2019, https://www.udiscovermusic.com/classical-features/max-richter-recomposed-vivaldi-four-seasons/ (accessed November 28, 2019).
[2] Igor Stravinsky in Robert Craft, *Conversations with Igor Stravinsky* (New York: Doubleday, 1959), 84.
[3] Bella Brover-Lubovsky, *Tonal Space in the Music of Antonio Vivaldi* (Bloomington, Indiana University Press, 2008), 101.

fixation with dusting, moreover, could be intended to convey the idea of "spring cleaning."

While playing with the Vivaldi prejudices by summarizing the seasonal cycle in a series of countryside views from summer to spring, Bozzetto simultaneously treats the audience with one of the rare *Allegro non troppo* explicit visual references to *Fantasia* (the other ones appear in the *Boléro*; see Part Two, Chapter 7). The short film begins with the view of a proscenium; its curtain then opens on an open-air scenery. The outline of the opening curtain becomes a graphic pattern for wipe effects in scene transitions. The *Dance of the Hours* short from *Fantasia* equally used the proscenium and curtain motif to introduce the action, which then continues among architectonic elements that allude to a theatrical stage. In the Disney film, however, the proscenium is not seen in its entirety: the camera frames the rising curtain only, after having traveled through heavy doors and a tall columned hall. Those elements are a likely attempt at substantiating the introduction by Deems Taylor, who concluded his speech by mentioning that the original ballet from the opera *La Gioconda* took place during a party hosted by the duke Alvise Badoero in the hall of a Venetian palace (the Ca' d'Oro); anyway, no resemblance exists between the hall in the *Dance of the Hours* and that of the actual Italian palace. In Bozzetto's case, even though the camera similarly moves toward the curtain, the proscenium is visible (but it depicts no real place, being quite abstract and brightly colored). The *Fantasia* quotation stays here not only in the opening curtain but also in the connective function it has in respect to the content of the live-action interstitials; it is not making an allusion to the narrative setting of the music, like in the case of Taylor's introduction, but it instates a thematic continuity with the main location of *Allegro non troppo*, which is precisely a theater, the Donizetti in Bergamo. Moreover, just before the beginning of the short, the host repeatedly (and awkwardly) calls "curtain!" to mark the beginning of the piece.

Another parallel with *Fantasia* is that soon after the beginning of the short film the theatrical context is dropped altogether; the space expands well beyond the reasonable limits of a stage, in a flight of fantasy that Robin Allan, in his commentary of the *Dance of the Hours*, connected with visual formulas found in American musicals:

> The theatrical setting is emphasized at the beginning, but it quickly becomes apparent that this is too large a stage to be contained within the bounds of a proscenium arch and within an ordinary theatre. Here is a reminder of the Hollywood tradition of the musical number extending beyond the theatre or cabaret setting in which it is placed.[4]

---

[4] Robin Allan, *Walt Disney and Europe* (London: John Libbey, 1999), 151.

The main role in Bozzetto's *Concerto RV 559* is played by a funny anthropomorphized animal; the female bee, however, is much more stylized and caricatural than the ostriches, the elephants, Hyacinth the Hippo, and the alligators in *Fantasia*. Moreover, the bee is not playing the role of a classic dancer (an archetype that has an arguably timeless quality) but that of an Italian housewife from the 1970s. Her movements are choreographed to the music, with an abundance of minute synchronizations that foreground strong temporal perceptual functions. It is a choreography of obsessive efficiency and practicality, though, and not of transcendent artistic passions. The *Dance of the Hours* was ironic also in this respect, as the graceful moves of the ballerinas were ridiculed by their use in the satisfaction of primal feeding needs. In Bozzetto's case, the bee's choreography tells that she contently controls every single detail of her "domestic" domain through a chain of automated actions. Her final goal is to enjoy a meal while watching TV, but only after having achieved absolute cleanliness and organization in her environment. This stereotype of the overefficient housewife is not new to Italian animation. During the economic boom, many female characters from the "Carosello" commercials were positively presented as resourceful and practical housewives or caregivers. This was to suggest that, by using the advertised products, women would have better dealt with the challenges of a household of the 1960s and the 1970s. This conservative and exacting view of the female role was evident, for example, in the Studio K animated "carosellos" for the Ambrosoli honey drops (1965–72, 1976), which starred a mother of many children who always knew how to step in and fix their mischiefs (and was praised by the children with a jingle that saluted her as a "beautiful, sweet, dear mommy").[5] Similarly, the "carosellos" for the Bertolini baking powder (1970, 1974–6) by the Studio Marosi presented a little girl named Mariarosa, who lived in a tidy small house, was a good cook, and was always ready to come help. A small marching band of children celebrated her inevitable success with a "brava, brava, Mariarosa" song.

The twist in Bozzetto's story, the arrival of an unexpected, uncontrollable external force in the form of a gigantic (from the bee's perspective) couple of humans in love, feels like an allegory of the rupture in the falsely safe life models that occurred to the 1970s Italian society (see Part One, Chapter 2). The bee's attempts at regaining control of her environment are all frustrated; she tries to readjust her plans, but she cannot flee the impending menace. It is likely not by chance that the threat comes from two people engaging in a rather innocent leisurely activity that should be supposed to vehicle positive feelings: a young couple enjoying their free time. This couple, though, is barely positive at all. They cast ominous shadows over the idyllic landscape. They seem completely alien to it, also because they are rotoscoped: their

---

[5] "Bella, dolce, cara mammina."

movements, unlikely those of the bee, are traced from a live-action performance by Guido Manuli and a female student from the acting school "QuellidiGrock."[6] They show no respect for the life of plants and animals. They act as if they are entitled to that place. In this, they might embody the sense of entitlement that many Italians developed during the economic boom in respect to leisure time, as it got largely commodified and made into a status symbol (see Part One, Chapter 2). The presence of an extravagant-looking car just reinforces this feeling, as well as the hint at stereotyped social roles in the attitude of the man, who gets ostentatiously impatient at the woman when she decides to take off her shoes. The tale of the bee and the couple might thus be Bozzetto's way to represent how the carefree years of the economic boom took a toll on the Italian social development. The old, crystallized ideals of richness and social order collapse over themselves, unable to coexist anymore; the entertainment of a well-to-do, conventional couple crushes the domestic efficiency. In the end, though, the bee goes apparently out of character, as she abandons the idea of sorting up the domestic chaos, and instead resorts to a weapon she had always had on her body, but that she had never used. The bee stings; the man finally becomes aware of her, and in the most painful way. In the 1970s, the struggle of Italian women for a proactive role in a patriarchal society started to raise awareness and controversies (see Part One, Chapter 2). The final resolution of Bozzetto's bee might be a funny way to represent the shocked reaction of the old mores to the puncture in carefree security imparted by one of the trusted pillars of society, the good housewife.

As already mentioned, the audiovisual workings of the *Concerto RV 559* episode are mostly at the service of temporal perceptual functions that also appear in connection with the fast camera movements inherent to Bozzetto's directing style. This makes the tone of the episode light, and the pacing fast. The usual care for making the editing correspond to the phrasing of the music is present and thoroughly developed. The dynamic attitude of the music–image relationship is also instated by spatial perceptual functions that make here their debut in *Allegro non troppo*. Those are instances where the music reinforces the motion on screen without close synchronies. This happens, for example, when the two lovers roll in the grass down the hill: the music is there playing a descending progression. Finally, there is also an elegant coincidence between the *solo* and *tutti* alternance typical of the Baroque concerto (the soloists and the whole orchestral ensemble take turns, creating a typical "terraced" pattern of symmetrical soft "proposals" and loud "answers"). At first, the soloists are reserved to the small bee, while

---

[6]Bozzetto in in the documentary "Ricordando *Allegro non troppo*," in the *Allegro non troppo* DVD, part of the DVD collection "Tutto Bozzetto (o quasi)" (Roma: Multimedia San Paolo, 2005).

the whole orchestra enters with the towering humans. This *compositional motivation*, which makes the sound of the solos almost a leitmotiv for the bee, is however later abandoned. The solo and tutti get freely associated with the characters, so as to allow a more tightly knitted mickey-mousing that enhances the growing frenzy.

10

The Firebird Suite (1919 Version)

Description

God, a single-eyed triangle, is about to create man. His hands come down from the heavens and, in a blue nothingness, they mold a creature from clay. The first attempt does not go well. The thing comes alive (changing from a greyish blue to fuchsia), but it is just a hand directly connected to a foot by the wrist. It wiggles around a bit, then it extends toward the sky and melts. God's eye widens in dismay. He tends to a new critter; this time, it comes out as a red, stumpy torso with arms and legs pointing in the wrong direction. The third attempt is finally successful: Adam is born first, a yellow, fidgeting clay puppet, and then Eve. They do not just change color when life pervades them, but they become animated cartoons.

Adam and Eve timidly touch each other with one finger. He then takes her hand. From the void that surrounds them, a green little snake pops out. He looks around and soon notices the two humans sitting on the ground. A blue tree appears and grows big yellow apples on its branches. The snake, Adam, and Eve look at it. One apple turns red. The snake grins and smirks at the couple, plotting something. His eye twitches repeatedly; it is a tic he will keep for the rest of the episode.

The reptile furtively tiptoes (by making small jumps) to the tree and picks the shiny red apple with his mouth. He reaches the humans. He first offers the apple to Adam, who refuses it with a smile. At first surprised, the snake malignantly glances at Eve; however, the woman has the same reaction. Astonished and then sadly disappointed, the snake crumples down to the ground while Adam and Eve walk away side by side.

At first intentioned to leave the apple, the snake has a sudden second thought. His eye twitches with malice; he puts the apple to his mouth with his tail and he swallows the fruit. Overcome by sleepiness he curls up, with a final eye twitch before resting his head on his spires.

A fire abruptly explodes. Everything turns red and orange on a black background. A giant, fat demon, with a grinning face and an orange bulbous body, manifests himself. The serpent is terrified; the monster picks him from the ground. He laughs in his face; a second demon, a purple one, arises. Several others follow, all in different colors; some of them tease the snake by showing them the tongue or making grimaces. The orange demon laughs again and then sends the snake flying and twirling around in the dark, until he falls on the ground. The eyes of the demons are around him; three giant devils arise and stretch their right arms forward. The limbs morph into three lines of speeding cars that chase the snake, who grows little legs and runs away. Headlights of live-action car speed away in the background. The line of cartoon cars resembles a long snake that raises its multicolored body like a cobra ready to attack.

The protagonist bumps into the orange demon. Details from real light billboards are visible behind him. The devil opens his mouth and a flight of stairs drops from it. It is an escalator that climbs upward, while the snake runs downward to escape. He holds to something elastic that however snaps. Now seated on one of the steps, the snake has no choice but to go up into the mouth of the demon; the front teeth of the giant stretch to the bottom lip and, like prison bars, they seal the snake inside.

The inner mouth of the demon is covered in TV screens. They show logos, advertisements, and commercials about sex, with real footage of naked women. Two couples of cartoon woman breasts extend from one screen to the dizzy snake, who tries to flee. A tongue-arm protrudes from a cartoon mouth and makes inviting gestures with its hand. Finally, two hands joined together (like those from the ending of the *Prélude à l'après-midi d'un faune*) come forward and then separate, revealing that they belong to a huge, bright pink naked woman. Her open mouth fills the whole screen, until the scene cuts to the round window of a washing machine. The snake is imprisoned inside it while the machine floats away. The window finally opens and ejects the snake together with soap and water.

Live-action lights and billboards keep appearing in the background. From a bunch of large beer cans, two blonde naked girls erupt and then throw themselves into the snake's mouth, turning into yellow liquid.

In the sky, the demons now sit on large toilets; from their bottom comes a shower of house appliances, canned food, TVs, and car pieces. They line up and chase the snake once again. When they reach him, a bright light flashes and then the screen turns black.

All the stuff expelled by the toilets lingers around the snake. It suddenly turns into paper bills and money, and back to objects afterward. The whole scene is taking place into a giant beating heart; the arteries keep pumping goods and money into it.

A small church floats on-screen; the heart comes too, and, like a cornucopia, it pours money through the open roof of the building. The church becomes a monumental building with a dome that opens like a lid to take in more money. The clueless snake is half-submerged in a sea of coins; one of them drops on his head, so he reacts with a scornful eye twitch.

The screen becomes black again. Small candle flames appear one by one. They line up in rows around the snake, while a small casket materializes, plank by plank, around the reptile. The lid falls on him. A rotating beacon light appears in the darkness. The snake peeks from inside the casket. The police signal is on the head of a blue demon, who comes forward with a grinning face. In an attempt to flee, the snake gets his tail stuck in the casket. The devil grabs him and, with needle and thread, sews the animal's mouth shut. The tongue of the monster protrudes in the shape of a gloved hand with a truncheon; it hits the snake on the head multiple times, while the character grows arms to shield himself from the blows. He finally frees himself from the clutches of the demon, but he ends up on a road that moves under his feet like a treadmill; while he runs in place, other gloved hands burst out from other treadmills nearby; they continue to abuse the snake with truncheons, syringes, guns, and rifles, until a cage falls on him. Trapdoors open on the treadmills and let out giant metallic springs. One of them pushes the cage in the air.

A flock of winged demons comes forward. The orange demon is ascending fast; he holds the snake on the palm of his hand. He repeatedly closes and opens his fingers; the snake gets progressively dressed as a middle-class man, with, a suit, a tie, and a hat.

The hand of the demon disappears. The black background breaks in half and reveals Adam and Eve in the pale blue scenery of the beginning. The distraught snake sits in front of them. The music by Stravinsky ends.

The snake looks at his own dress. He has a fit and, in despair, he acts out in mime (while speaking in gibberish) all his misadventures. Adam and Eve calmly look at each other. Finally, the snake removes his clothes (and reabsorbs his limbs). He sticks out his tongue: the apple is on it. He rests the fruit on the ground and scornfully crawls away.

The action continues for a little while over the live-action interstitial: the snake appears in front of the orchestra and the old ladies get scared. They all run away, while the host tries to stop them, to no avail.

Program Notes

Just like the *Concerto RV 559*, the final number in the *Allegro non troppo* program is a multimovement piece that gets only partially set to Bozzetto's animation. The original is the five-movement second suite[1] that Igor

---

[1] The first one was compiled in 1911; the third and last one came in 1945.

Stravinskj compiled, in 1919, from his own two-act (with an introduction) ballet *The Firebird*. It was staged for the first time in Paris on June 25, 1910, by the Ballets Russes, the dance company of the Russian impresario Sergej Djagilev, who also commissioned the work. *The Firebird* marked a turning point in Stravinsky's career: according to composer and musicologist Roman Vlad, "its success was overwhelming, and Stravinsky's name was made: he found himself overnight enjoying an enviable position in western musical life."[2] It was also the first time that the revolutionary orchestral writing of Stravinsky's early maturity started to become evident, with occasional rhythmic violence and sharp sound contrasts that foreshadowed the primal sound brutality of the *Rite of Spring*.

The Firebird was conceived as a *ballet d'action*,[3] which is to say a music tightly knitted to plot events that get expressed by choreography and pantomime. Its story came from a mixture of two items from the narrative Russian folklore. The first one is the Firebird, a benign female character that appears in many stories. The musicologist Richard Taruskin called her "a part of every Russian's prepackaged dreamworld."[4] Her archetype was mixed with the tales about Kašèj the Deathless, an immortal evil being. The two authors of the ballet scenario, the art historian Alexandre Benois (1870–1960) and the choreographer Michel Fokine (1880–1942), took inspiration from Russian fairy tales collected by Aleksandr Nikolaevič Afanas'ev (1826–1871). However, another source was a poem by Jakov Petrovič Polonskij (1819–1898), *Zimnij put'* (*A Winter's Journey*, 1844) that is an early example of a work where the Firebird and Kašèj are featured together; Polonskij drew inspiration from an older anthology of Russian popular prints (*lubki*) that, in 1830, presented Kašèj as a king for the first time,[5] just like he is in Stravinsky's ballet. The storyline devised by Benois and Fokine was summarized by Vlad as follows:

> The young Czarevitch Ivan ... having captured the Firebird sets it free out of pity and thus attains the moral right to liberate the world from the diabolical Katschei. The liberation is the work of the Firebird, which at the very moment when Ivan is about to be turned to stone, sends everyone to sleep with the enchanted lullaby and gives the Czarevitch the chance to seize and destroy the eggshell containing the soul and with it the pledge of Katschei's immortality.[6]

---

[2]Roman Vlad, *Stravinsky* (Oxford: Oxford University Press, 1985), 14.
[3]Ibid., 11.
[4]Richard Taruskin, *Stravinsky and the Russian Traditions* (Oxford: Oxford University Press), 556.
[5]Ibid., 565.
[6]Vlad, *Stravinsky*, 12–13.

The Firebird also helps by trapping in a forced dance Kašèj's minions, who were chasing Ivan. In the finale, several characters that were petrified by the evil king come back to life, including thirteen princesses, one of which is Ivan's love interest. The movements of the 1919 *Suite* chosen by Bozzetto, the second and the third one, are in fact about both the princesses and the dance of the minions: they are the *Princesses' Khorovod* (a round dance) and the *Infernal dance of King Kastchei*. The only similarity between the story of the short film and that of the original ballet stays in the "infernal" theme attributed to the dance of the minions, which Bozzetto played out by visualizing the persecution of the snake by humongous colored demons. Also, the two selected movements refer to the two worlds that get reciprocally confronted in the ballet, the human and the supernatural one. The *Princesses' Khorovod* is about the human world, just like in the *Allegro non troppo* episode, even though the context is a religious one: it is that of the creation of mankind according with the Judeo-Christian tradition, as the music accompanies a retelling (with comedy twists) of the biblical story from the Book of Genesis. The *Infernal dance of King Kastchei* is instead heard in the second half of the episode, when Bozzetto definitely departs from the Bible and introduces demons as harbingers of the most degenerate sides of the civilization that will come after the loss of the pristine Edenic state.

In respect to these major plot points, the *Firebird* of *Allegro non troppo* seems to be revealing about Bozzetto's stance on religious themes. The topic is foregrounded also in the *Boléro*: in that case the symbol of Christianity, the cross, barges into the scene with ominous solemnity together with the musical event that the director mostly charged with meaning, the final modulation that made him think about the last-minute appearance of man at the end of evolution. The cross is not presented in a positive light: the angle, the color, and the attitude of the characters make it seem intimidating and oppressive. Moreover, it comes at a focal point in a narrative that tells how the late arrival of man disrupted the natural order, by means of brutal violence and cunning malice. Religion gets similarly referenced in other works by Bozzetto, like *Grasshoppers*, where high priests who abuse of their powers, or ruthless fundamentalists, have key roles in the relay race of mutual violence recounted by that short film. In *Rapsodeus*, the light that everyone seeks through the ages, and that triggers merciless killings, might be a metaphor for religious truth; at one point, two popes fight each other over it, on mechanic cathedrals. However, during a 2017 screening of *Rapsodeus* in Padova,[7] the director said that he did not want the light to be associated with a specific meaning, and that it might represent all the things humans hold as worthy of taking someone else's life. Moreover, it must be noted that in *Grasshoppers* the cross appears too, but not to scare or oppress people;

---

[7]Cinema Pio X, Padova, June 30, 2017.

instead, it causes the warring men to momentarily pause in awe. Their fight rages on soon, though, and the cross, disregarded, sinks in the dust they kick up. It might be argued, then, that Bozzetto's films do not present religion as something inherently detrimental for the world, but they do elaborate on the way religion has historically appeased greed and violence. In this respect, Bozzetto situates religion among the tools that mankind wrongly used, just like the fire that appears in the hand of the ape during the *Boléro*, and that soon gets turned into a weapon. The premise about the negative relationship between men and their tools seems to be twofold: tools become weapons as soon as men sees them as means to obtain more power over their peers. This has been a constant in Bozzetto's output since his very first film, *Tapum! The History of Weapons*, which is a satire of the ridiculous variety of deathly contraptions that have been created through the ages. So, humans might not be inherently evil; they are just dangerously inclined to make the worst possible choice in their pursue for power. This seems confirmed by the way Adam and Eve are presented in the *Firebird*. They are two rare Bozzetto characters who are not malignant, neurotic, or frustrated. They appear instead as peaceful, affectionate, and dignified; and, evidently, they do not own or desire anything. They do not have any clothes on, and they live in a pale blue void; more importantly, differently from the Bible, they make a choice that goes against the acquisition of more power. They do not need the apple, which stands for the fruit that, in Book of Genesis, came from the tree of the knowledge of good and evil. When eaten by the snake, such fruit reveals its devastating potential: the demons that torment the serpent throw at him a whirlwind of visual metaphors about material desires in the contemporary society. The theme is the rampaging commodification of everything, including sex and, of course, religion; a telling scene, in this sense, is the one where a small church gets flooded with money and morphs into a towering cathedral. When contextualized as a thread in the director's pessimist view about how men pursue their goals, Bozzetto's references to religion suddenly appear even in good resonance with some teachings of Christianism and their theological elaboration. For example, according to the theologian and philosopher Augustine of Hippo (354–430), what was evil about the forbidden fruit in the garden of Eden was just how it got used by Adam and Eve,[8] who anyway, even when still innocent, had already in them the seeds of the pride and self-love that led to their disobedience.[9] Bozzetto's opinion on mankind seems to be quite the same: humans might be good but only when not given a chance to act out their natural propension to increase their power. The presence of such position in Bozzetto's films

---

[8] Allan D. Fitzgerald, ed., *Augustine through the Ages* (Grand Rapids, MI: William B. Eerdmans, 1999), 351.
[9] Ibid.

has however nothing to do with the religiousness or less of the director. Instead, this is likely another consequence of Bozzetto's keen ability to catch and expose through satire the main cultural and social issues of his own country. Catholicism has always been a huge presence in the culture of Italy; Bozzetto grew up and worked in an environment imbued with it. It is also because of this that the religious visual references that appear in Bozzetto's films mostly come from the Christian Catholic repertoire: it is the religion the director has always been more exposed to, and whose contradictions he knows best.

In *Allegro non troppo*, *The Firebird* is actually the piece that more explicitly targets the cultural shortcomings of Italy in the 1970s. Its second half, set to the *Infernal Dance*, is replete with provocative imagery referring to several sensible issues of that decade: the celebration of hedonistic consumerism in advertisements, the sexual liberation turned into a commodification of the female body, and the violence used by the state to maintain the status quo and censor the dissidents (see Part One, Chapter 2). This last point is touched by the sequence when the mouth of the snake gets sewn shut by a devil wearing a police beacon light; then, a multitude of hands donning white gloves and blue sleeves, as well as white truncheons, suggests an association with the colors and equipment of the Italian State Police. The use of live-action footage (shot by Bozzetto himself) as backgrounds to the animations was intended to make it even clearer that the satire was about the contemporary society.[10]

The animation itself, instead, falls in the "rough" part of the stylistic spectrum of *Allegro non troppo*. Only the *Slavonic Dance* looks sketchier; there are, however, design differences even within the short film itself. The outline of the snake and the demons is made of a succession of small curves that gives them a "squishy" appearance, particularly prone to metamorphosis. In fact, the characters are continuously shape-shifting; the skin of the demons sometimes emits even "bubbles" of matter that burst up and disappear, just like the initial dark amoeba in the *Boléro*. This morphing attitude is enhanced by the flatness of the designs by Manuli, which allows them to change without hindering too much the consistency (e.g., when the snake ends up with legs and arms). Adam and Eve, instead, have a more solid appearance. Such design is actually a consequence of the multiple animation techniques used on them: before they turn into drawings, they get introduced as plasticine puppets in the introductory sequence produced by the studio Master Programmi Audiovisivi. So, the drawing style "inherits" the solid design of the puppets. That sequence is

---

[10]Bozzetto in the documentary "Ricordando *Allegro non troppo*," in the *Allegro non troppo* DVD, part of the DVD collection "Tutto Bozzetto (o quasi)" (Roma: Multimedia San Paolo, 2005).

a quite unique occurrence of Claymation in an Italian animated full-length feature. Its presence is justified by the screen action, as God models the first human beings from the substance of earth. There might be here also an implied parallel between the hands of the animator, which give life to characters on screen, and that of God as "animator" in the sense that he gave an *anima* (Latin and Italian for "soul") to Adam and Eve. Interestingly, Bozzetto did not follow the biblical tale about the creation of the woman; she gets created second, but not from Adam's rib. She is instead modeled independently, in the same way of her husband. This might be a sensible touch by Bozzetto, in a decade when women became vocal about their rights but were nonetheless struggling hard to get the attention they deserved from the patriarchal Italian society. In fact, the detail about Adam's rib was one of the major points that consolidated the woman as a vicarious figure, at the service of man, in the most conservative Christian view; Augustine of Hippo, in his *On the Literal Meaning of Genesis (De Genesi ad litteram)*, even declared that "woman deserved to have her husband for a master. But if this order is not maintained, nature will be corrupted still more, and sin will be increased."[11]

The two parts of the short film are different also in the interaction between music and animation. The more quiet and melodic *Princesses' Khorovod* is mainly used as a source of emotive functions. The uncorrupted world of Adam and Eve is described by the section of the music that starts one bar before rehearsal number 5 in the original score. The *Firebird* is in fact the only other episode of *Allegro non troppo*, after the *Boléro*, that features a single movement in a less than complete form. There is even a diegetic justification for this: while the other pieces in the program are supposed to be performed by the orchestra of old ladies, the *Firebird* plays from a record after all the musician have left the theater. The music starts in the live-action interstitial, while the record and the gramophone are on screen; the diegetic impression gets even reinforced by an artificially superimposed sound effect, the rhythmic scratching of the needle through the grooves. According to Audissino's terminology, this gives the music a realistic motivation.

The transition to the Claymation sequence, however, repositions Stravinsky's music to an artistic motivation, with an emotive function that however is replete with implicit synchronies that cleanly outline the phrasing, just like it largely happens in the *Prélude à l'après-midi d'un faune* and the *Valse triste*. A few explicit synchronies are anyway present, like the one that emphasizes the birth and growth of the tree: the animation starts exactly with a new section (rehearsal number 11) where the thematic material and the instrumentation make a radical change.

---

[11]Augustine of Hippo, *The Literal Meaning of Genesis*, vol. 2, ed. John Hammond Taylor (New York: Newman Press, 1982), 171.

The *Infernal Dance*, instead, is mostly a matter of temporal perceptual functions, and rightly so: it is the place of *The Firebird* where Stravinsky unleashed for the first time a daring rhythmic treatment of the orchestra and a writing that violently cuts from one timbre to another, a future trademark of his so-called "Russian period" and of works like the *Rite of Spring*. Bozzetto took advantage of the many sounds that get aurally "pinpointed" by accents or sudden alternances to create an intense choreography of synchronies, expressed through character animation, editing, and camera movements. The vast majority of functions is of the temporal perceptual kind, but there are also spatial perceptual ones, like the one that describes the speeding of the cars that pursue the snake. Their relentless motion catches and visualizes the sense of urgency conveyed by an insistent repetition of a melodic fragment that gets passed through the woodwinds, while the strings accompany it with fast repetitions of a motivic cell of two short notes followed by a longer one (rehearsal number 6). Anyway, Bozzetto's inventiveness in devising synchrony ideas is probably at its wildest in *The Firebird*; in some of its most memorable moments, the director reframes Stravinsky's most outstanding timbrical ideas as "cartoony" sound effects that work like onomatopoeias. This is the case of the synch of the trombone glissandos with the female breasts popping out from the TV screens, or of a "pulsating" passage with pizzicato strings and timpani to suggest the sound of the beating heart. The most surprising case in this selection might however be the creation of the orange demon's laughter with the two trombones that play two bars before rehearsal number 1: the head movement and the staging of the action make the synchrony unmistakable, expressive and funny at once.

As in the *Valse triste*, the animation of *The Firebird* goes on for a little while after the music has already finished. When the snake reenacts his experience with the future miseries of civilization, he speaks in gibberish like Mr. Rossi and his sound effects get rendered in the fashion of a "regular" sound cartoon. This choice eases the transition of the animated snake to the sound film context of the live-action sequence, to create the gag that justifies the whole orchestra fleeing at once and leaving the film without a finale. However, this could be also an aesthetic transition to the finale itself, the last animated episode of *Allegro non troppo*, and the one that abandons the *Fantasia* model to embrace a traditional pattern of cartoon sonorization, even if paired with a highly anarchic narrative content.

Finale(s)

Description

Now left with no orchestra, no conductor, and no animator, the desperate host, in need of a conclusion for the film, gives a phone call to an unspecified archive that seems to have a reserve of prefabricated finales in stock.

The answer comes from a cartoon world that dialogues with the live-action one in a cross-cut short sequence. The supposed archivist is a bizarre hunchback named Franceschini.

When the call ends, Franceschini comes out of a door that seems to open on the grid over the proscenium. He mutters half-articulated words; while he goes on with his slurred speech with a stolid smile on his face, he plods over a wooden beam and then among the cordage, with a lantern in his hand. He finally reaches a pile of small theater stages, each one with their red curtains closed. With slow and heavy movements, he grabs one of the stages and rests it on the ground. Excited, he applauds and then sits down, getting ready to review the finales.

The curtain opens. A scene from Shakespeare's *Romeo and Juliet* appears: the two lovers (portrayed as slim cartoon characters) are parting, and Romeo comes down from Juliet's balcony. A loud orchestral finale, with a unison of brasses and a cymbal crash, plays in the background: Romeo jumps to the ground in one single leap and then, as the curtain closes and immediately reopens, he goes again upstairs and repeats his stunt while Juliet takes an ostentatiously graceful pose. The action gets repeated over and over, each time with the same music and the curtains closing and opening again. Romeo's leap becomes progressively more disastrous; Juliet contributes to this, first by kicking him down with an oversized shoe and then picking him up from the ground, returning to the balcony and throwing Romeo from there piece by piece.

Franceschini is not satisfied. He sticks out his tongue and then smashes the small stage out of sight. He picks another one and sits again in front of it, full of expectations.

The curtain opens. A tenor is concluding the aria *Celeste Aida*, from the first act of the famous opera by Giuseppe Verdi. While he keeps his high note, an extremely fast zoom-out makes the point of view drift away to show the city, the whole planet, and finally God on a cloud, who, disturbed by the opera singer, covers his ears.

Curtain. A bipedal mouse hunts a cat with a knife in hand. The cat closes a door behind himself and rests his back on it; however, the door is actually a giant mousetrap that snaps on his neck.

Curtain. A ballerina with giant legs is interpreting the finale of the *Dance of the Seven Veils* from Richard Strauss's opera *Salome*. She tries to pick a flower, but its stem and roots are unexpectedly long. While the flower is still stretching out, she gets swallowed by the ground. He ends up with her feet sticking out from the place where the flower was, while the latter has now its root in the previous place of the ballerina.

Curtain. An athlete, drawn in a black-and-white shaded style slightly more realistic than the other finales, is about the reach the finish line of a race. However, the string that marks the goal severs him in two.

Curtain. The camera travels through a seemingly never-ending series of opening doors. This is actually the perspective of a little man running inside a hamster wheel that has four doors on the inside. A giant cartoon hamster observes the scene with satisfaction. Meanwhile, the final measure from Beethoven's *Piano Sonata No. 8 Op. 13 (Pathétique)* plays for three times.

Curtain. Two quite realistic black-and-white caricatures of Humphrey Bogart and Audrey Hepburn exchange a passionate kiss. When they try to separate their lips, their mouths stay glued together. Their scared faces go off-screen while their mouths stretch in a ridiculously long string of flesh that ultimately breaks and falls down. They slowly return back, horrified, with all their teeth exposed.

Franceschini is again not amused. He goes for another stage; the sequence that ensues this time has no curtain cuts but presents a single chain of catastrophic events in Manuli's drawing style.

The wind blows the hat off the head of a man. He bends to pick it from the ground; however, he raises a leg that bumps into a garbage collector, who falls down with his trash bin. The bin hits a car, throwing the driver out of it; the car bounces and hits an airplane, which in turn hits a liner ship that takes fire. The ship smashes onto a dock and triggers an explosion; the flames reach some skyscrapers, driving out of the buildings a crowd of terrorized people. The fire then spreads to a missile on its launch pad. It takes off and hits a location somewhere over the horizon: the mushroom cloud of an atomic bomb rises. Other missiles respond to the attack, from all over the planet; the whole Earth gets bombed and finally blows up in pieces.

The last live-action sequence ensues, with the host and the conductor that resolve to make a new film, a sexy remake of *Snow White and the Seven Dwarfs*; but there is also an animated denouement. It reveals that this is one of the finales reviewed by Franceschini, who seems to be enjoying it while looking at it through one of his little theaters. In a last twist, the snake from *The Firebird* appears in front of Franceschini and bites him on the nose; the hunchback runs away until a "happy end" sign crushes him.

Program Notes

Under the appearance of an ultimate admission of inadequacy and incompetence, brought forward by the staging of a search for an ending that spirals out of control, the last animated sequence in *Allegro non troppo* actually provides a solid conclusion to the feature, as it ties together and confirms its storytelling and expressive premises. To achieve this, the finale(s) sequence works simultaneously at several levels: narrative, structural, stylistic, satirical, and musical.

The narrative meaning of the episode is the most straightforward one. It develops to the extreme the presentation of *Allegro non troppo* as a mindless low-budget imitation of the "serious" feature that *Fantasia* was. Not only the orchestra, the conductor, and the animator are gone; now the host, after having dropped his fake air of confidence, desperately admits that he has no clue on how to conclude his show. Instead of providing some idea of his own, he entrusts the search for a finale to someone who is possibly more incompetent than himself, a goofy, babbling hunchback with a dazed face. The rapid fire of alternate (and unlikely) ending scenes that ensues plays yet again on the supposed derivativeness of *Allegro non troppo*; the finale has to be chosen from a stock of preexisting materials, disregarding their actual pertinence to the story. The message becomes obsessively clear: *Allegro non troppo* does not aspire to reach *Fantasia*'s heights, as its very plot is a blatant rip-off, with no original ideas. After all, among Bozzetto's early title ideas there were "Senza Fantasia" ("Without Fantasia") and "Poca Fantasia" ("Not Much Fantasia").

However, this is only for the sake of comedy and narrative consistency. By observing the finale(s) sequence from the structural point of view, it does not seem just some sort of self-diminishing denouement. The short animations reviewed by the hunchback Franceschini create an alternate and condensed version of the omnibus structure that defines the whole picture. They increase the established pace of the changes in narration and animation styles to an exhilarating extreme, while keeping the feeling of a variegate collection of short films; so, it is as if the film model of *Allegro non troppo* suddenly shifted gears and changed its tempo. Should the musical meaning of its title be literally taken, it might be said that in the finale(s) *Allegro non troppo* turns into an *allegro con brio*, or even a *presto*. In fact, if the film were a musical composition, this would have made perfect sense: a faster tempo at the climactic concluding section of a piece is a well-established formula to give out a sense of closure, by means of a rhythmic intensification. Such sections are often headed *stretto* or *stretta*, which means "tight"; they are a quite common conclusive device in arias from Italian operas. A couple of renowned examples are the end of the duet with chorus *Libiamo ne' lieti calici* from Act I of Giuseppe Verdi's opera *La Traviata* or the ending of Adina's aria *Prendi, per me sei libero* from Act II of Gaetano Donizetti's *L'elisir d'amore*. There are instances of *stretta* also in instrumental compositions, as in the fourth and conclusive movement of Beethoven's *Fifth Symphony*. The finale(s) sequence could thus be considered, structurally, as *Allegro non troppo*'s *stretta*.

The structural positioning of the finale(s) as an operatic *stretta* might be understood also in light of the similarities between this sequence and *Opera*, a 1973 short film codirected by Bozzetto and Guido Manuli, who was the main responsible for the style and gags that the conclusion of *Allegro non troppo* displays. *Opera* was Manuli's first directorial experience and was based on a concept of his own: excerpts from operas by Puccini, Gounod, Verdi, and Rossini (plus a few fragments of compositions by Bach, Beethoven, Chopin, Paganini, and Wagner) become a backdrop to absurdist visual gags happening on stage during an opera concert gala. In the first half, directed by Manuli, the gags flow one into the other with no narrative direction; each segment is introduced by the name of the featured opera (or composition), but then the original librettos gets referenced only by means of basic allusions to the clothes or actions of the characters (like William Tell trying to hit an apple on someone's head with an arrow or Romeo singing under Juliet's balcony). For the rest, anything can happen; the metamorphosis and the surreal twists are continuous. The music is used as a comedy tool. It is largely cut and reassembled so as to articulate and accentuate the gags. In some cases, it is quite difficult to make out the particular aria or piece that is being quoted. The audiovisual setting changes in the part directed by Bozzetto, who has anyway never liked the opera repertoire very much (Manuli, instead, enjoyed it a lot), being more interested in instrumental music.[1] As the aria *Largo al factotum* from Rossini's *Barber of Seville* starts, the gags remain absurd but they more coherently revolve around Figaro and his crazy hair-cutting routine, which becomes an excuse to introduce and mock a few icons of the pop culture and history of the 1970s (Charlie Brown, Batman, Richard Nixon, Moshe Dayan). The aria by Figaro stays recognizable, as the cuts are far less frequent than before; it is interspersed with the beginning of *Un bel dì vedremo* from Puccini's

---

[1]Personal communication to the author via Skype, January 20, 2019.

Madama Butterfly, sung by the Statue of Liberty on the backdrop of a sea that, at each return of the music, gets more polluted, to the point that the statue needs to wear a gas mask. So, under Bozzetto's direction, the second half of *Opera* gets more goal-oriented: it focuses on the director's typical discourse on the wrong use of power and the subsequent future of the world (in one scene, an overpopulated earth is consumed by people looking like a bunch of ravenous insects; its remains look like an apple core). A few ideas destined to end up in *Allegro non troppo* are already present in the second half of *Opera*—most notably, the derailment of the story of Adam and Eve (a giant apple crushes Adam; Eve is inside it) and the gloomy skyline of a polluted city taking over the whole landscape. The first half, instead, uses the proscenium-curtain visual device to stage and mutually separate the gags, as in the finale(s) of *Allegro non troppo*. In hindsight, *Opera* feels like a general rehearsal to the 1976 full-length feature that had however a too fast pace for the expressive intentions of Bozzetto, not only because of the shorter run time but also because of the presence of Manuli, the most creative gagman of the Bozzetto Film, in a directing position. So, it seems that the heritage of *Opera*, and especially of its Manuli-helmed first half, mostly found an outlet just in the finale(s). The "operatic" argument of the 1973 short goes well with the idea of making an *Opera*-like sequence into a sort of *stretta*, a typical closure for opera arias; at the same time, however, the fact that Bozzetto left Manuli in charge of the finale(s) gives to the *Opera* reference also a stylistic consistency. The drawing manner of Manuli is in fact clearly distinguishable in the slender characters with wide eyes and a kind of "rubber hose" anatomy in their limbs, always ready to morph or dismember themselves; it is the same style that can be appreciated in the first half of *Opera*, and that quite clearly differs from that of Bozzetto, which is less polished and based on stumpy and more geometric character designs (Mr. Rossi can be easily compared with Figaro from *Opera*, for example). Because of this, the finale(s) work as a marker of continuity with the most absurdist vein of the Bozzetto animated production, which had been partially tamed in the rest of *Allegro non troppo* in order to not hinder the more varied and, at time, pathetic tone Bozzetto was aiming for in this feature. It is as if, after having restrained him for the whole of the six musical shorts, Bozzetto finally "unleashed" Manuli to have his own way during the finale(s). If observed carefully, though, the style of the finale(s) is by no means a "pure Manuli" one. In a clear attempt to reinforce the sense of continuous variation in the spectator, so as to convey a hectic visual rhythm, the drawing style is not homogeneous. Sometimes it is Manuli himself who alters his own graphic approach, as in the scene with the athlete at the finish line; in another occasion, though, a different artist provides the visuals. This is the case of the kiss between Bogart and Hepburn, rendered by Mirna Masina with a grotesque caricatural approach full of realistic shadowing and details. Even the animation style changes; the essential but fluid approach by Manuli is superseded by transitions between still images; when the two heads come together, after having had their lips ripped off, they slide on-screen like paper cut-outs. But ultimately, Bozzetto's touch also remains visible, as in the camerawork that features agile whip pans and, most of all, an extreme zoom-out (from the inside of a theater to a cloud in the heavens, where God is covering his ears) that could be compared with the camera movement that goes on through the whole 1967 short film *Man and His World*. The final image, the explosion of the world, is a staple of Bozzetto's repertoire, too; *Opera* also featured it, with the earth being eaten like an apple, in the section of the short that was in fact directed by Bozzetto. So, the finale(s) concede a lot to the wildest sides of Bozzetto and Manuli's inspiration, without losing sight of the stylistic imprint of *Allegro non troppo*.

The finale(s) might be a *stretta* also in respect to the satirical content of the film. Their whole contextualization as a last resort measure by a host left without an ending reinforces the whole TV variety show metaphor that pervades the live-action parts of *Allegro non troppo* (see the Program Notes to Chapter 7), and confirms the attribution of incompetence and superficiality traits to this form of entertainment. Mass entertainment also gets targeted by presenting screen stories (or parts of them, like a finale) as interchangeable stock goods. The concept of the film genre as a disposable commodity was critically addressed before by Bozzetto: his two previous features, *West & Soda* and *Vip, My Brother Superman*, were in fact based on the ironic subversion of clichés from classic Western and superhero films. The conclusion of *Allegro non troppo* dares to go beyond that, as it subverts the classic Hollywood narrative scheme as a whole, by tampering with one of its key elements: the ending. As Bordwell described, the narrative device of the classic Hollywood film is all about chained causes and effects, and "the ending becomes the culmination of the spectator's absorption, as all the causal gaps get filled. The fundamental plenitude and linearity of Hollywood narrative culminate in metaphors of knitting, linking, and filling."[2] *Allegro non troppo* seems to argue about how empty this model had become in the 1970s, by (seemingly) avoiding an ending altogether, and even reinforcing this impression by slapping on-screen a forced "happy end" sign at the very last moment, and in English, too: the language of Hollywood, the place from which reportedly came the phone call that, at the beginning of *Allegro non troppo*, complained about the *Fantasia* rip-off. That Bozzetto is targeting Hollywood, and its outdated norms about films, is rendered even more evident by the gruesome derailment of Bogart and Hepburn's performance during one of the key moments in classical cinema narratives, which is

---

[2] David Bordwell, in David Bordwell, Janet Staiger, and Kristin Thompson, *The Classical Hollywood Cinema: Film Style & Mode of Productions to 1960* (London: Routledge, 2005), 18.

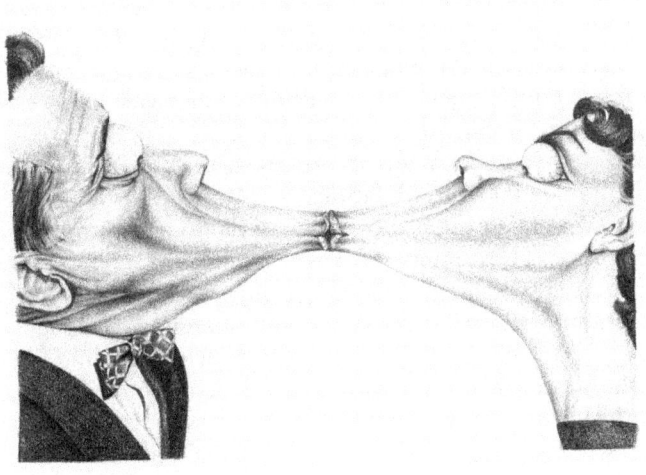

FIGURE 7 *Humphrey Bogart and Audrey Hepburn literally lock their lips together, during the finale(s) of* Allegro non troppo. *The art, by Mirna Masina, demonstrates the stylistic eclecticism that Bozzetto reserved to the conclusive animated episode; it also homages and satirizes the classical Hollywood film (by referencing Billy Wilder's* Sabrina, *1954) and its outdated genres and conventions, by derailing one of the narrative and visual tropes of old romantic comedies (the kiss exchanged by the main players).*

the kiss (Figure 7). In fact, the two actors starred together in a renowned romantic film from the late classical Hollywood, by one of the directors who contributed to define such classical canon: *Sabrina* (1954), by Billy Wilder. All those elements are well in tune with the modern parody attitude of *Allegro non troppo*: works from the past get ironically referenced to show a distance from them, but also how they can get reshaped into a new expressive form. The finale(s) might even remark this by subtly joking about another film that was itself a modern parody[3] of a Hollywood film genre,

---

[3]Bendazzi defined it as neither a satire nor a parody, but a paraphrase of *Frankenstein* (James Whale, 1931), *The Bride of Frankenstein* (James Whale, 1935), and *The Son of Frankenstein* (Rowland V. Lee, 1939). Bendazzi, Mel Brooks. *L'ultima follia di Hollywood* (Milano: Il Formichiere, 1977), 124–5.

Young Frankenstein. Bozzetto seems to tip his hat at Mel Brooks's spoof of horror films through the black-and-white cinematography of the live-action interstitials, but also by making the theater archivist a possible send-up to Igor, the hunchback played by Marty Feldman. Both the characters play a similar narrative role: they are the incompetent helpers of an equally incompetent main character with an air of grandiosity, who sends them off to retrieve an object for them (a brain, in the case of Igor, and a finale in *Allegro non troppo*). The name of the cartoon hunchback, Franceschini, is a very likely pun on "Frankenstein."

The finale(s) give also some space to Bozzetto's core satirical themes, about mankind and its greedy relationship with its environment. A hint of this resides in the "finale" that shows a giant hamster taking his revenge on a man, who has to keep running in a wheel while the animal looks at him in amusement; the switching of the roles, which exposes what pets have to bear to entertain their owners, resonates with Bozzetto's advocacy of animal rights. However, the chain of events that starts with the wind blowing the hat off a man's head and ends with the destruction of the earth, is more explicit in this respect; it not only forwards a new ridiculous variation on the role of self-destruction in the history of mankind that Bozzetto has started to chronicle since his first short, *Tapum!*, but it also lets the real fears of atomic warfare as a catastrophic development of the Cold War, which were very well alive in the 1970s, crawl into *Allegro non troppo*. The idea of global destruction ensuing a series of trivial events, as well as the high-spirited music (the final bars of Liszt's *Hungarian Rhapsody No. 2*) accompanying the end of the world, seems to pay homage to how Stanley Kubrick concluded his 1964 film *Dr. Strangelove Or: How I Learned to Stop Worrying and Love the Bomb*.

There is also a musical meaning to the finale(s). The sequence, just like it concentrates many gags that Manuli did not have a chance to fit into the rest of *Allegro non troppo*, became a virtual repository for several music pieces that Bozzetto considered for the film program, but that did not make it to the final selection. Even if they are presented in tiny bits that make them barely recognizable, in a follow-up to the music strategy of *Opera*, the compositions featured in the finale(s) include the aria *Celeste Aida*, from Verdi's *Aida*; the *Dance of the Seven Veils*, from Strauss's *Salome*; the "Pathétique" and *"Moonlight"* piano sonatas by Beethoven; the *String Quintet in C major* D. 956, Op. posth. 163 by Schubert; the orchestral version of the *Hungarian Dance* No. 5 by Brahms; the first movement of Mahler's *Symphony No. 1*, the *Toccata and Fugue in D minor* by Bach; and, as said earlier, Liszt's *Hungarian Dance No. 2*, in its orchestral variant. There is also a fragment from a piece that played earlier in the film, the *Slavonic Dance No. 7* by Dvořák. While the presence of all this works is a small payback to Bozzetto's painstaking and hidden work of musical selection during the preproduction, the use of very specific bits from each one of those pieces—the cadences—makes for a bold musical reinstatement of the whole satire about the meaningless perpetuation of stock formulas in entertainment. From Baroque to late Romanticism, in the European musical language, the cadence is precisely a formula that brings a sense of conclusion to a phrase, a section, or even to a whole piece. The effect is not just functional but even psychological; according to Arnold Schönberg, "The meaning of the harmonic cadence is the restoration of the state of rest."[4] It is, thus, a cliché that signals the end of dramatic tension; in the finale(s) of *Allegro non troppo*, though, this already formulaic trope is completely emptied of meaning by the fact the cadences are no longer reliable indicators of an ending, as a new story starts again right after each one of them. Moreover, while the audiovisual strategy is mainly based on synchronies (temporal perceptual functions) between the cadences and the cartoon action, the whole concept behind the music–animation relationship in *Allegro non troppo* gets here completely disproved. The integrity of the music is no longer respected, and the compositions, reduced to their tritest formulas, are there just to support a frantic mickey-mousing with no emotional depth. The finale(s) seem tinged with audiovisual nihilism.

It might not be nihilism, though. It is true that, as recalled throughout this book, negations have often been used by Bozzetto to talk about himself and his work. He says he is not able to draw; he reacted to the prospect of making a full-length feature by warning that he was no Disney. Mr. Rossi debuted by demonstrating that he was no filmmaker; Minivip, from *Vip, My Brother Superman*, was no superhero. In respect to *Allegro non troppo*, the whole film is about it not being *Fantasia*; the music is not played by a real orchestra, the conductor is a fake one as well, and the same goes for the host. The list could go on for quite a while. If paired with the disillusionment the director nurtures about mankind, the whole situation might be commented with the tongue-in-cheek remark that ended Bozzetto's first short film, *Tapum!*: "Mamma mia che pessimista," "my goodness, what a pessimist!"

In truth, Bozzetto's pessimism, while it might be based or not on a true personality trait, works as a storytelling device. It is a premise and a context; it frames an expressive space that actively challenges the negativity. The point is not to have a forced happy ending that might look as fake as the sign falling on Franceschini's head. Instead, the characters are free to lose their battles, at the end (as often happens to Mr. Rossi, who even gets burned to ashes in *Allegro non troppo*); but they will do so after having tried their best to succeed. *Una vita in scatola*, Bozzetto's 1967 short film, makes this concept an existential one: life is a succession of obligations and suffering,

---

[4] Arnold Schönberg, *The Musical Idea and the Logic, Technique and Art of Its Presentation*, ed. Patricia Carpenter and Severine Neff (New York: Columbia University Press, 1995), 249.

but on the way one can meet fleeting moments of extreme beauty and bliss that are worth the effort.

Allegro non troppo is just like one of Bozzetto's "pessimistic" characters: by claiming the absence of any artistic quality, and positioning itself as a crude imitation of an admirable predecessor (just as Minivip was the shameful descendant of a genetically remarkable ancestry), it actually freed itself from expectations and challenged the music–image relationship with no preconceptions. With no need for being a sequel or a remake, and with no target audience in mind, it let itself open to the sociocultural background of its makers, becoming a condensate of themes and visual solutions that drew both from the context of Italy in the 1970s and from the achievements and shortcomings of the "Carosello" age, the most productive, creative, and controversial years of Italian animation.

After all, Bozzetto found a solution to not being able to draw. He put a line around an idea; he ended up making *Allegro non troppo*, and much more. It might not have been a cure for pessimism, but it worked quite well for sure.

A GUIDE TO FURTHER RESEARCH

The resources on Bozzetto in English are quite scarce and, in most cases, they only offer a succinct presentation of his life and works. The only exception is a monograph by Bendazzi that was translated into English in 1998, but that however became quite outdated through the years, having been first printed in 1972. Anyway, it received an updated new English edition, as a chapter of the essay collection *A Moving Subject* (Boca Raton, FL: CRC Press, 2020). Even though not as diverse as the books that have been published in Italian, the few English resources on Bozzetto make for a profitable entry-level gateway into the scholarly discourse on the director.

Bendazzi, Giannalberto. *Bruno Bozzetto. Animazione primo amore.* Milano: ISCA, 1972

The first monograph ever published on Bozzetto was written by Bendazzi, who based his research also on direct information coming from the director himself; in fact, Bendazzi and Bozzetto have been close friends since their youth. However, there is no bias in Bendazzi's critical commentary: the interpretative reasoning is objective and keeps itself far from any personal involvement, as it even elaborates on some shortcomings of Bozzetto's films and style. The book got soon quite outdated from the historical point of view, as it was published when Bozzetto was at his creative peak (he had yet to work on *Allegro non troppo*). Nonetheless, the agile book was reprinted twice (as a long chapter in edited books, as in Alfio Bastiancich, ed. *Bruno Bozzetto: 1958–1988.* Savona: Centro Promozionale Coop, 1988), because Bendazzi's points stayed valid through the years and, as such, useful to understand Bozzetto's later production, too. An English edition (featuring also a Croatian translation) was published in 1998 by the Animafest Zagreb. An updated English edition is now part of the CRC Press book *A Moving Subject*, from the "Focus Animation" series.

Green, Kerry. "What's New in Italian Animation. The World of Bruno Bozzetto." *Film Library Quarterly* XIII, no. 4 (1980): 30–6.

This article by Kerry Green is mostly a report of facts on Bozzetto, his films, and a few of his collaborators.

Halas, John. *Masters of Animation.* London: BBC, 1987.

Bozzetto studied with John Halas at the beginning of his career, right after his 1958 debut. They made together *The History of Inventions*, Bozzetto's second short film—and his least favorite one. Even though the two clashed on their different visions of cartoon comedy, they greatly respected each other. In this book, a companion to a BBC TV series of the same name, Halas dedicates a complementing but matter-of-fact article (p. 90) to Bozzetto, full of sharp observations about his style. However, he seems to have kind of missed the point of *Allegro non troppo*, as he deems it "a parody of a grand symphony concert and the unexpected happenings which could occur during such a concert."

Grant, John. *Masters of Animation*. New York: Watson-Guptill, 2001.

The chapter on Bozzetto (pp 43–7) of this encyclopedia of renowned animation artists, which has by coincidence the same name of a previous book by John Halas (see above), has been for years one of the most lengthy and detailed English-language sources on the director. Not only it provides reliable biographic and production data, but it also integrates them with appropriate critical observation. The brief discussion on *Allegro non troppo* seems to be a weak point though, just like in Halas: the author argues that "one of the movie's sequences, done to Ravel's *Boléro*, is such a close homage to *Fantasia*'s *Rite of Spring* segment that it is difficult to see it as anything other than parody." While the *Boléro* does feature visual quotations of *Fantasia*, it is hardly a mere parody of it, being instead very far from it in terms of style and content.

Antonini, Anna. "Bruno Bozzetto: Wit and Wisdom." *Animation Journal* 25 (2017): 38–48.

This essay by Antonini is part of the final issue of the *Animation Journal*, which since 1992 had been one of the most respected scholarly publications on animation, founded and edited by Maureen Furniss. The theme of the issue, guest edited by Giannalberto Bendazzi and the author, is Italian animation; so, the purpose of Antonini's essay is to give a critical assessment of Bozzetto's whole body of work in this context, with international readers in mind.

APPENDIX 1

Musical compositions listed in the *Allegro non troppo* diaries

* used in the film
° partially used in the finale of the film
+ developed into a one-page plot

Name of the composer	Title	Year of composition
Adam, Adolphe	*Le Diable à quatre* (ballet)	1845
Albinoni, Tomaso	*Concerto Op. 5 No. 7* Title redacted by Bozzetto	1707
Bartók, Béla	*The Wooden Prince Op. 13, Sz. 60* (ballet suite)	1914–17
Beethoven, Ludwig Van	°*Piano Sonata No. 8 in C minor Op. 13* ("Sonata Pathétique") Title redacted by Bozzetto	1798
	°*Piano Sonata No. 14 in C# minor* "*Quasi una fantasia*" *Op. 27, No. 2* ("Moonlight Sonata")	1801
	Piano Sonata No. 23 in F minor Op. 57 ("Appassionata") Title redacted by Bozzetto	1804–6
Bellini, Vincenzo	*Guerra, guerra!* Choir from the opera *Norma* - Story idea: "war and its foolishness" Title redacted by Bozzetto	1831

APPENDIX 1

Name of the composer	Title	Year of composition
Bernstein, Leonard	*Fancy Free* (ballet)	1944
Bizet, Georges	*Farandole*, from *L'Arlésienne, Suite No. 2* (incidental music) - Story idea: "chase consumer goods"	1872
Boito, Arrigo	*Mefistofele* (opera)	1861–81
Brahms, Johannes	+*Hungarian Dance No. 1* (for orchestra)	1852–69
	°*Hungarian Dance No. 5* (for orchestra)	1852–69
Bussotti, Sylvano	*Tableaux vivants (avant La Passion selon Sade)*, for two pianos	1964
Čajkovskij, Pëtr Il'ič	+*Danse des petits cygnes* from *The Swan Lake* (ballet)	1875–6
	Francesca da Rimini Op. 32 (tone poem)	1876
	Capriccio Italien Op. 45 (fantasy for orchestra) - Story idea: "slow"	1880
Chopin, Fryderyk	*Étude Op. 10 No. 3*	1833
	Nocturne No. 7 Op. 27 No. 1 (for piano)	1836
Debussy, Claude	+**Prélude à l'après-midi d'un faune* (symphonic piece) - Story ideas: "desires. Temptations. Warm. Three-dimensional. Watercolor-like"	1894
	Fêtes, from *Nocturnes* (for orchestra)	1899
De Falla, Manuel	*La vida breve* (opera; probably the act 2 music published as *Interlude and Dance*)	1904–5
	El amor brujo (ballet; probably the shortened orchestral version)	1916

APPENDIX 1

Name of the composer	Title	Year of composition
Delibes, Léo	+*Pizzicato Polka*, from *Sylvia* (ballet) - Story ideas: "funny"; "prank"; "amusing"; "relaxing"	1876
Dvořák, Antonín	*Slavonic Dance Op. 46 No. 1* - Story idea: "dictators. Servility"	1878
	Slavonic Dance Op. 46 No. 5	1878
	°**Slavonic Dance Op. 46 No. 7* - Story idea: "one does something, the crowd copies him"; "the TV hypnotizes the people, someone buys goods, the crowd copies him"	1878
	Slavonic Dance Op. 46 No. 10 - Story idea: "surreal ballet"	1878
	Symphony No. 9 in E minor, "From the New World" Op. 95, B. 178	1893
Gershwin, George	Unspecified.	
Gounod, Charles	*Faust* (opera; probably the Introduction, for orchestra)	1839–58
	Funeral March of a Marionette (for piano or orchestra)	1872 (piano); 1879 (orchestra)
Grieg, Edvard	+*In the Hall of the Mountain King*, from *Peer Gynt* (incidental music)	1875
Händel, Georg Friedrich	*Water Music* (three suites of orchestral movements)	1717
	Hallelujah from the *Messiah HWV 56* (oratorio, for choir and orchestra)	1741
	Music for the Royal Fireworks HWV 351 (suite for wind instruments)	1749

Name of the composer	Title	Year of composition
Haydn, Franz Joseph	*L'isola disabitata* Hob. *XXVIII/9* (ouverture from the opera)	1779
	Symphony No. 100 in G major Hob. *I/100* ("Military")	1793–4
	Symphony No. 101 in D major Hob. *I/101* ("The Clock") Title redacted by Bozzetto	1793–4
Hendrix, Jimi	Unspecified - Story idea: "hell"	
Henry, Pierre	*The Liverpool Mass* (electronic music)	1967
Hindemith, Paul	*Symphonic Metamorphosis of Themes by Carl Maria von Weber*	1943
Holst, Gustav	*Mars*, from *The Planets* (symphonic suite) - Story idea: "war and its foolishness"	1914–16
	Jupiter, from *The Planets* (symphonic suite) - Story idea: "supermarket-advertising"	1914–16
	+*Uranus*, from *The Planets* (symphonic suite)	1914–16
Kabalevskij, Dmitrij Borisovič	*Comedians' Galop*, from *The Comedians* (orchestral suite of incidental music) - Story ideas: "funny"; "factory assembly line?"	1938–9
Kachaturian, Aram	*Sabre Dance* from *Gayane* (ballet)	1942
Liszt, Franz	*Au lac de Wallenstadt*, from *Années de pèlerinage, Première année: Suisse*, S.160 (for piano)	1848–54

Name of the composer	Title	Year of composition
	+°*Hungarian Rhapsody No. 2 in C-sharp minor*, S.244/2 (orchestral version by Liszt and Franz Doppler; Bozzetto mentions a version for piano and orchestra; there is no such version, so Bozzetto was probably referring to the arrangement by Scott Bradley for the MGM short *The Cat Concerto*, 1947) - Story idea: "to fly"	1857
Mahler, Gustav	°*Symphony No. 1 in D major* ("Titan")	1887–8
	+*Symphony No. 3 in D minor*, first movement (*Kräftig. Entschieden*)	1893–6
Milhaud, Darius	*La Mort du tyran Op. 116* (cantata for mixed choir, piccolo, clarinet, tuba, and percussions)	1932
Mosolov, Aleksandr Vasil'evič	*Factory: machine-music* ("The Iron Foundry"), from the ballet suite *Steel*	1926–7
Mozart, Wolfgang Amadeus	*Benedictus sit Deus K. 117* (choir and orchestra) - Story idea: "The Garden of Eden" Title redacted by Bozzetto	1768
Musorgskij, Modest	*Pictures at an Exhibition* (possibly the orchestral version by Maurice Ravel)	1874 (Ravel's version: 1922)
Offenbach, Jacques	*Belle nuit, ô nuit d'amour* (*Barcarole*) from the opera *Les contes d'Hoffmann*	1880
Paganini, Niccolò	*Violin Concerto No. 2 in B minor Op. 7* ("La Campanella")	1826
	Perpetual Motion Op. 11 (for violin and piano, or violin and guitar; it was also arranged for violin and orchestra by other composers)	1835

APPENDIX 1

Name of the composer	Title	Year of composition
Ponchielli, Amilcare	Dance of the Hours, from the opera La Gioconda	1874–6
Prokof'ev, Sergej	The Love for Three Oranges Op. 33 (opera)	1918–21
	The Fiery Angel Op. 37 (opera)	1919–27
Rachmaninov, Sergej	Isle of the Dead Op. 29 (tone poem)	1908
	Symphonic Dances Op. 45 (orchestral suite)	1940
Ravel, Maurice	Pavane pour une infante défunte (for piano or orchestra) - Story idea: "sad"	1899 (piano); 1910 (orchestra)
	+Daphnis et Chloé (ballet) - Story idea: "metropolis"	1909–12
	La valse (choreographic poem for orchestra)	1919–20
	+*Boléro	1928
Respighi, Ottorino (after Gioachino Rossini)	La Boutique fantasque (ballet) - Story idea: "action"	1919
Rimskij-Korsakov, Nikolaj Andreevič	Scheherazade Op. 35 (tone poem) - Story idea: "war and its foolishness"	1888
Rossini, Gioachino	Il barbiere di Siviglia (ouverture from the opera) - Story idea: "too zealous"	1816
	Semiramide (ouverture from the opera) - Story idea: "war"	1822–3
	+Guillaume Tell (ouverture from the opera) - Story ideas: "war"; "comedy"	1829

APPENDIX 1   221

Name of the composer	Title	Year of composition
Saint-Saëns, Camille	*Danse macabre* Op. 40 (tone poem) - Story idea: "horror"	1874
	The Carnival of the Animals (chamber suite)	1886
Satie, Erik	*Parade* (ballet)	1916–17
Schubert, Franz	*Piano Quintet in A major D. 667 ("The Trout")* Title redacted by Bozzetto	1819
	°*String Quintet in C major D. 956, Op. posth. 163*	1828
Sibelius, Jean	*Finlandia* Op. 26 No. 7 (tone poem) Title redacted by Bozzetto	1899
	+**Valse triste* Op. 44 No. 1 (for orchestra) - Story ideas: "romantic"; "sentimental"; "the old age"	1903
	Tapiola Op. 112 (tone poem) Title redacted by Bozzetto	1926
Smetana, Bedřich	+*Dance of the Comedians*, from *The Bartered Bride* (opera) - Story idea: "many Mr. Rossis at the office. Ballet"	1863–6
	The Moldau (tone poem) - Story idea: "graphic"	1874
	The Devil's Wall (opera; probably the ouverture)	1881–2
Šostakóvič, Dmítrij Dmítrievič	Unspecified piece	
Stockhausen, Karlheinz	+*Kontakte* (electronic music) - Story ideas: "modern hell. Comedy. Horror"	1958–60

Name of the composer	Title	Year of composition
Strauss, Johann II	Die Fledermaus (operetta; probably the ouverture)	1874
Strauss, Richard	Death and Transfiguration Op. 24 (tone poem)	1888–9
	Till Eulenspiegel's Merry Pranks Op. 28 (tone poem) Title redacted by Bozzetto	1894–5
	°Dance of the Seven Veils (from the opera Salome Op. 54)	1902–5
Stravinsky, Igor	Feu d'artifice Op. 4 (fantasy for orchestra)	1908
	*The Firebird (ballet suite) - Story idea: "spectacular"	1919
	Jeu de cartes (ballet)	1936–7
Tijuana Brass	Unspecified	
Verdi, Giuseppe	+King for a Day (ouverture from the opera)	1840
	°Aida (opera)	1871
Vivaldi, Antonio	Concerto for 2 Trumpets in C major, RV 537 - Story idea: "experimental"	Unknown
	+Gloria RV 589 - Story ideas: "flying saucers"; "religion"	1715
	Concerto in F major Op. 10 No. 1 RV 433 ("The Sea Storm")	1728
	Concerto in G minor Op. 10 No. 2 RV 439 ("The Night")	1728
Wagner, Richard	Ride of the Valkyries (from the opera Die Walküre) - Story idea: "sexy"	1852–6

APPENDIX 1

Name of the composer	Title	Year of composition
	Forest Murmurs (from the opera *Siegfried*)	1851–2; 1856–71
Weber, Carl Maria Von	+*Invitation to the Dance* Op. 65, J. 260 (for piano; orchestrated by Hector Berlioz) In one instance, title redacted by Bozzetto	1819 (Weber); 1841 (Berlioz)
	Oberon (opera; performing edition by Gustav Mahler)	1824–6 (Weber); 1907 (Mahler)
Unspecified	Modern Music (unspecified)	
	Spiritual song (unspecified)	

APPENDIX 2

The *Allegro non troppo* that never was

One-page plots from Bozzetto's notebooks, translated in English by the author

1. Johannes Brahms
   Hungarian Dance No. 1
   2'40"
   Animated drawings musical short film
   War parody. Exploitation and perils of the soldier against the higher officers. Presentation of the soldier alone, sweeping the floor, surrounded by ten boorish officers. Study of the map and attack plan. The heavily loaded soldier attacks. The head guys ride on a jeep or a helicopter. They comfortably follow him. Seas-mountains-swamps-mosquitoes. He finally finds the enemy (Vietnamese). He surrounds him with ten mortars—Fire! Giant hole—The Earth gets swallowed like in an hourglass and the generals too. The Earth empties itself out and disappears.

2. Pëtr Il'ič Čajkovskij
   Danse des petits cygnes from *The Swan Lake*
   1'43"
   The TV, tempting, lures a chicken in a supermarket. Then the doors suddenly close down.

3. Claude Debussy
   Prélude à l'après-midi d'un faune
   9'40"
   Visions and desires of a satyr who walks away from his huge and ugly sleeping wife to stroll around the wood with his flute.

4. Léo Delibes
   Pizzicato Polka, from *Sylvia*
   1'30"
   Animated drawings musical short film
   A pervert has fun pinching girls in the streets, at the cinema etc. He is admonished by the judge, but he returns at it as soon as he steps out from the court hall. (Mr. Rossi?) (Contour only?)

5. Edvard Grieg
   In the Hall of the Mountain King, from *Peer Gynt*
   2'8"
   Animated drawings musical short film
   The hall of the king.
   Ugly and microscopical larvae blow up and become pompous, rich and beautiful like kings. They explode one after another. A janitor sweeps the empty hall.

6. Gustav Holst
   Uranus, from *The Planets*
   5'30"
   Animated drawings musical short film
   War parody.
   Presentation of a small-time dictator. A little Napoleon. A deserter—chase—they bring him back in line. Humorous parade.
   Fortress on the edge of a ravine. They surround it but they self-destruct while attempting a night ambush.
   At dawn, reaction and self-destruction of the attackers, too, because of stupid errors.
   One lone survivor (the deserter?) enters the manor and everything collapses down the ravine.

7. Franz Liszt
   Hungarian Rhapsody No. 2 in C-sharp minor, S.244/2
   8'
   Crystal ball—Witch.
   He steals it and sees a woman. They chase him to recover it. In the end, they all have a TV.

   —
   Clairvoyant witch.
   She shows a crystal ball to a customer. Funerals—disasters ... atomic bombs. He (hunchback?) steals it. He flees.
   1st version interrupted striptease. Intercalated by her who searches around. She swoops onto him. Chase. Crystal ball like a football. The people chase the ball. The witch changes her shape and becomes bigger. She swallows it/a beating/naked women come out from everywhere.

It starts with a dark abyss. It ends with the darkness that swallows everything.

8. Gustav Mahler
   Symphony No. 3 in D minor, first movement *(Kräftig. Entschieden)*
   4′50″
   Animated drawings musical short film
   City at sunset.
   Waste dump. Underwater panoramic shot. Wasted cars. A monster forms and comes out of the water—fight to destroy it. Symbols to defeat it (statue of liberty—justice—cross).
   It looks for gasoline. It devours gas stations. It finds an oilfield. It extracts oil and the world empties out and disappears. It falls in an empty space.[1]

9. Maurice Ravel
   Daphnis et Chloé
   15′
   A monster city creates on its own. Two children who break into its streets make the citizens-slaves understand that it is time to run away. They fly away like freed birds. Fight between the citizens and the city that wants to get them back.

10. Maurice Ravel
    Boléro
    15′30″
    The race of life. A tiresome march of all living beings toward something that attracts them. Life or death? Colors—from black to light. Red in the finale.

11. Gioachino Rossini
    Guillaume Tell (ouverture from the opera)
    In search of an apple (mix-ups and misunderstandings). Rears of women—horse—hippopotamuses—elephants—etc.
    He wants the apple of Adam and Eve. In the end it hits the world that breaks into pieces / only the apple remains.

---

[1] In Manuppelli, "Intervista a Bruno Bozzetto," Bozzetto added that he imagined also a shot featuring a line of trucks seen as silohuettes, loaded with wasted cars that they proceeded to dump into a lake. However, Bozzetto mistakenly attributed this story idea to the first movement of Mahler's *Symphony* No. 1.

12. Jean Sibelius
    Valse triste Op. 44 No. 1
    Life of a man. Birth—death (piano—sad music).
    Life changes. City—civilization. Invasion of concrete.
    An old man sees again his life through pictures that become animated.
    An old man comes back home at evening and, in front of the window, sees his whole life backwards.
    Colors—from grey to the colors of summer through the seasons—return to grey.

13. Bedřich Smetana
    Dance of the Comedians, from *The Bartered Bride*
    5'32"
    Animated drawings musical short film
    Satire of bureaucracy. Big shots and servility.
    Clock—everyone rushes to the office—When the head of the office is not there, the mice dance. When the chief returns—servility. Handkiss.
    At 6 PM everyone runs to the elevator.
    Manicure—hairdryer—nails—teeth.
    They become butterflies outside. Enraged, the chief chases them on the skyscraper. He tries to catch them with a butterfly net, but he falls down.
    King Kong as finale? Airplanes shoot at him.
    2nd version.
    A military base is like an office. In and out times. Return back home with flowers. Christmas tree. All brothers. Fireworks—explosions.
    Final title "Pax in terra."

14. Karlheinz Stockhausen
    Kontakte
    6'–8"?
    The snake steals and eats the apple of Adam and Eve. He falls down to hell. He sees the life and the tortures that will be inflict to mankind. He climbs back and offers the apple to them. Red.

15. Giuseppe Verdi
    King for a Day (ouverture from the opera)
    5'45"
    Animated drawings musical short film
    A never-ending military parade. A satire of war.
    Among the tanks and the ships wounded people parade, more and more moribund, up to the dead and the medals.
    Incredible weapons. Extremely long cannon. It fires in the finale and destroys the tribune with state leaders, priests, beautiful women etc.

16. Antonio Vivaldi
    Gloria RV 589
    Like flying saucers, the priests come from the sky and colonize a free and happy planet, making it into a cluster of churches and cathedrals where the inhabitants are imprisoned.

17. Carl Maria Von Weber
    Invitation to the Dance Op. 65, J. 260
    8'43"
    Animated drawings musical short film
    Politics.
    Dance of nations.
    Servile little ambassadors bring messages. Hypocrisy and nice faces for those who are convenient for them.
    As they dance, they eliminate each other with diabolical tricks.
    In the end they all disappear, wiped out.

BIBLIOGRAPHY

Alberti, Walter. *Il cinema d'animazione, 1832–1956*. Torino: Edizioni Radio Italia, 1957.
Alberti, Walter, and Claudio Bertieri. *Cinema di animazione. Quaderni del cineforum genovese 2*. Genova: Carbone, 1960.
Allan, Robin. *Walt Disney and Europe*. London: John Libbey, 1999.
Aloi, Dino, ed. *Bruno Bozzetto. Cinquant'anni di cartoni animati*. Torino: Edizioni Il Pennino, 2005.
Angela, Piero. *Il mio lungo viaggio. 90 anni di storie vissute*. Milano: Mondadori, 2017.
Angela, Piero, and Bruno Bozzetto. *Noi e la collera*. Milano: Garzanti, 1987.
Angela, Piero, and Bruno Bozzetto. *Noi e la gelosia*. Milano: Garzanti, 1987.
Angela, Piero, and Bruno Bozzetto. *Noi e la paura*. Milano: Garzanti, 1987.
Antonini, Anna. "Bruno Bozzetto: Wit and Wisdom." *Animation Journal* 25 (2017): 38–48.
Audissino, Emilio. *Film/Music Analysis: A Film Studies Approach*. London: Palgrave Macmillan, 2017.
Augustine of Hippo. *The Literal Meaning of Genesis*, vol. 2, edited by John Hammond Taylor. New York: Newman Press, 1982.
Baragli, Enrico. "Requiem per Carosello." *La civiltà cattolica* 3036 (December 18, 1976): 580–7.
Barrier, Michael. *Vita di Walt Disney. Uomo, sognatore, genio*. Translated by Marco Pellitteri. Latina: Tunué, 2009.
Bastiancich, Alfio, ed. *Bruno Bozzetto: 1958–1988*. Savona: Centro Promozionale Coop, 1988.
Bastiancich, Alfio, and Carla Rezza Gianini, eds. *Gianini e Luzzati. Cartoni animati*. Milano: Silvana Editoriale, 2013.
Beckerman, Howard. *Animation—The Whole Story*. Mattituck, NY: Amereon House, 2001.
Beckerman, Michael. "The Master's Little Joke: Antonín Dvořák and the Mask of Nation," in *Dvořák and his World*, edited by Michael Beckerman, 134–54. Princeton, NJ: Princeton University Press, 2012.
Bellano, Marco. "*I fratelli Dinamite* di Nino Pagot (1949) e l'idea di 'bello' in musica," in *Estudios sobre la influencia de la canción popular en el proceso de creación de música incidental*, edited by Sergio De Andrés Bailón, 335–57. Salamanca: Ediciones Universidad de Salamanca, 2016.
Bellano, Marco. "Il Veneto e l'animazione dopo il 2000: botteghe al centro del mondo," in *Veneto 2000: il cinema. Identità e globalizzazione a Nordest*,

edited by Antonio Costa, Giulia Lavarone, and Farah Polato, 112–17. Venezia: Marsilio, 2018.

Bellano, Marco. " 'Oh ... Musica moderna!'. Hollywood, satira e 'modernismo' nella musica di Giuseppe Piazzi per *I fratelli Dinamite*." *Cabiria* 178 (2014): 57–70.

Bellano, Marco. "Origini dell'animazione italiana: epopee di pionieri solitari," in *Fantasmagoria. Un secolo (e oltre) di cinema d'animazione*, edited by Davide Giurlando, 43–50. Venezia: Marsilio, 2017.

Bellano, Marco. "Painted Orchestras: Orchestration and Musical Adaptation in *Fantasia* and *Fantasia 2000*," in *Relaciones Música e Imagen en los Medios Audiovisuales*, edited by Teresa Fraile and Eduardo Viñuela, 277–87. Oviedo: Ediciones de la Universidad de Oviedo, 2015.

Bellano, Marco. "Silent Strategies: Audiovisual Functions of the Music for Silent Cinema." *Kieler Beiträge zur Filmmusikforschung* 9 (2013). http://www.filmmusik.uni-kiel.de/KB9/KB9-Bellano.pdf (accessed March 3, 2021).

Bellano, Marco, Marco Vanelli, and Giovanni Ricci. *Animazione in Cento Film*. Recco: Le Mani, 2013.

Bendazzi, Giannalberto. *Animation–A World History*, 3 vols. Boca Raton, FL: CRC Press, 2015.

Bendazzi, Giannalberto. *Appeso a una matita. Il cinema d'animazione di Guido Manuli*. Genova: Incontri internazionali con gli autori di cinema, 1984.

Bendazzi, Giannalberto. *Bruno Bozzetto: animazione primo amore*. Milano: ISCA, 1972; now in Bastiancich, Alfio, ed. *Bruno Bozzetto: 1958–1988*. Savona: Centro Promozionale Coop, 1988.

Bendazzi, Giannalberto. "Bruno Bozzetto cineasta." *La Rivista del Cinematografo* 6 (June 1975): 244–53.

Bendazzi, Giannalberto. *Cartoons*. Venezia: Marsilio, 1988.

Bendazzi, Giannalberto. "The First Italian Animated Feature Film and Its Producer: Anton Gino Domeneghini." *Animation Journal* 3, no. 2 (Spring 1995): 4–18.

Bendazzi, Giannalberto. "Il Signor Rossi." Catalogo del Festival Videopolis. Vicenza, 2002.

Bendazzi, Giannalberto. *Mel Brooks. L'ultima follia di Hollywood*. Milano: Il Formichiere, 1977.

Bendazzi, Giannalberto. *Topolino e poi. Cinema d'animazione dal 1888 ai giorni nostri*. Milano: Il Formichiere, 1978.

Bendazzi, Giannalberto, and G. Michelone. *Il movimento creato. Studi e documenti di ventisei saggisti sul cinema d'animazione*. Torino: Edizioni Pluriverso, 1993.

Bendazzi, Giannalberto, M. Cecconello, and G. Michelone, eds. *Coloriture. Voci, rumori, musiche nel cinema d'animazione*. Bologna: Pendragon, 1995.

Bendazzi, Giannalberto, and R. De Berti. *La fabbrica dell'animazione. Bruno Bozzetto nell'industria culturale italiana*. Milano: Editrice Il Castoro, 2003.

Bertozzi, Marco. *Storia del documentario italiano. Immagini e culture dell'altro cinema*. Venezia: Marsilio, 2008.

Bettetini, Giancarlo, Paolo Braga, and Armando Fumagalli. *Le logiche della televisione*. Milano: FrancoAngeli, 2004.

Bordwell, David. *Poetics of Cinema*. New York: Routledge, 2012.

Bordwell, David, Janet Staiger, and Kristin Thompson. *The Classical Hollywood Cinema: Film Style & Mode of Productions to 1960*. London: Routledge, 2005.
Bordwell, David, and Kristin Thompson. *Film Art: An Introduction*, 10th ed. New York: McGraw-Hill, 2012.
Boscarino, Antonio Vincenzo. *L'estetica di Bruno Bozzetto. Teoria e prassi tra movimento e spettacolo*. Roma: Bulzoni Editore, 2002.
Boulez, Pierre. *Notes of an Apprenticeship*. New York: Alfred A. Knopf, 1968.
Bozzetto, Anita, and Irene Bozzetto. *Bruno Bozzetto: Dal bozzetto al pixel*. Bergamo: Grafica Monti, 2008.
Bozzetto, Bruno. "Adagio, accelerando," in *Fantasmagoria. Un secolo (e oltre) di cinema d'animazione*, edited by Davide Giurlando, 79-90. Venezia: Marsilio, 2017.
Bozzetto, Bruno, ed. *Allegri ... non troppo. 40 anni di cinema di animazione*. Bergamo: Edita, 2001.
Bozzetto, Bruno. *Il signor Rossi e le donne*. Milano: Sperling & Kupfer, 1970.
Bozzetto, Bruno. *Le avventure di Ventun Din, fotoamatore*. Milano: Il Castello, 1972.
Bozzetto, Bruno. *Mille piccoli cretini*. Milano: Sperling & Kupfer, 1971.
Bozzetto, Bruno. *Viva gli abominevoli sciatori*. Milano: Sperling & Kupfer, 1970.
Brover-Lubovsky, Bella. *Tonal Space in the Music of Antonio Vivaldi*. Bloomington, Indiana University Press, 2008.
Brunetta, Gian Piero. "Il cinema italiano dal boom agli anni di piombo," in *Storia del cinema mondiale*, edited by Gian Piero Brunetta, vol. III, 2. Torino: Einaudi, 2000.
Bruno Bozzetto Film. Milano, 1970.
Bruno Bozzetto. Mostre, Cinema, Teatro, Incontri. Catalogo della manifestazione "I segni e i colori dei maestri dell'animazione: Bruno Bozzetto, Lele Luzzati, Pino Zac". Parma: Assessorato alle attività culturali del Comunce di Parma, 1985.
Budassi, Enzo. *Arte e tecnologia del film di animazione*. Roma: Edizioni Bizzarri, 1972.
Caldiron, Orio, and Turi Fedele, eds. *Il film d'animazione in Europa: atti del Convegno svoltosi nell'ambito della Rassegna internazionale del film d'animazione: Abano Terme 13-14 marzo 1970*. Este: Tipografia Euganea, 1971.
Candia, Renato. *Sul filo della matita. Il cinema di Bruno Bozzetto*. Mestre: Cinit, 1992.
Causo, Massimo, and Carlo Chatrian, eds. *Maurizio Nichetti. I film, il cinema e ...* Cantalupa, TO: Effatà Editrice, 2005.
Cawelti, John G. "Chinatown and Generic Transformation in Recent American Films," in *Film Theory and Criticism: Introductory Readings*, edited by Gerald Mast, Marshall Cohen, and Leo Braudy, 498–511. Oxford: Oxford University Press, 1992.
"Cento anni di vita dell'Istituto d'Arte di Urbino. Capitolo Quarto." https://www.prourbino.it/ScuolaDelLibro/StoriaCarnevali_cap4.htm (accessed October 18, 2019).

Cereda, Chiara, Shirin Chehayed, Priscilla Mancini, and Andrijana Ružić, eds. *Allegro non troppo. Un tesoro dell'arte italiana*. Milano: Agema, 2016.
Chatman, Seymour. *Story and Discourse: Narrative Structure in Fiction and Film*. Ithaca, NY: Cornell University Press, 1978.
Chion, Michel. *Audio-Vision: Sound on Screen*. Translated by Claudia Gorbman. New York: Columbia University Press, 2017.
Cinema di animazione italiano. Catalogo della settimana del cinema di animazione italiano—Istituto italiano di cultura di Vienna. Milano: ISCA, 1973.
Code, David J. "Hearing Debussy Read Mallarmé." *Journal of the American Musicological Society* 54, no. 3 (2001): 493–554.
Colombo, Fausto. *La cultura sottile. Media e industria culturale in Italia dall'ottocento agli anni novanta*. Milano: Bompiani, 1998.
Cook, Nicholas. *Analysing Musical Multimedia*. Oxford: Clarendon Press, 1998.
Cotte, Olivier. *... Il était une fois le dessin animé*. Paris: Dreamland, 2001.
Craft, Robert. *Conversations with Igor Stravinsky*. New York: Doubleday, 1959.
Culhane, John. *Walt Disney's Fantasia*. New York: Harry N. Abrams, 1987.
Culhane, John. *Fantasia/2000: Visions of Hope*. New York: Disney Editions, 1999.
Daniels, David. *Orchestral Music: A Handbook*, 4th ed. Lanham, MD: Scarecrow Press, 2005.
Darwin, Charles. *The Origin of Species*. London: Wordsworth, 1998.
Davis, Amy. "The Fall and Rise of Fantasia," in *Hollywood Spectatorship: Changing Perceptions of Cinema Audiences*, edited by Melvyn Stokes and Richard Maltby, 63–78. London: BFI, 2001.
Della Torre, Roberto, and M. Pagot, eds. *The Dynamite Brothers. Una storia molto animata*. Milano: Il Castoro, 2004.
Della Torre, Roberto, and M. Pagot, eds. *Un mondo perfetto. Le pubblicità cinematografiche dei fratelli Pagot*. Milano: Il Castoro, 2005.
Di Marino, Bruno. "Integrati e apocalittici. Appunti per una storia dell'animazione italiana prima del 2000," in *Il mouse e la matita. L'animazione italiana contemporanea*, edited by Bruno Di Marino and Giovanni Spagnoletti, 17–39. Venezia: Marsilio, 2014.
Di Marino, Bruno. "Vite in scatola: opere e autori del cinema d'animazione," in *Storia del cinema italiano 1965/1969*, edited by Gianni Canova, 219–30. Venezia: Marsilio, 2003.
Dorfles, Piero. *Carosello*. Bologna: Il Mulino, 1998.
Eco, Umberto. *Lector in fabula. La cooperazione interpretativa nei testi narrativi*. Milano: Bompiani, 1979.
Ellwood, David W. "Containing Modernity, Domesticating America in Italy," in *The Americanization of Europe: Culture, Diplomacy, and Anti-Americanism after 1945*, edited by Alexander Stephan, 253–76. New York: Berghahn Books, 2006.
Faeti, Antonio. "Quasi un Bozzetto al giorno, il nostro Bozzetto quotidiano," in *Cinema a passo uno: maestri dell'animazione*. Mantova: Publi-Paolini, 1983.
Falabrino, Gian Luigi. *Storia della pubblicità in Italia dal 1945 a oggi*. Roma: Carocci, 2007.
Ferkiss, Victor C. *Technological Man: The Myth and the Reality*. New York: Braziller, 1969.

Field, Christopher D. S., E. Eugene Helm, and William Drabkin. "Fantasia." *New Grove Dictionary of Music and Musicians*, Grove Online, https://www.oxfordmusiconline.com/grovemusic/view/10.1093/gmo/9781561592630.001.0001/omo-9781561592630-e-0000040048?rskey=x541Fd (accessed August 1, 2019).

Film sul pentagramma: giornate del cinema d'animazione 11–14 ottobre 1984. Forlì: Comune di Forlì, 1984.

Finch, Christopher. *L'arte di Walt Disney. Da Mickey Mouse ai Magic Kingdoms*. Translated by Marta Fornasier. Milano: Rizzoli, 2001.

Fiori, Fulvio, and Marco Pagot, eds. *The Art of Pagot*. Milano: Edizioni BD, 2008.

Fitzgerald, Allan D, ed. *Augustine through the Ages*. Grand Rapids, MI: William B. Eerdman, 1999.

Formenti, Cristina. "Dal neorealismo al documentario animato scientifico: le animazioni 'realiste' di Gibba." *Cabiria* 178 (2014): 4–19.

Formenti, Cristina. "Note sul documentario animato italiano e il suo periodo delle origini." *Immagine. Note di storia del cinema* 15 (2017): 65–77.

Francis, Richard C. *Domesticated: Evolution in a Man-Made World*. New York: W.W. Norton, 2015.

Furniss, Maureen. *Animation: The Global History*. London: Thames & Hudson, 2017.

Garity, William E., and Watson Jones. "Experiences in Road-Showing Walt Disney's Fantasia." *Journal of the Society of Motion Picture Engineers* 39 (1942): 6–15.

Garofalo, Damiano. *Storia sociale della televisione in Italia, 1954–1969*. Venezia: Marsilio, 2018.

Gerbino, Giuseppe, and Alexander Silbiger. "Folia." *New Grove Dictionary of Music and Musicians*. Grove Online. https://www.oxfordmusiconline.com/grovemusic/view/10.1093/gmo/9781561592630.001.0001/omo-9781561592630-e-0000009929#0000009929.3 (accessed September 21, 2019).

Gianeri, Enrico, aka Gec. *Storia del cartone animato*. Milano: Omnia Editrice, 1960.

Ginsborg, Paul. *Storia d'Italia dal dopoguerra a oggi*. Translated by Marcello Flores and Sandro Perini. Torino: Einaudi, 2006.

"Giorgio Valentini." Motusfilm.com. http://www.motusfilm.com/SitoItalia/CvGiorgio.htm (accessed October 18, 2019).

Giovannetti, Viviana, ed. *Ai margini del cartoon. Supplemento a Cineclub 25*. Roma: FEDIC, 1995.

Giovannetti, Viviana, ed. *I mondi animati di Bruno Bozzetto. Fuori Quadro: supplemento a Cineclub 24*. Roma: FEDIC, 1994.

Giovannini, Attilio. *Guida alla pubblicità cinematografica*. Milano: L'ufficio moderno, 1957.

Giurlando, Davide, ed. *Fantasmagoria. Un secolo (e oltre) di cinema d'animazione*. Venezia: Marsilio, 2017.

Goldmark, Daniel. *Tunes for 'Toons: Music and the Hollywood Cartoon*. Berkeley: University of California Press, 2005.

Goldmark, Daniel, and Yuval Taylor. *The Cartoon Music Book*. Chicago: Chicago Review Press, 2002.

Grant, John. *Masters of Animation*. New York: Watson-Guptill, 2001.

Grasso, Aldo. *Storia della televisione italiana*. Milano: Garzanti, 2004.
Grasso, Aldo, Luca Barra, and Cecilia Penati, eds. *Storia critica della televisione italiana*. Milano: Il Saggiatore, 2019.
Green, Kerry. "What's New in Italian Animation. The World of Bruno Bozzetto." *Film Library Quarterly* XIII, no. 4 (1980): 30–6.
Guido, Francesco Maurizio, aka Gibba. *Diario. Un uomo di grande insuccesso*. Alassio: Città di Alassio, 2008.
Gut, Serge. "Le phénomène répétitif chez Maurice Ravel. De l'obsession à l'annihilation incantatoire." *International Review of the Aesthetics and Sociology of Music* 21, no. 1 (June 1990): 29–46.
Halas, John. *Masters of Animation*. London: BBC, 1987.
Halas, John, and Bob Privett. *How to Cartoon for Amateur Films*. London: Focal Press, 1951.
Halas, John, and Roger Manvell. *Art in Movement: New Directions in Animation*. New York: Hastings House, 1970.
Halas, John, and Roger Manvell. *The Technique of Film Animation*. London: Focal Press, 1959.
Hanslick, Eduard. *The Beautiful in Music: A Contribution to the Revisal of Musical Aesthetics*. Tranlsated by Gustav Cohen. London: Novello, 1891.
Harries, Dan. *Film Parody*. London: British Film Institute, 2000.
Hassen, Marjorie, ed. *Bach-Stokowski Toccata and Fugue for Organ, D Minor*. http://www.library.upenn.edu/exhibits/rbm/stokowski/bach.html (accessed August 17, 2019).
Hight, Craig. "Mockumentary: A Call To Play," in *Rethinking Documentary: New Perspectives, New Practices*, edited by Thomas Austin and Wilma de Jong, 204–16 (Berkshire: Open University Press)..
Hodge, Robert, and Gunther Kress. *Social Semiotics*. Ithaca, NY: Cornell University Press, 1988.
Honess Roe, Annabelle. *Animated Documentary*. London: Palgrave Macmillan, 2013.
Honolka, Kurt. *Dvořák*. London: Haus, 2004.
Hume, David. *Treatise Concerning Human Nature*. Edited by Lewis Amherst Selby-Bigge. Oxford: Oxford University Press, 1888.
Hutcheon, Linda. *A Theory of Parody: The Teachings of Twentieth Century Art Forms*. New York: Routledge, 1985.
Incontri internazionali con gli autori di cinema d'animazione. Pegli: Manni, 1983.
Incontri internazionali con gli autori di cinema d'animazione. Pegli: Manni, 1984.
Incontri internazionali con gli autori di cinema d'animazione. Pegli: Manni, 1985.
Kletschke, Irene. *Klangbilder. Walt Disneys "Fantasia" (1940)*. Stuttgart: Franz Steiner Verlag, 2011.
Lloyd, Rosemary. *Mallarmé: The Poet and His Circle*. Ithaca, NY: Cornell University Press, 2005.
Lombardo, Daniele. *Guida al cinema d'animazione. Fantasie e tecniche da Walt Disney all'elettronica*. Roma: Editori Riuniti, 1983.
Luckett, Moya. "Fantasia: Cultural Constructions of Disney's 'Masterpiece'," in *Disney Discourse: Producing the Magic Kingdom*, edited by Eric Smoodin, 214–36. London: Routledge, 1994.

Maisetti, Massimo, ed. *Cinema d'animazione italiano—Bruno Bozzetto 1956/1977*. Catalogo della rassegna. Roma: L'Officina Filmclub, 1977.
Maisetti, Massimo. "Il cinema d'animazione a Milano." *Ciemme* no. 98 (Oct.–Dec. 1991): 23–8.
Maisetti, Massimo, and Nedo Zanotti. *A scuola col cinema d'animazione. Guida pratica per insegnanti e alunni*. Venezia: Marsilio, 1979.
Manassero, Roberto, ed. *Infinity Festival 2005*. Cantalupa, TO: Effatà Editrice, 2005.
Manghini, Franca. "Apprendere con il cinema." *ISCA Informazione* 4–5, July–October, 1981.
Marnat, Marcel. *Ravel*. Paris: Fayard, 1986.
Massimino-Garniér, Max. "Contributi sul cinema d'animazione. Un'analisi non apocalittica. Rapporti tra il cinema d'animazione e le pubblicità." *Azimat*, May–October, 1971.
Massimino-Garniér, Max. "Scuole europee di cinema di animazione." *ISCA Informazione*, July–October, 1981.
Merritt, Russell, and J. B. Kaufman. *Walt Disney's Silly Symphonies: A Companion to the Classic Cartoon Series*. Gemona: La Cineteca del Friuli, 2006.
Miceli, Sergio. *Musica per film. Storia, Estetica, Analisi, Tipologie*. Milano: Ricordi LIM, 2009.
Michelone, Guido, and Giuseppe Valenzise. *Bibidi bobidi bu: la musica nei cartoni animati da Betty Boop a Peter Gabriel*. Roma: Castelvecchi, 1998.
Molinari, Vito. *Carosello… e poi tutti a nanna. 1957–1977: i vent'anni che hanno cambiato l'Italia*. Sestri Levante: Gammarò edizioni, 2019.
Montagna, Carlo. "Cinema d'animazione." *La Vernice*, December, 1970.
Montanaro, Carlo. "C'era una volta l'animazione italiana." *Cabiria* 177 (2014): 6–11.
Montanelli, Indro, and Mario Cervi. *L' Italia degli anni di piombo, 1965–1978*. Milano: BUR Rizzoli, 2018.
Moretti, Chiara. "Girolamo Poloni," in *I pittori bergamaschi dell'Ottocento*, edited by Rossana Bossaglia. Azzano San Paolo: Bolis, 1992. Now at https://girolamo-poloni.weebly.com (accessed July 19, 2019).
Newmarch, Rosa. Frontispiece notes to *Valse triste. From the Music to Arvid Järnefelt's Drama "Kuolema". By Jean Sibelius. From Op. 44. Arranged for Pianoforte Solo*. New York: Schirmer, 1904.
Nichetti, Maurizio. *Autobiografia involontaria*. Milano: Bietti, 2015.
Nin, Joaquín. "Comment est né le Boléro de Ravel." *La Revue Musicale* 19, no. 187 (December 1938): 211–13.
Osmond, Humphry Fortescue. "A Review of the Clinical Effects of Psychotomimetic Agents." *Annals of the New York Academy of Sciences* 66, no. 3 (1957): 418–34.
Pallant, Chris. *Demystifying Disney: A History of Disney Feature Animation*. London: Bloomsbury, 2013.
Pasolini, Pier Paolo. *Scritti corsari*. Milano: Garzanti, 2008.
Perucca, Sabrina. *Il cinema d'animazione italiano oggi*. Roma: Bulzoni, 2008.
Pintus, Mario. *A … come animazione*. Milano: ISCA, 1975.
Pistoia, Marco. *Maurizio Nichetti*. Milano: Il Castoro, 1997.

Pollone, Matteo, and Vittorio Sclaverani, eds. *Bruno Bozzetto*. Special issue of *Mondo niovo 18–24 ft/s*, 96, 2014.
Querin, Mario, ed. *Bruno Bozzetto*. Trento: Centro di Documentazione Visiva, 1992.
Rall, Hannes. *Animation from Concept to Production*. Boca Raton, FL: CRC Press, 2018. ePub.
Ramsey, Grant, and Charles H. Pence. "Chance in Evolution from Darwin to Contemporary Biology," in *Chance in Evolution*, edited by Grant Ramsey and Charles H. Pence, 1–11. Chicago: University of Chicago Press, 2016.
Reich, Willi. "In Memoriam Maurice Ravel." *La Revue Musicale* 19, no. 187 (December 1938): 275.
Retrospective Bruno Bozzetto. Annecy: Journées Internationales du Cinema d'animation, 1985.
Rigoni, Alberto, and Giovanni Russo. "All Roads Lead to Animation: Gianini, Luzzati, Cavandoli, and Manuli." *Animation Journal* 25 (2017): 49–61.
Rolf, Marie. "Semantic and Structural Issues in Debussy's Mallarmé Songs," in *Debussy Studies*, edited by Richard Langham Smith, 179–200. Cambridge: Cambridge University Press, 1997.
Rondolino, Gianni. *Bruno Bozzetto Pubblicitario*. Torino: STIP, 1969; now in Bastiancich, Alfio, ed. *Bruno Bozzetto: 1958–1988*. Savona: Centro Promozionale Coop, 1988.
Rondolino, Gianni. *Storia del cinema d'animazione*. Torino: UTET, 2003.
Roscoe, Jane, and Craig Hight. *Faking It: Mock-Documentary and the Subversion of Factuality*. Manchester: Manchester University Press, 2001.
Rubin, David S. *Psychedelic: Optical and Visionary Art since the 1960s*. Cambridge, MA: MIT Press, 2010.
Santillo, Maria Pia. *Conversazioni Animate. Interviste a dodici registi d'animazione italiani*. Berlin: RAUM Italic, 2016.
Sbravatti, Valerio. *Allegro non troppo. Vedere la musica e ascoltare i disegni*. Roma: Il glifo, 2015. Kindle.
Schönberg, Arnold. *The Musical Idea and the Logic, Technique and Art of Its Presentation*. Edited by Patricia Carpenter and Severine Neff. New York: Columbia University Press, 1995.
Schopf, J. William. *Cradle of Life: The Discovery of Earth's Early Fossils*. Princeton, NJ: Princeton University Press, 1999.
Scollo Lavizzari, Marco. "INCOM," in *Enciclopedia del Cinema*. Roma: Treccani, 2003.
Scrimitore, Raffella. *Le origini dell'animazione italiana. La storia, gli autori e i film animati in Italia 1911–1949*. Latina: Tunué, 2013.
Scrimitore, Raffaella. "Luigi Liberio Pensuti, film d'animazione oltre la propaganda." *Cabiria* 178 (2014): 47–56.
Scrimitore, Raffaella, Mario Verger, and Emiliano Fasano. "Chronology of Italian Animation, 1911–2017." *Animation Journal* 25 (2017): 6–37.
Sette, Alessandra Maria. *Personaggi e interpreti. L'animazione dalla réclame allo spot*. Roma: Garamond, 1996.

Shoemaker, Pamela J., and Tim P. Vos. *Gatekeeping Theory*. New York: Routledge, 2009.
Speciale cinema d'animazione. Portfolio illustratori, VI, no. 8. Cuneo: Editrice Azzurra—Associazione Illustratori, May 1986.
Stephenson, Ralph. *The Animated Film*. London: Tantivy Press, 1973.
Suarès, André. "Ravel. Esquisse." *La Revue Musicale* 19, no. 187 (December, 1938): 48–52.
Taruskin, Richard. *Stravinsky and the Russian Traditions*. Oxford: Oxford University Press, 556.
Thomas, Frank, and Ollie Johnston. *The Illusion of Life: Disney Animation*. New York: Disney Editions, 1981.
Tirapelle, Roberto (wrongly attributed to A. Camon), ed. *Il cinema di Bruno Bozzetto. Sequenze* 9. Verona: Nuova Grafica Cierre, 1990.
Toninelli, Fabio, ed. *Bruno Bozzetto. La lina intorno all'idea*. Cremona: Tapirulan, 2019.
Tyrrell, John. "Skočná". *Grove Music Online*, 2001. https://www.oxfordmusiconline.com/grovemusic/view/10.1093/gmo/9781561592630.001.0001/omo-9781561592630-e-0000043852 (accessed November 17, 2019).
uDiscover Team. "'I Fell in Love with the Original Again': Max Richter on Recomposing Vivaldi's Four Seasons." uDiscovermusic, 31 August 2019. https://www.udiscovermusic.com/classical-features/max-richter-recomposed-vivaldi-four-seasons/ (accessed November 28, 2019).
Valoroso, Nunziante. "Stagioni cinematografiche Walt Disney Italia 1938–2000." *Cabiria* 171 (2012): 43–64.
Vlad, Roman. *Stravinsky*. Oxford: Oxford University Press, 1985.
Walker, Steven F. "Mallarmé's Symbolist Eclogue: The 'Faune' as Pastoral." *PMLA* 93, no. 1 (January 1978): 106–17.
Weber, William. "Concert (ii)." *New Grove Dictionary of Music and Musicians*. Grove Online. https://www.oxfordmusiconline.com/grovemusic/view/10.1093/gmo/9781561592630.001.0001/omo-9781561592630-e-0000006240 (accessed August 16, 2019).
Wenk, Arthur. *Claude Debussy and the Poets*. Berkeley: University of California Press, 1976.
Zane, Marcello. *Scatola a sorpresa. La Gamma Film di Roberto Gavioli e la comunicazione audiovisiva in Italia da Carosello a oggi*. Milano: Jaca Book, 1998.
Zangrando, Fiorello. *Ombre italiane. Storia dei disegni e pupazzi animati*. Milano: Quaderni dell'osservatore, 1968.
Zanotto, Piero. *Disegni e pupazzi animati di ieri e di oggi. Quaderni della Rivista del cinematografo* 12. Roma: Arti Grafiche Scalia, 1966.
Zanotto, Piero. *I disegni animati*. Padova: RADAR, 1968.
Zanotto, Piero, and Fiorello Zangrando. *L'italia di cartone*. Padova: Liviana, 1973.

Press Articles

Abbattista Finocchiaro, Antonia. "Bruno Bozzetto, un giovane autore di cinema." *La Rivista di Bergamo* 29, nuova serie, January–March, 2002.

"Addio ad Albicocco, grande cartoonist." *Il Resto del Carlino*, April 15, 2011, 27.

"Addio al regista e animatore Giuseppe Laganà". *Il Blog di Fumodichina*, January 5, 2016. https://ilblogdifumodichina.blogspot.com/2016/01/addio-al-regista-e-animatore-giuseppe.html (accessed October 17, 2019).

"Allegro non troppo." *L'Ordine*, February 26, 1978.

"Allegro non troppo di Bruno Bozzetto." *Libertà*, January 20, 1978.

Alvarez, Raul. "Dal Bozzetto al computer." *Nuovo Cinema Europeo*, March 1981, 10, 12.

Andrews, Rena. "*Allegro non troppo*. Adult's Fantastic Journey of *Fantasia*." *Denver Post*, September 22, 1977.

Azzano, Enrico, and Raffaele Meale. "a Bruno Bozzetto—Parte Seconda." *Quinlan. Rivista di critica cinematografica*, April 4, 2014. https://quinlan.it/2014/04/04/intervista-bruno-bozzetto-parte-seconda/ (accessed July 24, 2019).

Azzano, Enrico, and Raffaele Meale. "Intervista a Bruno Bozzetto." *Quinlan. Rivista di critica cinematografica*, April 4, 2014. https://quinlan.it/2014/04/04/intervista-bruno-bozzetto/ (accessed August 2, 2019).

Balducci, Maurizio. "Storie a ritmo di cartoons. Intervista a Bruno Bozzetto." *Segnocinema* 28, May 1987.

Bandettini, Anna. "Allegro non troppo. Ho settant'anni." *La Repubblica*, March 2, 2008.

Bastiancich, Alfio. "Italie: visages de Bruno Bozzetto." *CinémAction* 51, April 1989.

Belpoliti, Marco. "Bruno Bozzetto. 78 anni di idee con linee attorno." *Ascolta!*, March 3, 2016. https://www.doppiozero.com/rubriche/3/201602/bruno-bozzetto-77-anni-di-idee-con-linee-attorno (accessed August 2, 2019).

Bendazzi, Giannalberto. "Atlas Ufo Robot contro il Signor Rossi." *Cinemasessanta* 135, September/October 1980.

Bendazzi, Giannalberto. "Bozzetto del sig. Bozzetto." *Linus* 4, no. 205, April 1982.

Bendazzi, Giannalberto. "Bruno Bozzetto: il più giovane, il più bravo." *King Cinema* 1, May 1969.

Bendazzi, Giannalberto. "I sogni del Signor Rossi." *Letture*, April 1979.

Bendazzi, Giannalberto. "Molti film, buone intenzioni ma poco arrosto per il turismo." *Turismo Italia*, June 30, 1975.

Bendazzi, Giannalberto. "Siamo in crisi: ah, se tornasse il bel Carosello," *Il Giorno*, August 17, 1981.

Bendazzi, Giannalberto. "Un'anima gentile." *Il Sole 24 Ore*, December 3, 2000.

Bologna, Carlo. "Allegro non troppo." *Il Giornale Nuovo*, February 4, 1978.

Bologna, Carlo. "È molto sospetto: fa pensare." *L'Arena*, February 4, 1978.

Bolsi, Daniela. "Ecco un sandwich di comiche per una satira in pillole." *Il Giornale*, December 18, 1984.

Bozzetto, Bruno. "Il Signor Rossi va in America. La lezione di Bozzetto." *La Repubblica*, May 13, 2012.

Brugnoli, Olinto. "Allegro non troppo." *La Voce dei Berici* 26, February 1978.

Bugliosi, Rita. "Il papà del Signor Rossi tra spazio e nanotecnologie." *Almanacco della Scienza* 7, July 5, 2017. http://www.almanacco.cnr.it/reader/cw_usr_view_facciaafaccia.html?id_facciaafaccia=8073&giornale=8074 (accessed August 2, 2019).
Cappa, Marina. "I miei spaghetti sono cattivissimi." *Il Giorno*, October 31, 1998.
Caroli, Clara. "Non chiamatemi papà. I miai cartoon? Tanta fortuna. E oggi il Signor Rossi direbbe … ." *La Repubblica*, May 10, 2013.
Carra, Luca. "Mazinga è mostruoso e impacciato, l'uomo di Bozzetto è umano, rigoroso, persino scientifico." *Italia Oggi*, March 25, 1987.
Casini, Stefania. "Ti convinco con il trucco." *Ciak* 1, May 1985.
Catena, Antonella. "I cartoni animati in cattedra." *Alba* 45, November 5, 1993.
Cattaneo, Marcella. "Cinema d'animazione. Bruno Bozzetto." *La Rivista di Bergamo* 33, nuova serie, 2003.
Cervasio, Stella. "Bozzetto: 'Napoli il top della fantasia'." *La Repubblica*, November 2, 2016.
Champlin, Charles. "*Allegro* in Time with *Fantasia*." *Los Angeles Times*, July 26, 1977.
Chiari, Francesco. "Bruno Bozzetto o del saper ridere." *Il popolo cattolico*, May 20, 1995.
Chiarullo, Enzo. "La firma di Bruno Bozzetto per gli spot natalizi di La7." *Italia Oggi*, December 20, 2002.
Cirio, Rita. "La tigre di cartoon." *L'Espresso*, September 19, 1976.
Codelli, Lorenzo. "Bruno Bozzetto, opiniâtre et solitaire." *Positif* 472, June 2000.
Colombo, Franco. "Allegro non troppo." *La Gazzetta del Mezzogiorno*, December 31, 1977.
Colombo, Franco. "Allegro non troppo." *L'Unità*, December 31, 1977.
Colombo, Franco. "Bozzetto spiega in una mostra i segreti dei cartoni animati." *L'Eco di Bergamo*, October 17, 1974.
Colombo, Franco. "Bruno Bozzetto con *Allegro non troppo* ha conquistato l'America prima dell'Italia." *L'Eco di Bergamo*, April 20, 1976.
Colombo, Franco. "Celebri pagine musicali alla base del nuovo film di Bruno Bozzetto." *L'Eco di Bergamo*, August 21, 1974.
Colombo, Franco. "Film di Bozzetto in Brasile." *L'Eco di Bergamo*, July 24, 1974.
Colombo, Franco. "I cartoons di Bozzetto fanno il giro del mondo." *L'Eco di Bergamo*, December 23, 1975.
Colombo, Franco. "Un'orchestra di anziane signore per il nuovo film di Bozzetto." *L'Eco di Bergamo*, April 20, 1976.
Comuzio, Ermanno. "A come animazione." *Il Giornale di Bergamo*, February 8, 1976.
Comuzio, Ermanno. "Allegro non troppo di Bruno Bozzetto." *Cineforum*, April 4, 1978.
Comuzio, Ermanno. "Arriva Bozzetto a New York." *Il Mattino di Padova*, February 14, 1979.
Comuzio, Ermanno. "Bozzetto ha messo in piazza i segreti del suo mestiere." *La Notte*, October 15, 1974.
Comuzio, Ermanno. "Bruno Bozzetto." *La Rivista di Bergamo* 5, April–June 1996.
Comuzio, Ermanno. "Bruno Bozzetto ci fa da maestro nella gaia epopea del sesso." *Il Giornale di Bergamo*, January 4, 1979.

Comuzio, Ermanno. "Bruno Bozzetto dal film animato al 'dal vero' attraverso la 'porta dei sogni'." *Cineforum* 266, August 1987.
Comuzio, Ermanno. "Bruno Bozzetto sta lavorando ad un nuovo lungometraggio animato." *Il Giornale di Bergamo*, July 20, 1974.
Comuzio, Ermanno. "Come ri-disegnare il mondo." *La Rivista di Bergamo* 5, nuova serie, April–June 1996.
Comuzio, Ermanno. "I sogni del Signor Rossi." *Ciao 2001*, February 4, 1979.
Comuzio Ermanno. "I sogni del Signor Rossi". *Il Giornale di Bergamo*, February 11, 1979.
Comuzio, Ermanno. "Il 'cartoonist' Bergamasco." *Il Giornale di Bergamo*, December 17, 1977.
Comuzio, Ermanno. "Questo è il più bel film di Bozzetto." *Il Giornale di Bergamo*, February 19, 1978.
Comuzio, Ermanno. "Successo a New York per Bruno Bozzetto." *Il Resto del Carlino*, February 15, 1979.
Comuzio, Ermanno. "Tre film in lizza per il 'Rizzoli'." *Il Giornale Nuovo*, April 22, 1978.
Comuzio, Ermanno. "Vip, My Brother Superman." *Cineforum* 79, November 1968.
Comuzio, Ermanno. "Vip! Mio fratello superuomo" *Cineforum* 79, November 1968, 669.674.
Comuzio, Ermanno. "Successo a New York per Bruno Bozzetto." *Il Resto del Carlino*, February 15, 1979.
Comuzio, Ermanno. "Tre film in lizza per il 'Rizzoli'." *Il Giornale Nuovo*, April 22, 1978.
Cosulich, Oscar. "Ci sono soldi soltanto per gli spot." *La Repubblica*, July 26, 1996.
Cosulich, Oscar. "Il fumetto." *L'Espresso*, January 9, 1997.
Cosulich, Oscar. "Joff il gatto firmato Bozzetto." *La Repubblica*, April 24, 1995.
Cosulich, Oscar. "Ora mi do del lei allo specchio." La Repubblica, March 9, 1991.
Crespi, Alberto. "*Sandwich* e *Il Corsaro Nero*: e chissà che la Tv non smantelli il ghetto …." *Cineforum* 247, September 1985.
Crist, Judith. "A Charming 'Allegro' Fantasy from Italy." *New York Post*, September 16, 1977.
De La Fuente, Léonardo. "Un grand dessinéaste." *Cinéma 72* 244, April 1979.
De Luca, Alessandra. "Bruno Bozzetto a Cartoons on the Bay: 'Il Signor Rossi potrebbe tornare sullo schermo'." *Ciak*, April 15, 2018. https://www.ciakmagazine.it/bruno-bozzetto-disegni-film/ (accessed August 2, 2019).
Demme, Enrico. "Bozzetto spiega il suo lavoro; Vesto un'idea con il disegno." *L'Unità*, May 15, 1982.
D. G. "Allegro non troppo." *Il Settimanale*, January 4, 1978.
D. G. "Il Signor Rossi umano e non umano." *L'Unità*, December 24, 1978.
D. G. "I sogni del Signor Rossi." *L'Unità*, January 2, 1978.
Di Fronzo, Luigi. "Allegro non troppo. Il film di Bozzetto musicato dalla Verdi." *La Repubblica*, April 16, 2005.
Di Fronzo, Luigi. "I cartoon di Disney e Bozzetto. Questa sì che è buona musica." *La Repubblica*, December 20, 2003.
Di Maria, Paolo. "Mazinga che noia (conversazione con Gianni Rondolino)." *Nuovo Cinema Europeo*, March 1981.

Di Stefano, Paolo. "Bruno Bozzetto: 'Ora il mio signor Rossi diventerà un blogger'." *Corriere della Sera*, September 29, 2018. https://www.corriere.it/cronache/18_settembre_29/bruno-bozzetto-ora-mio-signor-rossi-diventera-blogger-fb6c27ec-c420-11e8-af74-9a32bd2d1376.shtml?refresh_ce-cp (accessed July 21, 2019).

Dividi, Fabrizio. "Bruno Bozzetto: 'L'ecologia? L'ho scoperta grazie a Bambi della Disney'." *Corriere Torino*, July 10, 2019.

F. C. "Bozzetto a Teheran nella giuria internazionale." *L'Eco di Bergamo*, October 27, 1972.

F. C. "Bruno Bozzetto senza sosta tra cinema, libri, festival." *L'Eco di Bergamo*, October 26, 1971.

Feo, Marco. "L'arte di Bruno Bozzetto." *Computer Graphics & Publishing*, November–December 2000.

Ferrari, Ilia. "La musica è una guida per entrare nella realtà." *La Repubblica*, December 14, 1977.

Festa, Anna. "Supergulp, i fumetti in TV." *Brescia Oggi*, October 18, 1977.

Fidi, Vittorio Emilio. "Bruno Bozzetto, Regista? Disegnatore? Fumettaro? Creativo a tempo pieno." *Qui Bergamo*, March 1994.

Filizzola, Renato. "Walt Disney 'revisionato'." *Il Nostro Tempo*, January 22, 1978.

Frerè, Pierfrancesco. "La fine di Carosello. Contro Calimero sparate a zero." *Il Settimanale*, August 4, 1976.

Garel, Alain. "Allegro non troppo." *Image et Son* 338, April 1979.

Gasparini, Barbara. "Marziani sfacciati e ventilatori volanti." *Virtual—Mensile di Realtà Virtuale e Immagini di Sintesi*, December 1993.

Gasparini, Barbara. "Sintetico ma non troppo." *Virtual—Mensile di Realtà Virtuale e Immagini di Sintesi*, March 1994.

Gavazzeni, Alberto. "I cartoni di Bozzetto." *Il Giornale di Bergamo*, April 21, 1971.

Gavioli, Gianni. "Bruno Bozzetto." *Creativi*, March 11, 1995.

Gavioli, Gianni. "Bruno Bozzetto." *Creativi*, March 18, 1995.

Gavioli, Gianni. "Bruno Bozzetto." *Creativi*, March 25, 1995.

Gavioli, Gianni. "Bruno Bozzetto." *Creativi*, April 1, 1995.

Gedda, Alberto. "Bozzetto, cinquant'anni come un graffito amaro." *La Repubblica*, April 27, 2005.

Ghigi, Giuseppe. "I sogni del Signor Rossi." *Il Diario*, December 27, 1978.

G. G. "Disney in Parodia nel 'cartoon' italiano." *Il Corriere della Sera*, December 29, 1977.

Giampaoli, Emanuela. "I maestri dell'animazione svelano arti e affinità elettive." *La Repubblica*, November 28, 2007.

Giovannini, Attilio. "Che lingua parla Alan Ford?" *La Repubblica*, April 21, 1977.

Giovannini, Attilio. "I sogni del Signor Rossi." *La Repubblica*, January 2, 1979.

Giovannini, Attilio. "I sogni del Signor Rossi in TV." *Linea Grafica*, January 2, 1979.

Giovannini, Attilio. "Il cartone animato dalla pubblicità al lungometraggio." *L'Ufficio Moderno*, May 1973.

Giovannini, Attilio. "Il mondo dei fumetti." *L'Avanti*, March 10, 1977.

Giovannini, Attilio. "La mosca e il cattivissimo." *Linea Grafica*, May 1979.

Giovannini, Attilio. "La parola come animazione del'immagine." *Linea Grafica*, August 1979.

Giovannini, Attilio. "Occhio allo schermo: libertà, censura e conformismo." *L'Ufficio Moderno*, March 1977.
Giovannini, Attilio. "Un cartoon anti-Disneyano per Bruno Bozzetto." *La Notte*, July 26, 1974.
Giovannini, Attilio. "Una rivoluzione estetica nei titoli dei film." *Linea Grafica*, November 1977.
Giuliano, Cristina. "Un mammut da 15 miliardi." *Punto.com*, April 17, 2001.
G. R. "Come sogna Bozzetto". *Il Corriere della Sera*, December 23, 1978.
Grazzini, Giovanni. "Allegro non troppo." *Corriere della Sera*, December 23, 1977.
Grazzini, Giovanni. "Vip, My Brother Superman." *Corriere della Sera*, November 1, 1968.
G. R. L. "Allegro non troppo." *Il Tempo*, December 23, 1977.
Guardini, Laura. "Nel mondo degli insetti con Bruno Bozzetto." *L'Occhio*, July 10, 1981.
Guarienti, Giovanni. "Bozzetto inventa storie." *Musica Viva*, February 1978.
Guarienti, Giovanni. "L'Allegro di Bozzetto." *La Voce del Popolo*, February 10, 1978.
Guarienti, Giovanni. "La parodia di Disney in un 'cartoon' italiano." *Il Giornale di Sicilia*, February 5, 1978.
Guarienti, Giovanni. "Questo non è un film." *L'Arena*, February 4, 1978.
Henné, Peter. "Bozo troppo. Visually Stunning, Comically Void." *Westwood Village View*, October 19, 1990.
Impellizeri, Paolo. "Coi cartoni animati all'origine dell'uomo." *Bergamo Oggi*, June 17, 1981.
"Intervista a Bruno Bozzetto." *Strane Storie—Altroquando* 8, Fall 2001.
"Intervista a Giorgio Valentini." Tesionline Cinema. https://cinema.tesionline.it/cinema/article.jsp?id=1296 (accessed October 18, 2019).
Lanfranco, Emanuela. "Bozzetto, un vip tutto da ridere." *La Voce*, April 26, 1996.
Lazzarin, Paolo. "Dieci consigli di Bruno Bozzetto." *Panorama*, December 19, 1974.
Lo Duca, Joseph-Marie. "Alice al paese delle meraviglie." *Cinema Nuova Serie* I, no. 6 (January 15, 1949): 176–7.
Lussana, Massimiliano. "Italiani brava gente (e anche furba)." *Il Giornale*, December 31, 1996.
Maisetti, Massimo. "Animatori alla riscossa." *L'Unità*, September 2, 1979.
Maisetti, Massimo. "Arriva Bozzetto, con i suoi disegni diverte e ci prende in giro." *Il Secolo XIX*, May 5, 1982.
Maisetti, Massimo. "Bruno Bozzetto: l'anti-Disney italiano." *Letture*, March 1974.
Maisetti, Massimo. "Cartoni animati d'importazione." *Il Giornale dello Spettacolo*, May 14, 1982.
Maisetti, Masismo. "Cartoons in lotta contro i minuti." *L'Unità*, August 8, 1979.
Maisetti, Massimo. "Il ritorno di Biancaneve, una bambina di 43 anni." *L'Unità*, January 11, 1981.
Maisetti, Massimo. "Sette cortometraggi di Bruno Bozzetto." *La Provincia*, July 22, 1979.
Maisetti, Massimo. "Sotto il ristorante cinese." *Letture* 10, October 1987.
Maisetti, Massimo. "Sul video cartoni animati scelti male o come tappabuchi. Ma per fortuna c'è braccio di ferro." *L'Unità*, July 18, 1979.

Maisetti, Massimo. "Tutti d'importazione i film d'animazione in TV?" *ISCA Informazione* 3–4, March–April 1982.
Maisetti, Massimo. "Vincono i premi ma sono disoccupati." *L'Unità*, August 13, 1979.
Manin, Giuseppina. "Quel primo 'bau' non si scorda mai." *Corriere della Sera*, March 9, 1996.
Manuppelli, Ivan. "Intervista a Bruno Bozzetto." *Piero Tonin Blog*, December 12, 2014 (http://pierotonin.blogspot.com/2014/12/intervista-bruno-bozzetto_12.html (accessed October 17, 2019).
Marchesano, Nino. "Bruno Bozzetto all'università 'Ecco come nascono i miei eroi'." *La Repubblica*, April 9, 2008.
Maritan, Massimo. "Quei gustosi *Sandwich* … alla Bozzetto. Cortometraggi comici prodotti dalla Tsi." *TeleRadio7—Rivista settimalae della Svizzera italiana sui programmi radiotelevisivi*, July 13–19, 1985.
Meek, Scott. "Allegro non troppo." *Monthly Film Bulletin* 547, August 1979.
Moneta, Francesco. "Bozzetto dà un'anima a un 'muletto' giallo." *Il Giornale di Bergamo*, October 8, 1979.
Morandini, Morando. "Bozzetto—Come *Fantasia* ma meglio di Walt Disney." *Il Giorno*, December 23, 1977.
Morandini, Morando. "Il successo 'made in Usa' gli ha aperto la strada." *Il Giorno*, December 20, 1977.
Morandini, Morando. "Un'orchestra di vecchie donne per un *Fantasia* all'italiana." *La Repubblica*, December 23, 1977.
Moskowitz, Gene. "Allegro non troppo." *Variety*, December 8, 1976.
M. T. "Da domani a Pescara i graffianti cartoni animati di Bozzetto." *L'Unità* November 12, 1978.
Nosari, Pier Giorgio, and Lucia Ferrajoli. "Il Signor Rossi è un pezzo da museo." *L'Eco di Bergamo*, December 5, 2000.
Novelli, Luca. "Tutta la forza del cinema d'animazione. Conversazione con Bruno Bozzetto, cineasta e pensatore per immagini." *Grafica & Disegno* 13, September/October 1994.
O. R. "Bruno Bozzetto spiega il successo dei cartoni animati giapponesi." *La Stampa*, December 2, 1979.
Orlando, Alessandra. "Bozzetto fa da guida per un viaggio tra i 'segreti' dei cartoni animati." *L'Eco di Bergamo*, March 28,1985.
Paganin, Patrizio. "Bozzetto il timido—La vita è una matita." *La Repubblica*, November 26, 1994.
Pasolini, Pier Paolo. "Una sfida ai dirigenti di Viale Mazzini." *Corriere della Sera*, December 9, 1973.
Perrone, Paolo. "Come si dice cartoon in italiano?" *Letture* 561, November 1999.
Pescatori, Vanna. "Tutti 'umoristi doc'." *La Stampa*, May 20, 1995.
Pianelli, Giuseppe. "Allegro non troppo." *Roma TV*, January 8, 1978.
Pianelli, Giuseppe. "Allegro quasi pessimista." *L'Osservatore Romano*, January 7, 1978.
Pianelli, Giuseppe. "Bella rivincita." *Il Tirreno*, January 11, 1978.
Pianelli, Giuseppe. "Bruno Bozzetto Allegro non troppo." *Stereoplay*, January 1978.
Pini, Luciano. "Allegro non troppo." *L'Unità*, December 23, 1977.

Pintus, Mario. "Si conclude l'incontro con il cinema d'animazione." *La Nuova Sardegna*, December 20, 1978.
Pintus, Mario. "Tutti i miei attori fatti di luce, colore e fantasia." *La Nuova Sardegna*, July 23, 1993.
Poggialini, M. "Bruno Bozzetto da trent'anni 'Signor Rossi' del cartone." *Avvenire*, October 19, 1988.
"Quando il cuore si anima." DVD Italy, December 9, 2005. https://www.dvd-italy.it/quando-il-cuore-si-anima/ (accessed August 2, 2019).
Quaianni, Maya. "È morto Giuseppe Maurizio Laganà." *Lo Spazio Bianco*, January 5, 2016. https://www.lospaziobianco.it/morto-giuseppe-maurizio-lagana (accessed October 17, 2019).
"Quelli dello Studio Bozzetto. Vale a dire: la Disney bergamasca." *Bergamopost*, December 14, 2014. http://www.bergamopost.it/vivabergamo/studio-bozzetto-disney-bergamasca/ (accessed July 30, 2019).
Raffaelli, Luca. "Il segreto della felicità di Bruno Bozzetto: 'Mia moglie, papà e una pecora'." *La Repubblica*, August 18, 2016.
Ransenigo, Gianfranco. "I fumetti al cinema. La matita sullo schermo." *Brescia Oggi*, November 9, 1977.
Rastagno, Remo. "Alla ricerca dell'animazione." *Scena*, September 1977.
Rastagno, Remo. "Cartoni animati educativi alla TV." *Il Giornale di Calabria*, October 8, 1977.
Rezoagli, Sandro. "Disney parodiato dal Signor Rossi." *L'Avvenire*, December 16, 1977.
R. F. "Alla corte del sultano il mastino diventa una pecora." *La Repubblica*, December 27, 1978.
R. F. "I sogni del piccolo 'Travet', i sogni del Signor Rossi." *Il Giornale di Sicilia*, December 31, 1978.
Riccardi, Francesco. "La musica di Jannacci per i cartoni di 'Carosello'." *Linkiesta*, April 2, 2013. https://www.linkiesta.it/it/article/2013/04/02/la-musica-di-jannacci-per-i-cartoni-di-carosello/12650/ (accessed July, 26, 2019).
Ronchetti, Pierluigi. "Una bottiglia di Coca-Cola ci verserà sulla Luna." *Il Tempo*, December 6, 1974.
Rondolino, Gianni. "Bozzetto quasi come Disney." *La Stampa*, February 22, 1978.
Rondolino, Gianni. "Sigmund di Bozzetto va alle Olimpiadi." *La Stampa*, April 3, 1984.
Rosa, Riccardo. "Dai film di Nichetti a Mastro Lindo: addio a Giovanni Ferrari, l'uomo capace di disegnare i sogni." *Corriere della Sera*, December 27, 2017.
Rossi, Giovanni, M. "Allegro non troppo anti-Disney senza fantasia." *L'Unità*, March 31, 1978.
Scaccabarozzi, Claudio. "Tao e la fatica della semplicità." *La Provincia*, May 20, 1992.
Schickel, Richard. "Neo-*Fantasia*—Allegro non troppo." *Time*, October 3, 1977.
Schupp, Patrick. "Allegro non troppo." *Séquences* 104, April 1981.
Serenellini, Mario. "Allegro non troppo." *La Gazzetta del Popolo*, December 24, 1977.
Serenellini, Mario. "Bozzetto cerca fondi per il suo film. 'L'Italia è disinteressata ai cartoon'." *La Repubblica*, March 6, 2016.

Serenellini, Mario. "Bozzetto: i roditori? Grandi attori. L'importante è che siano minuscoli." *La Repubblica*, October 17, 2007.
Serenellini, Mario. "Bozzetto: il cinema snobba i cartoon italiani ma mi vuole Disney." *La Repubblica*, April 6, 2009.
Serenellini, Mario. "Bozzetto: 'la mia passione in 3D'." *La Repubblica*, November 4, 2005.
S Serenellini, Mario. "Bozzetto, la sfida americana di un disegnatore da premio." *La Repubblica*, November 27, 2014.
erenellini, Mario. "Bozzetto racconta i segreti dei cartoon." *La Repubblica*, May 11, 2002.
Serenellini, Mario. "Bozzetto si dà all'ecologia." *La Repubblica*, January 2, 1991.
Serenellini, Mario. "Bruno Bozzetto festeggia 50 anni molto animati." *La Repubblica*, April 28, 2005.
Serenellini, Mario. "'Fantasiaspaghetti', ma in Usa trionfò." *La Repubblica*, December 6, 2000.
Serenellini, Mario. "Il Signor Bozzetto." *La Repubblica*, December 6, 2000.
Serenellini, Mario. "Macchè cinquant'anni, West & Soda è attuale." *La Repubblica*, November 24, 2015.
Serenellini, Mario. "Variazioni su Fantasia." *Il Giornale Nuovo*, December 27, 1977.
Sereni, Silvio. "Tornano gli eroi di carta." *Paese Sera*, March 15, 1977.
Signorelli, Angelo. "West and Soda, 1965 e Vip, My Brother Superman, 1968." *La Rivista di Bergamo* 33, nuova serie.
Solmi, Angelo. "Un west tutto da ridere." *Oggi*, October 28, 1965.
Solomon, Charles. "*Allegro non troppo* Returns with Expansion of Live Action." *Los Angeles Times*, October 19, 1990.
Spaventa, Simona. "Bruno Bozzetto: Allegro non troppo quarant'anni dopo." *La Repubblica*, October 11, 2016.
Spaventa, Simona. "Casa, prato e vignette. La Favola di Beelen, pecora popstar di Bruno Bozzetto." *La Repubblica*, January 2, 2019.
Spaventa, Simona. "Il mago dei cartoon." *La Repubblica*, January 16, 2011.
Spaventa, Simona. "Il Signor Rossi e i nuovi Cartoon. Bruno Bozzetto ritorna al futuro." *La Repubblica*, January 11, 2014.
Specchia, Francesco. "Bozzetto, il destino di un uomo nel cognome." *Libero*, January 16, 2001.
Specchia, Francesco. "Bozzetto in corsia e il gatto grida ...." *Il Giornale*, May 30, 1996.
Stone, Judy. "A Delightful Italian Bow to Disney's *Fantasia*." *San Francisco Chronicle*, November 18, 1977.
Strano, Gualtiero. "Fa il verso a Disney il nuovo mago dei cartoni animati." *Il Secolo*, March 25, 1978.
Strauss, Bob. "*Allegro*'s Fantasia of Inspiration." *Daily News*, October 19, 1990.
Tanzarella, Mariella. "Bruno Bozzetto 'Con lui lavorare era divertimento'." *La Repubblica*, January 4, 2004.
Tanzarella, Mariella. "Noi Grock, quarant'anni di pura passione c'eravamo." *La Repubblica*, April 4, 2014.
Tournès, Andrée. "Allegro non troppo." *Jeune Cinéma* 118, April–May 1979.

Valdata, Achille. "Bozzetto al lavoro per un nuovo film." *L'Eco di Bergamo*, December 5, 1973.
Valdata, Achille. "Bozzetto dichiara guerra ai cartoon." *Stampa Sera*, August 1, 1973.
Valdata, Achille. "Opere e premi di Bruno Bozzetto." *L'Eco di Bergamo*, December 5, 1973.
Valdata, Achille. "Un terzo lungometraggio d'animazione nei prossimi programmi di Bozzetto?" *L'Eco di Bergamo*, August 3, 1973.
Vecchi, Bruno. "Parolacce e fumetti in tv. Per il Signor Rossi è tutto un imbroglio." *L'Unità*, January 15, 2000.
Venantino, Gianni. "Bozzetto in giuria al festival di Zagabria." *Il Giornale di Bergamo*, April 26, 1974.
Venantino, Gianni. "Umiliato e offeso il 'cartoon italiano'." *Il Piccolo*, April 6, 1974.
Verger, Mario. "Addio Walter Cavazzuti." *Note di tecnica cinematografica*, April 2003–January 2004, 28–9.
Verger, Mario. "Il mondo di Bruno Bozzetto." *Rapporto Confidenziale* 14, May 2009, 26–33.
Vigorelli, Vittorio. "Bozzetto ha esplorato i classici della musica." *Il Giornale di Bergamo*, May 9, 1978.
Voltolini, Alberta. "Bruno Bozzetto. 'Campiglio quanto m'ispiri'." *CampiglIO* 4 no. 6 (Summer 2018): 16–24.
"Walter Cavazzuti." *Girodivite.it*. https://www.girodivite.it/antenati/xx3sec/_cavazzuti.htm (accessed October, 18, 2019).
Zanotto, Piero. "Anche l'umorismo depura il fegato." *Momento Sera*, September 28, 1976.
Zanotto, Piero. "Assurda emarginazione perseguita i cartoni animati." *Avvenire*, April 5, 1974.
Zanotto, Piero. "E adesso il Signor Rossi diventa latin lover." *Il Gazzettino*, December 28, 1970.

Documentaries

"Behind the Scenes," a documentary in the *Vip, My Brother Superman* DVD, part of the DVD collection "Tutto Bozzetto (o quasi)." Roma: Multimedia San Paolo, 2005.
Bozzetto non troppo (Marco Bonfanti, 2017).
Gente di Milano—I mondi di Bruno Bozzetto (Daniela Trastulli), in the DVD "I corti di Bruno Bozzetto," part of the DVD collection "Tutto Bozzetto (o quasi)." Roma: Multimedia San Paolo, 2005.
"I segreti di West & Soda," a documentary in the West & Soda DVD, part of the DVD collection "Tutto Bozzetto (o quasi)." Roma: Multimedia San Paolo, 2005.
L'arte è un delfino. Intervista a Bruno Bozzetto (Stefania Gaudiosi, September 30, 2019). https://www.artribune.com/television/2019/09/video-l-arte-e-un-delfino-intervista-a-bruno-bozzetto/ (accessed December 14, 2019).
L'intervista di Enzo De Bernardis, 7 gennaio 1977, https://www.swissinfo.ch/ita/compie-50-anni--west-and-soda-/42645310 (accessed July 24, 2019).
"Ricordando *Allegro non troppo*," a documentary in the *Allegro non troppo* DVD, part of the DVD collection "Tutto Bozzetto (o quasi)." Roma: Multimedia San Paolo, 2005.

INDEX

Note: Page numbers followed by "n." indicate endnotes in the text.

2001: A Space Odyssey (Kubrick) 176

Abano Terme 16
Abbado, Claudio 111
Academy Award 2, 16, 38, 57
Adam, Adolphe 215
Adam and Eve 71, 107, 110, 193, 195, 198–200, 207, 227–8
Adobe Flash (software animation tool) 59, 115
advertising
  agencies 12
  campaign 128
  cartoon 12
  consumers/consumerism and 17, 109
  effectiveness 49
  ethics 100
  industry 46
  Italian animation 12
  market 11, 14
  Pagot Film studio 13
  program 4
  psychedelia 79
  "sensationalist" 78
Advertising Council 77–8
A filo d'erba (On a Blade of Grass) (Bozzetto) 29
Aida (Verdi) 210, 222
Aida degli Alberi (Aida of the Trees) (Manuli) 115
Albéniz, Isaac 171
Alberti, Walter 33
Albicocco, Paolo 113
Albinoni, Tomaso 215
Alfa Omega (Alpha Omega) (Bozzetto) 48
Alice in Wonderland (Geronimi) 80

Allan, Robin 64
Allegro non troppo (Bozzetto) 63–100, 90n.84, 101–29, 169–70, 207–14
  animation crew 112–22
  approaching 17–18
  audiovisual analysis 133–8
  Boléro 174
  Concerto RV 559 195
  and *Fantasia* 23, 63–9, 80–100, 188, 205
  fictitious arcadian world 149
  Firebird Suite 42, 197, 200
  Italy in the 1970s 72–80
  live-action frame 57, 139–47
  live-action scenes 122–7
  minuscule players 31
  Mr. Rossi 43–5
  music–image synchronizations 173
  origin 102–6
  Prélude (Debussy) 19, 153, 155
  scientific literature 176
  scouting and discarded ideas 106–11
  screenplay 111–12
  Slavonic Dance 32, 160
  storyboard 111–12
  stretta 206, 208
  structuring repertoire 106–11
  tales of 69–72
  in theaters 127–9
  and *Tico-Tico* 48
  Valse triste 36, 179
Allen, Woody 54
Allied invasion of Italy 10
Alpini Corps 27
American Indians 48
Andersen, Hans Christian 10

Angela, Piero 58, 85
animated advertising 13.
    See also advertising
Animated Cartoons: How They Are made, Their Origin and Development (Lutz) 34
Animation Band, The 60, 117
animation crew 112–22.
    See also Italian animation
Animation Journal 214
Animation Studio 117
Anschluss 25
Anselmi, Guido 52
Antonini, Anna 36, 214
Apollo Moon missions 165
Arrigo e il suo tigrotto ("Arrigo and his tiger cub") 12
Arrigoni (food company) 12
artistic motivation 137.
    See also motivations
Asimov, Isaac 57
audiovisual analysis 133–8
audiovisual function 137.
    See also specific functions
Audissino, Emilio 134, 135, 136n.12, 170
Augustine of Hippo 198
Au lac de Wallenstadt, from *Années de pèlerinage, Première année: Suisse*, S.160 (Liszt) 218
Austria 25
Ave Maria (Schubert) 82–5, 89, 94, 96, 169
Avery, Tex 29, 34–5, 51n.81, 77, 114

Babbut (character) 118
Bacchini, Romolo 6, 6n.20
Bach, Johann Sebastian 81, 84, 86, 89, 92, 92n.89, 97–8, 98n.98, 206, 210
Badoero, Alvise (character from Ponchielli's opera *La Gioconda*) 188
Baeus (Bozzetto) 32, 43
Baffo (cartoon character) 47
Baffoblù (cartoon character) 32, 47
ballet d'action 196

Ballets Russes (dance company) 196
Bambi (animated film) 5n.17, 23
Banca Nazionale dell'Agricoltura (National Bank of Agriculture) 74
Barbera, Joseph 60, 109
Barks, Carl 28, 109
Bartered Bride, The (Smetana) 108
Bartók, Béla 215
Bassi, Giancarlo 45
Bassi, Pier Emilio 45
Bastiancich, Alfio 213
Batman (character) 206
Beatles, The 79
Beeella (sheep) 61, 61n.105
Beethoven, Ludwig van 82–3, 94
    Piano Sonata No. 8 in C minor Op. 13 ("Sonata Pathétique") 204, 215
    Piano Sonata No. 14 in C # minor "Quasi una fantasia" Op. 27, No. 2 ("Moonlight Sonata") 106, 210, 215
    Piano Sonata No. 23 in F minor Op. 57 ("Appassionata") 215
    Symphony No. 5 Op. 67 206
    Symphony No. 6 Op. 68 "Pastoral" 82
Be Leery of Lake Eerie (Barks) 109
Belgium 10
Belle nuit, ô nuit d'amour (Barcarole) (Offenbach) 106, 219
Bellini, Vincenzo 215
Bellow, Saul 28
Bendazzi, Giannalberto 24–5, 30, 41–2, 44, 65–6, 209n.3, 213–14
Benedictus sit Deus K. 117 (Mozart) 106, 219
Benois, Alexandre 196
Beretta, Angelo 113
Berliner Philharmoniker 90
Berlinguer, Enrico 73–4
Berlin International Film Festival 2, 57, 116
Berlusconi, Silvio 55
Bernstein, Leonard 216
Bettetini, Giancarlo 146
Biagi, Enzo 73
Bianchi, Paul 9, 12

Bianchi, Pietro 34
Bible 76, 197–8
  Book of Genesis 198
Bioletto, Angelo 11
Bizet, Georges 216
Blair, Lee 98
Blechman, R. O. 2
Bogart, Humphrey 97, 204, 208
Boito, Arrigo 216
Boléro (Ravel) 96–7, 102–4, 109–12, 165–76, 170n.6, 198–200, 220
  Allegro non troppo 117
  and *Fantasia* 83, 87, 214
  program notes 168–76
  sfumato 17
  uncanny creatures 79
  and the *Valse triste* 90, 95, 141, 179
Bolex Paillard (16mm) 30
Bolognin, Mauro 105
Boneschi, Giampiero 52
Bonfanti, Marco 1n.1
Bordwell, David 134–5
Borghese, Junio Valerio 74
Borowczyk, Walerian 16
Bottini, Giovanni 6
Boulez, Pierre 153
Bourek, Zlatko 3
Bozzetto, Andrea 44, 60–1
Bozzetto, Bruno 13, 23–61, 65, 82–3, 168, 171, 180–1, 189, 197, 210, 213
  advocacy for animal rights 61
  Alfa Omega (Alpha Omega) 48
  Allegro non troppo (See *Allegro non troppo* (Bozzetto))
  Baeus 32, 43
  "Bruno the Great" 56
  "Carosello" 30, 39, 45–9, 48n.73, 53–61
  Cavallette (Grasshoppers) 2, 32, 197
  Come si realizza un cartone animato (How to Make an Animated Cartoon) 46
  contemporary animation 3
  domestic success 2
  Due ragni nel piatto (Two Spiders on a Plate) 31
  early years 25–8

Ego 49
"eternal amateur" 14
Europe & Italy 59
Fantasia indiana (An Indian Fantasy) 30
A filo d'erba (On a Blade of Grass) 29
first attempts 28–31
full-length animated film 49–53
I cosi (The Things) 59–60
I due castelli (The Two Castles) 31, 160
I gatti che furbacchioni (The Cats Are So Slick) 29
I ladri che mascalzoni (Thieves Are Such Troublemakers) 31
Il cerchio si stringe (The Net Is Closing In) 31
Il rudere (The Wreck) 29
Il signor Rossi al campeggio (Mr. Rossi Goes Camping) 41
Il signor Rossi al fotosafari (Mr. Rossi Goes to a Photo Safari) 39, 41
Il signor Rossi al mare (Mr. Rossi Goes to the Beach) 41–2
Il signor Rossi a Venezia (Mr. Rossi Goes to Venice) 41
Il signor Rossi cerca la felicità (Mr. Rossi in Search of Happiness) 17
Il signor Rossi compra l'automobile (Mr. Rossi Buys a Car) 39
Il signor Rossi e lo sport (Mr. Rossi and Sport) 44
Il signor Rossi va a sciare (Mr. Rossi Goes Skiing) 41, 114
Il solito documentario (The Usual Documentary) 29
insects matter 31–3
inspiration 3
international recognition 2
inventions of his father 31n.42
I sogni del signor Rossi (Mr. Rossi's Dreams) 17, 44
La cabina (The Cabin) 56
"La Macchina della Musica" ("The Music Machine") 105

INDEX

La storia delle invenzioni (The History of Inventions) 34, 37, 213
Le vacanze del signor Rossi (Mr. Rossi's Vacations) 17
Looo 59
"Los Prinziamo" 80
l signor Rossi e le donne (Mr. Rossi and Women) 43
L'uomo e il suo mondo (Man and His World) 32
Mammuk 57
Mistertao 2, 57–8
Mr. Rossi (cartoon character) 32, 38–45
"Musicanimata" ("Musicanimation") 105
Opera (short film) 206–7, 210
Oppio per oppio (The Household Drug) 56
parents 27, 46
Partita a dama (A Game of Checkers) 30
Piccolo mondo amico (Small Friendly World) 29, 38
"Poca Fantasia" ("Not Much Fantasia") 205
quality commercials 4
quote 1
Rapsodeus 60, 197
"Sandwich" 56
Self Service 32
self-taught drawing skills 2
"Senza Fantasia" ("Without Fantasia") 205
Small Friendly World 30
So Far 107
Sotto il ristorante cinese 56
Strip Tease 77
structuring repertoire 106–11
"Supermano" 80
Tapum! La storia delle armi (Tapum! The History of Weapons) 2, 7, 29–30, 33–7, 45, 198, 210–11
"The Italian Disney" 23–5
Tico-Tico 30, 48
Un Oscar per il signor Rossi (An Award for Mr. Rossi) 38–9, 41, 43, 45

Vip, Mio fratello superuomo (Vip, My Superman Brother) 5, 16, 42, 51, 53–5, 59, 104, 117, 208, 211
West and Soda 16, 28, 42–3, 51–4, 59, 112, 117, 208
Bozzetto non troppo (Bonfanti) 1n.1
Bradbury, Ray 57
Braga, Paolo 146
Brahms, Johannes 108, 160–1, 210–16, 225
Brdečka, Jiří 34
Brera Academy of Fine Arts in Milan 117
Brigate Rosse (Red Brigades) 71n.29, 74–5
British Museum 29
Brooks, Mel 71, 145, 210
Brover-Lubovsky, Bella 187
Brown, Fredric 57
Brunetta, Gian Piero 40
Bruno Bozzetto: 1958–1988 (Bastiancich) 213
"Bruno Bozzetto: Animation, Maestro!" (exhibition) 2
Bruno Bozzetto. Animazione primo amore (Bendazzi) 213
BrunoBozzettoChannel (YouTube channel) 2, 59
Bruno Bozzetto Film 2 13, 45–9, 55–7, 59, 101, 113–15, 207
Bruno Bozzetto Pubblicitario (Rondolino) 5n.16
"Bruno Bozzetto: Wit and Wisdom" (Antonini) 214
"Bruno the Great" (Bozzetto) 56
Bufalini, Marcello 68n.24
Bugs Bunny (cartoon character) 31
Bussotti, Sylvano 107, 216
Busto Arsizio 16
Buzzati, Dino 28

Cabiria (Pastrone) 5n.17
Čajkovskij, Pëtr Il'ič 81, 92, 105, 109, 216, 225
Dance of the Plum Fairy (from Čajkovskij's *Nutcracker Suite*) 92–3

INDEX

Danse des petits cygnes (from Čajkovskij's *The Swan Lake*) 109–10, 216, 225
Calabresi, Luigi 75
Caldarelli, Gero 116
Cameo-Poly Cinema (now Regent Street Cinema) 29
Campani, Paul 14
Campogalliani, Carlo 9
Canale 5 (broadcaster) 55
Candia, Renato 39
Candide (Voltaire) 3
Cannes Film Festival 3, 33, 116
Cannon, Robert 3
"Canzonissima" (play) 146
Capriccio all'italiana 105
Capriccio Italien Op. 45 (Čajkovskij) 105, 216
CARAN (animation production company) in Turin 6
Carnelutti, Francesco 78
Carnival of the Animals, The (Saint-Saëns) 221
"Carosello" ("Carousel") (TV advertising program) 4–5, 11–15, 17–18, 72–3, 115, 189
  Baffo (cartoon character) 47
  Baffoblù (cartoon character) 32, 47
  Bozzetto, Bruno 30, 39, 45–9, 48n.73, 53–61
  Buc the Buccaneer (cartoon character) 47
  Guglielmone (cartoon character) 47
  Kuko (cartoon character) 32, 47
  "Los Prinziamo" (Bozzetto) 80
  Magno (cartoon character) 47
  Peroni (beer brand) 76
  Pildo (cartoon character) 32, 47
  Poldo (cartoon character) 32, 47
  "Sapore di Citta" 79
  SuperShell (gasoline brand) 76
  Unca Dunca (cartoon character) 47–8, 117
Carpi, Cioni 15
Cartoni Animati Italiani Roma (CAIR) 6
Cartoon Film 117

Cassano, Riccardo 8
Cat Concerto, The (Hanna and Barbera and Hanna) 60, 109
Catholic University in Milan 116
Cavallette (Grasshoppers) (Bozzetto) 2, 32, 197
Cavandoli, Osvaldo 12
Cavazzuti, Walter 113, 168
Cawelti, John G. 65
cel animation 6, 17, 30
Celeste Aida 204, 210
Centro Sperimentale di Cinematografia 116
C'era una volta il West (Once Upon a Time in the West) (Leone) 137
Cereda, Giancarlo 45–6, 50, 52, 113, 168
Cervi, Mario 73
Chaplin, Charlie 43
Charlie Brown (cartoon character) 206
Chatman, Seymour 134
Chernabog (fictional character) 82, 84, 97, 97n.96, 169
Chesani, Sergio 45, 52
Chi ha paura ...? (Monster Mash) (Manuli) 115
Chinese Dance 92
Chion, Michel 91
de Chomón, Segundo 8
Chopin, Frédéric 206, 216
Christian Democracy 73–5
Cinderella (Jackson) 144
cinema advertisement 12
Cingoli, Giulio 80
Civic Cinema School in Milan 116
Clampett, Robert "Bob" 35
Claymation 84, 97, 112, 200
Code, David J. 153
cognition 137
cognitive functions 137
cognitivism 135
Cold War 210
Collodi, Carlo 11, 16
Colombo, Fausto 146n.7
Comedians' Galop (Kabalevskij) 218
Come si realizza un cartone animato (How to Make an Animated Cartoon) (Bozzetto) 46

Come si realizza un cartone animato (Re) 46n.68
Comin, Jacopo 6
Comitato Italiano Cotone ("Italian Cotton Committee") 117
Commedia all'italiana 40
compositional motivation 136, 191
"concert feature" 18, 63, 87, 143
Concerto for 2 Trumpets in C major RV 537 (Vivaldi) 222
Concerto in C Major RV 559 (Manuli) 32, 42, 114–15, 118, 185–91
Concerto in C Major RV 559 (Vivaldi) 72, 88, 91, 108, 142, 185
Concerto in F major Op. 10 no. 1, RV 433 ("The Sea Storm") (Vivaldi) 222
Concerto in G minor Op. 10 no. 2, RV 439 ("The Night") (Vivaldi) 222
Concerto Op. 5 No. 7 (Albinoni) 215
connotative cognitive function 137
Constitutional Court Resolution no. 202 of 1976 55
constructivism 135
Conversations with Igor Stravinsky (Craft) 187
Coppola, Mario 36
Cori (clothing brand) 76
Corona Cinematografica 14
Corra, Bruno 8
Corradini, Ginanni 8
Corriere della Sera (newspaper) 44
Cosmopolitan (magazine) 118
Cossio, Carlo 6, 9, 12
Cossio, Vittorio 6, 12
Craft, Robert 187
"Cuccioli" (Gruppo Alcuni) 56
Culhane, James "Shamus" 113
Culhane, John 91n.86, 99
Cydalise et le chèvre-pied (Cydalise and the satyr) (Pierné) 82

Dalì, Salvador 98
Dallapiccola, Luigi 187
D'Alò, Enzo 25, 55, 118
Danse macabre Op. 40 (Saint-Saëns) 94, 221

Daphnis et Chloé (Ravel) 108–10, 171, 220, 227
Darwin, Charles 83, 174–5
Davis, Marc 113
Dayan, Moshe 206
De Ambrosis, Luciano 10
De Barberis, Alessio 6
De Berti, Raffaele 65
De Sica, Vittorio 10, 41
Death and Transfiguration Op. 24 (Strauss) 222
Debussy, Claude 83, 90, 95, 140, 216
Prélude à l'aprè s-midi d'un faune (Debussy) 149, 151–7, 225
Decroux, Étienne 116
Delibes, Léo 109, 217, 226
Denmark 10
denotative cognitive function 137
Denti, Riccardo 113
De Patie-Freleng Enterprises 38
Desire under the Elms (Mann) 34
Destino (Dalì) 98
Deutsche Grammophon 90, 90n.83
Devil's Wall, The (Smetana) 221
Die Abenteuer des Prinzen Achmed (The Adventures of Prince Achmed) (Reininger) 10
Die Fledermaus (Strauss) 222
Dionysus (god) 82
Disney (mass media company) 3–5, 10–12, 15, 17, 23, 25, 29, 34, 36, 50, 53, 59–60, 63–4, 67–70, 80, 82–5, 87, 91, 93, 95–8, 100, 105, 113–15, 143–4, 168–70, 180, 188, 211
Disney Channel 56
Disney-Formalism (artistic paradigm) 98
Ditz, Bruno 12
Djagilev, Sergej 196
"DoDo, the Kid from Outer Space" (Halas and Batchelor TV) 54
Domeneghini, Anton Gino 10–12, 10n.35
Donald Duck (cartoon character) 28, 30, 30n.37, 39
"Donate sangue" ("Donate Blood") 78
Donizetti, Gaetano 206

Donizetti Theatre in Bergamo 139–40, 146, 188
Don Quichotte à Dulcinée (Ravel) 172
Dosso Dossi (art school in Ferrara, Italy) 118
Dostoevskij, Fëdor 142
Dovniković, Borivoj 3
Dragić, Nedeljko 3
Dreamer's Dictionary, The (Robinson) 54
Dr. Strangelove Or: How I Learned to Stop Worrying and Love the Bomb (Kubrick) 210
Due ragni nel piatto (Two Spiders on a Plate) (Bozzetto) 31
Dukas, Paul 81, 93
Dumbo (Sharpsteen) 5n.17, 169
Dunning, George 79
Dvořák, Antonín 108, 141, 160–1, 210, 217

East European 9
Eco, Umberto 69
economic recovery, Italy 12
Edelmann, Heinz 80
Edwards, Blake 38
Ego (Bozzetto) 49
Èjchenbaum, Boris 135
El amor brujo (De Falla) 216
Ellens dritter Gesang (Ellen's Third Song) (from Schubert's song cycle *Liederzyklus vom Fräulein vom See*) 89
emotive function 155
Étude Op. 10 No. 3 (Chopin) 216
European Common Market 39
European Enlightenment 175
Europe & Italy (Bozzetto) 59
Expo Milano 2015 60

Facebook 59, 60
Factory: machine-music ("The Iron Foundry") (Mosolov) 219
Falabrino, Gian Luigi 72
Falana, Lola (showgirl) 146
Falena, Lola (cartoon character) 146
Falk, Lee 28, 53
De Falla, Manuel 216

Fancy Free (Bernstein) 216
Fantabiblical (Manuli) 114
Fantasia (anthology animated film) 5n.17, 17–18, 23, 48, 87n.78, 101, 103–6, 133, 143, 145, 147, 168–70, 170n.6, 174, 188–9, 201, 205, 208, 211
and *Allegro non troppo* (Bozzetto) 63–9, 80–100
and *Boléro* (Ravel) 83, 87, 214
Fantasia 2000 91n.86
Fantasia indiana (An Indian Fantasy) (Bozzetto) 30
Fantozzi (Salce) 41
Fantozzi, Ugo (film character) 41
Farandole (Bizet from Georges Bizet's *L'Arlésienne, Suite no. 2*) 216
Faust (Gounod) 217
Faust band 107
Feldman, Marty 71, 210
Felix 2—The Mechanical Rabbit and the Time Machine (Laganà) 118
Felix—Ein Hase auf Weltreise (Felix—All Around the World) (Laganà) 118
Felix the Cat (cartoon character) 31
Fellini, Federico 52
Ferragosto 40
Ferrari, Giovanni 113, 118, 168, 180–1
Festival International de la Publicité Cannes Lions 13
Festival internazionale del film d'arte e sull'arte (International Festival of Art Films and Films on Art) 38
Festival Internazionale del Film Pubblicitario ("Advertising Film International Festival") 13
Fêtes (Debussy) 216
Feu d'artifice Op. 4 (Stravinskij) 222
Fiaschi, Giorgio 78
FIAT 74
Field, Rachel 94
Fiery Angel, The Op. 37 (Prokof'ev) 220
Figliut (character) 118
"Film a soggetto" ("Narrative films") 10

Film/Music Analysis. A Film Studies Approach (Audissino) 134, 136n.12
finale(s) 203–12
Finch, Christopher 82
Finding Nemo (Stanton) 137
Finlandia Op. 26 No. 7 (Sibelius) 221
Finn, Will 59
Finocchiaro, Angela 116
Fior di Vite Ramazzotti 76
Firebird, The (Stravinskij) 42, 72, 76–8, 90, 91n.86, 97, 104, 107–8, 110, 112, 114–15, 118, 142, 144, 193–201, 205, 222
Fischinger, Oskar 98
Flach, Marise 116
"Flintstones, The" (Hanna-Barbera Productions) (TV series) 4
Floris, Alessandro 75
Fokine, Michel 196
Forest Murmurs (Wagner) 223
Forlani, Giorgio 113
formalism 99
Foster, Hal 28
Francesca da Rimini Op. 32 (Čajkovskij) 216
Franceschini (character) 143, 203–5, 210–11
Franceschini, Alberto 71n.29
Frattini, Roberto 58, 60
Fronte Nazionale (political party) 74
Frusta, Arrigo 8
full-length animated film 49–53
Fumagalli, Armando 146
Funeral March of a Marionette (Gounod) 217
Furniss, Maureen 214
Fyrtøjet (The Tinderbox) (Methling) 10

Gagliardo, Elio 14
Gagliardo, Ezio 14
Gagliardo, Fulvio 14
Gagosian Gallery in Genève, Switzerland 1n.3
Gamma Film 12–14, 51, 112, 117–18, 168
Garay, Nestor 70, 99, 134, 139, 142
Garbancito de la Mancha (Little Garbanzo Bean from the Mancha) (Moreno) 10
Garibaldi, Giuseppe 115
Garity, William E. 86
Gassman, Vittorio 40
Gastone (cartoon character) 32
Gatto Filippo licenza d'incidere (Philip the Cat—Licence to Hack) (Zac) 16
Gauthier-Villars, Henri 152
Gavioli, Gino 12–13, 16, 113
Gavioli, Roberto 12–13, 16, 113
Gazzolo, Nando 52
Gelsi, Ugo 12
Gente di Milano—I mondi di Bruno Bozzetto (Trastulli) 4n.14
Gerald McBoing Boing (Cannon) 3
Germany 10–11, 68
Geronimi, Clyde 80, 96
Ghislanzoni, Antonio 115
Gianeri, Enrico 12
Gianini, Giulio 15–16, 103
Gibba. *See* Guido, Francesco Maurizio
Ginna, Arnaldo 8, 17
Giobbe, Luigi 6
Giovannini, Attilio 12, 25, 50, 52
Giovannini, Maria Luisa 70, 139
"Gli eroi di cartone" ("Cartoon Heroes") (program) 16
Gloria RV 589 (Vivaldi) 108, 222, 229
Godi, Franco 48, 54, 80, 89, 133, 144
Golden Bear award 2, 57
Gomas, Guido 16
Gonzo, Luigi Guido 16
Gorgosaurus 168n.3
Gottfredson, Floyd 28
Gounod, Charles 107, 206, 217
Grant, John 80, 214
Great Britan 10
Green, Kerry 213
Grgić, Zlatko 3
Grieg, Edvard 106, 108, 217, 226
Gruppo Alcuni 56
Guerra, guerra! Chorus from Vincenzo Bellini's opera *Norma* (Bellini) 215
Guido, Francesco Maurizio 9, 13, 16–17

Guillaume Tell (Rossini) 104, 109–10, 220, 227
"Guinness at the Albert Hall" (Williams) 38

Habanera (Ravel) 171
Halas, John 33–4, 37, 54, 213–14
Halas and Batchelor Studio 37, 54
Hallelujah (from Händel's oratorio *Messiah*) 217
Hand, David 23, 113
Händel, Georg Friedrich 217
Hanna, William 60, 109
Hanna-Barbera Productions 4
Hanslick, Eduard 89
Hardy, Oliver 99, 140
Harries, Dan 66
Harris, David Campbell 77
Haydn, Franz Joseph 218
Heavy Metal (Potterton) 57
"Heigh-Ho" (song from the film *Snow White and the Seven Dwarfs*) 113
Help! (Hanna and Barbera) 57, 118
Hemingway, Ernest 28
Hendrix, Jimi 106
Henry, Pierre 218
Hepburn, Audrey 97, 204, 208–9
Herzog (Bellow) 28
Hess, Harry 117
Hight, Craig 37n.55
Hindemith, Paul 218
H Is for Head Game (Plympton) 98
Hitchcock, Alfred 136
Hitler, Adolf 25
Hodge, Robert 66
Hollywood 64, 208, 209
Holst, Gustav 108, 218, 226
Home on the Range (Finn and Sanford) 59
"Hot Autumn" 73–4
How to Cartoon for Amateur Films (Halas and Privett) 34
How to Kiss (Plympton) 98
Hubley, Faith 96n.95
Hubley, John 3, 34, 96n.95
Huckleberry Hound (Hanna-Barbera Productions) 4
Hugues, Robert 82
Hume, David 175
Hungarian Dance No. 1 (Brahms) 216
Hungarian Dance No. 5 (Brahms) 108–9, 160–1, 210, 216, 225
Hungarian Rhapsody No. 2 in C-sharp minor, S.244/2 (Liszt) 60, 109, 210, 219, 226
Hutcheon, Linda 66–8, 99

I bambini ci guardano (*The Children Are Looking at Us*) (De Sica) 10
Iberia (Albéniz) 171
I cosi (*The Things*) (Bozzetto) 59–60
Idea-Metodo-Arte ("Idea-Method-Art") (IMA) 11–12
I due castelli (*The Two Castles*) (Bozzetto) 31, 49, 51, 160, 162, 173
I fratelli Dinamite (*The Dynamite Brothers*) (Pagot) 10–11, 10n.35, 50
I gatti che furbacchioni (*The Cats Are So Slick*) (Bozzetto) 29
I ladri che mascalzoni (*Thieves Are Such Troublemakers*) (Bozzetto) 31
Il barbiere di Siviglia (*The Barber of Seville*) (Rossini) 220
Il boom (*The Boom*) (De Sica) 41
Il cerchio si stringe (*The Net Is Closing In*) (Bozzetto) 31
Il Cimento dell'Armonia e dell'Inventione (*The Contest between Harmony and Invention*) (Vivaldi) 186–7
Il cinema d'animazione, 1832–1956 (Alberti) 33
Il Corriere dei Piccoli (magazine) 9, 118
Il Corriere della Sera (newspaper) 118
"Il Corsaro nero" ("The Black Pirate") (TV series project by Bozzetto) 55–6
Il deserto dei tartari (*The Tartar Steppe*) (Buzzati) 28
Il Giorno (newspaper) 34
Illusion of Life: Disney Animation, The (Thomas and Johnston) 4n.11

Il nano e la strega (King Dick) (Gibba) 16–17
Il padre di famiglia (The Head of the Family) (Loy) 41
Il rudere (The Wreck) (Bozzetto) 29
Il signor Rossi al campeggio (Mr. Rossi Goes Camping) (Bozzetto) 41
Il signor Rossi al fotosafari (Mr. Rossi Goes to a Photo Safari) (Bozzetto) 39, 41
Il signor Rossi al mare (Mr. Rossi Goes to the Beach) (Bozzetto) 41–2
Il signor Rossi a Venezia (Mr. Rossi Goes to Venice) (Bozzetto) 41
Il signor Rossi cerca la felicità (Mr. Rossi in Search of Happiness) (Bozzetto) 17
Il signor Rossi compra l'automobile (Mr. Rossi Buys a Car) (Bozzetto) 39
Il signor Rossi e le donne (Mr. Rossi and Women) (Bozzetto) 43
Il signor Rossi e lo sport (Mr. Rossi and Sport) (Bozzetto) 44
Il signor Rossi va a sciare (Mr. Rossi Goes Skiing) (Bozzetto) 41, 114
Il sogno del bimbo d'Italia (The Dream of the Italian Child) (Cassano) 8
Il solito documentario (The Usual Documentary) (Bozzetto) 29
Il sorpasso (The Easy Life) (Risi) 40
Il topo di campagna e il topo di città (The Country Mouse and the City Mouse) (Bianchi) 9
Il turco in Italia (The Turk in Italy) (Rossini) 16
IMA. *See* Idea-Metodo-Arte ("Idea-Method-Art") (IMA)
I mostri (The Monsters) (Risi) 41
Impresa Pubblicita Cinematografica ("Cinema Advertising Enterprise") (IPC) 12
INCOM. *See* Industria CortiMetraggi (INCOM)
incompetence 145–6, 205, 208
India ink 50–1
Industria CortiMetraggi (INCOM) 5, 9

Infernal dance of King Kastchei (from Stravinskij's *Firebird Suite*) 197, 201
Innocenti (firm) 5, 46
insects 31–3
"Inspector, The" (theatrical cartoon) 38
Institute for the Study and Diffusion of Animated Cinema. *See* Istituto per lo Studio e la Diffusione del Cinema di Animazione (ISCA)
"Intervista a Bruno Bozzetto" (Manuppelli) 227n.1
In the Hall of the Mountain King (from the *Peer Gynt Suite* Op. 46 by Edvard Grieg) 106, 108, 217, 226
Invitation to the Dance Op. 65, J. 260 (Weber) 108, 223, 229
I paladini di Francia (The Paladins of France) (Luzzati and Gianini) 15
IPC. *See* Impresa Pubblicita Cinematografica ("Cinema Advertising Enterprise") (IPC)
I quattro moschettieri (The Four Musketeers) (Campogalliani) 9
ISCA. *See* Istituto per lo Studio e la Diffusione del Cinema di Animazione (ISCA)
Isle of the Dead Op. 29 (Rachmaninov) 220
I sogni del signor Rossi (Mr. Rossi's Dreams) (Bozzetto) 17, 44
Istituto Nazionale Luce 5–6
Istituto per lo Studio e la Diffusione del Cinema di Animazione (ISCA) 16, 213
Italian animation 5–17
 advertising 12
 animated documentary 9
 cel animation technique 6
 full-length features 10
 impact on audiovisual culture 5
 market 10
 niche repertoire 9
 production costs 7, 10
 renaissance 56
 rodovetro 7

stop-motion tricks 8
Technicolor process 7
Italian Communist Party (PCI) 73
"Italian Disney, The" 23–5
Italian Social Movement (MSI) 74–5
Italicus Rome-Brennero express train 75
Italy 6, 12, 50
  economic recovery 12
  first animated features 10
  liberation and violence (1970) 72–80
  orchestral music 103
  social progress 75
IULM University 116
Ives, Burt 34

Jackson, Wilfred 99, 144
Jacovitti, Benito 47
Jannacci, Enzo 48
Järnefelt, Arvid 91, 180
Jesus (jeans brand) 76
"Jetsons, The" (Hanna-Barbera Productions) (TV series) 4
Jeu de cartes (Stravinskij) 106, 222
Johnston, Ollie 4
Jones, Charles Martin "Chuck" 34, 113
Jones, Watson 86
Jungle Book, The (Reitherman) 113
Jupiter (from Gustav Holst's *The Planets, Op. 32*) 218
Jutriša, Vladimir 3

Kabalevskij, Dmitrij Borisovič 218
Kachaturian, Aram 218
Karajan, Herbert Von 90
Kaufman, J. B. 81
Keaton, Buster 43
Keil, Bill 113n.33
Kessler, Alice 155
Kessler, Ellen 155
"Kim" (Laganà) 118
Kimball, Ward 3
Kiss of the Earth, The (The Oldest and Wisest One) (from Stravinskij's *The Rite of Spring*) 93
Koffka, Kurt 136

Köhler, Wolfgang 136
Kontakte (Stockhausen) 107, 110, 221, 228
Kress, Gunther 66
Kristallnacht (Night of Broken Glass) 25
Kubrick, Stanley 176, 210
Kuko (cartoon character) 32, 47
Kuolema (Death) (Järnefelt) 91, 180
Kuri, Yōji 34, 49

La Boutique fantasque (Respighi) 220
La cabina (The Cabin) (Bozzetto) 56
La civiltà cattolica (magazine) 73
La cura contro il raffreddore (The Treatment for the Common Cold) (Bottini) 6
La danse (Matisse) 154
Ladd, Alan 52
Ladri di saponette (The Icicle Thief) (Nichetti) 116
Lady of the Lake, The (Scott) 89
"La famiglia Spaghetti" ("The Spaghetti Family") (Laganà) 56, 118
La gabbianella e il gatto (Lucky and Zorba) (D'Alò) 25, 118
Laganà, Giuseppe 51, 111–13, 117–18, 154, 168
La gazza ladra (The Thieving Magpie) (Rossini) 16
La Gioconda (Ponchielli) 82, 188
La Guerra e il sogno di Momi (The War and Momi's Dream) (de Chomón) 8
La Linea ("The Line") (character) 12
"La Macchina della Musica" ("The Music Machine") (Bozzetto) 105
La malia dell'oro (The Enchantment of Gold) (Velle) 6n.20
La Mort du tyran Op. 116 (Milhaud) 219
Lanterna Magica Studio 116
L'après-midi d'un faune (The Afternoon of a Faun) (Mallarmé) 151, 153
Largo al factotum (aria from Rossini's opera *Il barbiere di Siviglia*) 206

L'Arlésienne, Suite no. 2 (Bizet) 216
La rosa di Bagdad (The Rose of Bagdad) (The Singing Princess) (Domeneghini) 10–11, 10n.35, 50
L'arte è un delfino. Intervista a Bruno Bozzetto (Bozzetto) 1n.2
Lasseter, John 59
"Last of the Mohicans, The" (Laganà) 118
La storia delle invenzioni (The History of Inventions) (Bozzetto) 34, 37, 213
La storia di Lulù (Lulù's story) (Frusta) 8
La Traviata (Verdi) 206
Laurel, Stan 99, 140
La valse (Ravel) 171, 220
La vida breve (De Falla) 216
"Le avventure di Neve & Gliz" ("The Adventures of Neve and Gliz") (Nichetti) 116
Le avventure di Pinocchio (Pinocchio's Adventures) (Collodi) 6
Le Diable à quatre (Adam) 215
L'elisir d'amore (Donizetti) 206
Leone, Giovanni 74
Leone, Sergio 16, 53, 137
Leoni Brothers 12–13
Le Quattro Stagioni (The Four Seasons) (Vivaldi) 186–7
L'eroe dei due mondi (The Hero of the Two Worlds) (Manuli) 115
Le Théâtre de monsieur et madame Kabal (Mr. and Mrs. Kabal's Theatre) (Borowczyk) 16
Le vacanze del signor Rossi (Mr. Rossi's Vacations) (Bozzetto) 17
Lever (agency) 13
Libiamo ne' lieti calici (aria from Verdi's opera *La Traviata*) 206
Liederzyklus vom Fräulein vom See (Schubert) 89
"Lilliput-put" (RTSI) 32, 55
Linus (magazine) 118
Lionello, Oreste 54
L'isola disabitata Hob. XXVIII/9 (Haydn) 218
Liszt, Franz 60, 109, 210, 218–19, 226

Little Matchgirl, The (Andersen) 10
Little Red Riding Hood (fairy tale) 35, 51n.81
live-action frame 122–7, 139–47
Liverpool Mass, The (Henry) 218
Lloyd, Harold 43
Lo Duca, Joseph-Marie 7–8
Looo (Bozzetto) 59
Loren, Sophia 34
Lorenz, Konrad 58
"Los Prinziamo" (Bozzetto) 80
Lotta Continua (Continuous Struggle) 75
Love for Three Oranges, The Op. 33 (Prokof'ev) 220
Loy, Nanni 41
L'ultimo sciuscià (The Last Shoeshine) (Gibba) 9
L'uomo e il suo mondo (Man and His World) (Bozzetto) 32
"Lupo Alberto" (Laganà) 118
Lutz, Edwin 34
Luzzati, Emanuele 15–17, 103

Maazel, Lorin 90
Macco Film 6
macro-emotive function 137, 155
Madama Butterfly (Puccini) 206–7
Maestro, Marcello 12
Magno (cartoon character) 47
Mahler, Gustav 107n.12, 108, 210, 219, 227
Maisetti, Massimo 1n.2
Make Mine Music (animated musical anthology film) 5n.17
Malamud, Bernard 28
Mallarmé, Stéphane 151–2, 154
Mammuk (Bozzetto) 57
Mammut (character) 118
Mandrake (Falk) 28
Manet, Édouard 151
Manfredi, Manfredo 15, 41, 115
Mann, Delbert 34
Mantova 16
Manuli, Guido 18, 39, 46, 51, 51n.81, 56, 79–80, 111, 113–16, 143, 154, 190, 199, 204, 206–8, 210
Manuppelli, Ivan 227n.1

Maraja, Libico 11
Marks, Aleksandar 3
Mars (from Gustav Holst's *The Planets, Op. 32*) 218
Marshall Plan 39
Marzetti, Luciano 27–8, 45, 52, 168
De Mas, Pierluigi 117
Masina, Mirna 97, 207, 209
Massimino-Garniér, Giorgio "Max" 16, 28
Master Programmi Audiovisivi S.r.l. 112, 199
Masters of Animation (Grant) 214
Masters of Animation (Halas) 37, 213–14
Mastroianni, Alberto 15
Mastro Lindo 118
Matisse, Henri 1, 149, 154
Matteo, Mario 75
Mayer, Ferry 13
McCay, Winsor 16
McLaren, Norman 3, 16, 24, 30, 33
Mefistofele (Boito) 216
Mengacci, Guido 77–8
Menuet antique (Ravel) 172
Merritt, Russell 81
Methling, Svend 10
MGM 29, 35
Miceli, Sergio 135, 156
Micheli, Maurizio 63–4, 67, 70, 79, 134, 139, 145, 157
Mickey Mouse (cartoon character) 28, 31, 81–2, 109n.17, 144, 156, 183
micro-emotive function 137, 155
Milan Cinematheque 33
Milan Fair 13
Milan Police Command 75
Milhaud, Darius 106, 219
Milion Film 6
"Mille e una sera" ("One Thousand and One Evenings") (TV program) 10, 16
Mimica, Vatroslav 3
Ministry of Defense 74
Ministry of Health 75
Ministry of the Interior 74
Minivip 54, 54n.84, 57, 211–12

Minivip & Supervip: il mistero del viavai (*Minivip & Supervip: The Mystery of the Come-and-Go*) (Panaccione) 42, 57, 108
Misseri, Francesco 14
Mistertao (Bozzetto) 2, 57–8
mockumentary 37, 37n.55, 170n.6
Moldau, The (Smetana) 221
Molnár, Ferenc 28
Monicelli, Mario 105
Montanaro, Carlo 8
Montanelli, Indro 73
Moore, Fred 81
Moore, Ray 53
Moravian Duets (Dvořák) 160
Moreno, Arturo 10
Moriconi, Nando (fictional character) 144
Moro, Aldo 75
Morricone, Ennio 53, 115, 137
Morris, Desmond 58
Mosconi, Elena 65
Moscow International Film Festival (16th) 116
Mosolov, Aleksandr Vasil'evič 106, 219
Mostra Internazionale del Cinema al Servizio della Pubblicita ("International Exhibition of Cinema at the Service of Advertising") 13
motivations 136–7
Moving Subject, A (Bendazzi) 213
Mozart, Wolfgang Amadeus 106, 219
"Mr. Hiccup" (RTSI) 55
Mr. Rossi (cartoon character) 2, 17, 32, 34, 38–45, 47, 56, 77, 85, 102, 108, 141, 145n.5, 154, 211
MSI. *See* Italian Social Movement (MSI)
Mulazzani, Giovanni 46–7, 50–2
Munari, Bruno 12
Münchener Kammerorchester 90
Murakami, Jimmy Teru 117
"Musicanimata" ("Musicanimation") (Bozzetto) 105
Musica per film (Miceli) 135
Music Box, The (Parrott) 99, 140

INDEX

Music for the Royal Fireworks HWV 351 (Händel) 217
Musorgskij, Modest Petrovič 82, 219
Mussio, Magdalo 15
Mussolini, Benito 25

National Film Board of Canada (NFB) 3
Nazi Germany 25
"Neighbor" (Silverberg) 57
Nel paese dei ranocchi (In the Land of Frogs) (Rubino) 9
Netherlands 10
Newmarch, Rosa 179, 180
NFB. *See* National Film Board of Canada (NFB)
Nichetti, Maurizio 18, 39, 42, 44, 46, 56, 78–9, 99, 111, 113–16, 118, 133–4, 140, 142–4, 145n.5, 177n.1
Nielsen, Kay 169
Night and Day (short film) 13
Night on Bald Mountain (Musorgskij) 82–4, 89, 94, 97–8, 107, 169
Night the Animals Talked, The (Culhane) 113
Nijinska, Bronislava 171
Nine Old Men 113
Ningen Dōbutsuen (Clap Vocalism) (Kuri) 49
Nixon, Richard 206
Noble, Maurice 34
Nocturne No. 7 Op. 27 No. 1 (Chopin) 216
Novelletta (Short Story) (Šebesta) 9
Nozze tragiche (Tragic Wedding) (Velle) 6n.20
Nutcracker Suite Op. 71a, The (Čajkovskij) 81, 83, 86, 89, 92–3
Nuvoli, Giuliana 71n.29

Oberkommando der Wehrmacht (High Command of the Armed Forces) 25
Oberon (Weber) 223
Offenbach, Jacques 106, 219
Of Stars and Men (Hubley and Hubley) 96n.95

Oh My Darling, Clementine (American western folk ballad) 52
Ondatelerama (company) 14
One Hundred and One Dalmatians (Reitherman) 97
One Thousand and One Nights (fairy tale) 11
On the Literal Meaning of Genesis (De Genesi ad litteram) (Augustine of Hippo) 200
Opec. *See* Organizzazione Pagot & C. ("Pagot Organization and Company") (Opec)
Opera (Bozzetto and Manuli) 18, 114, 206-7, 210
Oppio per oppio (The Household Drug) (Bozzetto) 56
Opus (Company) 13
Orchestra Sinfonica Giuseppe Verdi di Milano 68n.24
Organizzazione Pagot & C. ("Pagot Organization and Company") (Opec) 13
Origin of Species, The (Darwin) 83, 175
Orsini, Vittorio 77–8
Osmond, Humphry Fortescue 79
OtiPi (association of advertising agencies) 77
Ouverture from Giuseppe Verdi's opera *Un giorno di regno (King for a Day)* 104

Paganini, Niccolò 206, 219
Pagot, Gi 13
Pagot, Marco 13
Pagot, Nino 7, 10–13
Pagot, Toni 7, 11
Pagot Film (studio) 13
Palermo, Ferdinando 11
Pallant, Chris 98
Pallavicini, Sandro 5
Pál utcai fiúk, A (The Paul Street Boys) (Molnár) 28
Panaccione, Gregory 57
Parade (Satie) 221
Parrott, James 99

Partita a dama (A Game of Checkers) (Bozzetto) 30
Pasolini, Pier Paolo 40–1, 73, 105
"Pastoral" Symphony 82–3
Paul Film 14
Pavane pour une infante défunte (Ravel) 220
PCI. *See* Italian Communist Party (PCI)
Peg Leg Pete (cartoon character) 144
Pellegrini, Elena 12
Pence, Charles H. 175
Pensuti, Luigi Liberio 9
perception 12, 39, 49, 79, 129, 135, 137, 155
perceptive function 137
Perkins, Anthony 34
Perpetual Motion Op. 11 (Paganini) 219
Per un pugno di dollari (A Fistful of Dollars) (Leone) 16, 53
"Pet Pals" (Gruppo Alcuni) 56
Petronio, Gustavo 12
Phantom, The (Falk and Moore) 28, 53, 54n.83
Philadelphia Orchestra 89
Piano concertos (Ravel) 172
Piano Quintet in A major D. 667 ("The Trout") (Schubert) 221
Piazza della Loggia, Brescia 75
Piazzi, Giuseppe 11
Piccardo, Osvaldo 12
Piccolo mondo amico (Small Friendly World) (Bozzetto) 29, 38
Piccolo Teatro of Milan 116
Pick-Mangiagalli, Riccardo 11
Pictures at an Exhibition (Mussorgskij) 219
Pierné, Gabriel 82
Pildo (cartoon character) 32, 47
Pinetti, Piero 60
Pink Elephants on Parade (informal denomination of a sequence from the film *Dumbo*) 169
Pink Panther, The (Edwards) 38
Pinocchio (Collodi) 5n.17, 11, 28
Pisicchio e Melisenda (Wooden Heads) (Saitta) 9
"Pista!" (Nichetti) 116

Pixar Animation Studios 59
Pixnocchio (Laganà) 117
Pizzicato Polka (Delibes) 109, 217, 226
plagiarism 64, 144
Planets, The Op. 32 (Holst) 108
Playboy (magazine) 118
Plympton, Bill 98
"Poca Fantasia" ("Not Much Fantasia") (Bozzetto) 205
Pogliaghi, Lodovico 26
Pojar, Břetislav 34
Poldo (cartoon character) 32, 47
Poloni, Girolamo 26–7
Poloni, Maria Giovanna 27
Polonskij, Jakov Petrovič 196
Ponchielli, Amilcare 82, 94, 220
  Dance of the Hours (from Ponchielli's opera *La Gioconda*) 82, 84, 89, 94, 188, 220
  Dance of the Hours of the Day (section of Ponchielli's *Dance of the Hours*) 94
"Portobello" (TV program) 78
Potere Operaio (Power of the Workers) 75
Potterton, Gerald 57
Prélude à l'après-midi d'un faune (Debussy) 83–4, 95–6, 115, 117–18, 140, 149–57, 162, 173, 179, 182, 194, 200, 216, 225
"Premio di qualità" ("quality award") 15
Prendi, per me sei libero (Aria from Gaetano Donizetti's opera *L'elisir d'amore (The Elixir of Love)* 206
Presepi, Guido 6
Princesses' Khorovod (from the *Firebird Suite* by Stravinskij) 197, 200
Prince Valiant (Foster) 28
Privett, Bob 34
program notes 143–7
  Boléro (Ravel) 168–76
  Concerto in C Major RV 559 (Manuli) 186–91
  finale(s) 205–12
  Firebird Suite, The 195–201
  live-action frame 143–7

Prélude à l'après-midi d'un faune (Debussy) 151–7
Slavonic Dance Op. 46 no. 7 160–3
Valse triste Op. 44 No. 1 179–83
Prokof'ev, Sergej 220
"PsicoVip" ("PsychoVip") (RAI) 54n.84, 56
psychedelia 79–80, 99
psychedelic 64, 79
Psycho (Hitchcock) 136
psychoanalysis 135
Pubblicità Progresso (Progress Advertising) 78
Publicitas (company) 12
Publicorona (company) 14
Publi-Enic (company) 12–13
Puccini, Giacomo 206–7
Pulcinella (Gianini and Luzzati) 16
Pupilandia ("The Land of Puppets") (short film studio) 12
Putiferio va alla Guerra (The Magic Bird) (Gavioli and Gavioli) 16, 146

"Quark" (TV program) 58, 85
"QuellidiGrock" ("TheGrockBunch") (acting school) 116, 190
"Quo Vadiz?" (Nichetti) 116

Rachmaninov, Sergej 220
RAI (Italian state television) 4, 10, 14, 16, 47, 52, 55–6, 74, 78
Rainbow 56
Rall, Hannes 101
Ramsey, Grant 175
Rapsodeus (Bozzetto) 60
Ratataplan (Nichetti) 116
Ravel, Maurice 17, 90, 102–3, 108–9, 141, 165–76, 214, 220, 227
Ravesi, Giacomo 15
RDA 70. See "Reparto di Animazione" ("Animation Division") (RDA 70)
Re, Carlo 46, 46n.68
realistic motivation 136, 156
Red Hot Riding Hood (Avery) 77
Reininger, Lotte 10
Reitherman, Wolfgang 97, 113

Rencontres Internationals du Film d'Animation 3, 33
"Reparto di Animazione" ("Animation Division") (RDA 70) 112–13, 118, 168
Respighi, Ottorino 220
Rever (studio) 13
Rhodia (firm) 7
Rhythmetic (McLaren) 30
Richter, Max 187
Ride of the Valkyries (from the opera *Die Walküre*) (Wagner) 222
Rigoni, Alberto 114
Rimskij-Korsakov, Nikolaj Andreevič 94, 220
Risi, Dino 40–1
Rite of Spring, The (Stravinskij) 82–3, 89, 91, 93, 96–8, 168–9, 175, 196, 201, 214
Robinson, Stearn 54
rodovetro 7
Romano, Carlo 52
Romanticism 211
Rome 6, 14
Romeo and Juliet (Shakespeare) 203
Ronde des princesses (from the *Firebird Suite* by Stravinskij) 90–1, 95
Rondolino, Gianni 5n.16, 48
Rooty Toot Toot (Hubley) 3
Roscoe, Jane 37n.55
Rossellini, Roberto 10
Rossi, Franco 105
Rossini, Gioachino 16, 104, 109, 206, 220, 227
Rota, Nino 52
RTSI 55, 78
Rubin, David S. 79
Rubino, Antonio 9
Rundfunk-Symphonieorchester Berlin 90
Russian Dance (from Čajkovskij's *Nutcracker Suite*) 93
Russo, Giovanni 114

Sabre Dance (Kachaturian) 218
Sabrina (Wilder) 209
Sadoul, Georges 3

Saint-Saëns, Camille 94, 221
Saitta, Ugo 9
Salce, Luciano 41
Salgari, Emilio 56
Salinger, J. D. 28
Salome (Strauss) 204, 210
Saludos Amigos (live-action/animated film) 5n.17
Salvi, Osvaldo 116
"Sandwich" (Bozzetto) 56
Sanford, John 59
San Remo Festival 146
"Sapore di Città" ("The Taste of the City") (Manuli and Nichetti) 79
Sappi, Osvaldo 141
Saragat, Giuseppe 74
Satie, Erik 221
"Scacciapensieri" (TV program) (Ferrari) 78, 118
Scaglioni, Massimo 5n.16
Scarpa, Roberto 45
Scatola a sorpresa. La Gamma Film di Roberto Gavioli e la comunicazione audiovisiva in Italia da Carosello a oggi (Zane) 113n.33
Scheherazade Op. 35 (Rimskij-Korsakov) 220
Schönberg, Arnold 211
Schubert, Franz 82, 89, 210, 221
Scott, Walter 89
screenplay 111–12
Searle, Ronald 2
Šebesta, Giuseppe 9
Secondo Canale (TV program) 10
Second World War 5, 8, 25, 77, 143
Self Service (Bozzetto) 32
Semiramide (Rossini) 220
"Senza Fantasia" ("Without Fantasia") (Bozzetto) 205
Shakespeare, William 203
Shane (Stevens) 52
Sharpsteen, Ben 169
Sheckley, Robert 57
Shoemaker, Pamela J. 163
Sibelius, Jean 90–1, 104, 179–81, 221, 228
Sicilian Opera dei Pupi 9

Silent Majority (movement) 74
"Silly Symphonies" (Disney) 60, 81, 94
Silverberg, Robert 57
Simrock, Fritz 160
Skeleton Dance, The (Silly Symphony) 94
Šklovskij, Viktor 135
Skočná 90, 161
Slavonic Dance Op. 46 No. 1 (Dvořák) 217
Slavonic Dance Op. 46 No. 5 (Dvořák) 90, 95–6, 104, 108, 110, 140–1, 159–63, 199, 210, 217
Slavonic Dance Op. 46 No. 7 (Dvořák) 217
Slavonic Dance Op. 46 No. 10 (Dvořák) 217
Sleeping Beauty (Geronimi) 96
Smetana, Bedřich 108, 110, 221, 228
  Bartered Bride, The (Smetana) 108
  Dance of the Comedians (from Smetana's opera *The Bartered Bride*) 108, 110, 221, 228
  Devil's Wall, The (Smetana) 221
  Moldau, The (Smetana) 221
Snow White and the Seven Dwarfs (animated musical film) 5n.17, 11, 71, 98, 113, 143, 205
So Far (album by Faust, krautrock band) 107
Soltanto un bacio (Just a Kiss) (Manuli) 114
Song of the South (live-action/animated musical drama film) 5n.17
Sorcerer's Apprentice, The (Dukas) 81, 83, 87–8, 93, 98, 101, 103, 169
Sordi, Alberto 41, 144
S.O.S. (Nichetti and Manuli) 114
Sottaceti (Pickles) 18
Sotto il ristorante cinese (Bozzetto) 56
"Spaccaquindici" (TV program) 78
Spain 10
Spanish Civil War 25
spatial perceptive function 137, 155
Spring Grounds (section from Stravinskij's *The Rite of Spring*) 93
Stadlmair, Hans 90

Stanton, Andrew 137
Starewicz, Władysław 16
Statue of Liberty 207
Steamboat Willie (animated short film) 156
Stegosaurus 168n.3
Steinberg, Saul 2
Steno 105, 144
Stevens, George 52
Stockhausen, Karlheinz 107, 110, 221, 228
Stokowski, Leopold 63, 81–2, 85, 89, 92–4 170
stop-motion 15
  "carosellos" 14
  clay animation 17
  science-fiction 30
  tricks 8
storyboard 111–12
storytelling 29–30, 35–7, 42, 47–8, 52, 85, 96, 100
"Strategy of Tension" 74
Strauss, Johann II 222
Strauss, Richard 107n.12, 204, 210, 222
  Dance of the Seven Veils (from Strauss's opera *Salome*) 204, 210, 222
  Death and Transfiguration Op. 24 (Strauss) 222
  Die Fledermaus (Strauss) 222
  Salome (Strauss) 204, 210
  Till Eulenspiegel's Merry Pranks Op. 28 (Strauss) 107n.12, 222
Stravinskij, Igor 11, 71, 82–3, 90, 93, 106, 187, 195–6, 201, 222
  Danse infernale du roi Kastchei (from Stravinskij's *Firebird Suite*) 90–1
String Quintet in C major D. 956, Op. posth. 163 (Schubert) 210, 221
Strip Tease (Bozzetto) 77
"Stripy" (RTSI) 55
Stubing, Solvi 76
Studio 3P 12
Studio Bozzetto & Co. 60, 102
Studio di Monte Olimpino 12

Studio K 14, 189
Studio Marosi 189
Studio Pagot 4
"Sul ritmo di ogni spiritual" ("To the Rhythm of Every Spiritual") (Laganà) 117
"Supermano" (Bozzetto) 80
SuperShell gasoline 76
Supervip 54, 57
Swan Lake, The (Čajkovskij) 109
Sylvia (Delibes) 109
Symphonic Dances Op. 45 (Rachmaninov) 220
Symphonic Metamorphosis of Themes by Carl Maria von Weber (Hindemith) 218
Symphony No. 1 in D major ("Titan") (Mahler) 210, 219
Symphony No. 3 in D minor (Mahler) 107n.12, 108–9, 219, 227
Symphony No. 9 in E minor, "From the New World" Op. 95, B. 178 (Dvořák) 217
Symphony No. 100 in G major Hob. I/100 ("Military") (Haydn) 218
Symphony No. 101 in D major Hob. I/101 ("The Clock") (Haydn) 218

Tableaux vivants (avant La Passion selon Sade) (Bussotti) 107, 216
Taiuti, Lorenzo 16
Tamburini, Pier Francesco 14
"Tante scuse" (TV program) 78
Tapiola Op. 112 (Sibelius) 221
Tapum! La storia delle armi (Tapum! The History of Weapons) (Bozzetto) 2, 7, 29–30, 33–7, 45, 170n.6, 171, 198, 210–11
Tarchi, Renzo 14
Taruskin, Richard 196
Tati, Jacques 116
Taviani, Franco 78
Taylor, Deems 81–2, 85, 92, 146, 188
Teatro delle Vittorie in Rome 146
Technicolor process 7
Tell, William 206
temporal perceptive function 137, 155–6, 172, 182, 201

Testa, Armando 14
Teste di legno (Saitta) 9
Theocritus (poet) 152
"There Will Come Soft Rains"
  (Bradbury) 57
Thomas, Frank 4
Thompson, Kristin 135
Three Caballeros, The (live-action/
  animated film) 5n.17
Tico-Tico (Bozzetto) 30, 48
Tijuana Brasses (music band) 106
*Till Eulenspiegel's Merry Pranks
  Op. 28* (Strauss) 107n.12, 222
Tim Tyler's Luck (Young) 28
Tiny. *See* Poloni, Maria Giovanna
"Tiramolla Adventures" (Laganà)
  117
*Toccata and Fugue in D minor BWV
  565* (Bach) 81, 84, 86, 89, 92,
  92n.89, 97–8, 98n.98, 210
Tognazzi, Ugo 41
Tomelleri, Paolo 48
"Tom & Jerry" (MGM) 29
*Tompitt e i banditi del Far Prest
  (Tompitt and the Fare Fast
  Outlaws)* (Cossio) 9
Toninelli, Fabio 61
Toot, Whistle, Plunk and Boom
  (Kimball) 3, 23–4, 34
Topolino (magazine) 109, 109n.17
"Topo Tip" ("Tip the Mouse")
  (Bozzetto and Pinetti) 60
Toscani, Oliviero 76
transtextual motivations 136
Trastulli, Daniela 4n.14
"Treasure Island" (Laganà) 118
Trilussa (poet) 9
Trintignant, Jean-Louis 40
"True-Life Adventures" (series of live-
  action documentaries) 31
Tynjanov, Yury 135
Tyrannosaurus 168n.3
Tyrrell, John 161
Tytla, Bill 84

Uberti, Emilio 78
*Un americano a Roma (An American
  in Rome)* (Steno) 143–4

*Un'avventura nella foresta (An
  Adventure in the Forest)*
  (Bianchi) 9
Un bel dì vedremo (aria from
  Giacomo Puccini's opera *Madama
  Butterfly*) 206
*Un burattino di nome Pinocchio
  (The Adventures of Pinocchio)*
  (Cenci) 16
Unca Dunca (Carosello character)
  47–8, 117
Uncle Scrooge (comic-book
  character) 28
UNESCO World Heritage 9
Un giorno di regno (King for a Day)
  (Verdi) 104, 108, 222, 228
United Productions of America
  (UPA) 3, 50
United States 6, 8, 11, 13, 68
University of Bergamo 57
University of Udine in Gorizia 118
unnamed child 1, 1n.2
*Un Oscar per il signor Rossi (An
  Award for Mr. Rossi)* (Bozzetto)
  38, 39, 41, 43, 45
UPA. *See* United Productions of
  America (UPA)
Uranus (from Gustav Holst's *The
  Planets, Op. 32*) 218, 226
USA Advertising Council 77

Valdi, Walter 44
Valentini, Giorgio 96, 113, 168,
  173, 180–1
Valse triste Op. 44 No. 1 (Sibelius)
  72, 84–5, 90–1, 97, 110–11, 118,
  141–2, 177–83, 200–1, 221, 228
Velle, Gaston 6n.20
Venice 13
Venice Film Festival (1949) 10
Verdi, Giuseppe 104, 108, 204, 206,
  222, 228
Via Melchiorre Gioia 46
Vicari, Angelo 74
Villaggio, Paolo 41
*Violin Concerto No. 2 in B minor
  Op. 7* ("La Campanella")
  (Paganini) 219

Vip, Mio fratello superuomo (Vip, My Superman Brother) (Bozzetto) 5, 16, 42, 51, 53–5, 59, 78, 104, 117, 163, 208, 211
visual music 91, 98
Vita di Mussolini (Mussolini's Life) (Presepi) 6
Vivaldi, Antonio 72, 88, 90–1, 104, 108, 142, 185–6, 222, 229
Volere volare (To Want to Fly) (Nichetti) 114, 118
Vos, Tim P. 163
Vukotić, Dušan 3, 33–4, 38
Vynález skázy (The Fabulous World of Jules Verne) (Zeman) 16

Wagner, Richard 206, 222–3
Walker, Steven F. 152
Walt Disney 24, 63, 91n.86, 94, 98
Walt Disney Family Museum in San Francisco 2
War Ministry 25
Warner Brother 34, 113
Water Music (Händel) 217
Weber, Carl Maria Von 223, 229
Weber, William 88, 108
Wenk, Arthur 153
Wertheimer, Max 136
West and Soda (Bozzetto) 16, 28, 42–3, 51–4, 59, 112, 117, 208
Wettach, Adrien 116
"What's New in Italian Animation. The World of Bruno Bozzetto" (Green) 213

Who Framed Roger Rabbit (Zemeckis) 114
Wilder, Billy 209
Williams, Richard 38
Willy. *See* Gauthier-Villars, Henri
"Winx Club" (Rainbow) (animated TV series) 56
Wooden Prince, The Op. 13, Sz. 60 (Bartók) 215
Wright, Kay 109

Xerox 97, 168

"Years of Lead" 74, 78
Yellow Submarine (Dunning) 79–80
Yogi Bear (Hanna-Barbera Productions) 4
Young, Lyman 28
Young Frankenstein (Brooks) 71, 145, 210
YouTube 2, 59–60

Zac, Pino 16, 105
Zaccaria, Giuseppe 16
Zagreb School of Animated Film 3, 15, 33–4
Zane, Marcello 113n.33
Zaninović, Ante 3
Zeman, Karel 16
Zimnij put' (A Winter's Journey) (Polonskij) 196
Zorry Kid (cartoon character) 47
Zucchelli, Nino 38

www.ingramcontent.com/pod-product-compliance
Lightning Source LLC
Chambersburg PA
CBHW052218300426
44115CB00011B/1737